Mikhail Bot

Sixth World Chess Champion

Isaak & Vladimir Linder

Foreword by Andy Soltis

Game Annotations by Karsten Müller

World Chess Champions Series

2020
Russell Enterprises, Inc.
Milford, CT USA

Mikhail Botvinnik
Sixth World Chess Champion

ISBN: 978-1-949859-16-4 (print)
ISBN: 949859-17-1 (eBook)

Published by:
Russell Enterprises, Inc.
P.O. Box 3131
Milford, CT 06460 USA

http://www.russell-enterprises.com
info@russell-enterprises.com

Cover by Janel Lowrance

Printed in the United States of America

Table of Contents

Foreword

When Bobby Fischer was storming his way to the world championship, one of the obstacles in his path was Mark Taimanov. The Leningrad grandmaster was Fischer's first opponent in the 1971 Candidates matches. Taimanov badly need advice and he turned to the man he referred to in his writing as "My Teacher."

Botvinnik had only played Fischer once, in a 1962 draw which had become legendary. He was retired from competitive chess and rarely attended major tournaments and matches as a spectator. But he was an ideal adviser because of his ability to analyze players. He dissected them as well as he evaluated positions.

Taimanov discovered that for years Botvinnik had been preparing what he called "dossiers" on each of the great players that he might meet one day over the board. His files went far beyond opening secrets and middlegame habits and included personality details and quirks that Botvinnik had detected and studied. The dossiers were so well researched that the methodology "could be instructive to the KGB," Taimanov said.

The files also revealed some of Botvinnik's idiosyncratic observations. For example, he concluded that if Max Euwe had a choice between two equally good candidate moves – and one of them moved a piece several squares, while the other moved a piece one or two squares – the former world champion would pick the "long" one. "Euwe is a tall man," Botvinnik wrote in the dossier, "and he needs room…"

Botvinnik's file on Fischer, which included improvements in some of Fischer's favorite openings, didn't help. Taimanov was trounced by Bobby 6-0 and his career went into a tailspin. Nevertheless, in 2003 when he wrote his memoirs (*Vspominaya Samykh, Samykh…*), Taimanov spoke of Botvinnik as if he had been the most important figure in his life, even more than his wife, who was also his longtime piano partner. "My entire chess fate is connected to the name Botvinnik," Taimanov wrote.

With the retirement of Vladimir Kramnik in 2019, it may appear that the Botvinnik era has finally ended. The "Patriarch" helped nurture three world champions, Kramnik, Anatoly Karpov and Garry Kasparov. No one else in chess history can make that claim. But to players born since 1990 – and that means roughly half of the world's top 50 grandmasters today – he is a figure out of the pages of history books.

This book by Isaak and Vladimir Linder will help ensure that he will be more than that to future generations. They will learn about Botvinnik's pathfinding discoveries in the openings. He was perhaps two or three years ahead of his rivals in many variations. That is not possible today. But you can see how Botvinnik managed to do it with the Winawer Variation of the French Defense. Rival players were stumped by his Winawer in the late-1930s. When they played him years later, armed with improvements for White, they found that that he had discovered new strategies for Black. His opponents fought a losing battle to catch up, until Botvinnik virtually gave up chess for three years after winning the world championship in 1948. By the 1950s, his dominance was gone. Younger opponents had the advantage of energy, endurance – and adopting Botvinnik's own pioneering method of preparation.

He was unique, even among world champions. He recognized the gap between the Marxist dream and the Soviet reality. But he remained a devout Communist – and Stalin apologist – even in his final days. In 1995, the 83-year-old Botvinnik telephoned another of his former students, Yuri Razuvaev. "I realized why I have lived so long," he said. Razuvaev expected him to continue with words of wisdom, of why fate had chosen him for a long life. But Botvinnik said: "I was never a patient in a Soviet hospital." (Three weeks later Botvinnik died, at home as he wished.)

Botvinnik was often super-secretive, even with friends. Taimanov recalled how Soviet sports officials had arranged a training camp for the national chess team before they were to leave for an international team tournament. Botvinnik had a natural loathing of these kinds of camps, where opening secrets were revealed. Instead, Botvinnik asked Taimanov to come to his home one evening, without telling anyone. Taimanov showed up on time. Botvinnik "was, as always, cordial" when he greeted him. But then he locked the door, closed the window and "confidentially" said, "Let us play a blitz match of ten five-munute games. But no one should know of them or the result."

Taimanov was surprised because Botvinnik had made his hatred of speed games well known. Taimanov won the match 7-3. As he left, Botvinnik said, "'Well, Mark Yevgenievich, not a word to anyone. Promise?" Taimanov, the faithful protege, kept the secret for four decades.

Botvinnik's approach to life was unlike almost all modern grandmasters. He stressed study and self-criticism over tournaments. Hw told his students to limit themselves to no more than 50 or so serious games a year. "It is not enough to play chess," he liked to say. "One must leave time to think about it." Another of his favorite sayings was, "If you choose a chess career for yourself, you have to learn your entire life.'"

Viktor Khenkin, a veteran journalist, recalled how a foreign graphologist wanted to see if the personalities of the world champions could be detected by their handwriting. He got veteran master Yakov Estrin to try to obtain the signatures.

When Estrin asked Vasily Smyslov, Smyslov said, "Try calling me in a month."

When Estrin called Tigran Petrosian, he answered, "Did Botvinnik agree to this?"

When Estrin encountered Mikhail Tal in a coat room at the Central Chess Club, Tal said "Give me a piece of paper." With one hand he scribbled his name and used the other to put on his coat.

And when Estrin called Botvinnik, he replied, "Tomorrow at 10:35 I will be waiting for you in the laboratory."

Estrin reported all this to the graphologist. But he didn't need the handwriting samples anymore. Estrin's experience revealed all he needed to know about the signers.

Andy Soltis
New York
November 2019

Everything about the
World Champions

For fifteen hundred years, chess has been acknowledged by the world to be the cleverest, wisest, and noblest of games that exist. And of course, those who achieve its full power excite in us special delight and honors. Over 130 years ago, the outcome of a lengthy match between two famous chess maestros – Wilhelm Steinitz and Johannes Zukertort – was that, for the first time, one of them could be called champion of the entire planet. Since that time, 16 chessplayers have ascended Olympus, crowned with laurel; their photographs grace the first page of this book. Before you stands the entire dynasty of the kings of chess: Wilhelm Steinitz, Emanuel Lasker, José-Raúl Capablanca, Alexander Alekhine, Max Euwe, Mikhail Botvinnik, Vassily Smyslov, Mikhail Tal, Tigran Petrosian, Boris Spassky, Robert Fischer, Anatoly Karpov, Garry Kasparov, Vladimir Kramnik, Viswanathan Anand and Magnus Carlsen.

Nowadays, when interest in events at the highest level has increased sharply, many chess aficionados would be interested in returning to the pages of the struggle for the world championship, rediscovering the details of the lives and creativity of every champion and of his chief opponents, their contribution to the golden treasury of the art of chess; they would immerse themselves in the inimitable aura of those major battles for the crown of chess.

The authors of this book wrote earlier at some length in their thousand-page work, *Kings of the Chess World* (Moscow, 2001). The lively story format employed by the authors was reviewed favorably by chess society. At the same time, it was said that we ought to break down that fundamental production, for ease of use, into separate books, each dedicated to one of the champions. And so, a few years later, we started work, since in that time, we had also managed to accumulate significant new material.

This is the next book in the series, concerning the first of the Soviet world champions Mikhail Botvinnik (1911-1995), who, by his victories and creative achievements, spread the fame of his native land's school of chess far and wide.

Here, you will learn all about the chess advances and achievements of the Patriarch of Soviet Chess, about his life and scholarly pursuit, and his contributions to the various phases of the game – opening, middlegame and endgame. This book presents over 100 of Botvinnik's best games and endings, and a number of tables and photographs. We present archival materials from his preparation for a match for the world championship against Alexander Alekhine, and other facts which have only recently been unearthed. The senior member of your authors was personally acquainted with Botvinnik, and beginning with 1948, was always present at his world championship events.

Every champion is a whole world of chess unto himself – one more step in the development of the art of chess. And the reader shall find, in these our books, much that will be notable about him as a person, as a great chessplayer, and as an active part of chess culture.

> Isaak & Vladimir Linder,
> Moscow
> July 2006

Signs and Symbols

!?	a move worth consideration
=	an equal position
±	White stands slightly better
±	White has a clear advantage
+−	White has a winning position
∓	Black stands slightly better
∓	Black has a clear advantage
−+	Black has a winning position
(D)	see the next diagram
1-0	White wins
0-1	Black wins
½-½	Draw agreed
+	check
#	mate
!	a strong move
!!	a brilliant/unobvious move
?	a weak move, an error
??	a grave error

Prologue

Mikhail Botvinnik (1911-95) was a man, and an epoch! He was born in the days of the last Russian emperor, Nicholas II, and he died in the time of the first President of Russia, Boris Yeltsin. He was taught by the second world champion, Emanuel Lasker, and he taught the 13th champion, Garry Kasparov.

When he was in school, he never used a logarithmic slide ruler; yet, at a respectable age, he played chess with a computer.

Botvinnik was not yet 25 years of age when he became one of the living symbols of great power, and remained so for the next 60 years.

His amazingly goal-directed nature sprang from a mix of his communistic upbringing, spartan regime, and innate intelligence. He was a two-sided person: champion and scholar, grandmaster of chess and doctor of electro-technology. Botvinnik's major qualities were his iron will, his scholarly approach, and clear vision of the goal ahead.

"On the front line of chess, without losing focus," is what Botvinnik's contemporaries used to call it during his 15 years as champion (1948-57, 1958-60, and 1961-63). Twice he regained the title of the world's strongest – a year after losing it, he reappeared, so changed that his opponents were unable to cope with him. As opposed to them, he never went through any feelings of euphoria.

In Botvinnik, there accumulated the best features of the Soviet School of Chess. And at the same time, this school embodied within itself many of the priorities it pronounced.

Botvinnik dedicated 30 years of his life to the creation of "artificial intelligence": a chess program that would not only "play like a master," but even "think like one." "Pioneer" was both his pride and his sorrow, as we;; as his "bluebird."

Misfortunes bedeviled him and forced his brain into constant tension. Thankfully, his mastery of the pen allowed him to write about his suffering continuously. He loved working in peace, preferring the quiet of his dacha office to his Moscow apartment. In his books, Botvinnik was transformed from an ascetic hermit into an ironical sage. Knowledge, the easy phrase, humor, the principled defense of his position, and with it, a unique ability to escape unnecessary politicization in a society raised on slogans and politics.

Botvinnik's multi-volume legacy is a classic of world chess; and his life was an example of unselfish service to the art of chess.

Chapter One

Life and Fate

Childhood and Youth

Mikhail Botvinnik was born on August 17, 1911 in Repino, near St. Petersburg. His mother was a dentist, his father, a dental technician. Moishe Botvinnik possessed great physical strength, and "could take the strongest bull in the state by the muzzle and wrestle it to the ground." However, his younger son bore not the slightest resemblance to Hercules – he did not participate in sports, and was frequently ill. In 1920, his father left the family, but continued to support, and otherwise materially aid, his sons, Misha and Isa.

Following the wishes of his mother, Mikhail started to attend music school, although he was more attracted to photography. One time, one of his mother's patients gave him a book by Muller on gymnastics, and from that point, his illnesses were forgotten, while gymnastics became an inseparable part of Botvinnik's life.

At 12, Mikhail Botvinnik learned how to play chess. Soon he became acquainted with his first chess books. One of them was José Raúl Capablanca's *Chess Fundamentals*. "The first chess book from which I

At 16, Botvinnik became a chess master (1927)

received a systematic idea of chess," wrote Botvinnik. As also the case with the Muller book, the youngster quickly absorbed all the necessary knowledge, and within a year, he began attending the city chess meetings. For this, he needed to "grow up" by three years, since they would not accept him there until he reached 16.

As Botvinnik recalled, he was given a pair of glasses – they gave him a

15

necessary gravitas. The novice quickly and confidently mounted the steps of the competitive hierarchy. Third category, second, first category! And all this in one year! Fate was fortunate in that it gave him the opportunity to play a game with the world champion. On November 20, 1925, Capablanca, on a free day from the Moscow International Tournament, came to Leningrad, and went to the smaller hall of the Philharmonic, where the strongest first-category players of the city awaited him. The youngest participant in the exhibition was Mikhail Botvinnik. The hall was full of chess fans. Each aficionado considered himself capable of telling a young player the only correct move to make, and to keep himself under control. Misha covered his ears. Despite the noise all around, he played quietly and confidently. An accurate Queen's Gambit unfolded, and, exploiting the unfortunate position of White's king, he began attacking. The world champion decided to jettison a pawn, and transpose into an endgame, evidently following the unwritten grandmaster's rule that "with youngsters, go for the endgame!"

But this was not enough. Botvinnik straightforwardly improved his position, realized his material advantage, and the grandmaster resigned.

(1) Capablanca – Botvinnik
Leningrad sim 1925
Nimzo-Indian Defense [D51]

1.d4 d5 2.c4 e6 3.♘c3 ♘f6 4.♗g5 ♘bd7 5.e3 Of course Capablanca does not fall into the opening trap 5.cxd5 exd5 6.♘xd5?? ♘xd5 7.♗xd8 ♗b4+ 8.♕d2 ♗xd2+ 9.♔xd2 ♔xd8–+

5...♗b4 6.cxd5 exd5 7.♕b3?! A bit artificial. 7.♗d3 is the main line. **7...c5 8.dxc5 ♕a5!** Botvinnik reacts forcefully. **9.♗xf6 ♘xf6**

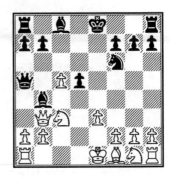

10.0-0-0? This is too optimistic as White's king is not safe. After 10.♗d3, the position is more or less equal. **10...0-0 11.♘f3 ♗e6 12.♘d4 ♖ac8!** Botvinnik brings fresh forces into the attack. **13.c6 ♗xc3** 13...bxc6!?–+ is even stronger. **14.♕xc3 ♕xa2 15.♗d3 bxc6 16.♔c2**

16...c5 This leads more or less by force to a clearly better endgame for Botvinnik. 16...♕a4+!? 17.b3 ♕a2+ 18.♕b2 ♕a5 19.♖a1 ♕c7 might be even better as White's open king is a factor with queens still on the board. **17.♘xe6 ♕a4+ 18.b3 ♕a2+ 19.♕b2 ♕xb2+ 20.♔xb2 fxe6**

21.f3 ♖c7 **22.♖a1** 22.♔c3 ♖b8 23.e4 ♖b4 24.♖a1 ♖cb7 25.♖hb1 is more active and therefore preferable, but Black should win in the long run in any case. **22...c4 23.b×c4 d×c4 24.♗c2 ♖b8+ 25.♔c1 ♘d5 26.♖e1 c3**

27.♖a3? 27.♖a4 to answer 27...♘b4 with 28.♖e2, making it much more difficult for Black to invade White's camp. **27...♘b4 28.♖e2?!** 28.♖g1 is more tenacious. **28...♖d8 29.e4 ♖c6 30.♖e3** 30.♖×a7 ♖d2 31.♖×d2 c×d2+ 32.♔×d2 ♖×c2+−+ **30...♖d2 31.♖e×c3 ♖×c2+ 32.♖×c2 ♖×c2+** "In a hopeless position," Mikhail Moiseevich recalls, "Capablanca swept away the pieces (as a sign that he had resigned) and moved on. The expression on his face was not very pleasant. Therefore I am skeptical about eye-witness reports that the world champion praised my play." (Kasparov in *My Great Predecessors* II) **0-1**

The next day, when Botvinnik went to school (well-known, prior to the revolution, under the name of the Vyborg eight-graded commercial school of Gherman), he was given a hero's welcome.

Mikhail studied assiduously. His teacher had no objection to his passionate enthusiasm for chess, and

looked the other way at his short-term absences. In the autumn of 1926, the 15-year-old Botvinnik was included on the Leningrad team for a match with a team from Stockholm. Horn-rimmed glasses, a suit and hat in the "borsalino" style that were bought for him before he traveled to Sweden lent him gravitas. "Like a London dandy dressed/ He went forth to the test," was the way he quoted his favorite poet. In Stockholm, on fifth board, Botvinnik played the 21-year old Gosta Stoltz (later to become a famous grandmaster) and won (1½-½).

(2) Botvinnik – Stoltz
Stockholm 1926
Queen's Gambit Declined [D55]

1.d4 d5 2.c4 e6 3.♘c3 ♘f6 4.♗g5 ♗e7 5.e3 0-0 6.♘f3 b6 7.♖c1 ♗b7 8.♗d3 ♘bd7 9.0-0 ♘e4 10.♗×e7 ♛×e7 11.c×d5 e×d5

12.♘×e4?! The following piece sacrifice is not completely convincing, so 12.♛b3 is the main line. **12...d×e4 13.♖×c7 ♗c8! 14.♗b5?** White has two better options: 14.♗e2 ♛d8 15.♛c2 e×f3 16.♗×f3 ♖b8 17.♖×a7; and 14.♗b1 e×f3 15.♛×f3, with compensation in both cases. **14...e×f3?** The first step in the wrong direction. 14...♛d8! 15.♖×c8 ♖×c8 16.♘d2 ♘f6 is clearly better for Black. **15.♛×f3**

15...♕d6? A tactical mistake. After 15...♖b8 16.♖xa7 ♕d8 17.♖c1 ♘f6, White has good compensation but not more. **16.♕c6!** The winning blow. **16...♕b4** 16...♕xc6 17.♗xc6 ♖b8 18.♗xd7 +– **17.♕xa8 ♗a6**

18.♕xf8+! The point, as the rooks will overpower the queen. 18.♕d5? ♘f6 19.♕c4 ♕xb5 20.♕xb5 ♗xb5 21.♖fc1 is better for White but not totally clear. **18...♘xf8 19.♗xa6 h5 20.♖xa7 ♕xb2 21.♗c4 ♘e6 22.♗b3 h4 23.d5 ♘d8** 23...♘c5 24.d6 ♘xb3 25.d7 ♕d2 26.♖a8+ ♔h7 27.d8♕ +– **24.♖d7 ♕f6 25.h3 b5 26.e4 ♔h7 27.e5 ♕b6 28.♖e1 b4 29.e6 fxe6 30.dxe6 ♘xe6 31.♖xe6 1-0**

The game was published in the chess column of the newspaper *Izvestia* (December 1, 1926) with the comments of Grigoriev. Summing up its various features, he wrote: "The game is not distinguished for its correctness, but it does credit to the resourceful play of the young Leningrader."

As Botvinnik recalled, one of the organizers of chess life in Leningrad, the chessplayer and translator of chess literature Samuel Osipovich Vainstein (1894-1942) literally made him annotate his game with Stoltz, and in two years induced him to collaborate with him on a book about the Alekhine-Capablanca match, written by Levenfish and Romanovsky.

Evaluating the analysis of the young Leningrader, Vainstein exclaimed, "Not even Bogoljubow would analyze like that!" Comparing him to a candidate for the world championship was undoubtedly flattering to Botvinnik. But early on, he learned to evaluate his own play critically, and his own possibilities also. "The habit of analyzing objectively is very important for the maturing of a chessplayer. Indubitably, this also was a help to my successes in future years," recalled Botvinnik.

Playing the role of Ernest in the Oscar Wilde play with the meaningful name *The Importance of Being Earnest*, Botvinnik excused himself from the school bench. He was not yet 16-years old, and the institute's starting age was 17. In 1927, he played in the candidates tournament for the USSR championship. In the double-round tournament of six, Botvinnik took second place, behind Petr Romanovsky, and soon made his debut in the national championship (see *USSR Championships*), where he shared fifth/sixth places and fulfilled the master norm. After the championship, Mikhail began to prepare for his entrance into the institute: he dreamed of studying at the Leningrad Polytechnic, with his favorite subjects being mathematics and physics.

The "draconian" acceptance rules – 95% workers and 5% by examination scores – did not frighten off this serious youngster. In September, he was accepted by the mathematics faculty, and by February 1928, Botvinnik entered the Polytechnic.

From that moment, chess and academics would always be "running a parallel course" in his life, without interfering with each other. When he was occupied with his studies, Botvinnik would put aside chess. When he played in tournaments, he would forget about electro-technology... Student years are a particular and unforgettable period of life's journey, which the "time express" passes by almost without stopping, leaving only memories of "stations" with the names of subjects and examinations, with the names of our teachers and classmates. For Mikhail Botvinnik, these clear memories were mixed with successful and unsuccessful tournament appearances.

HIs Family
"On May 1, 1934 I traveled to Vassievsky Island," recalled Botvinnik, "to Y. Rochlin. At that time my friend was married to a young ballet soloist, Valentina Lopukhina. I was late: everyone had gathered already. They were seated at table. I sat and glanced at my neighbor on the right, and sat stupefied... Within a year, she became

Valerina Gaiane Ananova

my wife – a fiery brunette, with black, black eyes, slim and elegant. She exuded magic." It was love at first sight! Gaiane Ananovna (Galyuchka, she was called, by her daughter and her husband) concluded her choreographic instruction with the famous Agrippina Vaganova and dedicated the next 24 years to the stage. Constant exercise – exercises at the bar, necessary for maintaining dancing technique – supported her ballet form. Her "bar" was the writing table and chessboard. Ballerina and chessplayer. The first word shows a certain lightness and even airiness, the second breathes seriousness and even dullness... Yes, they were complete opposites – and complemented each other ideally. She was sweet, and kind, and a believer; he was strict, principled, and believed that Communism would win out.

She dedicated herself to family, and considered it necessary to be of service to society. Her moral support and

Botvinnik, surrounded by family

constant presence in the hall aided him in difficult moments. He was stubborn in his dealings with authority, negotiating for the necessity of bringing his wife along to Nottingham, to the AVRO tournament, to Groningen, to The Hague... When Gaiane could not accompany him, she gave instructions for daily living: "On playing days, don't get distracted. Don't pay attention to anything else. Take a lesson from Ulanova: on the day of celebration, from the morning she never speaks with anyone. Remember that a person has but one nervous system."

In August, 1941, the Botvinnik couple were evacuated to Molotov (Perm), along with the Opera Theater and the Kirov Ballet, where Gaiane worked. Here, in April 1942, their daughter Olya was born. In the spring of 1944, they obtained a two-room apartment in Moscow, which looked good to them, after the one-roomer for six in Molotov. But the favorite little living space for the whole family became the dacha, which was built, according to Botvinnik's plan, in 1950, near Moscow in the settlement of Nikolina Gora. Here, Botvinnik would prepare for his next matches for the world championship, here he would rest. "He always took care to rest well – to restore his labor-readiness," recalled his daughter Olga. "In the winter, when he was younger, he would go skiing, and then clear the snow off the dacha. In the summertime, he would clear the paths, and sometimes go canoeing." Time passed. The family grew. Olga got married. "...His grandson, Yurochka, appeared. And then Lenochka. And their grandma grew, too." wrote Botvinnik, in his recollections of his wife. Caring for their grandchildren helped improve the health of Gaiane, who frequently suffered from depression. In 1985, Gaiane Davidovna and Mikhail Moiseevich celebrated their golden anniversary. And two years later, on December 4, 1987, Gaiane died. Botvinnik survived his wife by almost eight years, and succeeded in helping raise his great-grandson Alyosha, and his great-granddaughter Mashenka.

His Personality

Botvinnik lived in an epoch that is easily raised onto a pedestal; but it could just as easily break, and burn up, many a fate. He lived in a world where today's hero could become a fallen idol tomorrow, and fanfares turn into funeral marches. He was of an amazing time, and belonged to that rare cohort who did not turn into its victims.

Alekhine said that "...by means of chess, I nurtured my character." Botvinnik could have said that thanks to his character, he became champion. "He was, as the Americans would put it, a 'self-made man'" – as his daughter Olga wrote of him.

The collectivization, industrialization, and "chessification" of the entire country proceeded simultaneously. This last was the most successful, and the least difficult; but it needed its own Stakhanov [a mythical working-class hero – Tr.], its own symbol. Mikhail Botvinnik, the Komsomolian, deservedly became the right-winger in the numberless army of Soviet chessplayers. He was distinguished by

his honorability, self-confidence and principledness, as well as by the fact that he knew that his mission was to bring home to the Motherland the title of world champion.

In addition to his chess talent and knowing how to defend his convictions, having newly completed the Leningrad polytechnic institute, he had a number of additional qualifications: he knew Russian literature well, giving pride of place to Alexander Pushkin. He was a witty conversationalist; and an excellent dancer, having completely mastered the foxtrot and the Charleston. One day, he heard the following from the lips of Galina Ulanova herself: "I never thought I'd see a chessplayer who could dance." Botvinnik the student, starting out, gained his first successes in electro-technology, and was not content to rest on his laurels. Knowing how to set down his thoughts simply and straightforwardly helped him out, both in his analytical work in chess, and when writing his dissertation.

Neither his frequent interactions with "the most powerful people of his world" – the procurator of the republic, and the executive of the chess section, Krylenko, nor his prizes and awards – the car presented to him by Ordzhonikidze for his victory in Moscow (1935), the order of "The Sign of Honor" for his success at Nottingham (1936) – made him a hypocrite. When he felt it necessary, he agreed to write a letter form report to comrade Stalin about his successes. When he thought it was impossible, he would decline to support a letter about the fabricated "doctors' matter" (1953), and a quarter-century later still, he refused to affix his signature beneath the letter of other

Soviet grandmasters condemning Viktor Korchnoi, when Korchnoi stayed behind in Amsterdam (1976).

Moises Botvinnik, the son of a dental technician, in the mid-1930s, became the pride of the country, His name was known in all corners of the Soviet Union. He was compared to Komsomolits, and was presented as an example to Pioneers. His colossal work ethic was established, once and for all, by his powerful regime. He set himself a goal, and planned out the methods of achieving it. "The business plan of the smartest kid in the world, Mikhail Botvinnik," is what his wife Gaiane wrote in the fall of 1936, not without pleasant irony, when her husband began to "set aside" 12 hours a day for his candidate's dissertation.

Wartime put off the achievement of his chief goal – the title of world chess champion. A serious "close-armedness" meant he did not have to serve, but it could not save him from the Leningrad blockade. His native sense of danger did not betray him, as it had been developed in his chess battles. A couple of years after his 30th birthday, Botvinnik and his wife left the theater, and in less than a month the epic blockade began which took away many thousands, among them his elder brother, talented inventor Isya Botvinnik, who created in Leningrad the first street-lighting system...

"The voice of the people is sacred," said Seneca the Elder. The people's voice pronounced Botvinnik the "Patriarch of the Soviet Chess School" while he was still alive. His authority was indisputable, and his opinion – defining. For a game against the maestro, his

opponents would dress, as for a "final battle": putting on dress clothes, and bringing in as witnesses to the historic event close relatives and their best friends. When he turned 60, he found within himself the strength to say, "Enough!" and ceased playing in tournaments. His experience and knowledge he passed on to students. Among the pupils of the great teacher were some great students: Anatoly Karpov, Garry Kasparov, Vladimir Kramnik (see the *School of Young Talent*).

This epoch went a long way towards defining the guarded and disbelieving attitude of Botvinnik to new encounters and his genuinely Bolshevist irreconcilability with those he considered his enemies. But to his friends, or simply those with whom he was well-acquainted, he always considered it his duty to be helpful. They say that he had no equal in composing letters to higher-ups, and he stood on the carpet of his superiors with distinction, and never begged.

Botvinnik's faith in himself was boundless. Belief in eventual success of his computer program "Pioneer" helped him find his place in life after the "chessic dumbbell." The expansiveness of his thinking defined the expansiveness of his goals. His nephew, Igor Botvinnik, remembers: "Back in September 1984, he sent off to the Central Committee of the KPSS a paper (of some pages' length) on economics. He was ready for any sort of heavy consequences (in those days, this was terrible sedition), but "I had to do it..." Having put together an economic program, he thought only of his unfortunate fellow-citizens. He said that a politician "taking it to heart, could ascend to heaven on a white horse." The program "Economical homo sapiens" was completed in his lifetime, and later given to 18 government functionaries (the list was dictated in the last days of his life).

He never separated himself from his country, and believed that Russia would rise again. Learned, and a humanist. Chernobyl happened – he looked back, and above it, in connection with the spread of atomic plants. He believed that they had to be constructed in the unpopulated regions of the far north, and then the energy could be dispersed throughout the "motherland." Then the work could be performed "in shifts."

Until the end of his days, he thought of work; he regretted that he had never finished his chess program. "I did not have enough time or means to do it..."

By his daughter's admission, Botvinnik, on her school notebook, wrote the following German proverb:

If you lose your money – you lose nothing;
If you lose your health – you lose much;
If you lose honor – you lose everything.

Scholar

"There is no royal road to geometry," said Euclid Ptolemy. There are no privileged paths to learning! Access to its secrets is given only to those of a thinking, inquisitive nature. Botvinnik started his investigations into electro-technology when he was still a student, gaining practical experience in Dneprostroye in 1931. Already then he understood that without "trial and error," it would be hard to find the truth.

Within a year, he became an aspirant of the electro-mechanical faculty, studying under the direction of the excellent Soviet electro-technician A. A. Gorev. Upon completing his internship, in 1937 he defended, in the Industrial institute of Leningrad, his candidate's dissertation on the theme of "On the Influence of Oscillations of Tension on Small Oscillations of the Rotor of a Synchronous Machine." In his work, he showed, for the first time, that it was possible to give a steady transmission of electrical energy over a great distance, if the generators were specially regulated, as was later called "strong" regulation. At the time of evacuation, he was a co-worker in the high-voltage laboratory of the city of Molotov, and suggested an original project: the "leaping" tank, and obtained an author's certificate for the "adaptation of a tank for executing a leap." Later, Botvinnik remembered his invention: "It seemed too fantastic to us. Perhaps. I was not a specialist, but who knows – perhaps, somewhere on the moon, Mars or on some star in Alpha Centauri, cosmonauts will overcome the unevenness of unearthly landscapes with cosmic tanks, armed with this kind of adaptation."

In 1950, the publishing house "Gosenerrproizdat" printed 1500 copies of a book by the world chess champion and electro-technical scholar Mikhail Botvinnik: *Regulation of the Startup and Statistical Permanence of the Synchronous Machine.*

A copy of this rare edition is in the library of one of the authors of this book, with the gifting inscription: *To my most dear friend, Isaac Maksovich Linder, from Botvinnik, 9/10/52"*

23

The next link in the chain of Botvinnik's scholarly pursuits was the defense of his doctoral dissertation, which took place a month and a half after the conclusion of his match for the world championship against David Bronstein – June 28, 1951. The theme was an exact repetition of the name of the above-cited book.

The scholarly laboratory of Botvinnik had no table. He considered that, as soon as a scholar had a fundamental table, he would cease to be a thinker.

"I never made anything special, except during wartime," said Botvinnik. "For us, everything flowed from the basic theme of the work." Study of the problem of the creation of regulated energetical machines of alternating current brought Botvinnik's scientific group yet another triumph. On September 17, 1958 – that is, soon after Botvinnik's victory in his return match with Vassily Smyslov – his invention was registered as a state invention of the USSR, number 119590. One can only marvel at Botvinnik's ability to switch from chess over to electro-technology, and with that gain tremendous success.

A short time later, Botvinnik's book, *The Asynchronous Synchronous Machine*, was published in the USSR, and later, in England. Botvinnik's experimental researches in electro-technology, partly his interesting methods of regulating the stimulation of synchronous generators and carrying out work, the first in the world, in the creation of principally new, asynchronous synchronous machines had significant influence on the progress in this offshoot of science and technology.

*Botvinnik in his
electro-technical laboratory*

At the beginning of the 1960s, Botvinnik the scientist was absorbed by a totally new idea – the creation of "artificial intelligence" – the chess program "Pioneer," playing at the strength of a contemporary grandmaster. To the realization of this, at first sight, fantastic idea he dedicated the next 30 years of his life.

Algorithm of the Master
The idea of creating an "electronic chessplayer" came to Botvinnik in 1958, during a tele-discussion he had with Max Euwe (cf. *Netherlands*). From that time until the end of his days, it unceasingly pursued the first Soviet world champion.

From the very beginning, when the computer still played at the level of a beginner, it attempted to "embrace the unembraceable" in each and every position, searching for the solution by exhaustively analyzing variations. Then Botvinnik set himself the task of reducing the "tree of variations" and shortening the length of those variations. Because a full "variations tree" would comprise, according to mathematicians' calculations, about 10 to the 120th positions! This compelled him to change the goal of the search itself – instead of exact play, leading to mate, aim for the win of material by less exact play, which allows a sharp reduction of choices.

Botvinnik started to spread his new approach to the study of the problem in his public appearances. Back in 1960-61, he read in Berlin, at Humboldt University, a lecture on the theme of "People and Machines at the Chessboard." Then he published an article in *Komsomolskaya Pravda*. And on May 13, 1966, he set up a debate in Moscow, with the participation of mathematicians and chessplayers, at the Central Chess Club of Moscow. He met with Claude Shannon. In 1968, the publishing house "Nauka" published Botvinnik's book, *The Algorithm of Chess Play*; within three years, it was printed in English in New York. In it, he formulated the method of modelling a chess master in the selection of a move, based on positional evaluation, tossing out every additional and unnecessary move in the variations.

Botvinnik showed the future of the "inexact goal" of the computer for the solution of certain tasks of economics, as in planning the refitting of the construction of massive "unified energo-systems" of the USSR. This aided him, in 1972, to break through the

"Chinese wall" of lack of understanding in the Goscommittee for Science and Technology, the Ministry of Energy and the Head Calculating Center of the USSR Gosplan. Agreement was obtained to open the scientific theme for work on a chess program and "machine time" was set aside for its research.

In an interview for the weekly *64*, Botvinnik mentioned the programmers' search – and was shortly inundated with letters – 20 from Moscow, 10 from other cities nationwide, one from Holland, and Australia (!). Four years later, his nameless program was named "Pioneer." By that time, it played a decent opening and endgame, and its logical thinking was similar to the thinking of a chessplayer. The first of the achievements of "Pioneer" was to solve the famous Réti study.

White to move and draw

1.♔g7 h4 2.♔f6 h3 3.♔e6 h2 4.c7; 2...♔b6 3.♔e5 h3 4.♔d6 h2 5.c7

There followed solutions to studies by Caminer and Nadareishvili. Finally, Botvinnik took great pride in showing how "Pioneer" had found the winning continuation in the game Botvinnik-Capablanca (see *Famous Games*). As far as Pioneer's ability increased, Botvinnik considered it his duty to make it an achievement for the larger society. In 1975, the publishers Sovietskoye Radio issued his book, *On the Cybernetic Goal of the Game*; within four years, the same publishing house issued his new book, *The Solution of Inexact Gradations.*

In an appendix to chess play, this theme was developed by Botvinnik in his book, *The Chess Method of Resolving Gradation Tasks*, which was released in 1989 from the publishers Sovietsky Sport.

At the basis of his researches, as we already noted, Botvinnik strove to establish the method of positional evaluation which the master uses when deciding upon a move. But, alas, there are also factors in chess which are not amenable to modeling – intuition and, to a great extent, the master's imagination, sometimes in contradiction to formal logic, but forming one of the bases of the art of chess. Perhaps, for this reason, the idea of the creation of an artificial chess intellect, in the form it was thought up in the course of many years, was *a priori* the dream of the sixth world champion, and scholar.

And though, toward the end of his life, Botvinnik grew more and more convinced that in the solution to the problem of the "electronic chessplayer" mankind would achieve ever greater success, by taking a different course – a sharp increase in the processing speed and the amount of memory in a computer – he would not give up hoping for "the understanding and formalization of the algorithm of the chess master." He opined that, in the future, the "electronic chessplayer" would kill off this ancient and clever game. Botvinnik was an optimist, and in answer to these complaints, he would say: "Many are afraid that the utilization of such machines will mean the technical end of chess. I don't believe it. It is been a hundred years since the invention of the automobile, but people still race in stadiums with pleasure. I think that a chess machine will result in a still greater popularization of chess."

The School of Young Talents
From his earliest years, Botvinnik had forced himself to be independent, to have self-control and self-discipline. He was a creative, independent personality. "You have no feeling of gregariousness," the famous mathematician N. A. Krilitsky once said to him. In society, as everybody always said, such a compliment was worth a great deal.

The principle of independence became a basic feature of the pedagogical activity of Botvinnik. The first examples of the students of the 25-year old Botvinnik were the scholars with whom he occupied himself in the mid-1930s in the "Don Quixote" room of the Leningrad House of Scholars. Soon his wards were young chessplayers, but of a considerably higher qualification level. The 27-year old instructor was now teaching in the office of Alexander III.

At the close of the 1930s, the Anichkov Palace was "converted" into a House of

A summer session of the Botvinnik-Kasparov School in the Lithuanian city of Druskininkai. Among the participants are: Kramnik, Tiviakov and Shirov.

Pioneers, in which a chess club also was opened. "We worked on Sundays," recalled Botvinnik, "once every two weeks (10-12 people) – one worked at a demonstration board, while the rest listened and critiqued. Discussions arose, the atmosphere was electric. The demonstrators were selected in advance. They mentioned tasks they had fulfilled, of the most varied types: theoretical collections of endgames, annotated games, the analysis of a particular opening, etc. The character of the tasks was defined by the chess qualities of the student: let's say, he played poorly in the opening phase of a game, or carelessly analyzed his own games – that was precisely what determined the type and theme of the task. For each attendee, the approach was individualized."

One of his students in this period was the future international grandmaster, Mark Taimanov, who recalled with gratitude his teacher and his method: "Emphasis was on the breadth and accuracy of analysis, attention to detail, and chiefly to the independence of your conclusions. Botvinnik required of his students a careful and critical breakdown of the tournament games they had played. Now, looking back, I understand how smart this was: Botvinnik taught us, not only to work carefully over the board, but to use the same approach to the literary novelties, so necessary to the chess life of a professional."

In 1939 Botvinnik, with royal generosity, shared with the world of chess his experience and views on his system of preparation, publishing it in a tournament collection dedicated to the 11th USSR championship: an article entitled "My methods of preparation for events; my tournament regimen."

One has to be firmly convinced of his powers, in order to, as a candidate for the world championship, reveal the secrets and particulars of one's creative laboratory. Additionally, this was the step of an Enlightener and Teacher.

In the mid-1960s in Moscow, the sport organization "Trud" put together a chess school of gifted young chessplayers, and made its first instructor Botvinnik. Three times a year, during vacations, twenty youngsters from different cities of the country came to the school for lessons. Among its students were Anatoly Karpov, from the Ural city of Zlatoust, Yuri Balashov, from the city of Sharinsk, Naum Rashkovsky from Karaganda, Yuri Razuvaev from Moscow. All of them became international grandmasters, while Karpov went on to become world champion.

Botvinnik always reminded his young students that chess is not just a battle of minds, but a battle of nerves as well. "The winner," he wrote, turning to youth, "is the one who has greater stamina, who does not get lost in difficult positions, keeps his self-control until the end of the game, who has the stronger will." Botvinnik did not advise playing "unceasingly," one tournament after another.

"In order to play successfully, one must endure chess hunger," he considered. And not infrequently, he would tell his students, "Don't play too often – leave yourselves time to think about chess." The veteran of chess taught his youngsters to think for themselves, work and analyze independently. It is interesting that one day, when he suggested that his students analyze his adjourned position against Fischer from the 1962 Olympiad, 13-year-old Baku student Garry Kasparov found still another road to the draw which had not been found before, either by Botvinnik or by the other grandmasters. This was

already representative of the next wave of young chess talents, including Dolmatov, Yusupov, Psakhis, Kharitonov, Ehlvest, Rozentalis, Sokolov, Ionov, Nenashev, Akhmylovskaya, Ioseliani, and Zaitseva. All of them candidates, champions, grandmasters. The winter and summer sessions of the Botvinnik school occurred in a rest home near Moscow; the fall sessions, on the banks of the Black Sea in the Pioneer camp "Orlenok" (near Tuapse).

The methods of exercises of Botvinnik have been exhaustively described by Kasparov in the second volume of his series, *My Great Predecessors* (2003). In it, he writes: "Botvinnik's lessons were given according to a system, which was tested by him back before the war in the Leningrad Hall of Pioneers: everybody would study the play of one of the students together. At first, he would reveal his work between sessions, his successes in his studies, his efforts at sports, his participation in tournaments and his fulfillment of homework assignments; then he would demonstrate four of his recent games. During the sessions, we would also play training games; then we would analyze everything in the world; after which, using the words of the maestro, a final diagnosis would be made, and a cure prescribed – that is, homework. Additionally, we would be taught priceless professional secrets of preparation for events...

"And towards these young talents he gravitated with his whole soul. The wise old teacher tried not to overwhelm us by his authority, not to attach the kids to his own style, but on the contrary, help us in every possible way to develop our own possibilities. No pressure; with his native pedagogical tact, he would indicate the right direction. Immediately sensing my striving for a dynamic attacking style, his assignments for my homework included analysis of Alekhine's games."

Something like 40 years passed since Botvinnik's first teaching experiences, but his method remained the same and continued to bear excellent fruit. "I am sure," emphasized Garry Kasparov in 1985, after he won the world champion's title, "that the five years I spent in the Botvinnik school (1973-78) played a decisive role in my formation as a chessplayer, and defined the path of my further maturation."

Many of Botvinnik's students became, not just famous chessplayers themselves, but also good trainers (Balashov, Yusupov, Dolmatov, Razuvaev), and Garry Kasparov, having become champion of the world, continued to help his teacher educate new talents. The school now became known as the Botvinnik-Kasparov School. In 1987, its enrollment included, at Botvinnik's insistence, an 11-year-old master-candidate from Tuapse, Vladimir Kramnik. In March, 1988, Botvinnik participated for the last time in a teaching session at his school.

Political Horizons

"To serve one's native land by doing good works is excellent, but it is also an excellent thing to serve it by good speech," as the Roman historian Gaius Sallust (86-35 B.C.) said. Botvinnik was a patriot, and citizen of his Motherland, serving it by word, deed, and with his pen. The breadth of his horizon, unrestricted by the extent of the 64

squares of the chessboard, let him "separate the wheat from the chaff." His journeys abroad and the chance for him to compare life "here" with the life "there" set him thinking and allowed him to conclude that did not always coincide with the "party line." But his own inclination and his standing with that party were sacred for Botvinnik, and he never exploited them for career purposes. Nevertheless, honor and his principled nature plus a definite courageousness and understanding of his "regal" position called him to action. During the course of three difficult decades in the life of the country (1954-84), Botvinnik approached the Central Committee of the CPSU. The first was a letter to the academic and secretary of the Central Committee of the CPSU, N. N, Pospelov, which he sent off on May 29, 1954. It was called, "Is it possible to have a socialist revolution in the West without a Third World War?"

In a few pages, Botvinnik gave his analysis of the political situation in the world of the "cold war." In the opposition of the two camps – the socialist and the communist – he saw the threat of another worldwide conflict, and the rise of nuclear weapons threatening nuclear catastrophe. Botvinnik suggested, in detail, point by point, his plan of action to isolate the monopolists without shootings or bombings. "In what circumstances should they be placed, so that they would not have need of atomic warfare?" That was Botvinnik's question; his answer to it was: "For this, apparently, we do not need to deprive the capitalists of their "paradise" entirely, nor their families of their sweet life, etc. If now the monopolists spend upon their needs a significant amount of their additional profit value (profit per Marxism), would it not be right to set aside some of this profit (e.g., 25%), so that they would not need an atom bomb?

"It is not without interest to note that the British communist party also examines the payment of partial compensation to their landowners 'who remain loyal to the peoples' government...'

"It seems to me that, if one guaranteed (in the Western world) to the petit bourgeoisie the retention of 100% of their profits after the revolution, one might isolate the monopolists from the people, free humanity from atomic catastrophe, and create the conditions for a rapid socialist revolution in the West."

An answer to this letter was a "Note from the Secretary of the Central Committee of the CPSR, P. N. Pospelov re: The Errors of M. Botvinnik" from June 19, 1954, with the threatening conclusion:

"The 'notes' of Botvinnik are of interest, as displaying bourgeois ideology of a Laborite type and a fear of capitalist encirclement.

"I suggest that we ask Botvinnik into the Department of Propaganda and Agitation of the Central Committee and explain to him the anti-Marxist nature of his notes. And if he insists on his non-Communistic views, then it seems to me that he can no longer remain a Party member."

On December 27, 1954, Botvinnik wrote another letter to P. N. Pospelov, in which he agreed that he had committed a number of oversights, but could not understand how it was that his position could be taken for laborism?

"You have stated, Peter Nikolayevich, that my suggestions, directed towards the resolution of this task, are naive. I cannot but take your instructions into consideration and guidance. However, if these suggestions are out of place, then, in my view, you are obligated to find other suggestions. Marxism-Leninism shows the people the way to a shining future; it must show humanity also the way to rid themselves of nuclear catastrophe. It seems to me that today this may be done; tomorrow, perhaps, it will be too late."

A quarter-century later, on December 12, 1978, Botvinnik wrote a letter to a new secretary of the Central Committee of the CPSR, V. Zimyanin, about another matter, the program "Pioneer": a request to provide all the help possible to his work, and aid in the exporting of his program to West Germany or to the USA, where it would be possible to finish work on the creation of artificial intelligence. Over the course of the next two months, Botvinnik would continuously remind him of his note, since he believed that "finishing the work on the program would be of great value to the Soviet Union."

Finally, on February 9, 1979, in the department of science and scholarly pursuits of the Central Committee of the CPSR, there arrived notification from Botvinnik, the outcome of which was a conclusion by S. G. Sherbakov: "Botvinnik is not alone in his concern over the development of science; many scientists think about this also."

The "Pioneer" program was "not to leave!"

Seven more years passed, and the name Botvinnik was once again mentioned in the corridors of the Central Committee of the CPSR, with a negative connotation. According to a secret file of the KGB of May 17, 1984, "a conversation occurred between ex-world chess champion Botvinnik and former Soviet citizen M. A. Feinberg, who exited the USSR for Israel in 1979. At the present time, Feinberg lives in the USA and works as a correspondent for the anti-Soviet edition of *Novoye Russkoye Slovo*, and regularly appears in the emigrant press with positions hostile to the USSR."

Zimyanin referred this to the chief of the propaganda department of the Central Committee of the CPSR, B. I. Stukalin: "Think about how to bring to order comrade Botvinnik. His behavior is cynical and completely impermissible with his civic positions."

As a result, Botvinnik was "called on the carpet" by the deputy president of the Sport Committee V. A. Ivonin, and Stukalin put together a "Reference for Propaganda of the Central Committee of the CPSR" for June 13, 1984, labelled "Secret." Among other things, it said that Comrade Botvinnik "affirmed that during his visit to the U.S. he had conversations with Feinberg, but the sense of part of his expressions is spoiled by the author. Instead, he noted that certain thoughts from the interview were said before in the Soviet press and in public appearances."

"Comrade Botvinnik, it was noted, made some non-allowable remarks, which could redound to the harm of our country or which carried an insulting character as regards Soviet chessplayers. Taking into account Botvinnik's behavior, and the unhealthy interest displayed towards him by our ideological opponents, we suppose it a good idea to restrict his external journeys."

When, in May of 1993, all the above-cited letters were being prepared for printing in the magazine, "Historical Archive" (1993, Nos. 1-2), Botvinnik summed up all of the above, by saying: "It may be that, when all of this material is read, there will be less prohibition of my work. Then the past will extend its hand to the present."

Guest Appearances

Botvinnik's name possessed amazing magical power. His match and tournament performances were followed with great interest the world over. His books enjoyed large print runs, and were always in demand, translated and reprinted in many countries. His lectures resulted in filled halls everywhere. To play against him in exhibitions was considered an honor, and brought joy to many, both in the USSR and elsewhere.

Although finding an "opening" for lengthy appearances in Botvinnik's busy calendar was not easy, he found the time for it, since he thought it his duty in every way possible to help popularize chess in the world by appearing, not just in tournaments, but in exhibitions and lectures, by giving interviews and publishing articles in the general and specialized press. It was quite natural that more often Muscovites and Leningraders had the chance to see and hear him by playing against him in exhibitions.

But at various times, he also traveled to Vladimir, Tula, Yaroslavl, Rostov-on-Don, Saransk, Minsk, Riga, Odessa, Yerevan, Baku, Ashkabad, and many other cities and republics of the Soviet Union. Twice – in August 1965 and 1968 – Mikhail Botvinnik and his Dutch friends Max Euwe and Wilhelm Mohring travelled all over Siberia and the Far East. They were guests in Sverdlovsk, Novosibirsk, Irkutsk, Krasnoyarsk, Khabarovsk, and Vladivostok. They gave exhibitions and lectures, which received wide acclaim in the press. For example, Scherbak's article on Botvinnik's clock simultaneous in Vladivostok, appearing in the paper *Krasnoye Znamya* of August 29, 1968, headlined "Botvinnik Accepts the Challenge":

"At the chess tables drawn into a circle, sit the players. They are nervous, ruffling their hair and thinking for a long time over every move. The opponent of each of them is the same, but what an opponent – Botvinnik himself!

"Ten first-category players, the majority of them students, "threw down the gauntlet" to the famous grandmaster and former champion of the world.

"Despite his 57 years, Mikhail Moiseevich is still youthfully hale and energetic. After each of his moves, a whisper makes the rounds of the spectators; some carefully note down the moves of each game, while others simply follow the play of the famed chessplayer.

"The three-hour battle is over. Only three out of the ten – students V. Baranov, V. Kovalenko, and L. Shabarov – were able to withstand the assault of the ex-world champion and brought their games to a draw. The rest suffered the agony of defeat. But losing to Botvinnik, before whom, for many years, the best chessplayers in the world laid down their arms – there is no shame in that!

"Mikhail Moiseevich analyzed the play of all the players in the exhibition in detail, and respectfully noted the abilities of his youthful opponents, calling on them to study harder and train themselves some more, increasing their mastery. After his appearance, which was greeted with applause, Botvinnik drew into a tight circle all those who respected his talent. The questions came down like rain, and requests for autographs... Even when the grandmaster left the Hall of Culture, heading for his hotel, a long line of his fans stretched behind him. Experienced and beginning players walked shoulder-to-shoulder, walking and talking about chess matters."

Botvinnik generated quite as much of a reaction and interest with his lectures and exhibitions in other appearances as well. And the opinions of the Patriarch of Soviet chess (as Botvinnik was often labeled by the Soviet press) were treated with special interest and respect. Two examples: some replies by Botvinnik to questions by the listeners of the Riga University of chess culture, after his lecture, which occurred right after the world championship match between Karpov and Korchnoi in Merano, 1981:

How do you evaluate the outcome of the world championship match in Merano, from a creative standpoint?

The candidate did not play at the necessary level. Whereas Karpov made practically no errors. It was like Capablanca in his best years.

Do you consider the current system of playing for the world championship these days to be correct?

I don't like the large number of participants in the Interzonals, or the Candidates' matches, or the world championship match to six wins. It would be more sensible to have the match for the world championship of 20 to 24 games, and a match-tournament for the Candidates'.

Which particular traits of Garry Kasparov enabled him so rapidly to become a world-class chessplayer?

This is an exceptional chess talent, but he is subjective and too hasty making decisions. Very respectful, genuine; but with little experience of life. His talent reminds me of Alekhine.

What, do you think, is the optimal age for competitive achievements in chess?

The optimal age for achieving the heights in chess is 30 to 40 years old. One must develop positional understanding, in order to compensate for the reduced calculating capacity of variations. A chessplayer-researcher can maintain his strength until 50 years of age.

Could you compare Fischer's fate with Morphy's?

Yes.

Who was the greatest world champion of all?

Capablanca. He played intuitively.

Which chess journalist do you consider the most objective?

Tal.

Botvinnik's appearances outside our borders also were of great interest. He made most of them after playing in tournaments. He played in Dutch tournaments especially often. Here he would appear also as the chief of the USSR-Netherlands society (cf. *Netherlands*). After the Hastings tournament of 1966/67, Botvinnik made a grand tour "of chess Albion" – this is how he described his English appearances in his memoirs (cf. *Great Britain*).

While still world champion, Botvinnik toured Switzerland and West Germany with Salo Flohr. The first of these occurred during the period from January 26 to February 6, 1956, and was marked by exhibitions in Zürich, Basel, Lucerne and Zoloturn. Chess society was focused, of course, on the clock exhibition in Zürich against eight of the strongest players in the country, who two years earlier had represented the Swiss team at the 11th Olympiad in Amsterdam. The world champion won six games, lost one to Kupper, and drew one with Zimmerman.

(3) Botvinnik – Grob
Clock Simul, Zürich 1956
Réti Opening [D06]

1.♘f3 ♘f6 2.c4 d5?! White's center will be very strong soon. **3.c×d5 ♘×d5 4.e4 ♘f6 5.♘c3 e6 6.d4 c5** 6...♗e7 is played most often, but White is already clearly for choice. **7.d5 a6 8.♗g5 ♕b6 9.♗×f6 g×f6 10.♕d2 h5 11.♗e2 ♘d7 12.0-0 h4 13.a4 ♗h6 14.♕c2 ♗f4 15.a5 ♕c7 16.♖fd1 ♘e5 17.♘×e5 ♗×e5 18.h3 ♗d7**

19.♘a4! The knight heads for b6. **19...♗×a4** 19...0-0 can be answered by 20.♘b6 ♖ad8 21.♗c4 e×d5 22.♘×d5 ♕d6 23.♖a3, when Black's king is not really safe. **20.♖×a4**

20...♖c8? 20...♔e7 is necessary to defend the dark squares and connect the rooks. **21.♖c4 ♕×a5?** Grob's capture

is too greedy. He should secure his king with 21...0-0, but White remains on top after 22.b4 ♖fd8 23.♖×c5 ♕b8 24.♗c4 **22.b4! ♕a3?** Now Black's king no longer has enough defenders. But White also wins after 22...♕b6 23.b×c5 ♕a5 24.c6 b5 25.♖c5 e×d5 26.e×d5 ♕c7 27.♗g4 +– **23.♖×c5 ♖d8** 23...♖×c5 24.♕×c5 +– **24.d×e6 ♗d6** 24...0-0 25.e7 ♖×d1+ 26.♕×d1 ♖e8 27.♕d8 ♕a1+ 28.♗f1 ♕a4 29.b5 +–

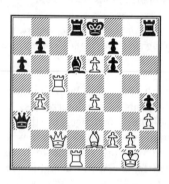

25.♖×d6! Botvinnik starts the final combination. **25...♖×d6 26.♖c8+ ♔e7** 26...♖d8 27.♕c7 0-0 28.♖×d8+ – **27.♕c7+ ♔×e6 28.♗g4+ f5** 28...♔e5 29.♕c5+ ♔×e4 30.♕f5+ ♔d4 31.♕f4+ ♔d5 32.♖c5 # **29.♗×f5+ ♔e5 30.♕c5+ 1-0**

At the end of September, 1959, Botvinnik completed a three-week journey through West Germany, accompanied by grandmaster Sal Flohr and master L. Abramov. The world champion's exhibitions in Bremen, Hamburg, Nurnberg and Hannover caused a real chessic stir. Botvinnik, as usual, played 25 boards at a time. In one of the exhibitions, by his own admission, he performed less than spectacularly (+9, -1, =15), but then read the next day in the newspaper that "Botvinnik destroyed the Bremenites."

During his appearances, literally everyone was interested in Botvinnik – he visited A. Sprinter, the famous publishing house in Hamburg, the ancient royal castle in Nurnberg, was a guest of the president of the West German chess union, Dr. Wildhagen, who was also famous for having issued a bibliography of the world's leading chessplayers, and gave him 400 games for the "Botvinnik" volume, attended the opening of the next West German championship, and a performance of a French ballet troupe.

*Botvinnik's exhibition
in West Germany*

From Germany, Botvinnik and Flohr set out for Sweden, where they had been invited by FIDE President Folke Rogard. The Swedes remembered that the 15-year-old Misha Botvinnik had made his first trip outside his borders into Stockholm (cf. *Youth and Childhood*). And here, 35 years later, world champion Mikhail Botvinnik was once again in the capital of Sweden, this time as an honored guest. And the following year, 1960, a congress of Swedish chessplayers made a unanimous decision to award Botvinnik a gold medal of the Swedish Chess Federation for his great efforts to develop the art of chess.

In 1973, Botvinnik visited 15 West German cities, among them Kiel, Hamburg, Bremen, Cologne, Bonn, etc. Along with his exhibitions, he also gave press conferences, and appeared on radio and television. One of the organizers of these trips was grandmaster Lothar Schmid, the chief arbiter of the Fischer-Spassky match. Having completed his tour, accompanied by the correspondence grandmaster Yakov Estrin, Botvinnik visited, in Tilburg, the 84-year-old widow of Efim Bogoljubow, who told him about the last years alive of the grandmaster and shared her impressions of the Russian participants in the 1914 Mannheim tournament, Selezniev, Rabinovich, and Romanovsky. In December 1975, Botvinnik read a lecture in West Berlin concerning the state of the chess world. Among other things, he said, "The appearance of Fischer on chess' Olympus, and the interest in him has led to a growth in the popularity of chess the world over – two-thirds of the nations in the UN belong to FIDE. But alas! Fischer's brief span of activity has also led to events in FIDE: the same disputes and arguments which were involved in the matches in 1972 and 1975, which were not possible in the period 1949 thru 1969, when a proper constitution for the world championship struggle was in place. Maybe this situation in FIDE will rouse an unhealthy interest on the part of the wider public. But this can hardly help in the creation of a genuinely creative atmosphere among the kings of chess. Nevertheless, there is no reason for pessimism. One hopes that the younger generation will serve the goddess Caissa with greater energy."

Among Botvinnik's memorable journeys in later years were transoceanic voyages to Toronto (1978) and New York (1983), for the World Computer Championships, and to Brussels (1991), where the quarterfinal matches for the world championship were held, and where he celebrated his 80th birthday.

In 1990, the Italian Chess Association awarded him the coveted prize in the name of Gioaccino Greco – "Una Vita Por Scacchi." Evaluating the contribution of this individual to the Renaissance era, Botvinnik wrote: "Greco was an outstanding representative of the Italian school of chess, who brought into chess praxis the combination as a full-fledged element of the algorithm of the master."

In this manner, by his unflagging and multi-faceted activity, Mikhail Botvinnik, one of the great players of the 20th century, aided the progress and popularization of the art of chess in the world.

Curiosities
Life did not deprive Botvinnik of this, either.

His Victorious Name
Botvinnik visited the Netherlands quite frequently.

"Do You know how your name sounds in Dutch?" asked a chess-fan once. "Bot-vin-ich" is translated to mean, "But I win."

Thirty years later, Botvinnik described this episode to his friend Grudkel – one of the leaders of the friendship society "USSR-Netherlands" – who laughed heartily. It turned out that "bot-vin-ich" has the same meaning as "win from an idiot!"

The Miraculous Pawn
On May 9, 1948, Botvinnik played his last game of the match-tournament for the world championship against Euwe, and, in making 14.b2-b4 with White, decided to offer a draw. After a little thought, the Dutch grandmaster agreed. What happened afterward was related by the one responsible for the celebration: "The noise and excitement in the hall was indescribable. The game on the next board had to be held up. It took the Chief Arbiter, Milan Vidmar, some time to quiet the crowd. Friends took me away to celebrate the victory."

Sometime later, the film crew was upset that they had not "preserved" forever the moment of my completing the move 14.b4, which brought the Soviet nation the champion's title. Then they pointed out that Estrin, who had been operating the demonstration board, had the same suit on that the newly-crowned champion was wearing. The filmgoers never suspected that the "historic" move, b2-b4, at the chess table in the movie was made, not by the champion, but by the demonstrator.

The b-pawn's "story" did not end there, however. Elizaveta Bykova took it as a talisman, for she was certain that this pawn would help her become world champion herself. And in fact, it did!

Also, the humble demonstrator, who touched this truly "miraculous" pawn, went on himself to become world correspondence champion!"

A Bad Sign

At the 16th Olympiad (1964), during the match USSR-Spain, the former world champion Mikhail Botvinnik was playing against the international master, Antonio Medina. Suddenly, Botvinnik rose and approached his team captain, Alexander Kotov, "My opponent will not let me concentrate. He whistles all the time, under his breath."

When Kotov complained to the captain of the Spanish team, he sadly shook his head and said,

"That's a bad sign."

"Why?"

"Look, if Medina starts whistling, it means that his position is absolutely hopeless!"

The Netherlands

Seven international tournaments, the match-tournament for the world championship, and an Olympiad – such was the Dutch service record of Mikhail Botvinnik.

An incomparable kingdom of cyclists, canals, and tulips. Here, Botvinnik negotiated for a world championship match with Alexander Alekhine after the conclusion of the AVRO tournament (1938). Here he outstripped the hero of the nation, Dr. Max Euwe (Groningen 1946). Here he laid the foundation for his historic triumph in the match-tournament for the world championship (1948). Here he won a famous game with Capablanca. And not

coincidentally, in 1960, Mikhail Botvinnik became president of the board of directors of the friendship society "USSR-Netherlands."

In his book, *Achieving the Aim* (1978), he wrote: "My chessic fate was so ordered, that in this country, I appeared many dozens of times. There are a lot of chessplayers in Holland: intellectuals and workers, children and grownups, Catholics and Protestants – all types of people play chess... The 'USSR-Netherlands' friendship society unites both large numbers of Soviet specialists, connected to the culture, economics, arts and history of the Dutch people, and everyone interested in this original and beautiful country. Our government, in its activity, strives to strengthen good relations between our two peoples."

During one of Botvinnik's trips to the Netherlands, in autumn 1958, at the invitation of his friend, Dr. Max Euwe, he was able to appear on a television broadcast devoted to the role of the computer in the life of contemporary society. And when Euwe put the question to the world champion, "Will the computer be able to play chess stronger than a man?," Botvinnik, without thinking, replied, "Yes!" And... he got 100 gulden for it!

In his book, *The Chessplayer and The Machine*, he jokingly said, "It is well-known that everything started with Eve... But in my creative path, a lot began, not with Eve, but with Euwe. It was, in fact, he who, in 1934, obtained an invitation for me to the New Year's tournament in Hastings – that was my very first international tournament. And now, after Euwe's question, I started to think, how to teach the computer to play well at chess." (cf. *Algorithm of the Master*)

By a caprice of fate, it was precisely in Holland, at the tournament in Leiden (1970), that Botvinnik closed out his competitive career. The competitive record of his Dutch appearances is impressive: five first places in international tournaments – Groningen 1946, Wageningen 1958, Amsterdam 1963 and 1966, Noodwijk 1965, one shared first/second places in Beverwijk 1969, one third place at AVRO 1938, and third/fourth places at Leiden (1970). In eight tournaments, he scored 41 wins, 37 draws, and only 8 losses (69.2%). He showed the best result on first board in the 1954 Amsterdam Olympiad (1954), with 8½ out of 11 (+6 -0 =5 77.3%). He also won confidently the first half of the 1948 world championship match-tournament in the Hague: 6 points out of 8 (+4 -0 =4).

Another direction of Botvinnik's activity proved particularly useful to Euwe's native land. In June 1988, at the invitation of a patron of the art of chess and all-around public figure Bessel Kok, he carried out in Moscow, together with Alexei Shirov and Gennady Sosonko, a special instructional session for the 19-year-old talent Jeroen Piket. "The result of our ten-day labors," said Botvinnik, "was a 'diagnosis' and 'cure': within a year, Piket became a grandmaster, and a few years later, one of the leading chessplayers of the Netherlands and Europe.

And an additional interesting note in Botvinnik's popularity in the Netherlands. Even a chess romantic like grandmaster Jan Timman, under the influence of Botvinnik above all others, noted in 1974: "I consider myself a student of the Soviet School of Chess... My chief 'guide' has been Botvinnik, with his instructive attitude toward chess, his deep penetration into the secrets of a position, his knowing how to induce the opponent to play his game."

Great Britain

Botvinnik played in four English tournaments, traveling there each time in a new role – as a debutant in international tournaments, candidate for the world championship, world champion, and former champion!

In 1934, the 23-year-old Soviet master Mikhail Botvinnik traveled across the border to participate in the Hastings New Year's tournament of 1934/35. In his memory, there always remained his difficult journey through all Europe in a "seated" railroad car: the train, following the Ostende-Dover route; the unfriendly English police at the passport desk. True, he only needed to see the invitation of the Hastings club for his whole behavior to change: he himself filled out all the forms and showed where his transport to London was. The policeman loved chess!

A year and a half later, Botvinnik and his young wife, Gaiane, traveled to the "tournament of champions" at Nottingham (1936). Following the wise advice of Emanuel Lasker, the

Botvinnik couple arrived a few days before the start of this respected event, so as to successfully acclimatize themselves. The day after arriving at the Victoria Station Hotel, Botvinnik and his wife were guests of the president of the Nottingham chess association and the tournament organizer, Mr. Derbyshire.

The tournament showed the world that, behind the "iron curtain," there had grown a worthy replacement generation for the Russian emigrés Alekhine and Bogoljubow. In the 1960s, Botvinnik played twice more at Hastings, and won first prize both times. Botvinnik always wrote with great sympathy for Great Britain.

In his essay published in the journal *Novy Mir* (1967/11), "Chess in Albion," speaking of his impressions of his guest appearances after the conclusion of the Hastings tournament, among other things, he gave a hint of the subtle humor peculiar to the English (and, we note, to himself also)... In Glasgow, for example, Botvinnik amazed the Scots with his familiarity with the works of Robert Burns, as the language of that famous poet was hard to understand even for contemporary Englishmen. And when he said that he read the poet in Marshack's translation, master Baruch Wood noted:

"That's something; now, if only one could translate Marshack, then the English could also learn to read Burns..."

Upon visiting the House of Commons in London, Botvinnik struck up a conversation about chess and international politics with a certain gentleman of impressively aristocratic bearing.

"How do you regard international society?," he asked Botvinnik.

"Pessimistically. The world is forever divided into two warring camps – chessplayers and non-chessplayers."

In 1981, his book, *Achieving the Aim*, was published in London. In the preface, Botvinnik wrote: "Some of my tournament appearances involved with the chess life of Britain, so it is pleasant, and an honor, for me that the book, *Achieving the Aim*, should come out in England." And as an introduction to his next production: "I hope that this book will aid in the development of British chess, which now stands at the highest level it has yet attained in the twentieth century."

Two years later, in 1983, the English asked Botvinnik to write an Introduction to the book *British Chess* for Pergamon Press. In it, the sixth world champion first of all gave exceptionally high marks to England's role in the progress of chess during the 19th century. "In the history of chess, British chess has played a wonderful role. The names Staunton, McDonnell, Blackburne, and Bird are well-known to the entire chessplaying world. And the first international tournament (1851) took place right in London."

Noting further, with regret, that in the first half of the 20th century the country "no longer possessed gifted masters," Botvinnik expressed hope for success soon for young Englishmen. Of this he was convinced, after giving exhibitions after the close of the 1966/67 Hastings tournament, in three universities (at Nottingham, Cambridge and Oxford): "It turns out that a young chess generation has grown up in England, so strong was the resistance of my opponents. Apparently, some sort of advance in the life-force of the people has begun, as if chess has become more popular.

Many years have gone by since then, and the expectations have been fulfilled. Young grandmasters have appeared. At the junior world team championship, the English team competed successfully with the Soviet one. Many chess books have appeared."

Botvinnik even predicted the early appearance in England of the elite master Short. He wrote: "We must expect that there is hope that a gifted chess master will soon appear in England – within a few years it may be young Short. Now he is only seventeen. But his games are easy to understand – his pieces do not move about, but 'live' on the board. One would wish him to become not just a strong practical player (this is fashionable nowadays, but the period of a chess practitioner is ten years shorter than the period of a researcher), but a chess researcher also. This would secure for a long period the interest in chess in the British Isles, which would undoubtedly be all to the good of the whole chess world..."

Need we say that the Short-Kasparov world championship match, ten years after these lines were written (London 1993), furnished the clearest possible support for Botvinnik's prediction.

Chapter Two

Matches, Tournaments and Opponents

AVRO 1938 (November 7-27)
A double-round event, organized by the Dutch radio company AVRO. On April 15, 1938, the newspaper *64* wrote: "The world's strongest players were invited to play in this tournament: world champion Alekhine (France), former champions Euwe (Holland) and Capablanca (Cuba), grandmasters Flohr (Czechoslovakia), Fine and Reshevsky (USA), Keres (Estonia), and decorated grandmaster Botvinnik (USSR)." Botvinnik appeared in the pages of the newspaper, talking about his planned preparations for this important contest and indicating the main contenders for first prize: Alekhine and Keres. World chess in general, as well as the organizers of the event, saw it as an unofficial candidates' tournament which would produce Alekhine's future opponent.

Botvinnik came to Amsterdam with his wife, Gaiane, and was struck by "the elegant old city with its countless bicyclists," with hardly a pedestrian among them. But the tournament was played in many cities of Holland. "We were moved all over the country. Before the game, instead of dinner, there were two hours of travel. The older

participants – Capablanca and Alekhine – could not take the pressure," Botvinnik remembered.

In the first round, Botvinnik lost to Fine. "He played the game excellently!" the loser acknowledged, and threw himself into overtaking the leaders. In the third round, in the next "Soviet-American struggle," he succeeded in taking a sort of revenge against this "transoceanic team" by beating Reshevsky.

(4) Botvinnik – Reshevsky
AVRO 1938
English Opening [A25]

1.c4 e5 2.♘c3 ♘c6 3.g3 g6 4.♗g2 ♗g7 5.e3 d6 6.♘ge2 ♘ge7 7.d4 e×d4 8.e×d4 0-0 9.0-0 ♘f5 10.d5 ♘e5 11.b3 a5 12.♗b2 ♘d7 13.a3 ♘c5 14.b4 ♘d7 15.♕b3

41

15...♘d4?! This exchange wastes a lot of time and gives White the initiative. 15...♖e8 16.♖ae1 ♘e5 17.♘e4 ♗d7 is more precise. **16.♘×d4 ♗×d4 17.♖ad1 ♗g7 18.♖fe1 a×b4 19.a×b4 ♘f6 20.h3 h5 21.c5 ♗f5 22.♘b5 ♗d7?** 22...♖e8 is more active. **23.c6! b×c6 24.d×c6 ♗c8?** This retreat runs into Botvinnik's strong reply. 24...♗f5 was forced.

25.♘×d6! ♗e6 25...c×d6 26.c7 ♕×c7 27.♗×a8 ♗×h3 28.♗f3+− **26.♖×e6 f×e6 27.♘f5 ♕e8?** Now White's bishops will reign supreme. The last chance to offer resistance was 27...♕×d1+ 28.♕×d1 e×f5 but White should be winning in the long run, e.g., 29.♗e5 ♖f7 30.♕b3+− **28.♘×g7 ♔×g7 29.♖d7+ ♖f7 30.♗e5 ♔g8 31.♖×c7 ♖×c7 32.♗×c7 ♖a1+ 33.♔h2 ♖a7 34.♗e5 ♖f7 35.c7 ♘d7 36.♕c2 ♖f8 37.c8♕ 1-0**

Winning game after game in methodical succession, Botvinnik beat Alekhine in round seven, then Capablanca in round eleven. And what victories those were!

It is hard to uncover what Alekhine's mistake was. Exploiting his opponent's tiniest error, Botvinnik methodically improved his own position, and although the world champion adjourned the game with even material, his position was hopeless. Interestingly, without seeing the position, but knowing that the position on the board was even, Savielly Tartakower, the grandmaster and famous chess journalist, in his report to the newspaper *Telegraaf*, told his readers that the draw was obvious. After filing his report, he quietly sat down to play cards with Flohr... Botvinnik came to his room. Without getting up from his game, Flohr asked, "Hasn't he resigned yet?" "Who?," questioned Tartakower. "Alekhine stands very badly," answered Flohr. "You're joking," worried Tartakower. But, upon discovering that it was true, he ran to call his editor, in order to correct the report... Upon resuming the game, White quickly established a material advantage, and soon Alekhine, who had just regained the title with his successful re-match with Euwe, resigned on move 51 (cf. *Endgame*).

AVRO 1938

		1	2	3	4	5	6	7	8	Total
1	Keres	x	1½	½½	½½	1½	½½	1½	½½	8½
2	Fine	0½	x	1½	10	10	11	½½	1½	8½
3	Botvinnik	½½	0½	x	½0	1½	1½	½1	½½	7½
4	Euwe	½½	1	½1	x	0½	0½	1	1½	7
5	Reshevsky	0½	1	0½	1½	x	½½	½½	1½	7
6	Alekhine	½½	0	0½	1½	½½	x	½1	½1	7
7	Capablanca	0½	½½	½0	10	½½	½0	x	½1	6
8	Flohr	½½	0½	½½	0½	0½	½0	½0	x	4½

Botvinnik ended his game with Capablanca with victory as a result of a spectacular combination, involving a double piece sacrifice. This game was spoken of highly also by the loser, who called it "a battle of minds!" (cf. *Famous Games*).

After his victory over Capablanca, Botvinnik had caught the leaders, Fine and Keres. But such inspired play took a lot of strength and nervous energy out of him. In the very next round, against Euwe, Botvinnik made a mistake in an even position, and lost. He ended up with 7½ points and third place, a point behind the winners, Keres and Fine, who passed through the whole tournament shoulder to shoulder. And all three world champions – Alekhine, Capablanca, and Euwe – wound up behind them.

Even before the tournament started, Alekhine read a specially prepared announcement that he would not meet the organizers' conditions, nor accept their nomination of a candidate, but would play against any well-known grandmaster who would guarantee his prize fund. Botvinnik, supported by high-placed government officials, carried on negotiations over a cup of tea. They worked out a sum that would be guaranteed Alekhine, whatever the contest's outcome ($6,700), and the location for their intended match (Botvinnik suggested Moscow, while Alekhine agreed to any country, as long as it was not Holland).

But here, in Amsterdam, when the AVRO tournament finished, as Botvinnik recalled, there was a historic meeting of the participants. "The question of the 'Eight Strongest Club' was discussed, with the idea that the club would secure the rules for holding matches for the world championship. Each member of the club would have a formal right to challenge the champion. Fine and Euwe were given the assignment to prepare and send out the projected rules (no one suggested that FIDE be brought into the matter of deciding this question.)"

Summing up the meaning of the AVRO tournament, the wins over Capablanca and Alekhine, the discovery of the creative potential of Botvinnik, and the acknowledgment by society worldwide of his claims for the crown of chess champion of the world, Kasparov writes: "In the thirties, Botvinnik had a number of notable successes, but the AVRO tournament, organized by the Dutch radio company that invited the strongest players of that time, forced people to take another look at him.

"The game with Capablanca [game 130] shows that Botvinnik's strategic vision was already at the level of the greatest geniuses of the old guard."

Alatortsev, Vladimir Alexeyevich (May 14, 1909-January 13, 1987), international grandmaster (1983), trainer, journalist, one of Botvinnik's chief opponents in national events at the start of the 1930s.

Vladimir learned early to play chess, but only felt the true beauty of the game when he began to study with the chess teacher and theoretician, two-time USSR champion Pyotr Arsenievich Romanovsky. He had successes in many local events, then in the

Vladimir Alatortsev

championships of his city and nation. In 1931, he took third place in the Leningrad championship, behind Botvinnik and Romanovsky. In the same year, he took part for the first time in the 8th USSR championship, and by sharing third/sixth places, became one of the leading players of the Soviet Union. In the 1932 Leningrad championship, he was Botvinnik's chief rival. But in both tournaments, he lost to him in their encounter, and took second place. The following year, Vladimir became Leningrad champion.

Botvinnik recalled: "I played many games against Vladimir Alatortsev. Many of those games, sometimes having decisive importance, I would win; but there were tense draws too. I only lost to him once, when we were playing an 'exhibition game' at a faster time-control, and whose moves were being transmitted by radio over the open airwaves. That was in Leningrad, in 1933 or 1934. Alatortsev played

especially well in complex, sharp positions. He was usually well prepared, especially with White. It was often difficult to play against him when you had Black..."

In 1935, Alatortsev played a drawn match, 6-6, against the Hungarian grandmaster, Andre Lilienthal (+4 -4 =4). and took part in a strong international tournament in Moscow for the first time, where he shared ninth/eleventh places with Ragozin and Romanovsky, drawing against the three top finishers, Botvinnik, Flohr and Lasker.

(5) Botvinnik – Alatortsev
Moscow 1935
English Opening [A25]

1.c4 e5 2.♘c3 ♘c6 3.g3 d6 4.♗g2 f5 5.e3 ♘f6 6.d4 ♗e7 7.♘ge2 0-0 8.b3 ♕e8 9.♗a3 ♖f7 10.♘d5 ♗f8 11.0-0 ♘d8 12.♕c2 c6 13.d×e5 d×e5 14.♗×f8 Preserving the dark-square bishop with **14.♘×f6+!? ♖×f6 15.♗b2 ♘f7 16.♖ad1** gives White a slight strategic initiative and he has more attacking potential than in the game. **14...♕×f8 15.♘×f6+ ♖×f6 16.♖ad1 ♘f7 17.♖d2 ♗e6 18.♖fd1 ♖e8 19.♕c3 ♗c8 20.♕a5 a6 21.♘c3 e4 22.♘a4 ♕e7**

23.♕c5? Without queens, White can no longer make real progress. 23.♘b6 ♘e5 24.♕c3 ♕c5 25.♘a4 ♕e7 26.c5 applies more pressure. **23...♕×c5 24.♘×c5 ♘e5!** Black's mighty knight gives him complete equality. **25.h3 ♖ff8 26.♔f1 h5 27.h4 ♔f7 28.♘a4 ♔e7 29.♘c3 ♗e6 30.♘e2 ♖d8 31.♘f4 ♖×d2 32.♖×d2 ♗f7 33.♔e2 ♖d8 34.♖d4 b5 35.c×b5 a×b5 36.♖×d8 ♔×d8 37.f3 e×f3+ 38.♗×f3 ♘×f3 39.♔×f3 ½-½**

After 1936, Alatortsev lived in Moscow, and won two championships of the capital (1936 and 1937). During the Second World War, he was the director of the Moscow Chess Club, and organized a series of tournaments in the capital, while working as a chef in the hospitals.

For many years, Alatortsev appeared "on the same team" as Vasily Smyslov, as his friend and helper. "Beginning with 1946, Vladimir Alatortsev was my official trainer," says Smyslov. "In 1948, during the match-tournament for the world championship, he was my second. This was our period of deeply creative interaction. We analyzed games and dissected positions together. I started to answer 1.d4 with 1...d5, on his recommendation. His influence on me, as far as working out my preferences of playing in closed positions, was indubitable. In any event, Alatortsev gave me the right idea, that in the battle for the world championship, one needed a wider creative palette – both in the openings, and in the middlegame. So his advice, experience and the depth of his understanding of position helped me very much in working out my style."

Chessplayers, among themselves, used to refer to Alatortsev as "the strategist."

"I became acquainted, as an 18-year old boy, with the games of Alatortsev, " said grandmaster Yuri Averbakh, "and saw that the greatness of his chess lay, first and foremost, in strategic and positional play."

"Alatortsev was a good strategist. We learned from his games," said the tenth world champion, Boris Spassky.

Alatortsev was a fine strategist, not just over the chessboard, but also in the politics of chess. He spent seven years heading the USSR Chess Federation (1955-61). During this period, Alatortsev was one of the organizers of the Olympiad (Moscow 1956), and together with Botvinnik, took an active part in the creation of the Central Chess Club on Gogolevsky boulevard. For more than 20 years, Alatortsev edited a chess column in the newspaper *Vechernyaya Moskva* (1943-64).

From his journalistic and training activities he moved on to the academic. He defended his dissertation, and was awarded the Candidate of Instructional Science. Over the course of 13 years, he headed up the laboratory of sports psychology in the All-Union Instructional-Research Institute of Physical Culture (1965-75), of which one of the "secret branches" of activity was analyzing the play of Robert Fischer.

Among family and friends, the "strategist," "politician" and "psychologist" was transformed into a loving husband and father, who lived for his family. From his early years, he demonstrated an affinity for drawing. He got along famously in this art, had encyclopedic knowledge in all areas of culture. He was a passionate fisherman. His apartment became a constant meeting place for encounters among the representatives of the established intelligentsia. Among his friends were Galina Vishnevskaya and Mstislav Rostropovich, husband and wife; the Rukavishnikov sculptor family; the academicians Anokhin and Kassirsky; and the writer Bogomolov.

In conclusion, two fine examples of the chess creativity of Alatortsev.

(6) Keres – Alatortsev
Moscow 1950
King's Gambit Accepted [C35]

1.e4 e5 2.f4 e×f4 3.♘f3 ♗e7 4.♗c4 ♘f6 5.e5 ♘g4 6.0-0 ♘c6 7.d4 d5 8.e×d6 ♗×d6

9.♘c3? This is too slow. 9.♕e2+ and 9.♕e1+ are the main options here. 9...0-0 10.♘e2 ♘e3 11.♗×e3 f×e3 12.a3 ♕f6 13.♕d3 ♕h6 14.♖ae1 ♗g4 15.h3 15.♘g3 ♖ae8 16.c3 is the alternative, but Black is still for choice of course. 15...♗h5 16.♘c3 ♖ae8

17.♘d5? 17.♘e4 ♗f4 18.♘h4 ♗g4 19.g3 ♗×g3 20.♘×g3 ♕×h4 21.♖×e3 limits the damage.

17...e2! This advance disrupts White's coordination completely. 18.♖f2 18.♖×e2 is met by 18...♖×e2 19.♕×e2 ♘×d4 20.♕f2 ♘×f3+ 21.g×f3 ♖e8 18...♗g3 19.c3 ♘a5 20.♖e×e2 ♗×f2+ 21.♖×f2 ♘×c4 22.♕×c4 c6 23.♘b4 ♗×f3 24.♖×f3 ♕c1+ 25.♔h2 ♕×b2 26.d5 a5 27.♘d3 ♕×a3 28.♖g3 ♕d6 29.♕d4 g6 30.c4 c×d5 31.c×d5 f5 32.♘c5 b6 33.♘b7 ♕c7 0-1

(7) Alatortsev – Lilienthal
Leningrad (m10) 1935
Budapest Gambit [A52]

1.d4 ♘f6 2.c4 e5 The Budapest. 3.d×e5 ♘g4 4.e4 4.♗f4 ♘c6 5.♘f3 is the main line. 4...♘×e5 5.f4 ♘ec6 6.♗e3 ♗b4+ 7.♘c3 ♕e7 7...♕h4+!? scores better. 8.♗d3 ♘a6 8...♗×c3+ 9.b×c3 ♘a6 10.♘f3 ♘c5 11.0-0 ♘×d3 12.♕×d3 d6 is more in the spirit of the opening and also played more often. 9.♘ge2 0-0 10.0-0 ♗c5 11.♗f2 d6 12.♘d5 ♕d8 13.a3 ♗×f2+ 14.♖×f2 ♘c5 15.♗c2 f5? This opens the position for White. 15...♗g4 limits the damage.

16.♘g3?! 16.exf5 ♗xf5 17.♗xf5 ♖xf5 18.b4 ♘e6 19.♕d2 ♖f7 20.♖e1 applies more pressure as more pieces are on the board. **16...♘xe4 17.♘xe4 fxe4 18.♗xe4 ♗f5 19.♗xf5 ♖xf5**

20.♕g4?! 20.♕b3 ♖b8 21.♖e1 ♕d7 22.♖e4 ♖ff8 23.♖fe2 is even better. **20...♖f7 21.♖e1 ♘e7**

22.♘c3 22.f5!? ♘xd5 23.cxd5 ♕d7 24.♖e6 is also very good for White. **22...♘g6?!** The knight is quite restricted here. 22...♘f5 23.♕f3 ♖b8 is preferable. **23.g3 ♕c8 24.♕f3** Alatortsev keeps his attacking potential as his king is safe while Black's king is not. **24...♖b8 25.♖fe2**

25...♖f8? This rook retreat is too passive. 25...♕d7 limits the damage. **26.♕d5+ ♔h8 27.♖e6 ♖d8 28.♘e4**

28...♘f8? Black does not have time for this retreat. 28...c6 29.♕f5 ♘f8 30.♘g5 ♕d7 was the last chance to fight. **29.♖e7 ♘g6 30.♘g5 h6** 30...♘xe7 runs into 31.♘f7+ ♔g8 32.♘h6+ ♔h8 33.♕g8+ ♘xg8 34.♘f7#. Lilienthal resigned in view of 31.♕f7 ♘xe7 32.♖xe7 ♖g8 33.♕g6 hxg5 34.♕h5#

Works: *Piece and Pawn co-ordination in Chess*, Moscow, 1958; *Problems of Modern Chess Theory*, Moscow, 1960; *Training Methods for Older Players*, Moscow, 1962; *Guide to Chess*, Moscow, 1965 (co-author); *Creativity in Chess*, Moscow, 1988.

Bibliography: Linder, Vladimir and Isaak, *The Two Lives of Grandmaster Alatortsev*, Moscow 1994.

Alekhine – Botvinnik
The Match That Was Not to Be

In 1936, Alekhine, taking note of Botvinnik's successes in the two Moscow tournaments in 1935 and 1937 and at Nottingham, called him "the most gifted of the young players" and "the most likely candidate for the world champion's title. I personally believe that he has every chance of becoming the world champion in the immediate future."

And so of course Botvinnik began dreaming of it, and in 1936 began preparing to wrest this title in a match with Alekhine. Not accidentally, in 1939 in Moscow, his book came out with detailed commentary on the games of the Alekhine-Euwe rematch.

Having regained the world champion's title, Alekhine indicated that he would play against any well-known grandmaster who could secure the prize fund. "Thus," wrote Botvinnik later, recalling (in his book, *Achieving the Aim*) during the AVRO tournament of 1938 in Holland, "I noted that it was necessary to decide right then and there, whether to challenge the champion to a match. I did not know when I would ever see Alekhine again. If I were to present the authorities the question of a match, I would have had to have: (1) the principle agreement of Alekhine; and (2) the details of the championship [match] all worked out."

During the closing ceremonies of the tournament, Botvinnik approached Alekhine and asked for "an audience. Alekhine quickly understood; joy flashed in his eyes – he understood that playing a world championship match against a Soviet player would be the simplest, and perhaps the only route to making peace with the Motherland."

"Tomorrow, in the Hotel Carlton, at 16:00," was his reply. And there, over a cup of tea, in the presence of Flohr, Alekhine gave his consent to a match with Botvinnik. The prize fund was agreed on, and when and to what address the official challenge would be sent to Alekhine.

Upon his return to Leningrad, Botvinnik laid out the particulars in a letter to the President of the Soviet Government. At the start of the New Year, he received a telegram from the government: "Should you decide to challenge chessplayer Alekhine to a match, we wish you complete success. The rest will not be difficult to secure. Molotov." Later, judging from the style of the telegram, Botvinnik understood that "it was most likely dictated by Stalin himself."

However, it was the Sport Committee, two months later and after lengthy wires, sent Botvinnik's challenge. By summertime, Alekhine's response came – the world champion accepted the challenge.

But alas, on September 1, World War II intervened, and discussions about the match could only be resumed six years later.

In autumn, 1945, an interview with Alekhine appeared in the British magazine *Chess* in which he reaffirmed that he was prepared to play the match against Botvinnik under the circumstances previously agreed. This eased Botvinnik's task, since a number of Western grandmasters had blamed, perhaps without justification, Alekhine for his cooperation with the Nazis. On this pretext, they suggested that he be deprived of his champion's title, and that an eight-man match-tournament be held in the summer of 1948 in the USA (as per a telegram to Moscow by Fine in November, 1945).

But Botvinnik figured that he would have to play a match for the world championship against the one who currently held that title – Alekhine. And on January 11, 1946, he sent off a letter to Stalin, in which he reminded him of the corresponding decision of the Soviet government in 1939, and asked him to "decide the question." (The letter, was discovered by Keres' Estonian biographer W. Heuer in the state archives of the Russian Federation. It was published by I. Yu. Botvinnik in the magazine *Shakhmatny Peterburg*, 2003, 1/42).

After receiving the favorable decision from the government, February 4, Botvinnik sent Alekhine his official challenge. Match negotiations quickly got underway through an intermediary, British Chess Federation president Derbyshire, who offered to start the

event in August of 1946 in Nottingham, with the prize fund underwritten by the Soviet Union. Although Botvinnik favored February 1947, he immediately began to prepare for the encounter, as witnessed by the "Preparatory materials for the world championship, 1946," discovered by the researcher into the life of Alekhine, Yu. Shaburov, in the above-mentioned archive.

Here he found the "Projected plan for preparing M. M. Botvinnik for his match with Alekhine." It examined two alternative methods of preparation, depending on whether the match was to begin on August 12, 1946, or February 3, 1947. In either case, they discussed signing the agreement around April 1, playing a training match with Keres, the analytical, competitive work by Botvinnik with Ragozin, his timely journey to England (about one month prior to the start of the match), and also taking into his preparation other Soviet players and securing many other needs for Botvinnik and Ragozin, brought about by postwar difficulties in national life (cf. *Chess in Russia*, Moscow, 1994, 1/83-85).

But Botvinnik's discussions about the world championship were cut short by his receipt of sad news: on March 24, 1946, in far-off Portugal, Alexander Alekhine had passed away.

Alekhine Memorial, 1956 (October 8-November 3, Moscow) Dedicated to the 10th anniversary of the death of the great Russian chessplayer and fourth world champion. 16 players, from 12 countries took part. Among them were Botvinnik, Smyslov, Bronstein, Keres, Taimanov (all USSR); Najdorf

Moscow 1956

		1	2	3	4	5	6	7	8	9	10	11	12	13	14	15	16	Total
1	Botvinnik	x	½	½	½	½	1	0	½	½	1	1	1	1	1	1	1	11
2	Smyslov	½	x		½	½	½	½	½	½	1	1	1	1	1	1	1	11
3	Taimanov	½	½	x	½	1	1	½	½	½	½	½	1	½	1	1	1	10½
4	Gligoric	½	½	½	x	0	½	½	½	1	½	½	1	1	1	1	1	10
5	Bronstein	½	½	0	1	x	½	½	½	½	½	1	½	1	½	1	1	9½
6	Najdorf	0	½	0	½	½	x	½	½	1	½	½	½	1	1	1	1	9
7	Keres	1	½	½	½	½	½	x	1	0	½	0	½	½	½	1	1	8½
8	Pachman	½	½	½	½	½	½	0	x	½	½	½	½	½	1	1	1	8½
9	Unzicker	½	½	½	0	½	0	1	½	x	1	½	½	½	1	0	1	8
10	Stahlberg	0	0	½	½	½	½	½	½	0	x	½	½	1	1	1	1	8
11	Szabo	0	0	½	½	0	½	1	½	½	½	x	½	½	½	0	½	6
12	Padevsky	0	0	0	0	½	½	½	½	½	½	½	x	0	½	1	½	5½
13	Uhlmann	0	0	½	0	0	0	½	½	½	0	½	1	x	1	½	½	5½
14	Ciocaltea	0	0	0	0	½	0	½	0	0	0	½	½	0	x	1	½	3½
15	Sliwa	0	0	0	0	0	0	0	0	1	0	1	0	½	0	x	½	3
16	Golombek	0	0	0	0	0	0	0	0	0	0	½	½	½	½	½	x	2½

(Argentina); Gligoric (Yugoslavia); Szabo (Hungary); Pachman (Czechoslovakia); Stålhberg (Sweden); and Golombek (England). The tournament was played in the Chaikovsky Concert Hall, and Alekhine's son attended as an honored guest.

(8) Padevsky – Botvinnik
Moscow 1956
Sicilian Defense [B88]

1.e4 c5 2.♘f3 ♘c6 3.d4 c×d4 4.♘×d4 ♘f6 5.♘c3 d6 6.♗c4 e6 7.0-0 ♗e7 8.♗e3 0-0 9.♗b3 ♘a5 10.f4 b6

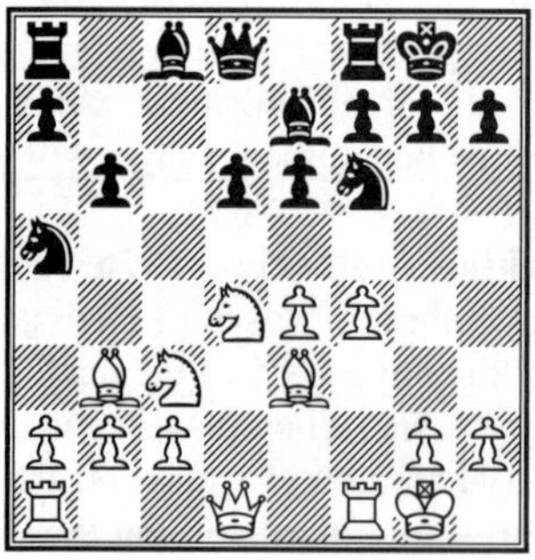

11.♕f3?! This approach is too slow. 11.e5! is the critical continuation. **11...♗b7 12.g4 ♖c8 13.g5**

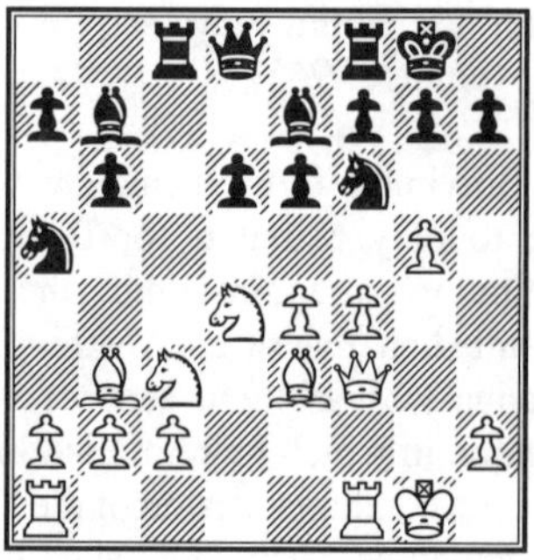

13...♖×c3! A typical and strong exchange sacrifice. **14.b×c3?** Now White's structure is in ruins, while his kingside attack leads nowhere. 14.g×f6 ♖×e3 15.♕×e3 ♗×f6 16.♖ad1 is unclear and critical. **14...♘×e4 15.♕g4** 15.♘×e6 f×e6 16.♗×e6+ ♔h8 17.♕h3 ♕e8 18.♗f5 ♖×f5 19.♕×f5 ♘c4 20.♗d4 ♘cd2. Against 15.♕h5, Black defends with 15...♕c8 16.♖f3 ♕×c3 17.♖af1 g6 18.♕h6 ♘×b3 19.a×b3 f5 20.♘×e6 ♖f7 **15...♕c8!**

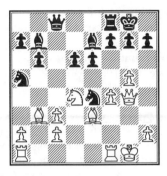

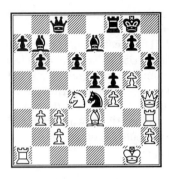

This strong prophylactic move stops White's attack in its tracks. **16.罝f3** 16.f5 e5 17.包e6 is met by 17...包xb3 18.axb3 fxe6 19.f6 豐xc3 20.豐xe6+ 罝f7-+ **16...包×b3** The computer's suggestion, 16...g6!, to meet 17.罝h3 with 17...e5, is even stronger. **17.a×b3**

23.h×g7 豐×g7+ (Chekhov) 24.含f1 d5-+; 22.魚×d4 豐×c2 23.g×h6 包f6-+ (Chekhov) **22...豐c6 23.g×h6 包g5 24.罝g3 豐h1+ 25.含f2 包e4+** and White resigned in view of 26.含e2 包×g3+ 27.h×g3 豐×h5+-+ **0-1**

Botvinnik was in the leading group the entire tournament, along with Bronstein, Najdorf, Smyslov, and Taimanov. After round 11, he led the tournament alone. Before the 15th and last round, he was a point ahead of Smyslov and Taimanov. For the third time in 11 years, fate brought Botvinnik and Keres together in the last round of a tournament. And for the third time – the previous two events being the 1948 match-tournament for the world championship and the 22nd USSR championship of 1955, Keres won! Botvinnik sustained his only loss in the Alekhine Memorial, choosing to play a complex system of the Sicilian Defense as Black. Smyslov, beating Ståhlberg after adjournment, caught up with the world champion. The outcome: Botvinnik and Smyslov shared first and second places with 11 points, third place went to Taimanov with 10½ points. Gligoric, and Bronstein rounded out the top five with 9½ points.

17...f5! 18.豐h4? 18.g×f6 is met by 18...罝×f6 19.f5 e×f5 20.包×f5 魚f8 (Chekhov in Megabase) 21.包e7+ 魚×e7 22.豐×c8+ 魚×c8 23.罝×f6 魚×f6 24.罝×a7 魚f5 and Black's minor pieces should prevail in the long run. 18.豐h3!? was the last chance, but Black has more than enough compensation after 18...a5 19.c4 g6 **18...e5! 19.罝h3 h6!** (D)

White's attack has been parried, which will not be said about Botvinnik's coming counterattack. **20.豐h5 豐×c3 21.罝d1 e×d4 22.魚d2** 22.g×h6 d×e3

Amsterdam Tournaments – 1963 & 1966

In the Dutch capital, the president of the society "USSR-Netherlands," Mikhail Botvinnik, considered it his duty to make every effort to perform as best he could. And he achieved the task he had set himself: two international tournaments resulted in as many triumphs!

December 11-16, 1963 The first international appearance by Botvinnik after the loss of his match for the world championship to Tigran Petrosian. This small tournament of six players, among whom were two Soviets – Botvinnik and Flohr, along with four Dutch players – Donner, Bouwmeester, Kuipers, and van Scheltinga – took place after a short series of guest appearances through the country, with lectures and exhibitions. The tournament ended in a confident triumph by Botvinnik, who amassed four points out of five games. Flohr was a half-point behind. The best of the Dutch players was Bouwmeester, with three points. The new leader of Dutch chess, Donner, did not perform up to par (2½ points). In his game with Donner, Botvinnik executed his favorite strategic technique: the occupation of

c6 by a knight, followed by an invasion into the enemy camp.

(9) Botvinnik – Donner
Amsterdam 1963
Catalan Opening [A14]

1.c4 ♘f6 2.♘f3 e6 3.g3 d5 4.♗g2 ♗e7 5.0-0 0-0 6.b3 b6 7.♗b2 ♗b7 8.c×d5 ♘×d5 9.d4 c5 This might be too early. 9...♘d7!? is played much more often. **10.d×c5 ♗×c5 11.♘bd2 ♘d7 12.a3 ♘5f6?!** 12...a5 is probably the lesser evil, but White retains some initiative with 13.♘e4 **13.b4 ♗e7**

14.♘d4! Botvinnik starts his play on the light squares by exchanging Black's main defender of this color complex. **14...♗×g2 15.♔×g2 ♕c7 16.♕b3 ♖fc8 17.♖fc1 ♕b7+ 18.♕f3**

Amsterdam 1963

		1	2	3	4	5	6	Total
1	Botvinnik	*	½	½	1	1	1	4
2	Flohr	½	*	½	½	1	1	3½
3	Bouwmeester	½	½	*	½	½	1	3
4	Donner	0	½	½	*	1	½	2½
5	Kuijpers	0	0	½	0	*	1	1½
6	Van Scheltinga	0	0	0	½	0	*	½

18...♘d5? With queens on the board, White's pressure is much stronger as his queen is more active and influential. So 18...♕×f3+ was called for to limit the damage, e.g., 19.♘2×f3 (19.♔×f3 ♗f8 20.♖×c8 ♖×c8 21.♖c1 ♖×c1 22.♗×c1 a5) 19...♗f8 20.♘c6 ♘c5 21.♘fd4 ♘a4 22.♖a2 ♘×b2 23.♖×b2 g6 24.♖bc2 ♔g7 and in both cases, Black can continue the fight. **19.e4!** The beginning of a strong powerplay on the light squares. **19...♘5f6 20.b5 a6?!** Opening the a-file helps White in the end and b6 is weakened. 20...♘e5 21.♕e2 ♗d6 makes it more difficult. **21.♘c6!** Botvinnik has reached his major strategic aim, as the powerful knight now rules the board almost singlehandedly. **21...♗f8 22.a4 a×b5** 22...♘c5 is met by 23.♗×f6 g×f6 24.♘c4 **23.a×b5 ♖×a1 24.♖×a1 ♖a8**

25.♖d1! Botvinnik keeps his strong rook of course to use his advantage in space and his greater mobility. **25...♘e8?** This retreat is too passive, but good advice is hard to give anyway. **26.♘c4 ♘c5** 26...♘ef6 27.e5 ♘d5 28.♘d6 ♗×d6 29.e×d6+– **27.e5**

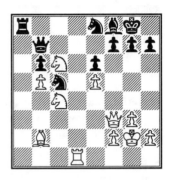

27...♖c8?! This loses immediately to the coming invasion on the a-file. But Black is already lost in any case, e.g., 27...h6 28.♗d4 ♔h8 29.♘×b6 ♕×b6 30.♕×f7 ♘c7 31.♘d8 ♖×d8 32.♗×c5 ♕b7+ (32...♕×c5 33.♖×d8+–) 33.♔h3 ♖×d1 34.♗×f8+– **28.♖a1 ♖c7** 28...♖a8 29.♖×a8 ♕×a8 30.♘e7++– **29.♖a7 ♕×a7** 29...♕c8 30.♘×b6+– **30.♘×a7 ♖×a7 31.♘×b6 1-0**

5-15 July, 1966 Just before his 55th birthday, Botvinnik extended his roster of triumphs with another successful performance in Amsterdam. The contest, organized by the IBM, was held in one of the sacred halls of contemporary architecture, "De Ark," and drew 10 participants, among those being Botvinnik, Flohr, Szabo and Pomar. Botvinnik scored seven wins, drew with Flohr, lost only to the Dutch master Barendregt, and outstripped by two full points the student of Alekhine, the Spaniard Arturo Pomar, who took second place.

Amsterdam 1966

		1	2	3	4	5	6	7	8	9	10	Total
1	Botvinnik	x	1	½	1	0	1	1	1	1	1	7½
2	Pomar	0	x	½	½	½	½	1	1	½	1	5½
3	Flohr	½	½	x	½	½	½	½	1	½	½	5
4	Zuidema	0	½	½	x	1	½	1	½	0	½	4½
5	Barendregt	1	½	½	0	x	0	0	½	½	1	4
6	Kuijpers	0	½	½	½	1	x	1	0	½	0	4
7	Szabo	0	0	½	0	1	0	x	1	½	1	4
8	Van Scheltinga	0	0	0	½	½	1	0	x	1	1	4
9	Robatsch	0	½	½	1	½	½	½	0	x	0	3½
10	Szilagyi	0	0	½	½	0	1	0	0	1	x	3

The powerful attack by Black in his game with Szabo was one of the tournament's highlights.

(10) Szabo – Botvinnik
Amsterdam 1966
English Opening [B37]

1.c4 c5 2.♘c3 g6 3.♘f3 ♗g7 4.d4 cxd4 5.♘xd4 ♘c6 6.♘c2 d6 7.e4 ♘h6 8.h4?! 8.♗e2 is the main move. **8...f5 9.h5 fxe4 10.hxg6?** This just opens the h-file for Black. 10.♘xe4 is called for. **10...hxg6 11.♘xe4 ♗f5 12.♘c3?** The wrong direction as Black can now continue his attack directly. 12.♘g3 limits the damage. **12...♕a5!**

Botvinnik continues to activate his forces forcefully. **13.♗d2 ♕e5+ 14.♘e3 0-0-0 15.♕a4?** This queen

sortie is too optimistic. 15.♘a4 ♘d4 16.♗c3 ♕e4 17.♗xd4 ♗xd4 18.♕e2 reduces the pressure but Black is still much better of course. **15...♘g4 16.♖xh8 ♖xh8 17.♕b5 ♕f4**

18.♘cd1? After this retreat, the coordination of White's forces is completely destroyed. He had two better options, 18.♘xg4 ♕xg4 19.♗e3 and 18.0-0-0 ♗xc3 19.bxc3 ♘xf2 20.♘xf5 ♕xf5 21.♕xf5+ gxf5 22.♖e1, but Black will win in the long run in both cases. **18...♘d4 19.♕a5** 19.♕a4!? is met by 19...♕e5 (however, not 19...♖h1?? 20.♕e8+ ♔c7 21.♘d5#) 20.♗c3 ♔b8 21.♖c1 ♕f4-+ **19...♖h1 20.♖c1** One refutation of 20.♕xa7 is the beautiful 20...♖xf1+ 21.♔xf1 ♗d3+ 22.♔e1 ♕f3-+ **20...♘e5 21.♕c7+** A last joke, which cannot save the game of course.

**21...♔×c7 22.♘d5+ ♔d7 23.♘×f4
g5** A powerful performance! **0-1**

"A thunderous crush, rare in grandmaster practice!" wrote world champion Tigran Petrosian, commenting on the game. He also said Botvinnik played with exceptional energy!

Konstantinopolsky labeled Botvinnik's game against Pomar "A brilliant strategic achievement."

(11) Botvinnik – Pomar
IBM Amsterdam (4), 1966
Slav Defense [D14]

**1.c4 c6 2.♘c3 d5 3.c×d5 c×d5 4.d4
♘f6 5.♘f3 ♘c6 6.♗f4 ♗f5 7.e3
e6 8.♗b5 ♗b4 9.♘e5 ♕a5** The alternative 9...0-0 scores better. **10.♗×c6+ b×c6 11.0-0 ♗×c3
12.b×c3**

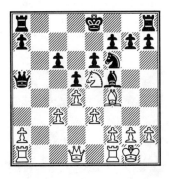

12...♖c8?! The capture 12...♕×c3? is too greedy: 13.♖c1 ♕b2 14.g4 ♗g6 15.h4 h6 16.♘×g6 f×g6 17.♕d3 and Black's numerous weaknesses will tell sooner or later. But 12...♕a6, to meet 13.g4 with 13...♗g6 14.f3 ♘d7, L.Portisch-Zhu Chen, Marbella 1999, was called for. **13.c4** The immediate 13.g4! was even better. **13...0-0**

14.g4! Botvinnik starts a dangerous initiative to restrict Black's pieces even further. **14...♗g6 15.c5 ♘e4 16.f3
♘d2?** 16...♘c3 17.♕d2 ♕a3 18.♖ac1 ♘b5 was the lesser evil. **17.♖f2 ♘c4
18.♘×c4 d×c4 19.♗d6 ♖fe8 20.e4**

Now White's superiority is clear as he will win Black's c-pawn. **20...f5
21.♕c2 f×e4 22.f×e4 ♕a3 23.♖e1
♕h3** 23...c3 24.♖f3 ♕b4 25.♕×c3 (Belov) is similar. **24.♖g2 ♖cd8
25.♖g3 ♕h6 26.♕×c4 ♕d2
27.♕c3 ♕×a2?** With the queens on the board, Botvinnik's attack must be winning. So 27...♕×c3 28.♖×c3 was forced from a practical point of view. **28.♖g2 ♕a6 29.h4 ♖d7 30.h5 ♗f7
31.♖a1 ♕c8 32.♕f3 ♕d8** (D)

33.g5! Feeding the pawns into the attack makes it unstoppable. **33...g6**

34.h6 e5 34...♖b7 35.e5+– **35.♗×e5**
35.♖b1!+– is even better. **35...♖b7?**
35...♖×d4? 36.♖×a7 ♖d7 37.♖×d7
♕×d7 38.♕f6 ♕d1+ 39.♔h2 ♕h5+
40.♔g3+– (Belov); 35...♗e6 is
relatively best, but White will win of
course sooner or later. **36.♕f4?!**
36.♗d6! wins more or less directly, e.g.,
36...♗e6 37.♕c3 ♗c8 38.♖f1 ♖×e4
39.d5 c×d5 40.c6 ♖be7 41.c7 and it is
over as 41...♕×d6? runs into 42.♕h8+
♔×h8 43.♖f8♯ **36...a5?** The computer
defense 36...♗c4 37.♕c1 ♗b5 is more
tenacious, but should not hold in the
long run. **37.♖f2 ♗b3**

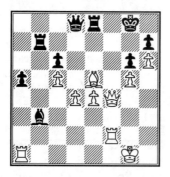

38.d5! Botvinnik breaks the blockade
forcefully. **38...c×d5 39.c6 ♖a7
40.c7 ♕e7 41.♗d6** and Black resigned in view of **41...♕×e4
42.♕f8+ ♖×f8 43.♖×f8♯ 1–0**

Belavienets, Sergei Vsevolodovich
(July 18, 1910, Smolensk-March 7,
1942) Soviet chess master and theoretician, one of the strongest players in the
country at the end of the 1930s.

While still a youth, Belavienets competed successfully in tournaments in
Smolensk and Byelorussia. By 1930,
he was living in Moscow; in 1932,
1937 (with Alatortsev), and 1938 (with
Smyslov), he took the title of Moscow
champion. In 1934, he became champion of the Russian Federation, and
played three times in the USSR championships.

"An unusually high, one could say –
grandmasterly – technique and skill in
defense. In particular, he knew how
clearly and accurately to calculate the
most complex and involved variations,
an almost complete absence of blunders, despite the occasional fierce time-
pressure – complete the characterization of this gifted master," is what the

Sergei Belavienets

chief arbiter of the 11th USSR championship (Leningrad 1939), Zubarev, wrote about the third prizewinner Belavienets, who finished just a half-point behind Kotov, who took second place. It is interesting that against the top ten placers, Belavienets had a plus score, 6½/9 (+4 -0 =5). This was a point more than the score of national champion Botvinnik against the same opponents, while his game against him ended in an 80-move draw.

By this time, Belavienets was a strong theoretician and teacher. In the first volume of the chess encyclopedia, *Sovremennyi Debyut* (1940), he was responsible for the major portion of the section on the Ruy Lopez.

Belavienets' games were distinguished for their depth of planning, elegant play in the endgame and amazing mastery in his defense of difficult positions. In this regard, for example, his encounters in tournaments with Lilienthal (Tbilisi 1937), Keres (Moscow 1939), and wins over Levenfish (Tbilisi 1937), and Tolush (Moscow 1939), or the following endgame with Flohr, were typical

(12) Belavenets – Flohr
Leningrad/Moscow 1939
Caro-Kann Defense [B15]

1.e4 c6 2.d4 d5 3.♘c3 d×e4 4.♘×e4 ♘f6 5.♘×f6+ e×f6 6.♗c4 ♗d6 7.♕e2+ ♗e7 8.♘f3 0-0 9.0-0 ♗g4 10.♖e1 ♗d6 10...♗×f3? is met by 11.♕×e7 **11.♕d3?!** 11.h3 ♗h5 12.♗d2 is more logical. **11...♘d7** The original 11...♕d7 12.h3 ♗f5 13.♕b3 ♘a6 is an interesting alternative. **12.h3 ♗h5 13.♗b3** 13.♘h4!? **13...a5**

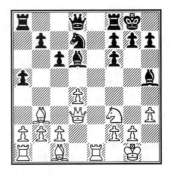

14.c3? A tactical oversight. 14.a4 gives White a slight plus. **14...♘c5! 15.♕d1** Of course not 15.d×c5?? ♗h2+ –+ **15...♘×b3 16.♕×b3?!** 16.a×b3 limits the damage. **16...♕d7** The alternative 16...♗×f3 17.g×f3 ♕d7 18.♔g2 a4 19.♕c2 ♖a5 is also good for Black. **17.♘h2 a4 18.♕c2 ♗c7 19.♗e3 f5?!** 19...♖fe8 is more precise as it keeps more options on the kingside open.

20.f4? White's bishop resembles an overgrown pawn now. 20.♕d2 ♕d6 21.g3 f6 22.♗f4 ♕d7 23.♗×c7 ♕×c7 24.♘f1 was the lesser evil. **20...f6!** Flohr prepares to regroup his bishop to increase his pressure on the queenside. **21.♘f1 ♗f7 22.c4 ♖fe8 23.♕d3 g6 24.b3 b5 25.g3 ♗a5 26.♖ed1 ♖ad8 27.♖ac1 ♗b6 28.♔f2?!** 28.♗f2 might be a bit more precise, but White's position is very difficult in any case. **28...♕a7 29.♔g2 ♕a8 30.♔f2 ♕a7 31.♔g2 ♕b7 32.♔f2 b×c4 33.b×c420.f4?** White's bishop resembles an overgrown pawn now. 20.♕d2 ♕d6 21.g3 f6 22.♗f4 ♕d7 23.♗×c7 ♕×c7 24.♘f1 was the lesser evil. **20...f6!** Flohr prepares to regroup his bishop to increase his pressure on the queenside. **21.♘f1 ♗f7 22.c4 ♖fe8 23.♕d3 g6 24.b3 b5 25.g3 ♗a5 26.♖ed1 ♖ad8 27.♖ac1 ♗b6 28.♔f2?!** 28.♗f2 might be a bit more precise, but White's position is very difficult in any case. **28...♕a7 29.♔g2 ♕a8 30.♔f2 ♕a7 31.♔g2 ♕b7 32.♔f2 b×c4 33.b×c4**

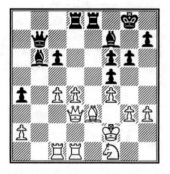

33...♗×d4 Flohr chooses a direct tactical solution. The positional 33...♖e4!? 34.c5 ♗a5 35.♘d2 ♗×d2 36.♕×d2 ♗d5 was also very strong. **34.♗×d4 c5 35.♕c3 c×d4 36.♖×d4 ♕a7 37.c5?!**

37...♗×a2? The wrong way around. 37...♖×d4 38.♕×d4 ♗×a2 39.♖a1 ♗b3 was called for, as 40.♘d2? runs into 40...♕e7-+ **38.♖×d8 ♖×d8 39.♕×f6 ♖c8?** 39...♖b8? is parried by 40.♘e3 a3 41.♕e5 ♖b2+ 42.♔g1 ♗f7 43.♘d5 ♗×d5 44.♕×d5+ ♔g7 45.♕d6 ♖e2 46.♕d3 ♕e7 47.c6 ♖e3 48.♕d7 ♖×g3+ 49.♔f2 ♕×d7 50.c×d7 ♖d3 51.♖a1 ♖×d7 52.♖×a3 and the rook endgame is tenable. But against 39...♖a8! White's defensive task is probably not solvable, e.g., 40.♘e3 a3 41.h4 (41.c6 ♖e8; 41.♕d6 ♗f7 42.♘d5 a2 43.♖a1 ♕b8) 41...♕g7 42.♕c6 ♖d8 43.♖c2 ♗f7 and Black has good winning chances in all cases as a result of his dangerous passed a-pawn. **40.♘e3 a3 41.c6?** 41.h4! ♗b3 42.h5 more or less forces the draw.

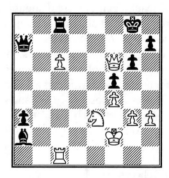

41...♗d5? Flohr does not have time for this retreat. 41...♖e8! gives Black good winning chances, e.g., 42.♕c3 ♗e6 43.c7 a2 44.g4 ♕a4 45.♔g3 g5 46.♘g2 f×g4 47.h×g4 ♔f7 **42.c7! ♕a5** 42...♖×c7? 43.♕d8++- **43.♖d1!** White has turned the tables completely. **43...♕×c7 44.♖×d5 ♖e8 45.♕d4** Strong centralization. **45...a2 46.♖d7** and Black resigned in view of 46...a1♕ (46...♕×d7 47.♕×d7 ♖×e3 48.♕d5+ ♔f8 49.♕×a2+-) 47.♕d5+ ♔h8 48.♖×c7 ♕b2+ 49.♖c2+- **1-0**

Belavienets successfully merged his chess activity with his work as an electrical engineer, working out new construction for livestock farms. Some of them were demonstrated at the All-Union Agricultural Exhibition in 1939. The life of this talented engineer and master was unfortunately cut short. At the start of World War II, he joined the home guard. On March 7, 1942, while commanding a small detachment of mortarmen, he died in the battle for control of the Staraya Russa-Novgorod route.

His daughter, Ludmilla (born 1940) became a well-known chessplayer herself, a grandmaster and women's world correspondence champion, and a trainer in the youth school named for Petrosian.

Biblio. Master Sergei Belavienets (edited by L. S. Belavienets), Moscow 1963.

Boleslavsky, Isaak Yefremovich (June 9, 1919, Zolotonosh, Ukraine-February 15, 1977, Minsk), international grandmaster (1950), world championship candidate during the 1940s and 1950s, chess theoretician and trainer. Learning chess at 9, Boleslavsky amazingly – without sufficient practice, relying basically on books – reached top-level master status. And the love for artistic literature, instilled by his mother from his early days, aided the development of a visual mode of thinking. "In my youth, it seemed to me that a chess game was like meeting a woman," he later wrote. "You know, for sure that both that kind of meeting, and a game played over the board, must begin, and must likewise end; in between, there is excitement, and at the midpoint, there will be something unexpected, unfore-

Isaak Boleslavsky

seen which you were not expecting, or a new and charming thing, or not so charming; or else you become happy, or sad..."

More often, chess brought him joy. In 1938, 1939, and 1940, Boleslavsky won three consecutive Ukraine championships!

In 1940, he appeared in his first USSR championship, and shared fifth/sixth places with Mikhail Botvinnik, but lost to him in their mutual game, and from that day forward he dreamed of getting even. Later on he recalled what sort of plans the 27-year-old, ambitious young master nurtured: "Here is where I decided, that by working systematically on myself, yes, I could beat him. Losing to Botvinnik again twice, in the match-tournament of 1941, and in a game from the 14th national championship, did not faze me at all. It seemed to me that I understood the play of Botvinnik, saw his strong and weak points. I began to prepare to meet him. Of course, I understood that this was a chessplayer of a wholly different style from mine of those days. But I believed I had chances of winning."

Over the next 10 years, Boleslavsky steadily improved his results: in the match-tournament for the title of Absolute Champion of the USSR, in 1941 – 4th place; at the USSR championships: 1944 – 3rd, 1945 and 1947 – 2nd and finally, 1950 – the acme of his competitive achievements – in the candidates' tournament, he shared first and second places with David Bronstein. An additional match was set up between them, and here Boleslavsky committed a psychological error: preparing for the match against Bronstein, he kept thinking all the time about the match with Botvinnik! Boleslavsky lost by just one point to Bronstein (7½-6½), but the price of that point was the loss of a chance for a match against the world champion, which remained but a dream.

Many of his contemporaries found Boleslavsky's combinative style attractive.

"For me," the Yugoslav grandmaster Gligoric shared with us, "Boleslavsky's style was always a chess ideal. In what other contemporary player is strategy and tactics, logic and fantasy, so well integrated?"

Boleslavsky took part once more in the 1953 candidates' tournament in Zürich, and played successfully in a string of tournaments – Bucharest 1953, Stockholm 1964, and Debrecen 1961, in which he shared first and second prizes. However, he showed an ever greater disposition towards training work.

At 37, Isaak was second to Vassily Smyslov in the 1956 candidates' tournament that Smyslov won, and three years later, Tigran Petrosian came to him for assistance. Theirs was to be a long and fruitful cooperation. In 1963, Petrosian defeated Botvinnik and became world champion; and three years later, he successfully defended the title against Spassky. "In all my successes achieved during the period of our cooperation," Petrosian later acknowledged, "Isaak Yefremovich was to 'blame'; his contribution was enormous."

Boleslavsky was distinguished for his phenomenal memory, encyclopedic knowledge, benevolence, and humility. Bronstein called him "a genuine artist in chess," and considered him one of the sharpest of Soviet chessplayers.

The paper *Izvestia* called the following game a pearl of the art of chess.

(13) Boleslavsky – Dzindzhichashvili
Minsk 1966
Queen's Gambit Accepted [D29]

1.d4 d5 2.c4 d×c4 3.♘f3 ♘f6 4.e3 e6 5.♗×c4 c5 6.0-0 a6 7.♘c3 b5 8.♗b3 ♗b7 9.♕e2 ♘bd7 10.♖d1 ♕b8 11.d5 e×d5 12.♘×d5 ♘×d5 13.♗×d5 ♗×d5 14.♖×d5 ♕b7 15.e4 ♗e7 16.♗g5 ♘b6 17.♖ad1

17...h6? Too provocative. 17...f6 is the main move, which equalizes. **18.♗×e7 ♘×d5 19.♗×c5! ♘e7?** 19...♘f4 20.♕e3 ♘e6 was called for, but White has more than enough compensation after 21.♗d6 ♖d8 22.e5 ♖c8 23.♘d2 **20.♘e5**

20...♖c8? Mistakes always seem to come in pairs. 20...♕c7! 21.♘d7 ♖d8 22.♗b6 ♕×d7 23.♗×d8 ♕e6 24.♕d3 ♘c6 25.♗b6 0-0 limits the damage. **21.♖d7 ♖c7** 21...♕×d7 22.♘×d7 ♔×d7 23.♕d2+ ♔e8 24.♕d6+- **22.♖d8+!! ♔×d8 23.♘×f7+**

23...♔d7? This try to escape runs into a beautiful refutation. 23...♔c8 24.♘d6+ ♔b8 25.♘×b7 ♔×b7 is forced, but White should be winning in the long run after 26.b4+- **24.♕g4+! ♔c6** 24...♔e8 25.♘d6++- **25.♕e6+** and Black resigned because of 25...♔×c5 26.♕d6+ ♔c4 27.♘e5#

Only once did Boleslavsky succeed in defeating Botvinnik. The game was notable for White's elegant positional play, aimed at the consistent breaking down of the enemy's blockade.

(14) Boleslavsky – Botvinnik
Voronovo 1952
Semi-Slav [D48]

1.d4 d5 2.c4 c6 3.♘f3 e6 4.♘c3 ♘f6 5.e3 ♘bd7 6.♗d3 d×c4 7.♗×c4 b5 8.♗d3 a6 9.e4 c5 10.d5 e5?! 10...c4 and 10...♕c7 are the main moves. **11.b3 ♗d6 12.0-0 0-0 13.a4** 13.♕c2!? **13...b4 14.♘e2**

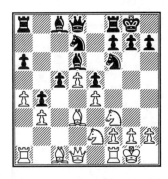

14...c4!! A very good strategic decision! Botvinnik sacrifices a pawn to blockade the queenside favorably. 14...a5? 15.♘g3 ♗a6 16.♗×a6 ♖×a6 17.♕e2 ♖a8 18.♘f5 ♕c7 19.♘d2 is clearly better for White. **15.b×c4 ♘c5 16.♘g3 a5 17.h3 ♕c7 18.♘h4 g6 19.♖e1 ♘e8** 19...♘fd7!? **20.♗h6 ♘g7 21.♖e3?!** 21.♘f3!? is more precise, but Black has almost equalized in any case. **21...f6 22.♘f1** **22...♖f7?!** Botvinnik decides just to keep the blockade and then regroup very slowly. Objectively it was better to be more active on the queenside with 22...b3 23.♘d2 ♖b8 24.♗b1 b2 25.♖a2 ♖b4 26.♕c2 ♕b6= **23.♘d2 ♗d7 24.♗c2 ♕d8 25.♘hf3**

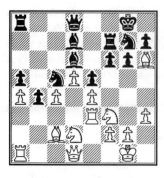

25...♘e8?! This retreat is quite slow and clumsy. 25...♘h5 is more active. **26.♘e1 ♘c7 27.♖g3 ♔h8 28.♘d3 ♘7a6 29.h4 ♘×d3 30.♗×d3 ♘c5 31.♗c2 ♕e7 32.♗e3 ♖c8**

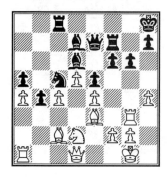

33.h5?! This gives Black more options on the kingside. Challenging the blockading forces with 33.♘b3! is called for. **33...♖g7 34.h×g6 h×g6 35.♘b3** 35.♕f3 is answered by 35...g5 36.♖h3+ ♖h7 37.♖×h7+ ♔×h7 38.♘b3 ♘b7 and like in the game, it is not easy to break Black's solid blockade. **35...♘×b3 36.♗×b3 g5 37.♖c1 ♗c5** A good way to keep the blockade, as 37...♖h7? runs into 38.c5 ♗×c5 39.♖×c5 ♖×c5 40.d6+− **38.♗×c5 ♖×c5 39.♖d3 ♖h7 40.f3?!** 40.♕f3!? is a better try.

40...♕f8? Botvinnik does not have time for this. The attack must be started with 40...♖h4! 41.♔f2 ♕h7 42.♕e2 g4 43.♕e3 ♖c8, and Black has enough counterplay. **41.♕e1 ♔g7 42.♕e3! ♕d6** 42...♕h8!? was a better practical try as 43.♕×c5?? runs into 43...♖h1+ 44.♔f2 ♕h4+ 45.♔e2 ♖×c1 which gives Black a draw. So 43.♔f2 is called for. **43.♖dd1 ♗e8 44.♔f2 ♗g6 45.♖h1 ♖×h1 46.♖×h1 ♖c7 47.♔e2 ♖c5 48.♔d2 ♕b6 49.g3 ♕d6 50.♔c1 ♕e7 51.♔b2 ♕d6 52.♖h2 ♕c7 53.♖d2 ♕d6 54.♖f2 ♕e7 55.♖f1 ♗h7 56.♕d2 ♕d6**

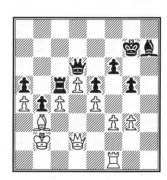

57.f4! Finally White opens the kingside for the final attack. **57...♗×e4 58.f×g5 f5 59.♕e3 ♕c7 60.♖f2 ♖×c4 61.d6 1-0**

Boleslavsky died at 57. Grieving over the sudden loss, one of his friends, and one who learned from him, grandmaster Alexei Suetin, wrote in the magazine *Shakhmaty v SSSR* (1977, No. 4):

Boleslavsky was a man of exceptional modesty, and a very cultured person. If it was hard to imagine Boleslavsky without chess, then it would have been simply impossible to imagine him without a book. He knew history, classic literature, poetry very well indeed... His notable systems in the Sicilian and King's Indian Defenses were truly innovative; his researches enriched a whole string of current openings. His deeply constructed books and clever analyses in the chess press long ago made Boleslavsky one of the world's leading theoreticians.

Books: XVIII USSR Chess Championship, Moscow 1952 (co-author); *Selected Games*, Moscow 1957; *Petrosian-Spassky 1969*, Moscow 1970 (co-author). *Bibliography:* A. Suetin, *Grandmaster Boleslavsky*, Moscow 1981.

Bondarevsky, Igor Zakharovich (May 12, 1913, on the independent Samsonov farm, near Rostov-on-Don-June 14, 1979, Piatigorsk), Soviet grandmaster, theoretician, arbiter, trainer, correspondence grandmaster. Igor learned the basics of chess when he was 9. In 1925, his country underwent "chess fever" as a result of the Moscow international tournament, and the 12-year old Igor began studying *Chess Fundamentals* by Capablanca. By day, he dedicated himself to his beloved mathematics; in the evenings, it was chess. And at the beginning of the 1930s, he started structured studies at the Rostov House of Pioneers.

He won the championship of Rostov-on-Don four years in a row (1933-36), and won the All-Union first category tournament in Leningrad in 1936. A year later, he was awarded the title of master. And in 1940, he won the USSR championship jointly with Lilienthal, ahead of Smyslov, Keres, Boleslavsky, and Botvinnik, and became a grandmaster of the USSR. "His chess talent is beyond all question... He always strives for active play, and figures out the most complicated positions," wrote Botvinnik a year before the tournament. Bondarevsky confirmed the flattering assessment of the strongest Soviet chessplayer by handing him the following defeat in the very first round.

(15) Bondarevsky – Botvinnik
Moscow 1940
Nimzo-Indian Defense [E29]

1.d4 ♞f6 2.c4 e6 3.♞c3 ♝b4 4.a3 ♝×c3+ 5.b×c3 c5 6.e3 0-0 7.♝d3 ♞c6 8.♞e2 d6 9.e4 e5 10.d5

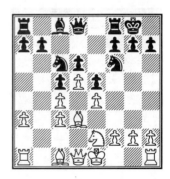

10...♞a5 A very risky sideline as the knight may find itself offside. 10...♞e7 is the main move. **11.0-0 a6 12.♞g3** 12.a4!? **12...b5 13.c×b5 c4 14.♝c2 a×b5 15.a4**

15...b×a4? Regrouping the misplaced knight with 15...♘b7 was better, e.g., 16.♗g5 b×a4 17.♗×a4 (17.♘h5 ♗g4 18.♘×f6+ g×f6 19.♕×g4 f×g5 20.♗×a4 ♘c5 21.♗b5 ♕f6=) 17...h6 18.♗×f6 ♕×f6 19.♕e2 ♘c5 20.♗b5 ♖b8 21.♗×c4 ♗d7 with compensation for the pawn. **16.♖×a4 ♘d7 17.♗e3 ♘c5?** This leads to a strategically lost position. 17...♕c7 was necessary. **18.♗×c5 d×c5 19.♕h5 f6 20.♖fa1 ♗d7 21.♖4a3 ♕b6 22.♕d1 ♖a7 23.♘f1 ♖fa8 24.♘e3 ♔f8 25.♖1a2 ♖a6 26.h3 ♕d8 27.♘×c4 ♗b5 28.♘×a5 ♖×a5 29.♕a1**

Bondarevsky has installed Alekhine's gun on the a-file. **29...♖×a3 30.♖×a3 ♖×a3 31.♕×a3 ♕c7** The defense 31...♕b6 32.♕a8+ ♔f7 33.♗d1 ♕a6 is parried by 34.♕b8 ♗e2 35.♗b3 c4 36.d6 ♔e6 37.♕f8 ♕×d6 38.♕g8+ ♔d7 39.♗a4+ ♔c7 40.♕×g7+ ♔b6 41.♗d7+− **32.♕a8+ ♔f7 33.♗d1**

♔g6?! 33...♗d7 34.♗a4 ♗×a4 35.♕×a4 ♔e7 36.♕a6 ♕d7 37.♕b6 +− **34.♗g4 ♗d7**

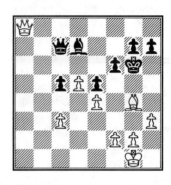

35.d6!? ♕×d6 **36.♕d8** The pin is decisive. **36...♕d2 37.♕×d7 ♕e1+ 38.♔h2 1-0**

In 1948, Bondarevsky participated in the first interzonal tournament, at Saltsjobaden, where he shared sixth/ninth places with Najdorf, Flohr and Stålhberg. But he did not play in the candidates' tournament because of illness. In the future, Bondarevsky mostly confined himself to trainer's work. He led the student team at the world student Olympiads. He worked with two eventual world champions –

Igor Bondarevsky

Smyslov (1956-1959), and over 10 years later, Spassky. He also prepared three candidates – Keres, Geller, and later Kozlovskaya, who became his wife.

"The main thing a trainer needs," he said, "is strong nerves and a strong heart!" One day, when a journalist asked Bondarevsky whether he had ever had a "knockdown" in his training work, he replied: "Yes. It was during the ninth game of the Spassky-Keres match. I had already settled in. The game, which would decide the match, was an easy win for Spassky. And suddenly, Spassky made a "long" queen move, after which Paul Petrovich was nearly winning. Any queen move of one or two squares would have won easily..."

On the whole, the Spassky-Bondarevsky collaboration would go down in history as one of the most fruitful ones, reminiscent of the duets Botvinnik-Ragozin, Tal-Koblents, Petrosian-Boleslavsky. Bondarevsky brought a valuable contribution to the theory of openings, working out, together with Tartakower and Makagonov, an original system of play in the Queen's Gambit. Bondarevsky Memorial tournaments have been held in Rostov-on-Don.

Books: *Twenty Games from the 12th All-Union championship*, Rostov-on-Don 1941; *Soviet Chessplayers in the USA, England and Sweden*, 1955; *1955 Göteborg Interzonal Chess Tournament*, Moscow 1957; *Learn to Play Chess*, Leningrad 1966; *Petrosian-Spassky 1969*, Moscow 1970 (co-author); *Combinations in the Middlegame*, 2nd ed., Moscow 1982.

David Bronstein

Bronstein, David Ionovich (February 19, 1924, Belaya Tserkov, Ukraine-December 5, 2006, Minsk) Russian chessplayer, international grandmaster (1950), played a match for the world championship with Botvinnik in 1951.

In childhood dreams, he would, quite often, promote his pawn to a vqueen in a game against the second world champion, Emanuel Lasker. In this way, the dream of winning the title of the world's strongest chessplayer was impressed upon the consciousness of the youngster. At that time, he was studying in the Kiev House of Pioneers, under Alexander Konstantinopolsky, who was destined to become his supporter and trainer in his match against Botvinnik. At 16, David received the silver medal of the Ukraine champion. After the war, he moved to Moscow, where he quickly achieved great successes. 1946 Moscow champion, third prize in the 1945 USSR championship, national champion in 1948 and 1949, winner of the 1948 Stockholm international tournament, and finally, he shared first and second places with Boleslavsky in the 1950 Budapest candidates' tournament, and victory in a playoff match against Boleslavsky.

In 1951, Bronstein played his match with Botvinnik. This was the first world championship encounter in 14 years – since the Alekhine-Euwe match of 1937. And the grandmasters gave the world a grandiose spectacle. In strategy, tactics, and finally, in the delicacy of their endgame play (many of the games finished deep in the endgame), they proved themselves worthy opponents. We now present one of the best games of the match.

(16) Bronstein – Botvinnik
Moscow (m22) 1951
Dutch Defense [A91]

1.d4 e6 2.c4 f5 3.g3 ♘f6 4.♗g2 ♗e7 5.♘c3 0-0 6.e3 d5 7.♘ge2 c6 8.b3 ♘e4 9.0-0 ♘d7 10.♗b2 ♘df6 11.♕d3

11...g5?! This bold advance is too optimistic. A more solid alternative is 11...b6 **12.c×d5?!** This exchange frees Black's position. The direct 12.f3 ♘×c3 13.♕×c3 is more logical. **12...e×d5 13.f3 ♘×c3 14.♗×c3 g4 15.f×g4 ♘×g4 16.♗h3 ♘h6** The computer

prefers 16...a5, e.g., 17.♗×g4 f×g4 18.e4 d×e4 19.♕×e4 ♗g5 20.♖×f8+ ♕×f8 21.d5 ♗f5 22.♕d4 ♖e8 23.♘f4 c5 24.♕d2 ♕d6= **17.♘f4 ♗d6 18.b4 a6 19.a4 ♕e7**

20.♖ab1 The direct 20.b5!? is probably somewhat stronger. **20...b5** 20...♗d7, to meet 21.b5 with 21...a×b5 22.a×b5 ♘g4 23.b×c6 b×c6 24.♖b7 ♖fb8=, was the alternative. **21.♗g2 ♘g4 22.♗d2 ♘f6 23.♖b2 ♗d7 24.♖a1 ♘e4** 24...b×a4!? 25.♖ba2 ♖fb8 26.♖×a4 ♗×b4 27.♗×b4 ♖×b4 28.♖×a6 ♖ab8 is also almost equal and might be easier to play for Black than the game continuation. **25.♗e1 ♖fe8 26.♕b3 ♔h8 27.♖ba2**

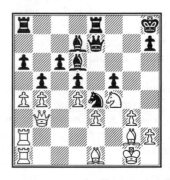

27...♕f8?! 27...b×a4 28.♖×a4 ♘f6 29.♗d2 (29.♖×a6 ♖×a6 30.♖×a6 ♘g4=) 29...♘e4 30.♗×e4 f×e4= gives Black sufficient counterplay on the kingside. **28.♘d3 ♖ab8?!** Now Bronstein can invade on the a-file with gain of time. 28...♕h6!? is more active. **29.a×b5 a×b5 30.♖a7 ♖e7 31.♘e5 ♗e8 32.g4 f×g4?** This loses by force as now the floodgates are open. After 32...♕g7, White still has a dangerous initiative as Black's light-square bishop and rook are passive, e.g., 33.♖×e7 ♕×e7 34.♗×e4 f×e4 35.♗g3 ♖c8 36.♕b2 ♔g8 37.♕f2, and White is for choice, but a draw is also still possible. **33.♗×e4! d×e4 34.♗h4**

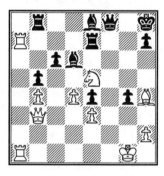

The awakening of White's sleeping dark-square bishop decides the game. **34...♖×e5** 34...♖×a7 35.♖×a7 ♕h6 36.♗g3 ♖c8 37.♗f4 ♕f6 38.♖f7 ♗×f7 39.♘×f7+ ♔g7 40.♘×d6+− **35.d×e5 ♗×e5 36.♖f1 ♕g8 37.♗g3 ♗g7** 37...♗×g3? 38.♕c3+ ♗e5 39.♕×e5+ ♕g7 40.♕×g7♯ **38.♕×g8+ 1-0**

"A beautiful conclusion. Bronstein played the concluding attack excellently, and makes a powerful impression." (Lilienthal)

Neither Botvinnik nor Bronstein was able to obtain a decisive advantage in the course of the match. In the 23rd game, Botvinnik evened the score. Now it was down to the final encounter, which ended up drawn. With the score 12-12, the champion retained his title.

"I understood," admitted Bronstein, "that it was impossible to play logical chess against Botvinnik: he would easily break down whatever I could set up. And I constantly set before my opponent unusual tasks – perhaps, at some point, I overreached. Whatever the outcome, it was an interesting match."

Here's Botvinnik's opinion of his opponent: *A brilliant master of the attack, able to make original decisions, he flung himself into the match for the world championship, shouldering aside such talented masters as Keres, Smyslov, Boleslavsky etc.*

Bronstein did a good job with complex piece play, setting up his pieces quite accurately according to general considerations. In the middlegame, he was dangerous. But where exact analysis was required, where it was necessary to find the exceptions to the rules, Bronstein was weaker. There was also another factor, which allowed me, in circumstances that were unfavorable to me – I had not played one tournament game in the past three years – to hold the match to a draw. This was a matter of personal and competitive shortcomings of my challenger: a tendency to a sort of extravagance and self-satisfaction, and also naivete in his competitive tactics...

Improvisation, playing by inspiration, breadth of view, the desire to introduce something new – these were all characteristics of the young candidate. He experienced a nostalgia for the discarded King's Gambit, and the "pre-rating" times, when the creative approach to chess was valued more than anything, when the spirit of combinations continuously flew over the board.

(17) Bronstein – Dubinin
Leningrad 1947
King's Gambit Accepted [C39]

**1.e4 e5 2.f4 e×f4 3.♘f3 g5 4.h4 g4
5.♘e5 h5 6.♗c4 ♖h7** 6...♘h6 is
played more often. **7.d4**

7...♗h6? 7...f3! is critical. **8.♘c3
♘c6?** Mistakes always seem to come
in pairs. 8...f3! 9.g×f3 d6 10.♘×f7 ♖×f7
11.♗×f7+ ♔×f7 12.♗×h6 ♘×h6 is still
called for to limit the damage. **9.♘×f7
♖×f7 10.♗×f7+ ♔×f7 11.♗×f4
♗×f4** 11...♔g7 12.♗×h6+ ♘×h6
13.♕d2 d6 14.0-0-0 is also very
promising for White. **12.0-0 ♕×h4?!**
12...♔g7 is more difficult to break, but
does not hold because of 13.♖×f4 d6
(13...d5 14.♘×d5 ♗e6 15.c4+–)
14.♕d2 ♗d7 15.♖af1 ♗e8 16.♖f5
♕×h4 17.♖g5+ ♗g6 18.♘e2 ♘f6
19.♕f4 ♖f8 20.♘g3 ♔h7 21.♘f5 ♘×d4
22.♘×d4 ♘×e4 23.♖f5 ♗×f5 24.♘×f5
♕g5 25.♕×e4+– **13.♖×f4+ ♔g7**

14.♕d2! Bronstein invites all his
forces to the party on the kingside.
**14...d6 15.♖af1 ♘d8 16.♘d5 ♗d7
17.e5!** Bronstein opens the position for
his attack. **17...d×e5** 17...♗b5 18.c4
♗×c4 19.♘e3 ♗×f1 20.♘f5++–;
17...♗c6 18.♘e3 ♘h6 19.e×d6 c×d6
20.d5 ♗e8 21.♕c3+ ♔h7 22.♖f8+–
**18.d×e5 ♗c6 19.e6! ♗×d5 20.♖f7+
♘×f7 21.♖×f7+ ♔h8** 21...♔g6?
22.♕d3+ ♔h6 23.♕h7+ ♔g5 24.♕g7‡
22.♕c3+ ♘f6 23.♖×f6 ♕×f6
23...g3? 24.♖h6+ ♔g8 25.♖h8‡
**24.♕×f6+ ♔h7 25.♕f5+ ♔h6
26.♕×d5 ♔g6 27.♕d7 1-0**

(18) Bronstein – Geller
Moscow 1961
Nimzo-Indian Defense [E27]

**1.d4 ♘f6 2.c4 e6 3.♘c3 ♗b4 4.a3
♗×c3+ 5.b×c3 0-0 6.f3 d5 7.c×d5
e×d5 8.e3 ♗f5 9.♘e2 ♘bd7
10.♘f4** 10.♘g3 scores better. **10...c5
11.♗d3** The original 11.g4!? is more
ambitious. **11...♗×d3 12.♕×d3 ♖e8
13.0-0 ♖c8 14.♖b1**

14...♕a5? Geller underestimates the
coming dangers for his king. After
14...♘b6, Black is by no means worse.
**15.♖×b7 ♘b6 16.g4 h6 17.h4
c×d4?** Geller had to take the exchange
with 17...c4 18.♕f5 ♕a6 19.♖×b6 ♕×b6
20.g5 ♘h7 and White has good
compensation, but not more than that.

18.g5 18.c×d4 is also very good for White, as 18...♖c3 can be met by19.♖×a7 **18...d×e3?** 18...♖×c3 19.♗d2 ♖×d3 20.♗×a5 ♖×a3 21.♗×b6 a×b6 22.g×f6 d×e3 is relatively best, but of course it is not likely that Black can survive. 18...h×g5? 19.h×g5 ♖×c3 20.♗d2 ♖×d3 21.♗×a5 ♖×a3 22.♗×b6 a×b6 23.g×f6 d×e3 runs into 24.♔h2!! ♖a4 25.♖e7+– **19.g×f6 ♖×c3 20.♕g6!!**

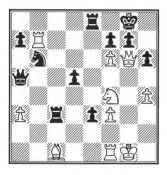

and Geller resigned in view of 20...f×g6 21.♖×g7+ ♔f8 22.♘×g6#

Bronstein constantly tried to bring something original into his praxis. One of his most important discoveries in the development of chess theory, as Garry Kasparov showed in the examples of the games against Pachman and Zita in the 1946 Moscow-Prague match, was successfully breathing new life into Black's attacking ideas in the King's Indian Defense.

To him belongs the idea of chess time-measurement – recording the time, to the second, taken by both players in thinking about each move, and also quick-chess tournaments, so popular in recent years. At the beginning of the 1970s, he played a series of matches against Tal and Vasiukov in which each player was given 15 minutes for the entire game. And in 1975, on the initiative of the English publishing house Batsford, an international tournament was held using that time-control at Teesside. Bronstein won, a half-point ahead of the young Jan Timman.

Bronstein was convinced that "the strongest chess computer will remain considerably inferior to the human brain in those cases, where the human uses his intuition," And he showed this by playing against the newest computers, right up until the middle of the 1990s. In his experiments, he "tried to create the most confusing positions possible... Intuition and experience told me that the computer, although it calculates millions of variations, on the whole does not always select the best move."

Back at the start of the 1960s, he admitted that he had played his own immortal game, concluding with a forced ten-move mating combination against the electronic black king. The point was that after the 13th move, the computer fell into deep thought, used up all its time, and the chief arbiter – that is, the chief programmer, wanted to adjourn... No, here it is: I announced mate in ten!"

(19) Bronstein – IBM "M20"
Moscow 1963
King's Gambit Accepted [C34]

1.e4 e5 2.f4 e×f4 3.♘f3 ♘f6 4.e5 ♘g4? 4...♘h5 is the main move. **5.d4?** 5.h3, to meet 5...♘×e5? with 6.♕e2, is called for. **5...g5?** Black's development should be combined with attacking the center with 5...d6 **6.♘c3 ♘e3?** 6...d6 7.♕e2 ♗e7 limits the damage. **7.♕e2?** 7.♗×e3 f×e3 8.♗c4 ♗e7 9.0-0 0-0

10.♕d3+− **7...♘×f1?** Black does not have time for this. 7...g4 is critical, e.g., 8.♗×e3 g×f3 9.♕×f3 f×e3 10.♗c4 ♕h4+ 11.g3 ♕h6 12.0-0, and White certainly has compensation, but it is not clear, if he is better. **8.♘e4**

8...♘e3?! The knight just makes too many moves. 8...♗e7 offers more resistance, but White simply must be clearly better after 9.♖×f1 **9.♘f6+ ♚e7 10.♗d2?** Bronstein probably wants the computer to take on c2 and a1. Objectively, 10.♗×e3 was better: 10...f×e3 11.♘×g5 d6 12.♕h5 ♗e6 13.d5 d×e5 14.♘×f7+− **10...♘×c2+ 11.♚f2 ♘×a1?** This is too greedy. The defense 11...♗g7! seems to hold, e.g., 12.♖ac1 d6 13.♖×c2 ♚f8 14.♘×g5 ♗×f6 15.e×f6 ♘c6 16.♘×f7 ♚×f7 17.♕h5± **12.♘d5+ ♚e6?** 12...♚e8 is forced, but Bronstein's attack is winning in all variations, e.g., 13.♘f6+ ♚e7 14.♘×g5 ♗h6 15.♗×f4 ♕f8 16.♕h5 ♘a6 17.♖×a1+− **13.♕c4! b5?!** Now the computer is mated by force, but the position was hopeless anyway. **14.♘×g5+ ♕×g5 15.♘×c7+ ♚e7 16.♘d5+ ♚e6 17.♘×f4+ ♚e7 18.♘d5+** (D)

18...♚e8 18...♚e6 19.♘c7+ ♚f5 20.♕d3+ ♚g4 21.♕h3# **19.♕×c8+ ♕d8 20.♘c7+ ♚e7 21.♗b4+ d6**

22.♗×d6+ ♕×d6 23.♕e8# A powerful demonstration of the strength of human intuition in the old days, when the computers were too greedy. **1-0**

Bronstein was the author of many books, in which were clearly revealed the soul of a chess romantic. They are all unusual, attractive, and interesting. A genuine chess bestseller was his book on the 1953 Zürich Candidates' Tournament in Switzerland, 1953.

In the last years of the 20th century, by his own admission, Bronstein finally knew the freedom of roaming throughout the world – "From my youngest days, the virus of freedom grew within me."

He lived in Spain, and occupied himself with the chessplayers of Oviedo University. Then he was attracted by England – a country with a long-standing chess tradition. He returned once again to Russia... and on February 19, 1999, the world of chess observed his 75th birthday. He passed away in Minsk on December 5, 2006 at the age of 82.

Books: 200 Open Games, Moscow 1970; *The Beautiful and Violent World*, Moscow, 1978 (co-author);

International Grandmaster Tournament, Neuhausen-Zürichm 1953, Moscow 1954; *Chess Self-Teacher*, Moscow 1987; *David vs. Goliath* (with co-author S. Voronkov), Moscow 2002; *The Sorcerer's Apprentice*, Moscow 2004 (with Tom Furstenberg).

Biblio: Wainstein, B.S., *Improvisation in the Art of Chess*, Moscow 1976.

Wageningen, 1958 (October 28-November 3) By invitation of Max Euwe, his country was again visited by his old friends, Mikhail Botvinnik and Salo Flohr, to participate in a small tournament of six players. The year before, a men's zonal tournament had been played there – one of the elimination stages towards the world championship, and the participants, living in the Wageningen Hills Hotel, proudly named this woodsy, hilly region by the Rhine the "Hollander Himalayas." For Botvinnik, this kind of idyllic little corner of nature was ideally suited. The mountain air, daily walks, and as a result – he played brilliantly. Three wins and two draws in five games assured him of first place. The results: 1. Botvinnik 4; 2-3. Donner & Flohr 3; 4. van Scheltinga 2; 5-6. Bouwmeester, Roussel 1½ .

Wijk Aan Zee, 1969 (January) This traditional chess festival was financed by the Dutch metallurgical complex "Hoogoven." Until 1967, the tournament was held in Beverwijk. In 1968, it moved to the small town of Wijk aan Zee. The main contenders, besides the 57-year old Botvinnik, were considered to be Yefim Geller, Paul Keres and Lajos Portisch – or, as the chess journalists still called him, the "Hungarian Botvinnik." Among the 16

players, the other most dangerous opponents were Fridrik Olafsson of Iceland, the Americans Pal Benko and William Lombardy, the Dutchman Johannes Donner, the Yugoslav Dragoljub Ciric, and Lubomir Kavalek, who had emigrated from Czechoslovakia in 1968. In the drawing of lots, Botvinnik drew Number 13. This highly experienced fighter was not superstitious, but this number complicated his tournament strategy: he would have to play seven games with White, and eight with Black.

At the beginning, Botvinnik managed to break away from his chief competitors – Keres and Geller were somewhat "under the weather," while Portisch started off by losing two games. Botvinnik won methodically from outsiders, and made draws with his pursuers. But after the tenth round, he was nearly overtaken by a group of his pursuers, which by now also included Olafsson and Benko.

A key game, as far as the prize distribution was concerned, was the "game of the two Botvinniks," in which the Hungarian version played White, and the Soviet had Black. The game was adjourned three times, and it looked as though it had to end in the ex-world champion's first loss. However, before the final adjourned session, Paul Keres found a study-like saving line in the tremendously difficult bishop vs. knight ending. The black knight, according to Botvinnik, "leapt about like a madman," constantly threatening to give itself up for one of White's two remaining pawns, while the other would be captured by the black king. After 88 moves, a draw was agreed. In the end, Botvinnik and Geller shared

Wijk aan Zee 1969

	1	2	3	4	5	6	7	8	9	10	11	12	13	14	15	Total
1. Geller	*	½	1	½	1	0	1	1	1	½	½	½	½	½	1	1	10½
2. Botvinnik	½	*	½	½	½	½	½	½	½	½	1	1	1	1	1	1	10½
3. Portisch	0	½	*	1	0	½	½	1	1	½	1	1	1	½	½	1	10
4. Keres	½	½	0	*	½	½	½	1	½	1	1	½	½	1	1	1	10
5. Olafsson	0	½	1	½	*	½	½	0	1	1	½	1	1	1	½	½	9½
6. Benko	1	½	½	½	½	*	½	0	½	0	½	1	½	1	1	1	9
7. Ciric	0	½	½	½	½	½	*	½	½	½	1	1	½	1	1	0	8½
8. Doda	0	½	0	0	1	1	½	*	½	½	½	1	½	½	1	0	7½
9. Donner	0	½	0	½	0	½	½	½	*	½	½	1	0	1	1	1	7½
10. Kavalek	½	½	½	0	0	1	½	½	½	*	½	0	1	1	0	½	7
11. Lombardy	½	0	0	0	½	½	0	½	½	½	*	1	1	1	0	½	6½
12. Ostojic	½	0	0	½	0	0	0	0	0	1	0	*	1	½	1	1	5½
13. Medina	½	0	0	½	0	½	½	½	1	0	0	0	*	0	½	1	5
14. Langeweg	½	0	½	0	0	0	0	½	0	0	0	½	1	*	1	1	5
15. Van Scheltinga	0	0	½	0	½	0	0	0	0	1	1	0	½	0	*	1	4½
16. Ree	0	0	0	0	½	0	1	1	0	½	½	0	0	0	0	*	3½

first/second places with 10 points, with Keres and Portisch sharing third/fourth places. And a half-point behind them were Olafsson, Benko, and Ciric.

There was an interesting encounter between Botvinnik and grandmaster Lombardy, who had until recently been a Catholic priest. He was a pleasant conversationalist, had a fine singing voice, and once, at Botvinnik's request, gave a heartfelt rendition of "Gospodi, pomilui!" ["Please, Lord!" - *Tr.*]. During his game against the Soviet grandmaster, no doubt, he would not have minded repeating it.

(20) Botvinnik – Lombardy
Wijk aan Zee 1969
English Opening [B38]

1.c4 c5 2.♘f3 g6 3.e4 ♗g7 4.d4 c×d4 5.♘×d4 ♘c6 6.♗e3 ♘f6 7.♘c3 0-0 8.♗e2 d6 9.0-0 ♗d7 10.♕d2 ♘×d4 11.♗×d4 ♕a5

12.♖fd1 ♖fc8

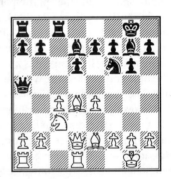

13.♗×f6 White's advantage in the resulting ending is most probably not enough to win. So 13.♖ab1 ♗e6 14.b3 ♕d8 15.♗f3 was played in Graf-Karagiannis, Athens 2008 **13...♗×f6 14.♘d5 ♕×d2 15.♘×f6+ ♔g7 16.♘h5+! g×h5 17.♖×d2 f6 18.b3 ♖c5 19.f4 ♖ac8 20.♖e1 ♗e8 21.♗f1 ♗f7 22.♔f2 a6 23.♖e3 ♖a5 24.a4 ♖ac5 25.♗e2 ♖8c7 26.♖g3+ ♔f8 27.♖h3 ♖7c6 28.f5 ♖b6 29.♖dd3**

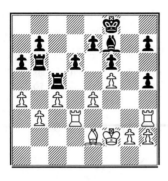

29...♖b4? As the counter ...b7-b5 is not in time and can often be met by c4×b5 followed by a4-a5, Black should play 29...♖e5! with good chances to defend. **30.♗×h5 ♗g8** 30...♗×h5 does not solve Black's problems in view of 31.♖×h5 b5 (31...♖e5 32.♖e3 d5 33.♖×h7 ♖×e4 34.♖×e4 d×e4 35.♖h3) 32.♖×h7 ♔e8 (32...b×c4? runs into 33.♖h8+ ♔g7 34.♖dh3 ♖×b3 35.♖3h7#) 33.c×b5 a×b5 34.a5 with good winning chances in both cases. **31.♖h4 e6?!** White's attack cannot be stopped in this way. Black should continue his own play with 31...b5, but White wins nevertheless because of 32.♖g3 ♖c8 33.♖hg4 ♗f7 34.♗×f7 ♔×f7 35.♖g7+ ♔e8 36.♖×h7 ♔d7 (36...b×a4 37.♖h8+ ♔d7 38.♖×c8 ♔×c8 39.b×a4 ♖×c4 40.h4 ♖×e4 41.h5 ♖h4 42.♖h3+−) 37.e5!! d×e5 38.♖d3+ ♔c6 39.c×b5+ a×b5 40.♖×e7+− **32.f×e6 ♗×e6 33.♗d1 ♗g8 34.♖×d6 ♔e7 35.♖d3 ♖e5 36.♖g4 ♗f7** 36...♖g5 37.♖×g5 f×g5 38.♖g3 h6 39.h4+− **37.♖g7 h6 38.♖h7 ♖e6 39.♗g4 ♔f8 40.♖d8+ ♗e8 41.♖h8+ ♔f7 1-0**

Olympiads Over the ten years from 1954 to 1964, Botvinnik took part in six Olympiads. Four times, he led the USSR team, and twice he played second board. In all of those events, the USSR

team took first place. Botvinnik was victorious twice on his board (in 1954, on first board, and in 1960, on second). In all, he played 73 games and scored 54½ points (+39 -3 =31), for 74.6%. He showed, once again, that he was an outstanding team performer.

1954, September 4-25, Amsterdam
The world champion made his debut at the 11th Olympiad. The USSR team (Botvinnik, Smyslov, Bronstein, Keres, with reserve boards Geller and Kotov) scored a convincing victory, scoring 34/44 in the finals), outstripping second-place Argentina by seven points. Their leader took first place on his board with 8½/11 (+6 -0 =5). Among Botvinnik's opponents were grandmasters Euwe (Holland), Najdorf (Argentina), Pirc (Yugoslavia), Pachman (Czechoslovakia), Unzicker (W. Germany), Szabo (Hungary), and Ståhlberg (Sweden). In the crucial match against Argentina, Botvinnik met with his Groningen vanquisher, Miguel Najdorf, and had sweet revenge.

(21) Botvinnik – Najdorf
Amsterdam 1954
King's Indian Defense [E65]

1.d4 ♘f6 2.c4 g6 3.g3 ♗g7 4.♗g2 0-0 5.♘c3 c5 6.♘f3 ♘c6 7.0-0 d6 8.e3 ♗f5 9.b3 ♕c8 10.♗b2 ♘e4 11.♖c1 ♘×c3 12.♗×c3 ♗e4 13.d5 ♗×c3 14.♖×c3 ♘d8 15.♘d2 ♗×g2 16.♔×g2 f5? This weakens many squares. 16...♕d7 is more circumspect. **17.f4 e6 18.e4! e×d5** (D)

19.c×d5! The right way to recapture, as the dynamic in the center gives White more active options. 19.e×d5? ♘f7 20.♖e3 ♖e8= **19...♘f7 20.♖e1 ♖e8**

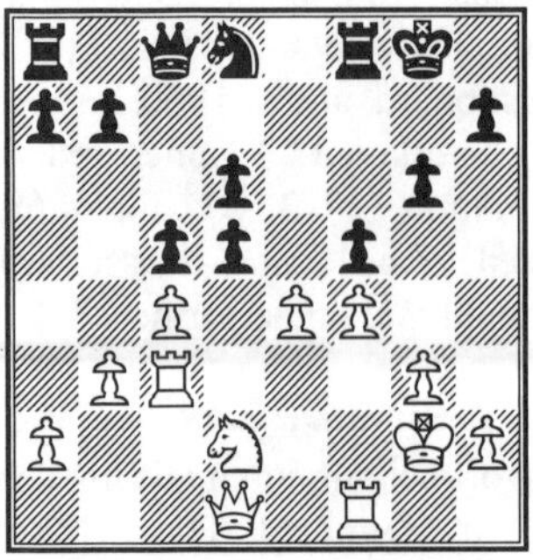

21.♖ce3 ♕d7 22.♕f3 ♖ad8 22...♘h6?! is met by 23.e5 **23.a4?!** The direct 23.e×f5 was better, as White is well placed for the opening of the e-file, e.g., 23...♖×e3 24.♖×e3 ♕×f5 25.g4 ♕c2 26.♖e2 ♕×a2 27.♘e4 ♕a1 28.g5 with a strong attack. **23...b6?** Now Botvinnik can open the position very favorably. Black's knight is particularly quite restricted. 23...♘h6! is needed as a preventive measure to stop White. **24.e×f5 ♖×e3 25.♖×e3 ♕×f5 26.g4 ♕c2 27.♖e2 ♖f8 28.♘e4**

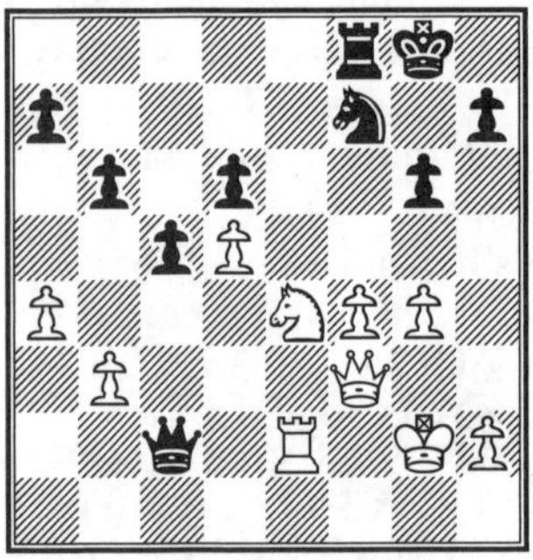

28...♕d1? 28...♕c1! is forced to meet 29.♘f6+ (29.h3 is called for, to preserve the clear advantage.) 29...♔g7 30.g5? with 30...♘×g5 31.f×g5? ♕×g5+ **29.♘f6+ ♔g7 30.g5 ♖c8 31.♖e3** Botvinnik heads for the endgame. 31.h4 c4 32.h5 ♕×b3 33.♕e4 wins as well. **31...♕×f3+ 32.♔×f3** This endgame is winning for White, as with rook and knight against rook and knight a slight initiative weighs heavily. **32...h6** 32...c4 33.b×c4 ♖×c4 34.♖e8 ♘h6 35.♖e7+ ♔f8 36.♖×a7+– **33.h4 h×g5 34.h×g5 a6** 34...c4 35.b×c4 ♖×c4 36.♖e8+– **35.♖e7 ♖b8 36.♖a7 b5 37.♖×a6 b×a4** 37...c4 is met by 38.b4+– **38.b×a4 ♖c8 39.a5 ♔f8 40.♖c6 ♖a8 41.a6 1-0**

1956, August 31 – September 15, Moscow The 12th Olympiad was held, for the first time, in the USSR. The basic roster of the Soviet team was unchanged. As before, it was led by world champion Mikhail Botvinnik; second board was held down by his challenger, Vassily Smyslov; while on third and fourth boards, Paul Keres exchanged places with David Bronstein (first reserve was Mark Taimanov; second reserve was Yefim Geller). In the finals, the USSR team lost only three games out of 44. Botvinnik won six games, without a loss, and with the top result – 9½/13 (73.1%). Among other players on first board, only the uncompromising Dane, Bent Larsen, was able to surpass him (14/18, or 77.8%).

(22) Botvinnik – Ståhlberg
Moscow 1956
Slav Defense [A11]

1.c4 ♘f6 2.g3 c6 3.♘f3 d5 4.b3 g6 5.♗b2 ♗g7 6.♗g2 0-0 7.0-0 ♘bd7 8.♕c2 ♖e8 9.♘c3 ♘f8 10.d4 ♗f5 11.♕c1 ♘e4 12.♖d1 ♘×c3 13.♗×c3 ♗e4 14.♘e1 ♗×g2 15.♔×g2 ♘d7 16.♕c2 ♕c7 17.♗b2 ♖ac8 18.♖ac1 d×c4 19.♕×c4 ♕a5 20.♘d3 (D)

20...e5? Ståhlberg opens the position for White. 20...♕d5+ is almost equal, e.g., 21.f3 ♕×c4 22.♖×c4 ♖cd8 23.♖cc1 e5= **21.d×e5 ♗×e5 22.b4** 22.♘×e5!? ♘×e5 23.♕f4 ♖e6 24.b4 ♕c7 25.♕d4

is even stronger. **22...b5 23.b×a5 b×c4 24.♘×e5!?** Most probably the right exchange as the double rook ending 24.♖×c4 ♗×b2 25.♘×b2 ♖×e2 26.♖×d7 ♖×b2 is better for White, but Black's practical drawing chances are better than in the game. **24...♘×e5 25.h3 ♖b8 26.♗c3 ♖e7?!**

27.♖b1! Again the right exchange. The double rook ending 27.♗×e5? ♖×e5 should only be drawn, e.g., 28.♖×c4 ♖×e2 29.♖d7 ♖×a2 30.♖f4 f5 31.♖×a7 c5 32.♖f3 c4 33.♖e3 ♔f8= **27...♖×b1 28.♖×b1 f6 29.a6 c5 30.♖b8+ ♔f7 31.♖c8 ♘d7** 31...♖e6 32.♖c7+ ♖e7 33.♖×c5 ♘d7 34.♖c7+- **32.♔f1 ♔e6?!** **33.♖c6+!** This strong *zwischenschach* destroys the harmony of Black's forces. **33...♔d5** 33...♔f7 34.♖c7 ♘b8 35.♖×c5 f5 36.♖×c4 ♘a6 37.♗d4+- **34.♖c7 ♔d6 35.♖×a7 ♖e8 36.♗a5 ♔c6 37.♔e1 ♘b6**

38.♗×b6? The resulting rook ending is not so clear. With the minor pieces White wins, e.g., 38.♖×h7 ♘a4 39.a7 c3 40.♖c7+ ♔b5 41.♖b7+ ♔×a5 42.♖b8+- **38...♔×b6 39.♖f7 ♔×a6 40.♖×f6+ ♔b5 41.♖f3 ♖d8 42.e4 ♖d4?** 42...♔c6 was the last chance, e.g., 43.♖c3 ♖e8 44.f3 ♖b8 45.a4 ♖b2 46.♖a3 c3 47.♖×c3 ♖a2 48.♖c4 ♖g2 and Black can still fight for a draw. **43.e5 ♔c6** 43...♔b4? 44.a3+ ♔b5 45.e6 ♔c6 46.♖e3+- **44.♖e3 ♔d7** 44...c3 45.♖×c3 ♖a4 46.a3 g5 47.♖e3 ♔d7 48.♔d2+- **45.f4 ♔e6 46.♔e2 ♖d8** 46...h5 47.h4 c3 48.♖×c3 ♖a4 49.♖×c5 ♖×a2+ 50.♔d3+- **47.a4 ♖b8 48.♖a3** The rook is well placed behind the passed pawn. **48...♖b2+ 49.♔d1 ♖b6 50.a5 ♖a6 51.♔d2 g5 52.♔c3 g×f4 53.g×f4 ♔d5 54.♖a1 h5 55.h4 1-0**

(23) Botvinnik – Gligoric
Moscow 1956
English Opening [A37]

1.c4 g6 2.g3 c5 3.♗g2 ♗g7 4.♘c3 ♘c6 5.♘f3 ♘h6 6.h4 d6 7.d3 ♖b8 8.h5 ♗d7 9.♗×h6 ♗×h6 10.h×g6 h×g6 11.♕c1!? (D)

11...♗g7 Of course not 11...♗×c1?? 12.♖×h8# **12.♖×h8+ ♗×h8 13.♕h6 ♗×c3+** 13...♗f6 14.♖b1 ♗f5 15.♔f1 ♔d7= is easier. **14.b×c3 e6 15.♘g5 ♔e7! 16.♔d2?! ♗e8?** Too passive.

The active 16...♕b6 more or less forces the draw, e.g., 17.♖c1 ♘d4 18.c×d4 ♕a5+ 19.♔c2 ♕b4 20.♖b1 ♗a4+ 21.♖b3 ♕a3 22.♔g7 ♗×b3+ 23.a×b3 ♕a2± **17.♕g7 ♔d7?!** 17...♘d4!? 18.♘h7 ♗c6 19.♗×c6 ♘×c6 reduces the pressure by exchanges, but White is much better nevertheless. **18.f4 ♕e7 19.♖h1 ♘d8 20.♘e4 ♔c7 21.♖h8 ♗c6 22.♘f6 ♕b6 23.♗×c6 ♘×c6 24.♖h7! ♘d8 25.♕×g6 ♕a6 26.a4! ♔a5 27.♕g5**

27...♔×a4?! This opens the roads for White's attack, but Black is lost in any case, e.g., 27...♕c7 28.♕h6 ♕b6 29.♕f8 ♕b2+ 30.♔e3 ♕×c3 31.♕×d6+− **28.♖h1!** The rook swings back to close the net around Black's king. **28...♔b3 29.♕h4 ♔b2 30.g4 1-0**

September 30-October 23, 1958, Munich The 13th Olympiad, once again, was a triumph for the USSR team (which had new reserves, Tal and Petrosian), and for its leader, who had recently regained the title of world champion, Mikhail Botvinnik. The opening ceremony, for the first time, featured the FIDE hymn (the author of which was the president of the Italian chess federation, J. dal Verme). Once again, there was a heated battle for first place between the Yugoslav and USSR teams, who fought to a draw (2-2) in their individual encounter. It was only in round six that the USSR team went into the lead, and finished first at the end with a score of 34½. 5½ points behind them was the Yugoslav team (29), who in turn were 3½ points ahead of Argentina. However, in the struggle between the team leaders, grandmaster Svetozar Gligoric was able to outstrip Botvinnik with a top result of 9/12 (+7 -1 =4 or 75%).

In Munich, Botvinnik suffered his first loss in an Olympiad. In the semifinals, he lost to the Austrian master, 31-year old Andreas Dückstein. Interestingly, Botvinnik exacted revenge on him in the finals: the Austrians ended up in last place, but they drew with the Yugoslav team (2-2), which deprived them of a chance to fight for the gold medals.

1960, October 16-November 9, Leipzig Botvinnik's first appearance at an Olympiad as a former world champion. The lineup for the USSR team was Tal, Botvinnik, Keres, Korchnoi, reserves Smyslov and Petrosian. With "Monomakh's Cap" temporarily lifted from his brow, Botvinnik gave his opponents a good beating on second board, racking up 10½ points in 13 games (+8 -0 =5 or 80.8%). When the world champion Tal asked which game from 1960 made the strongest impression on him, he named Botvinnik's game against the German grandmaster, Lothar Schmid, played at Leipzig, and annotated it for the newspaper *Pravda*.

(24) Botvinnik – Schmid
Leipzig 1960
Modern Benoni [A43]

1.d4 c5 2.d5 d6 3.e4 g6 4.♘f3 ♗g7 5.♗e2 ♘f6 6.♘c3 ♘a6 7.0-0 ♘c7 8.a4 a6 9.♘d2 ♗d7 10.♘c4 b5 11.e5!? d×e5 11...b×c4 12.e×f6 ♗×f6 might be the lesser evil. **12.a×b5 a×b5 13.♖×a8 ♕×a8 14.♘×e5 b4 15.d6**

15...b×c3? The resulting passed c7-pawn decides the game in White's favor. 15...♘e6 16.♘b5 ♕d5 should have been played. **16.d×c7 ♕c8 17.♗f4 c×b2?!** 17...0-0 18.b×c3 ♗a4 19.♕d3 e6 20.♕c4+–; 17...♕×c7 18.♗c4+– **18.♘×d7 ♘×d7 19.♗b5 ♗d4 20.c3 e5 21.c×d4 e×f4 22.♗×d7+ ♕×d7 23.♕e2+** The computer move 23.♕a4 is also possible, e.g., 23...♕×a4 24.c8♕+ ♔e7 25.♖e1+ ♔f6 26.♕×h8+ ♔g5 27.♖e5+ f5 28.h4+ ♔×h4 29.♕×h7+ ♔g5 30.♕e7+ ♔h5 31.♖e6 b1♕+ 32.♔h2+– **23...♔f8 24.♕e5!?** 24.♕×b2 ♕×c7 25.d×c5 ♖g8 26.♖a1

wins as well. **24...♔g8 25.♖b1 f6 26.♕×c5 ♔g7** 26...♔f7 27.♖×b2 ♖c8 28.♖b8 ♖×c7 (28...♕×c7 29.♖×c8+–) 29.♕f8+ ♔e6 30.♖e8+ ♔d5 31.♖e1 ♖c2 32.♕b8+– **27.♖×b2 ♖e8 28.♖b1 f3 29.g×f3 ♕h3 30.♕c6 1-0**

1962, September 16-October 10, Varna At the 15th Olympiad, Botvinnik assumed his usual place at the head of the USSR team, leading a team of "superstars": Petrosian, Spassky, Keres, with reserves Geller and Tal. Botvinnik demonstrated solidity, scoring 8/12 (+5 -1 =6 or 66.7%), and outscoring, on his board, the 19-year-old "Brooklyn wunderkind," Bobby Fischer, who scored 11/17, for 64.7%. The game between them became the story of the rook ending: Botvinnik and Geller together found a miracle saving line for White (cf. *Defense*).

1964, November 2-25, Tel Aviv Botvinnik's last appearance on a USSR team at the Olympiads was also his first appearance in the Holy Land. The roster of the USSR team was Petrosian, Botvinnik, Smyslov, Keres, reserves Stein and Spassky. As before, the team left no possibility for the other teams to compete with them for first place. Botvinnik played as though liberated, scoring 9/12 (+7 -1 =4 or 75%). 2,000 games were played at the Olympiad, but best of all was Botvinnik's win over the Israeli master Aloni.

(25) Aloni – Botvinnik
Tel Aviv 1964
King's Indian Defense [E71]

1.d4 ♘f6 2.c4 c5 3.d5 g6 4.♘c3 d6 5.e4 ♗g7 6.h3 0-0 7.♗e3 e6 8.d×e6 ♗×e6 9.♘f3 ♕a5 10.♕d2 ♘c6 11.♗e2 ♘d7 11...♕b4!? **12.0-0**

♘de5 13.♘×e5 d×e5 14.♖ad1 ♘d4 15.♗d3? 15.♘d5! is called for as 15...♕×a2? runs into 16.♗×d4 c×d4? 17.♖a1 ♕b3 18.♖a3+−

15...♗×h3! 16.b4! The best reaction to muddy the waters. 16.g×h3? ♘f3+−+ 16...c×b4 The alternative 16...♕×b4!? 17.♖b1 ♕a5 18.♖×b7 ♖ab8 19.♖fb1 ♖×b7 20.♖×b7 ♗c8 came strongly into consideration. 17.♘d5 ♗g4 18.♖b1?! 18.f3 ♗e6 19.a3 limits the damage, e.g., 19...♗×d5 20.a×b4 ♕b6 21.e×d5 ♗h6 22.♖fe1 18...♕d8?! 18...♘c6 applies more pressure, e.g., 19.♖b3 ♖fc8 20.a3 b×a3 21.♕×a5 ♘×a5 22.♖×a3 ♘c6 19.♗×d4?! It is better to preserve the strong bishop with 19.♖×b4 19...e×d4 20.♖×b4 b6 21.a4 f5?! 22.e×f5 ♗×f5 23.a5!? b×a5

24.♖b5? 24.♖b7! ♗×d3 25.♕×d3= is more active. 24...♗×d3 25.♕×d3

♕h4?! Too aggressive. The prophylactic 25...♖f7 gives Black a clear plus. 26.g3?! The first step in the wrong direction. 26.c5 gives White sufficient compensation. 26...♕g4 27.♖e1? This runs into a devastating counterattack. White must fight for the light squares with 27.♔g2! 27...♖f3! 28.♕b1? 28.♘e7+ ♔h8 29.♖g5 is more or less forced, but Black should win in the long run after 29...♕×g5 30.♕×f3 ♖f8 31.♕d3 a4−+ 28...♖af8 29.♖e4

29...♖×g3+!! 30.f×g3 ♕×g3+ 31.♔h1 d3! Black just has too many attackers. 32.♘e7+ ♔h8 33.♕e1 ♕h3+ 34.♔g1 d2 35.♘×g6+ 35.♕×d2? ♖f1＃ 35...h×g6 36.♕h4+ 36.♖h4+ ♔g8−+ 36...♔g8 and Aloni resigned in view of 37.♕×h3 d1♕+ 38.♔h2 ♖f2+ 39.♕g2 ♕f3−+ 0−1

During the event, Botvinnik managed to acquaint himself with the landmarks of the land of Israel: Mount Sinai, Nazareth, a trip to Jerusalem, and to read a lecture and give an exhibition in Haifa. To the question, "What nationality do you consider yourself?" he replied: "My situation is complicated. I am a Jew by blood, a Russian by culture, and a Soviet by upbringing."

The Soviet team for the 16th Olympiad, Tel Aviv 1964.
Left to right: Leonid Stein, Vassily Smyslov, Mikhail Botvinnik, Boris Spassky,
Paul Keres, Tigran Petrosian

This would be a good place to mention that, as the second Russian (Alekhine being the first) and the first Soviet player to win the world championship, proudly representing the USSR in that image in the international arena, Botvinnik was not, however, indifferent to the fate of the Jewish people and the nation of Israel, now reborn from the ashes. The very next day after he was crowned, in Moscow, with the laurels of a world champion, on May 19, 1948, he wrote a letter, in which he praised the recognition of Israel by the Soviet Union.

The letter began as follows: "The noble decision of the Soviet Government to acknowledge the Jewish state in Palestine will be taken with joy and gratitude by that long-suffering population." This letter was not published at that time, landed in the Ministry of Public Safety and was directed to the "Affairs of the Jewish Anti-Fascist Committee" who followed it up. It was only printed at the time of *perestroika*, and a facsimile of Botvinnik's letter was reprinted in the magazine *64-Shakhmatnoye Obozreniye*, 5/1998, three years after his death, when the world was observing the 50th anniversary of the State of Israel.

Hastings, 1934/35, 1961/62, 1966/67
Botvinnik played three times in the traditional Christmas tournament at Hastings. His first appearance was his international debut and brought him no laurels: fifth place in a company full of well-known names. His second and third appearances took place almost thirty years later, when the "student" had, in the eyes of the chess world, become the "professor," and ended in two convincing wins for him.

1934/35, December 27-January 15
The well-known Leningrad chess activist, S.O. Weinstein (1894-1942), who accompanied Botvinnik, wrote about his impressions of the tournament and Botvinnik's "baptism by fire" in the chess bulletin dedicated to the Second Moscow International Tournament (8/February 28, 1935). Here are some fragments of his "Hastings Impressions."

Hastings 1934/35

		1	2	3	4	5	6	7	8	9	10	Total
1	Euwe	*	1	½	½	½	1	1	½	½	1	6½
2	Thomas	0	*	½	1	1	1	0	1	1	1	6½
3	Flohr	½	½	*	½	½	½	1	1	1	1	6½
4	Capablanca	½	0	½	*	0	½	1	1	1	1	5½
5	Lilienthal	½	0	½	1	*	½	1	½	½	½	5
6	Botvinnik	0	0	½	½	½	*	½	1	1	1	5
7	Michell	0	1	0	0	0	½	*	½	1	1	4
8	Menchik	½	0	0	0	½	0	½	*	½	1	3
9	Norman	½	0	0	0	½	0	0	½	*	0	1½
10	Milner Barry	0	0	0	0	½	0	0	0	1	*	1½

"Hastings: a seaside resort on the shore of La Manche – 199 kilometers from London and just as far from Dover – the harbor where steamships arrive from the mainland. We arrived in Hastings on the day the tournament was officially opened. La Manche was bustling. The sea heaved with enormous waves, and flung itself on the shore. The rain fell in buckets, and the wind tore off our brand-new English hats. We soon settled into our hotel, and hurried to look for the tournament site. The Hastings Chess Club, which had been in existence for some six hundred years, has its own three-story edifice, but two of its floors were leased out, and the third floor could hardly hold fifty players. So the club held its holiday congress in a special building made available to them by the city government.

"The 'White Pavilion' – the building in which the Hastings Tournament was held – was constructed a few years ago. Operas are performed in the upper two tiers. The lower pavilion, reserved for the tournament, is usually given over to dancing. The hall generally holds from 250 to 300 persons and has a stage where the tournament committee and the representatives of the press sit. Each of the English papers has its own special correspondent, and the foreign papers covered the tournament participants.

"Botvinnik, champion of the USSR, was the "sensation" of the tournament. They wrote of him that he looked like a student at Oxford University, that his manners were refined, that he always acted "gentlemanly." We were representatives of that great country, which had long been regarded in other lands as the "chess Eldorado." We alone had been sent by our government. We represented an association that had organized a very strong international tournament. But what made the greatest impression on the foreigners was our daily hour-and-a-half telephone call with Moscow. And only the Soviet Union showed exceptional interest in the events of Hastings and the performance of their representative there. And when an encouraging telegram from comrade Krylenko accidentally fell into the hands of the representatives of the press, it circulated throughout the English press, reaching even Madrid.

"On April 15, we crossed the Soviet border once again. The first overseas voyage of the Soviet champion ended not as we had expected, but nevertheless, it turned out quite satisfactorily." In this tournament, Botvinnik shared fifth/sixth places with Lilienthal. He played to a draw with Capablanca, and finished a half-point behind him. The first three places were shared by Euwe, Thomas and Flohr. The Dutch player, selecting the Caro-Kann Defense as Black, beat the Soviet champion in 58 moves.

December 27-January 5, 1961/62
After winning his return-match against Tal, and the gold medal of the championship of Europe at the head of the USSR team at Oberhausen, Botvinnik came to Hastings, where he continued his victorious journey. For the first time in the history of this tournament, first prize was taken by the reigning world champion. All of the victories at Hastings by Botvinnik's predecessors – Capablanca, Alekhine and Euwe – were achieved by them, either before they acceded to the title, or after they had added the "ex-" to it.

Two rounds before the end, Botvinnik had already assured himself of a share of first place, with 6½/7. He started quickly and built a two-point lead ahead of Gligoric, Penrose and Flohr, and he maintained that distance right to the end. Botvinnik became the only participant not to suffer defeat. In every game, he played only for the win, and his game against the four-time winner of the Hastings tournament, Yugoslav champion Svetozar Gligoric, as Flohr wittily observed, lasted two years! It started in 1961, was adjourned three times, on the 101st move Botvinnik "went right past" the winning line, and after 104 moves, their encounter wound up a draw – and it was already 1962!

The world champion's play is sharply delineated by the following game.

(26) Botvinnik – Bisguier
Hastings 1961
Réti Opening [A14]

1.g3 d5 2.♘f3 ♘f6 3.♗g2 e6 4.0-0 ♗e7 5.c4 0-0 6.b3 c6 7.♗b2 b5 8.d3 ♘bd7 9.♘bd2 ♗b7 10.♕c2 ♖c8 11.e4 ♕b6 12.e5 ♘e8 13.d4 c5 14.b4!?

Hastings 1961/62

		1	2	3	4	5	6	7	8	9	10	Total
1	Botvinnik	*	½	½	1	1	1	1	1	1	1	8
2	Gligoric	½	*	1	0	½	0	1	1	1	1	6
3	Flohr	½	0	*	½	½	½	½	1	1	1	5½
4	Bisguier	0	1	½	*	½	0	1	½	½	1	5
5	Penrose	0	½	½	½	*	½	1	1	0	1	5
6	Littlewood	0	1	½	1	½	*	0	0	1	0	4
7	Robatsch	0	0	½	0	0	1	*	½	1	1	4
8	Wade	0	0	0	½	0	1	½	*	½	1	3½
9	Barden	0	0	0	½	1	0	0	½	*	1	3
10	Aaron	0	0	0	0	0	1	0	0	0	*	1

A curious picture! White's initiative is difficult to deal with. **14...c×b4 15.c5 ♕c7 16.♕d3 ♗c6 17.♖fe1 g6 18.a3** 18.♗c1!? **18...b×a3 19.♕×a3 19...♖a8?!** This and the following moves are too passive as White can start a long-term initiative on the kingside sooner or later. 19...♘b6! 20.♕×a7 ♘c4 is more or less equal. **20.♗c3 ♗d8?!** 20...♘b8 21.♘b3 ♗d7 22.♘a5 ♘c6 is a better regrouping. **21.♘b3!**

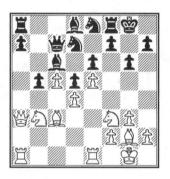

The knight strengthens the blockading forces on the queenside. **21...♘g7 22.♗a5 ♕b7 23.♗×d8 ♖f×d8 24.♘a5 ♕c7 25.♖e2 a6 26.♘e1 ♘f5 27.♕c3 b4?!** A desperate measure, but good advice is hard to give as White's long-term plan to attack on the kingside is difficult to resist. **28.♕×b4 ♖db8 29.♕c3 ♖b5?!** 29...♗b5 30.♖c2 ♔g7 31.♗h3 ♘e7 is more harmonious. **30.♖ea2**

30...f6? Opening the kingside in this way only helps White. 30...♘e7! 31.♗f1 ♖bb8 32.♘×c6 ♘×c6 33.♖×a6 ♖×a6 34.♖×a6 ♖b1 was the last chance to offer resistance. **31.♘×c6 ♕×c6 32.♗f1 f×e5 33.♗×b5 ♕×b5 34.d×e5 d4 35.♕d3 ♕×c5 36.♖×a6 ♖×a6 37.♕×a6 ♕×e5 38.♘d3 ♕f6 39.♕c8+ ♘f8 40.♖a8 ♘d6 41.♕d8 ♕×d8 42.♖×d8 ♘b5 43.♘e5 ♔g7 44.♘c6 1-0**

December 28-January 6, 1966/67 The major tournament of the 42nd annual chess festival in Hastings drew an unusual lineup of players. One of them was the 14-year old champion of Brazil (the youngest participant in Hastings history), Enrique Mecking; and the 19-year old world junior champion Bojan Kurajica of Ljubljana; the 17-year old Moscow student Yuri Balashov; the 18-year old English master Raymond Keene; and his countrymen, 20-year old Michael Basman, and 19-year old William Hartston. Providing competition for these youngsters were the 55-year old Mikhail Botvinnik; the 56-year old Israeli international master Moshe Czerniak; the 32-year old Jonathan Penrose, the leader of English chess; and the strongest grandmaster in East Germany, 31-year old Wolfgang Uhlmann.

Hastings 1966/67

		1	2	3	4	5	6	7	8	9	10	Total
1	Botvinnik	*	½	½	1	1	1	1	0	½	1	6½
2	Uhlmann	½	*	1	0	1	½	½	½	½	1	5½
3	Basman	½	0	*	1	0	½	1	½	1	½	5
4	Kurajica	0	1	0	*	½	½	1	½	½	1	5
5	Balashov	0	0	1	½	*	1	0	1	1	½	5
6	Penrose	0	½	½	½	0	*	1	½	½	1	4½
7	Mecking	0	½	0	0	1	0	*	1	½	1	4
8	Keene	1	½	½	½	0	½	0	*	½	0	3½
9	Hartston	½	½	0	½	0	½	½	½	*	0	3
10	Czerniak	0	0	½	0	½	0	0	1	1	*	3

The tournament proved "bloody" enough: just 19 games out of 45 (42.2%) were drawn. Botvinnik played the whole tournament confidently, losing only one game to Keene (blundering a rook in a level position), winning five games and drawing three. In the end he took home first prize – a "golden knight," a point ahead of Uhlmann (5½ points), and a point-and-a-half ahead of the "young guard": Balashov, Basman, and Kurajica (5 points).

(27) Botvinnik – Czerniak
Hastings 1966
Modern Defense [A42]

1.c4 g6 2.e4 ♗g7 3.d4 d6 4.♘c3 c6 5.♘f3 ♗g4 6.♗e3 ♘d7 7.♗e2 e5 8.d5 c5 9.0-0 ♘e7 10.♘e1 ♗×e2 11.♕×e2 0-0 12.f4 e×f4 13.♗×f4 ♘e5 14.♘f3 a6? Now Botvinnik can change the structure favorably. 14...♘×f3+ 15.♕×f3 (15.♖×f3 ♕d7 16.♖af1 a6=) 15...♕d7 16.♕g3 ♖ad8= **15.♘×e5 d×e5 16.♗e3 b6 17.a3** (D)

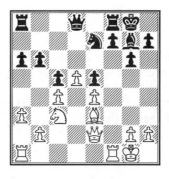

17...♕d7? This allows Botvinnik to seize the initiative on the queenside too easily. 17...a5 is necessary. **18.b4! ♖ac8 19.b×c5 b×c5 20.♕c2 f5 21.♘a4 ♕d6 22.♖ab1 f×e4**

23.♖×f8+ ♗×f8 24.♖b6?! 24.g4+– is more precise. **24...♕d7** 24...♕d8 25.g4+– **25.♘×c5 ♖×c5?** 25...♕d8 offers more resistance, but White will win in the long run, e.g., 26.♘b7 ♕×d5 27.c×d5 ♖×c2 28.d6 ♘c6 29.h4 ♖c3 30.d7 ♖×e3 31.♖×c6 ♗e7 32.♖×a6+– **26.♗×c5 ♕c7 27.♕f2 ♘f5 28.♖c6 ♕b7 29.♗×f8 e3 30.♕e1 ♘d4**

31.♗c5 However, not 31.♕×e3? ♕b1+ 32.♔f2 ♕c2+ 33.♔e1 ♕b1+= **1-0**

Groningen, 1946 (August 12-September 7) The first strong international tournament after the close of World War II. Twenty chessplayers from twelve countries took part. It was organized to honor the 75th anniversary of the Groningen chess club, and was planned, by its organizers, as a demonstration of the superiority of Max Euwe over the strongest contemporary opponents. In the event he won, they would have a strong basis for declaring ex-champion Euwe the world champion. For, after the death of Alekhine, for the first time in 60 years, the chess world was without a king.

Botvinnik arrived, with his wife Gaiane and their 4-year old daughter Olga. They would help him "re-establish his aura" after tough chess battles. The main competition for the top prize at Groningen was, as expected, between Botvinnik and Euwe.

After nine rounds, the hard-charging Botvinnik had racked up 8½ points! His rival, Euwe, had seven points. A lot was riding on the Euwe-Botvinnik game in the 10th round. Botvinnik later recalled, "This was our fifth game since 1934. Until then, the score between us was 3-1 in the Dutchman's favor, with two draws. It was difficult for me to play him: I had a hard time understanding his game. He could easily alter the situation on the board, making sort of "lengthy" moves with his pieces (I would overlook these). You had to give him his due – he would begin a powerful onslaught at the first opportunity, calculated variations accurately, and made a deep study of

the endgame... His nature was to be practical, in life as well as over-the-board. So it was hard for me, a logician, and in many ways a dreamer, to play him. Our encounter at Groningen was no exception. At first, I got a good game (Euwe played rapidly, but somewhat superficially). Then I decided that I could squeeze more out of the position than was possible. Euwe immediately seized the initiative, and I fought myself out of that with great difficulty. In that game, Euwe showed how carefully he had studied the ending: at the adjournment, he adroitly steered the game into a rook endgame, which was as much like the famous Lasker-Rubinstein (St. Petersburg, 1914) game, with colors reversed, as two drops of water. The rook ending inexorably transposed to a lost pawn ending, when it was time for me to resign."

However, analysis showed that the ending might have been saved, which Botvinnik showed to Euwe and his 2,000 supporters who filled the hall (cf. *Defense*). However, in the 14th and 15th rounds, Botvinnik lost two games – to the Soviet grandmaster Kotov and the Canadian master Yanofsky. With four rounds remaining, Euwe now led Botvinnik by a half-point. The leader of the Soviet delegation, master Gavriil Veresov, asked Gaiane to go into the "Harmony" hall with their daughter, for moral support.

Within Botvinnik, the "king of beasts" once again awoke... In every game, he played only for the win, and won three in a row: against the Czech, Cenek Kottnauer, against the Swiss Martin Kristofferson, and the Argentine, Carlos Guimard. Euwe had tougher opposition, and made three draws. In the final and

Groningen 1946

		1	2	3	4	5	6	7	8	9	10	11	12	13	14	15	16	17	16	19	20	Total
1	Botvinnik	x	½	1	0	1	½	1	1	1	0	1	½	1	0	1	1	1	1	1	1	14½
2	Euwe	½	x	0	½	1	½	1	½	½	0	½	1	1	1	1	1	1	1	1	1	14
3	Smyslov	0	1	x	½	½	½	1	½	½	½	½	½	1	½	½	½	1	1	1	1	12½
4	Najdorf	1	½	½	x	1	½	1	0	½	½	½	½	0	1	½	½	½	1	½	1	11½
5	Szabo	0	0	½	0	x	½	1	0	1	1	½	0	1	1	½	1	½	1	1	1	11½
6	Flohr	½	½	½	½	½	x	½	½	½	0	½	½	½	1	½	1	½	½	1	1	11
7	Boleslavsky	0	0	0	0	0	½	x	1	1	1	1	1	½	½	½	½	½	1	1	1	11
8	Lundin	0	½	½	1	1	½	0	x	½	½	1	0	0	1	0	½	½	1	1	1	10½
9	Stoltz	0	½	½	½	0	½	0	½	x	½	½	1	1	½	1	1	0	½	1	1	10½
10	Kotov	1	1	½	½	0	1	0	½	½	x	½	1	0	½	0	1	½	0	1	0	9½
11	Tartakower	0	½	½	½	½	½	0	0	½	½	x	½	1	½	½	1	1	½	½	½	9½
12	Denker	½	0	½	½	1	½	0	1	0	0	½	x	0	½	1	½	½	1	1	½	9½
13	Kottnauer	0	0	0	1	0	½	½	1	0	1	0	1	x	1	1	0	½	½	0	1	9
14	Yanofsky	1	0	½	0	0	0	½	0	½	½	½	½	0	*	½	1	1	1	½	½	8½
15	Bernstein	0	0	½	½	½	½	½	1	0	1	½	0	0	½	x	½	½	½	0	0	7
16	Guimard	0	0	½	½	0	0	½	½	0	0	0	½	1	0	½	x	1	½	½	1	7
17	Vidmar	0	0	0	½	½	½	½	½	1	½	0	½	½	0	½	0	x	½	½	0	6½
18	Steiner	0	0	0	0	0	½	0	0	½	1	½	0	½	0	½	½	½	x	1	½	6
19	O'Kelly	0	0	0	½	0	0	0	0	0	0	½	0	1	½	1	½	½	0	x	1	5½
20	Christoffel	0	0	0	0	0	0	0	0	0	1	½	½	0	½	1	0	1	½	0	x	5

decisive round, which unlike the previous rounds was played in the morning, all eyes were focused on the games Botvinnik-Najdorf and Kotov-Euwe. What was amazing was that all four of them were playing for the win! Botvinnik wished to secure first prize for himself, Najdorf wanted to get into the top five, and Kotov was "collecting the scalps" of the winners.

In these exceptionally nervous circumstances, fortune smiled upon Najdorf and Kotov, with the result that Botvinnik took first place, with 14½ points; Euwe finished a half-point behind (14); Smyslov was third (12½); and Najdorf and Szabo split fourth/fifth (11½).

(28) Botvinnik – Vidmar
Groningen 1946
Catalan Opening [E01]

1.d4 d5 2.♘f3 ♘f6 3.c4 e6 4.g3 d×c4 5.♕a4+ ♕d7 6.♕×c4 ♕c6 7.♘bd2 ♕×c4 8.♘×c4 ♗b4+ 9.♗d2 ♗×d2+ 10.♘f×d2 ♘c6 11.e3 ♘b4 12.♔e2 ♗d7 13.♗g2 ♗c6 14.f3 ♘d7 15.a3 ♘d5 16.e4 ♘5b6 17.♘a5 ♗b5+ 18.♔e3 0-0-0! 19.♖hc1

19...♘b8? Black should start direct counterplay with 19...f5 20.b3 ♘f6

20.b3?! 20.♖c5!? is more precise. **20...♗d7 21.♗f1 ♘c6?** Vidmar ends up in a very passive position after this loss of time. The active 21...f5 22.b4 ♘c6 23.♘×c6 ♗×c6 gives him more counterplay. **22.♘×c6 ♗×c6 23.a4!** ♗e8 23...♔b8 24.a5 ♘c8 25.a6 f5 26.b4 is also very promising for White. **24.a5 ♘a8 25.a6 b6 26.b4 ♔b8 27.♖c3?** Now Vidmar has time to construct a pawn barrier, which is not easy to break down. 27.b5! is better, restricting Black. **27...c6! 28.♖ac1 f6! 29.♘b1 ♗d7 30.♘a3 ♘c7?** Vidmar must close the queenside with 30...b5! **31.b5!!** Botvinnik opens the floodgates.

31...♘×b5?! 32.♗×b5?! The endgame after 32.♘×b5! c×b5 33.♖c7 ♖c8 34.♖b7+ ♔a8 35.♖×c8+ ♗×c8 36.♖×g7 ♗×a6 37.♖f7 +– is even better. **32...c×b5 33.♖c7 ♖c8?** 33...♗c8! was the last chance, e.g., 34.♘×b5 ♗×a6 (34...♖d7 35.♖×d7 ♗×d7 36.♘×a7 ♔×a7 37.♖c7+ ♔×a6 38.♖×d7 (ChessBase Megabase) 38...b5 39.♖×g7 b4) 35.♘×a7 ♗b7 36.♘b5 ♖c8 37.♔d2 ♗a6 38.♖1c6 (Megabase) 38...♗×b5 39.♖×c8+ ♖×c8 40.♖×b6+ ♔c7 41.♖×b5 ♖a8 with practical drawing chances in both cases. **34.♖b7+ ♔a8**

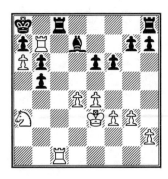

(29) Bernstein – Botvinnik
Groningen 1946
Sicilian Defense [B73]

1.e4 c5 2.♘f3 d6 3.d4 c×d4 4.♘×d4 ♘f6 5.♘c3 g6 6.♗e2 ♗g7 7.♗e3 ♘c6 8.0-0 0-0 9.♕d2 ♘g4 10.♗×g4 ♗×g4 11.f3 ♗e6 12.♘×c6?! 12.♖ad1 is played more often. **12...b×c6 13.♗d4 f6 14.b3 ♕a5**

35.♖×d7!! A deep exchange sacrifice. Botvinnik's activity will win in the long run. **35...♖×c1 36.♘×b5 ♖hc8 37.♖×g7 h6 38.♖×a7+ ♔b8 39.♖b7+ ♔a8 40.♖a7+ ♔b8 41.♖b7+ ♔a8 42.g4 e5 43.d5 ♖1c5 44.♖a7+ ♔b8 45.♖b7+ ♔a8 46.♖×b6 ♖b8 47.♖×b8+ ♔×b8 48.a7+ ♔b7** 48...♔a8 does not help in view of 49.d6 ♖c8 50.♔d3 ♔b7 51.♘c7 ♔×a7 52.♔c4+– (Megabase) **49.♘d6+ ♔×a7 50.♘e8 ♔b6 51.♘×f6 ♖c3+ 52.♔f2 ♖c7 53.h4 ♖f7 54.♘h5 ♔c7 55.g5! h×g5 56.h×g5 ♖h7 57.♘f6 ♖h2+ 58.♔g3 ♖h1 59.♔g2 ♖h8 60.g6** and Vidmar resigned because of 60...♖h6 61.g7 ♖g6+ 62.♔f2 ♖×g7 63.♘e8+ ♔d7 64.♘×g7+– **1-0**

And here, in Groningen, Botvinnik played his lone game with the famous veteran, grandmaster Ossip Bernstein (1882-1962).

As Botvinnik noted, in an afterword to his notes on this game, "playing with him, I involuntarily remembered, that back in the year I was born, Capablanca played a brilliant game against him at San Sebastian, 1911, which entered the golden treasury of chess."

15.♘b1? The resulting endgame is very good for Black because of his bishops and the initiative on the queenside. After 15.♖ad1, the position is more or less equal. **15...♕×d2 16.♘×d2 ♗h6 17.♖ad1 c5 18.♗f2 a5 19.a4 ♖fc8 20.♖fe1 c4!** A strong undermining blow. **21.♗e3 ♗g7!?** Botvinnik keeps his valuable bishop. The alternative, 21...♗×e3+ 22.♖×e3 c×b3 23.c×b3 ♖ab8, is also very strong. **22.b×c4 ♗×c4 23.♘b3 ♗f7 24.♖e2 ♖c4 25.♖d4 ♖c3 26.♖dd2 ♖c4 27.♖d4 f5 28.♖×c4 ♗×c4 29.♖e1 f×e4 30.♗d2?** 30.f×e4 limits the damage. **30...e×f3 31.♖×e7?!** f×g2 **32.♘×a5?** This leaves the mighty g2-pawn alive. 32.♔×g2 offers more resistance. **32...♗d5 33.c4 ♗f3 34.♔f2 ♖f8 35.♗e3 ♗c3 36.♖a7 ♗c6+ 37.♔g3 ♗×a5** 37...♖e1+ 38.♔h3 ♗f2 wins quicker. **38.♖×a5 ♖f3+ 39.♔×g2 ♖×e3+ 40.♔g1 ♖c3 41.♖a7 ♖×c4 42.♖c7 ♖c1+ 43.♔f2 ♖c2+ 0-1**

Ilyin-Zhenevsky, Alexandr Fedorovich (April 16, 1894, St. Petersburg-September 3, 1941, Novaya Ladoga, near Leningrad) Master, theoretician, journalist and highly visible organizer of Soviet chess life in the 1920s and 1930s. In 1920, it was through his efforts that the All-Russian chess Olympiad was held in Moscow, and became the first championship of the Soviet Union. He participated in it himself (sharing 9/10th places), and after that, in seven more USSR championships. He was twice champion of Leningrad (1926 and 1929), won the championship of the VTsSPS (1927), and shared first place in the Trans-Caucasian championship (1932).

He played Botvinnik more than once in the tournaments of Leningrad masters, and all of their games featured tense struggles, more often than not ending up as draws. He lost twice to his young opponent. In the national championship, they beat each other once each: in the fifth championship (1927), Botvinnik triumphed, while in the seventh (1931), it was Ilyin-Zhenevsky.

(30) Ilyin Zhenevsky – Botvinnik
Moscow 1931
Ruy Lopez [C90]

1.e4 e5 2.♘f3 ♘c6 3.♗b5 a6 4.♗a4 ♘f6 5.0-0 ♗e7 6.♖e1 b5 7.♗b3 d6 8.c3 0-0 9.d3 ♘a5 10.♗c2 c5 11.♘bd2 ♘c6 12.♕e2 ♖e8 13.♘f1 d5 14.e×d5 ♘×d5 15.♗d2 ♗f8 16.♘g3 ♗b7 17.a4 b4 18.♘g5 h6 19.♘5e4 g6 20.♕f3 (D)

20...f5? This bold advance is asking for trouble. 20...♘a5 is better. **21.♘×f5! g×f5 22.♕×f5 ♗g7?** 22...♔h8! 23.d4 ♕c7 was more or less forced to stop the first wave of the attack. **23.♘×c5?** Taking the pawn slows down White's

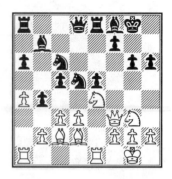

attack. 23.♕g6! is more to the point, e.g., 23...♕e7 (23...♘ce7? 24.♕e6+ ♔h7 25.d4 ♘g6 26.♕f7+−) 24.♗×h6 ♕f7 25.♕g3 ♖ad8 26.♘×c5 ♗c8 27.d4 ♖d6 28.♗×g7 ♕×g7 29.♗b3+− **23...♗c8 24.♕g6?!** 24.♕h5! ♘f6 25.♕h4 ♘d5 26.♕g3 applies more pressure. **24...♘ce7! 25.♕h5 ♗g7?** 22...♔h8! 23.d4 ♕c7 was more or less forced to stop the first wave of the attack. **23.♘×c5?** Taking the pawn slows down White's attack. 23.♕g6! is more to the point, e.g., 23...♕e7 (23...♘ce7? 24.♕e6+ ♔h7 25.d4 ♘g6 26.♕f7+−) 24.♗×h6 ♕f7 25.♕g3 ♖ad8 26.♘×c5 ♗c8 27.d4 ♖d6 28.♗×g7 ♕×g7 29.♗b3+− **23...♗c8 24.♕g6?!** 24.♕h5! ♘f6 25.♕h4 ♘d5 26.♕g3 applies more pressure. **24...♘ce7! 25.♕h5**

25...♘f5? Botvinnik's defensive forces lose coordination. 25...b×c3

Aleksandr Ilyin-Zhenevsky

26.b×c3 (26.♗×h6 ♗×h6 27.♕×h6 ♘f5 28.♕g6+ ♔h8) 26...♗f5 27.♗×h6 ♕d6 28.♗×g7 ♔×g7 29.♘e4 ♕g6= holds the position together. **26.d4! ♖f8 27.d×e5 b×c3 28.b×c3 ♕e7?** This loses more or less by force, but there is most likely no defense in any case, e.g., 28...♕c7 29.e6 ♘de7 30.♘d7 ♗×d7 31.e×d7 ♖ad8 32.♗b3+ ♔h7 33.♗e6 ♖×d7 34.♗×d7 ♕×d7 35.♖ad1 +– **29.e6!** The pawn cuts the board into two halves. **29...♕×c5 30.♗×f5 ♕e7 31.♗×h6 ♖×f5** 31...♗×h6 32.♕×h6 ♖×f5 33.♕g6+ +– **32.♕×f5 ♗×h6 33.♕×d5 ♗b7 34.♕d7 ♗g5 35.♖ab1 ♗c8 36.♕c6 1-0**

"Ilyin-Zhenevsky played the entire game excellently," – Botvinnik.

In the first Moscow international tournament in 1925, Ilyin-Zhenevsky shared 9/10th places, and inflicted a sensational loss on the world champion Capablanca.

(31) Capablanca – Ilyin Zhenevsky
Moscow 1925
Sicilian Defense [B25]

1.e4 c5 2.♘c3 ♘c6 3.g3 g6 4.♗g2 ♗g7 5.♘ge2 d6 6.d3 ♘f6 7.0-0 0-0 8.h3 a6 9.♗e3 ♗d7 10.♕d2 ♖e8 11.♘d1 ♖c8 12.c3 ♕a5?! 12...b5 is more natural. **13.g4 ♖ed8?! 14.f4 ♗e8 15.g5 ♘d7 16.f5 b5 17.♘f4 b4**

18.f6!? An enterprising way to open the gates. The normal 18.♘d5 is also good of course. **18...♗f8** White has good compensation after 18...e×f6 19.♘d5 f×g5 20.♗×g5 f6 21.♗h4 b×c3 22.b×c3 ♖b8 23.♘1e3 in view of his attacking prospects. **19.♘f2 b×c3 20.b×c3 e6** 20...e×f6 is still answered by 21.♘d5! **21.h4 ♖b8 22.h5 ♖b6?** This approach is too slow. This was the last chance to counter White's flank attack with the central thrust 22...c4!, for example, 23.d4 e5 24.d×e5 ♘c×e5 25.♘d5 ♘c5 with counterplay. **23.h×g6 h×g6 24.♘d1 ♘de5 25.♕f2** 25.♕e1!?+– is more precise. **25...♘g4** 25...d5 26.♕h4+– **26.♕h4 ♘ce5** (D)

27.d4? Capablanca is impatient and underestimates Black's defensive resources. The prophylactic 27.♗d2 wins. One sample line runs 27...♕a4

(27...d5 28.e×d5 e×d5 29.♘f2 ♘×f2 30.♔×f2 ♖b2 31.♔g3 ♖×d2 32.♖h1 +−) 28.♗f3 ♘×f3+ 29.♖×f3 ♖db8 30.♖h3 ♘h6 31.♘e3 ♖b1+ 32.♖×b1 ♖×b1+ 33.♔f2 ♖b2 34.g×h6 ♖×d2+ 35.♔e1 ♖×a2 36.h7+ ♔h8 37.♘×g6+ f×g6 38.f7 ♗×f7 39.♕f6+ ♗g7 40.♕×g7+ ♔×g7 41.h8♕‡ **27...♘×e3 28.♘×e3 ♕×c3 29.d×e5 ♕×e3+ 30.♔h1** 30.♔h2 ♖b2 31.♖ad1 ♖db8 32.e×d6 (32.♔h1 ♖d2 33.♖de1 ♕d4 34.♖f3 ♖d1 35.♖h3 ♖×e1+ 36.♕×e1 ♖b2 37.♘d3 ♖×g2 38.♔×g2 ♗c6 39.♕h4 ♕×e4±) 32...♗c6 33.d7 ♖d8 34.♘×g6 ♖×g2+ 35.♔h1 ♖g1+ 36.♔h2 ♖g2± **30...d×e5**

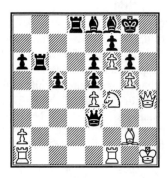

31.♖f3? This runs into an amazing refutation. 31.♘×g6! leads to a more or less forced draw: 31...f×g6 32.♖f3 ♕e2 33.♖af1 ♖d1 34.f7+ ♗×f7 35.♖×f7 ♖×f1+ 36.♗×f1 ♕h5 37.♕×h5 g×h5 38.g6= **31...e×f4!! 32.♖×e3 f×e3**

33.♕e1 33.♖e1 ♖b2 34.♖×e3 ♖d1+ 35.♖e1 ♖dd2−+ **33...♖b2 34.♕×e3 ♖dd2** Black's pieces are just too active. **35.♗f3** 35.♗f1 ♖h2+ 36.♔g1 ♗b5 37.♗×b5 ♖bg2+ 38.♔f1 a×b5 39.♖d1 ♖×a2 40.♔g1 ♖ag2+ 41.♔f1 b4−+ **35...c4 36.a3 ♗d6 37.♕a7** 37.♖d1 ♖h2+ 38.♔g1 ♗g3−+ **37...c3 0−1**

Among Ilyin-Zhenevsky's theoretical discoveries was the one in the Dutch Defense that bears his name: 1.d4 f5 2.g3 ♘f6 3.♗g2 e6 4.♘f3 ♗e7 5.0-0 0-0 6.c4 d6 7.♘c3 ♕e8.

Many literary works on international tournaments and of an autobiographical type belong to this master's pen. Ilyin-Zhenevsky showed himself to be a talented journalist also, as the chief editor of *Shakhmatny listok* (Leningrad 1925-30) and *Shakhmaty v SSSR* (Moscow 1936-37).

In his recollections of Ilyin-Zhenevsky after the start of World War II, Abramov said, "He evacuated himself and his wife from Leningrad. In Novaya Ladoga, Leningrad region, he set off in a barge on reconnaissance, and was severely wounded in the stomach by a splinter from an aerial bombardment. This was on August 31, and he died on September 3. His wife, Tansey Alexandrovna (née Vyazovskaya) committed suicide four days after her husband died."

Books: Moscow International Tournament (A Participant's Diary), Moscow 1926; *The 1927 Alekhine-Capablanca Match*, Leningrad 1927; *Notes of a Soviet Master*, Leningrad 1929; *The International Worker's Chess Movement and Soviet Chess Organization*, Moscow 1931.

Keres, Paul (January 7, 1916, Narva-June 5, 1975, Helsinki), Estonian player, international grandmaster (1950), Candidate for the world championship, participant in the match-tournament of 1948 for the title of world champion.

Paul learned how to play as early as Capablanca, at 4-years old. His regular opponent was his 7-year old brother Harald, later to become a well-known teacher of physics. At 13, Paul first attended the Parnu Chess Club and unexpectedly won the blitz tournament, winning all his games. At a young age, Paul was already composing his first chess problems, and playing correspondence (playing 150 games at one time!). Keres occasionally did both later on. He created about two hundred compositions. The following problem was created by the 16-year old Keres.

White to move and mate in two moves

1.♕h8! Playing for *zugzwang*. **1...e4 2. ♖×g1+! ♔×g1 3. ♕a1#; 1...e2 2. ♕×h2+! gh 3. ♘f2#**

At 19, Keres showed that he was a strong practical player as well, winning the Estonian championship and leading their team in the Olympiad at Warsaw

Paul Keres

(1935). In the very first round, he met world champion Alekhine... and lost. Nevertheless, even then his talent for combinations made a strong impression; they called him "the new Morphy." A year later, at the tournament in Bad Nauheim, Keres achieved his first international success, sharing first/second places with Alekhine. In 1937, there came a series of brilliant victories in Margate, Ostend, Prague, Vienna and Semmering/Baden. After Semmering, the *Times* wrote that "Keres brings to play an atmosphere of high adventure... Only he and Alekhine can bring us freedom from the endless sameness of positional play."

It became obvious that Keres was becoming one of the candidates for the world championship. This was also underscored by his brilliant result in the notable event of 1938, where, in a double-round tournament of the eight strongest chessplayers in the world, he shared first and second places with Reuben Fine. When, 32 years later, during the "USSR-Rest of the World" match, they asked Keres, who gave the best performance of the Soviet team (3-1 against Borislav Ivkov), for the best game of his career, he replied, "I can say, the most important one, beating Fine in the AVRO 1938.

(32) Fine – Keres
AVRO 1938
Ruy Lopez [C86]

1.e4 e5 2.♘f3 ♘c6 3.♗b5 a6 4.♗a4 ♘f6 5.0-0 ♗e7 6.♕e2 b5 7.♗b3 d6 8.a4 ♗g4 9.c3 0-0 10.a×b5?! 10.h3 is the main line. **10...a×b5 11.♖×a8 ♕×a8 12.♕×b5 ♘a7!**

Now White has difficult problems to solve. **13.♕e2 ♕×e4 14.♕×e4 ♘×e4 15.d4 ♗×f3 16.g×f3 ♘g5 17.♔g2 ♖b8 18.♗c4 e×d4 19.c×d4 ♘e6 20.d5 ♘c5 21.♘c3 ♘c8 22.♖e1 ♔f8 23.♖e2 f5** 23...♖b4!? **24.♘b5 ♘b6 25.b3 ♘×d5!** The point of Keres' previous play. **26.♘d4 ♘b4 27.♗d2?!** 27.♘×f5 ♗f6 28.♗e3 is the lesser evil. **27...d5! 28.♗×b4 ♖×b4 29.♘c6 d×c4 30.♘×b4 c×b3** (D)

31.♘d5? This runs into a direct refutation. 31.♖b2 was forced. **31...♘d3! 32.♖d2** If 32.♘×e7?, then 32...♘f4+–+ and 32.♖×e7? is met by 32...b2–+ **32...b2 33.♖d1 c5** 33...♘c1 34.♘c3 ♗f6 35.♘b1 c5, also winning.

34.♖b1 c4 35.♔f1 ♗c5 36.♔e2 ♗×f2 37.♘e3?! This retreat runs into a powerful refutation. But good advice is hard to give as 37.♔d2 ♔f7 38.♔c3 ♔e6 is also losing in the long run. **37...c3! 38.♘c2** Now Keres breaks the blockade very forcefully: **38...♘e1!! 39.♘a3** 39.♘×e1 ♗×e1 40.♔×e1 c2–+; 39.♘b4 ♗h4 40.♘a2 ♗f6 41.♔×e1 c2 42.♖×b2 ♗×b2 43.♔d2 c1♕+ 44.♘×c1 ♗×c1+ 45.♔×c1 ♔f7–+ **39...♗c5?** 39...♗h4! wins as White cannot untangle because of 40.♖×e1 ♗e1 41.♔×e1 c2–+ **40.♔×e1?** Now White is too slow. Activating the rook with 40.♖×e1 ♗×a3 41.♔d3 ♗b4 42.♔c2 was the last chance to offer resistance. **40...♗×a3 41.♔d1 ♗d6 42.♔c2** 42.h3?! ♗f4 43.♔c2 ♗c1–+ **42...♗×h2 43.♖h1** 43.♔×c3 ♗e5+ 44.♔c2 g5 45.f4 ♗×f4 46.♖×b2 ♔f7–+ **43...♗e5 44.♖×h7 ♔f7 45.♖h1 g5 46.♖e1 ♔f6 47.♖g1 ♔g6 48.♖e1 ♗f6 49.♖g1 g4 50.f×g4 f4! 51.g5 ♗d4 52.♖d1**

52...♗e3! The final point. Black's two remaining pawns will decide the day. **53.♔×c3 ♗c1 54.♖d6+ ♔×g5 55.♖b6 f3 56.♔d3 ♔f4 57.♖b8 ♔g3 0-1**

In 1948, Keres took part in the match-tournament for the world championship, and shared third/fourth places. And starting in 1953, he played in four straight candidates' tournaments; with amazing persistence, he would always finish second. Such consistency was the mark of the highest class. It was no accident that Petrosian said, "It is easier to be first once, than to be second four times." And Botvinnik called Keres the strongest of tournament battlers. Keres played in 70 international events, and was victorious in over twenty of them. He was also champion of the USSR three times (in 1947, 1950 and 1951).

He was always polite and correct, an excellent tennis player (he played in the championship of Estonia!), highly erudite ("There was no language on the planet that Keres did not know a few words of, and not a book that he would not read" – Mikhail Tal). And as a legacy, he left a flood of 42 books, among them opening monographs, analytical endgame works, and collections of his selected games. Among his best games, there were many that, at various times, he had won against all the former or future world champions, e.g., Capablanca (AVRO 1938), Alekhine (Margate 1938), Euwe (Noordwijk 1938; and the match-tournament of 1948), Tal and Fischer (Candidates' Tournament, Bled 1959), Petrosian (1949 USSR Championship), Spassky (Interzonal Göteborg 1955), Botvinnik (match-tournament, 1948, 1955 USSR Champi-

onship, and Alekhine Memorial Tournament, Moscow 1956).

(33) Keres – Botvinnik
Moscow 1956
Sicilian Defense [B63]

1.e4 c5 2.♘f3 ♘c6 3.d4 c×d4 4.♘×d4 ♘f6 5.♘c3 d6 6.♗g5 e6 7.♕d2 h6 8.♗×f6 g×f6 9.0-0-0 a6 10.f4 h5 11.♔b1 ♗d7 12.♗e2 ♕b6 13.♘b3 0-0-0 14.♖hf1 ♘a5?! 14...♗e7 and 14...♔b8 are the main moves. **15.♖f3 ♘×b3 16.a×b3 ♔b8 17.♘a4 ♕a7 18.f5**

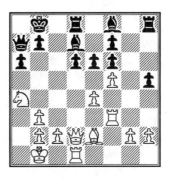

18...♗e7? This runs into a surprising combination. 18...b5 19.♘c3 ♗e7 is called for. **19.f×e6 f×e6 20.♖×f6!! ♖h7?** 20...♖hf8 21.♖×f8 ♖×f8 22.♕h6 b5 23.♘c3 h4 is a better practical try. Of course not 20...♗×f6? 21.♕×d6+ ♔c8 22.♘b6++– **21.♖g6 b5?! 22.♘c3 ♕c5**

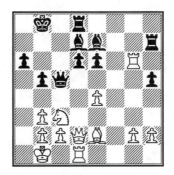

23.♘a2! A strong regrouping of the knight to increase the pressure on the light squares on the queenside. White's initiative cannot really be stopped. **23...♔a7 24.♘b4 ♖f8 25.♗f3 h4 26.h3 ♗c8 27.♘d3** 27.e5 d5 28.♘d3 is also very strong. **27...♕c7 28.♘f4 ♖f6 29.♗g4 ♖×g6 30.♘×g6 ♗b7 31.♗×e6 ♗d8 32.♗d5 ♗×d5 33.♕×d5 ♖f7 34.e5 1-0**

"Not a bad revenge for his previous losses!" – Kasparov

Beating Botvinnik, naturally, brought Keres special satisfaction, since from the experience of playing him in the match-tournaments of 1941 and 1948, he knew "that seizing victory from him was nearly impossible." These were words he said during an interview that he gave in 1963. The evaluation Keres gave Botvinnik in his book on the 1948 match-tournament is also significant: "His play was distinguished for its great depth and many facets, and from a competitive standpoint, it was simply outstanding. He won the title of world champion, undoubtedly, because he was the most worthy."

In his turn, Botvinnik more than once underscored that Paul Keres was always one of his toughest opponents on his chessic path toward the heights of Olympus. "Of course, when we competed together," wrote Botvinnik in 1991, on the occasion of the 75th anniversary of the birth of Keres, "as always in such situations, relations would be tense; but afterwards, we would be best of friends. Keres' life was an excellent example of serving the art of chess."

Botvinnik ended his recollections of the Estonian grandmaster with these words: "When I am in Tallinn, I go to his mausoleum, on the shore, so that I may bow to the great chess artist of our century." The traditional international tournaments in Tallinn are dedicated to Keres' memory. And there, in 1957, a House of Chess was opened, named after him. In January 2006, in Tallinn, a solemn gathering was held on the occasion of the 90th anniversary of the birth of Keres, to which chessplayers from all over the world were invited.

Books: *School of Chess*, Tallinn 1948; *Match-tournament for the World Chess Championship*, The Hague-Moscow, 1948, Tallinn 1950; *Theory of Chess Openings, Open Games*, ch. 1-2, Tallinn 1949-53; *French Defense*, Moscow 1948; *Selected Games*, Tallinn 1961 (in Estonian); *One Hundred Games*, Moscow 1966.

Biblio: Heuer, V., *Our Keres*, Tallinn 1977 (in Estonian); Neishtadt, Y., *The Paul Keres Chess University*, Moscow 1982; *Paul Keres*, Tallinn 1985.

Team Events From the start, when he debuted on the Leningrad team for its match against Stockholm in 1926, Botvinnik was involved in team matches. He was there when twin responsibilities lay upon his shoulders, when a comrade's misfortune on a neighboring board would affect tenfold those adjacent to him; when the joy of overall victory would overshadow one's own modest personal success. One of Botvinnik's last appearances in chess events was his participation in the "Match of the Century" on the USSR team in 1970.

In the 40-year interval between his "start" and "finish," Botvinnik often played various team events for the national team, his city, his society. The most significant, of course, were the Olympiads. Among team competitions, the USSR-USA and USSR-Great Britain matches, the European championships, the Spartakiads of the USSR, and the USSR team championships stand out.

USSR-USA Matches Botvinnik played in three matches. The first was the famous radio match which took place right after the end of the Second World War (September 1-4, 1945). It consisted of two rounds on ten boards. Botvinnik's opponent was U.S. champion Arnold Denker. The Soviet player won both games (cf. Ch. 3, *Attack*), and the overall score of the match (15½-4½) was a sensation. No one expected such a crushing defeat of the many-time winner of the "Tournament of Nations."

A year later, there was a face-to-face meeting in Moscow (September 12-16, 1946). Each team consisted of 10 players. This time, Botvinnik faced one of the world championship candidates, Samuel Reshevsky, and again won (1½-½). The match score was 12½-7½.

The third time Botvinnik played in a match against the USA in 1955, again held in Moscow (July 26-September 6). As in the previous matches, he took first board, leading an eight-man team. They played four rounds, and for the first time, Botvinnik lost to Reshevsky 1½-2½ (+0 -1 =3). The overall match score was 25-7 in favor of the Soviet team.

USSR-Great Britain Radio Match This took place on July 19-22, 1946. Each team consisted of twelve players (ten men, two women). The leader of the Soviet team played against Alexander, a master whom he had known since Nottingham, and concluded their mini-match by a score of 1-1 (both games were drawn). The overall match score was 18-5 in favor of the Soviet team.

Soviet chessplayers, participants of the USSR – USA radio-match. Seated (left to right): Aleksandr Kotov, Vassily Smyslov, Mikhail Botvinnik, Vyachislav Ragozin, Salo Flohr. Standing: Andre Lilienthal, Isaak Boleslavsky, Vladimir Makogonov, Igor Bondarevsky, David Bronstein

"Match of the Century," Belgrade 1970 In the encounter USSR vs. The Rest of the World, Botvinnik played a four-game mini-match against the 35-year-old Yugoslav grandmaster Milan Matulovic. As early as the first game, playing The Modern Defense with Black, Botvinnik courageously went in for complications, and managed to wrest the initiative. They castled on opposite sides, but thanks to his fianchettoed bishop at g7, like a laser lighting up the long diagonal, Black developed a powerful attack against the b2-square.

(34) Matulovic – Botvinnik
Belgrade 1970
Modern Defense [B06]

1.e4 g6 2.d4 ♗g7 3.♘f3 d6 4.♗c4 ♘f6 5.♕e2 c6 6.♗b3 0-0 7.♗g5 h6 8.♗h4 e5 9.d×e5 d×e5 10.♘bd2 10.♘×e5?? **♕a5+–+ 10...♕c7 11.♘c4 ♘h5 12.♗g3?! ♘f4 13.♗×f4 e×f4 14.0-0-0 ♗g4 15.e5?** This takes time and weakens the pawn. 15.♕d2 limits the damage. **15...♘d7 16.♕e4 ♖ad8?!** 16...b5!? 17.♘d6 ♗×f3 18.g×f3 ♘×e5 is even stronger. **17.♕×f4 ♗×f3 18.♕×f3 b5 19.♘e3 ♘×e5 20.♕g3 a5 21.a3 ♔h7 22.♘g4?! h5 23.♘×e5 ♗×e5 24.♕f3 ♔g7 25.♖he1 ♗f6 26.c3?! c5 27.♖×d8?! ♖×d8**

28.g3? White does not have time for such a slow move. But good advice is hard to give anyway. Even a radical approach like 28.♖d1!? should be considered. **28...c4! 29.♗c2 b4! 30.a×b4?!** Opening lines accelerates defeat, but White has no real defense anyway, e.g., 30.♕f4 ♖c8 31.♕e3 b×c3 32.b×c3 ♕b7 33.♖d1 ♖b8–+ **30...a×b4 31.c×b4 ♕b6 32.♖d1**

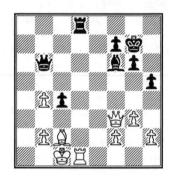

32...♕×b4? Without rooks White still has slim chances to hold. 32...♖b8! wins, e.g., 33.♖d7 (33.♕a3 ♕×f2–+) 33...♕×b4 34.♕d5 ♕e1+–+ **33.♖×d8 ♕×b2+ 34.♔d1 ♗×d8 35.♕d5 ♕f6 36.♔e2 ♗b6?!** 36...♕e7+ 37.♔f1 ♕c7 38.f4 ♗f6 applies more pressure as White cannot exchange queens easily. **37.f4! ♕c3 38.♕e4?** With queens, Black's pressure is very dangerous. 38.♕e5+ was necessary, e.g., 38...♕×e5+ 39.f×e5 ♗d4 40.e6 f5 41.♗a4 ♔f8 42.♗b5 c3 43.♗a4 ♔e7 44.♗b3 and White should be able to defend. **38...♗d4 39.f5?** 39.h4? f5 40.♕e7+ ♔h6–+; 39.♔f1! was the last chance to limit the damage. **39...g×f5 40.♕×f5 ♕e3+ 41.♔f1 ♕g1+ 42.♔e2 ♕×h2+ 43.♔d1 ♕g1+ 44.♔e2 ♕e3+ 45.♔f1 ♕×g3 46.♕h7+ ♔f8 0-1**

The following three games featured uncompromising draws, and Botvinnik secured the victory by a score of 2½-1½ (+1 -0 =3). The international press and many of the participants dubbed him one of the heroes of this historic match.

European Championships Botvinnik took part in the second and third continental championships, which took place in Germany in 1961 (Oberhausen) and in 1965 (Hamburg). Mikhail Botvinnik, on first board, turned in the top result: 6/9 (+4 -1 =4). Four years later, he did not perform as well on second board (+2 -3 =3).

(35) Botvinnik – Unzicker
Oberhausen 1961
Catalan Opening [D34]

1.c4 ♘f6 2.♘f3 e6 3.g3 d5 4.♗g2 c5 5.0-0 ♘c6 6.c×d5 e×d5 7.d4 ♗e6 8.♘c3 ♗e7 9.♗e3 c4 10.♘e5 0-0

11.♘×c4! A strong shot which is still the main line nowadays. **11...d×c4 12.d5 ♘×d5 13.♘×d5 ♗f6 14.♖c1 ♗d4 15.♗×d4 ♗×d5 16.e4 ♗×e4?** In the resulting open position, White's bishop and initiative give Botvinnik a clear advantage. 16...♗e6! should have been played. **17.♗×e4 ♘×d4 18.♖×c4 ♘e6 19.♕c2 g6 20.♗×b7 ♖b8 21.♗g2 ♕f6 22.b3 ♘d4 23.♕e4 ♖fd8 24.♖e1 ♘f5 25.♖c6 ♕b2 26.♖c2 ♕a3 27.♕e5 ♕b4**

28.♔f1?! 28.♖c7 is more precise, e.g., 28...♖b5 29.♕a1 ♖c5 30.♖d7+− **28...♖b6 29.♗d5 ♕b5+ 30.♗c4 ♕d7**

31.♕e4? Now it becomes very difficult to make progress in view of Black's counterplay. After 31.g4! ♘g7 32.♕e7, White is clearly better and his position is much easier to play than in the game. (32.♖ce2, to meet 32...♕×g4 with 33.♗×f7+, might be even stronger.) **31...♖d6 32.♖ce2 ♘d4 33.♖e3 ♘f5 34.♖3e2 ♘d4 35.♖b2 ♕h3+ 36.♕g2?!** The computer suggests the amazing 36.♔g1 ♖f6 37.♖d2 ♘f3+ 38.♕×f3 ♖×f3 39.♖×d8+ ♔g7 40.♖e7 with more than enough compensation for the queen. **36...♕f5?** This attack can be parried. After 36...♕h5!, Black has sufficient compensation: 37.♖d2 ♘f3 38.♖×d6 ♖×d6 39.♗e2 ♘d2+ 40.♔g1 ♕a5 41.♖d1 ♔g7= **37.f4 ♕h5 38.♖f2 ♕a5?!** 38...♕c5 gives more counterchances. **39.g4! ♘e6 40.f5** The prophylactic 40.♕g3!?, to meet 40...♖d1 with 41.♕e3, is more precise. **40...♖d1! 41.♕e4** (D)

41...♖8d4?! The resulting endgames are very critical. The computer prefers 41...g×f5 42.♖×f5 ♕c3 43.♗×e6 (43.♖×d1 ♖×d1+ 44.♔g2 ♖d4) 43...♕h3+ 44.♔g1 ♖×e1+ 45.♕×e1 ♕×g4+ 46.♔h1 ♖d1 47.♖g5+ ♕×g5

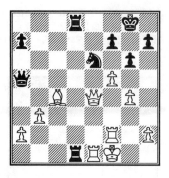

48.♗xf7+ ♔xf7 49.♕xd1 ♔e6 50.♕e2+ ♕e5 with practical drawing chances. **42.♕e3 ♕xe1+ 43.♔xe1 ♘f4 44.fxg6 hxg6 45.h4 ♔g7 46.♖c2 ♖xe1+ 47.♔xe1 f5 48.gxf5 gxf5 49.♗f1 ♔g6 50.♖c5 ♔h5?** The rook ending 50...♘d3+ 51.♗xd3 ♖xd3 offers much better chances because of the drawish tendencies of rook endings in general and Black's passed f-pawn. **51.♖xf5+ ♔xh4 52.♖a5?!** 52.♔f2 is more precise. **52...♖d7 53.♔f2**

53...♖e7? Black's king is too passive now. 53...♔g4 was the last real chance to fight. **54.♔f3 ♘g6 55.♗c4 ♘e5+?! 56.♔f4 ♘g4 57.♖a6 ♔h5?! 58.♗d5! ♘e5?!** 58...♖g7 59.♗f3 ♔h4 60.♗xg4 ♖xg4+ 61.♔f5 ♖g7 62.♖h6+ ♔g3 63.♖g6++− **59.♗e4 1-0**

Spartakiad of USSR In the Moscow team lineup, Botvinnik played in three Spartakiads (1959, 1963 and 1967); in two of them, the Moscow team was victorious. Botvinnik showed his best result in 1963 (after losing his world championship match with Petrosian). In nine games, Botvinnik took eight points (+7 -0 =2). But personal success does not always guarantee a win for the team. Moscow wound up taking second place, a half-point behind the team from the Russian Federation.

(36) Kholmov – Botvinnik
Moscow 1963
Pirc Defense [B07]

1.e4 d6 2.d4 ♘f6 3.♘c3 g6 4.♗g5 h6 5.♗f4 ♗g7 6.h3 c5 7.dxc5 ♕a5 8.♕d2 ♕xc5 9.♗e3 ♕a5 10.♗d3 ♘c6 11.♘ge2 ♘d7 12.0-0 ♘de5 13.f4 ♘xd3 14.cxd3 e6 15.♖ae1 ♗d7 16.a3 ♘e7 17.♗d4 ♗xd4+ 18.♘xd4 ♕b6 19.♕f2 0-0-0 20.♘f3 ♕xf2+ 21.♔xf2 ♔b8 22.♖c1 f6 23.d4 ♖hf8 24.h4 d5 25.exd5 exd5 26.♖fe1 ♖f7 27.g3 ♗g4 28.♘h2 ♗c8 29.♖c2 ♘c6 30.♖ce2 ♖ff8 30...♘xd4 31.♖d2 ♘f5 32.♖xd5= **31.♖d2 g5 32.♘f3 gxf4 33.gxf4 ♖g8 34.♖g1 ♖xg1 35.♘xg1 ♗g4 36.♘f3 ♘e7 37.♘e1 ♘f5 38.♘g2 h5 39.♘e3 ♘xh4 40.♘exd5 f5 41.♖d3 ♘g6 42.♖e3 h4 43.♖e6 h3 44.♖xg6 ♖h8**

45.♘e2! The right way to deal with the dangerous h-pawn. **45...♗×e2 46.♖g1! ♗g4 47.♘e3 h2 48.♖h1 ♖h3 49.♘×g4 f×g4 50.♔g2 ♖f3 51.♖×h2 ♖×f4 52.d5 ♖d4 53.♔g3 ♔c7 54.♖h7+ ♔b6 55.♖h6+ ♔c5 56.♖h7 ♔b6 57.♖h6+ ♔b5 58.♖h7 ♔a6 59.♖h6+ b6**

60.♖h7? This sells White's precious d-pawn too cheaply. 60.d6 ♔b5 61.♖g6 ♔c6 62.d7+ ♔c7 63.♖×g4 ♖×d7 64.♔f3 ♖d3+ 65.♔e2 ♖b3 66.♖b4= **60...♖×d5 61.♔×g4** 61.♖h2 ♖d4 should also be lost in the long run. **61...♖d2 62.b4 ♖b2 63.♖h3 ♖a2 64.♔f4 ♔b5 65.♔e4 ♔a4 66.♖h7 ♖×a3 67.♖×a7+ ♔×b4 68.♖h7 b5 69.♔d4 ♖a8** and Kholmov resigned because of 70.♔d3 ♔b3 71.♔d2 b4 72.♔c1 ♖a1+ 73.♔d2 ♔b2–+ **0-1**

Botvinnik's total score at Spartakiads: 18/24 (+13 -1 =10).

USSR Team Championships
"Revenge is no longer? Then, long live revenge!" This is what the ex-world champion, Mikhail Botvinnik, might have said, in his soul, after his convincing win over the world champion, Tigran Petrosian, in the Trud-Spartak match, in the 1964 USSR team championship. The 53-year-old veteran also defeated the 42-year old former world champion Vassily

Smyslov ("Burevestnik") and the talented 19-year old, USSR champion Leonid Stein ("Vo'oruzhenykh Sil"). Botvinnik drew three other games, and did not lose any (4½/6!).

(37) Botvinnik – Petrosian
Moscow 1964
English Opening [A14]

1.c4 c5 2.♘f3 ♘f6 3.♘c3 e6 4.g3 b6 5.♗g2 ♗b7 6.0-0 ♗e7 7.b3 d5 8.e3 0-0 9.♗b2 ♘c6 10.c×d5 e×d5 11.d4 ♖e8 12.♖c1 ♖c8 13.♗h3 ♖b8 14.♖e1 c×d4 15.e×d4 ♗b4 16.♖×e8+ ♕×e8 17.a3 ♗f8 18.♕d3 g6 19.♖e1 ♕d8 20.♘e5 ♗g7 21.f3 ♘a5 22.♕d1 a6 23.♘a2 ♘c6 24.♗c3 ♕c7 25.♕d2 a5 26.♗b2 ♕d6 27.♘c1 27.♘c3!? **27...♗c8 28.♗f1 ♗e6 29.♘cd3 ♘e7 30.b4 a×b4 31.a×b4 ♘e8 32.b5 f6 33.♘g4 ♗d7?** Petrosian loses coordination. After 33...♘c7, he should be able to defend.

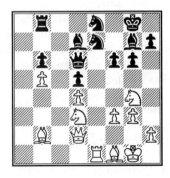

34.♗c3! The threat ♗b4 cannot really be parried. **34...♘f5 35.♘f4 ♕f8?! 36.♘×d5 ♔h8 37.♗b4 ♕f7 38.♘e7 ♘ed6?! 39.♘×f5?!** 39.♗×d6 ♘×d6 40.♕f4 wins directly. **39...♘×f5 40.d5 ♖e8 41.♖e4** 41.♘e3!?+– **41...h5 42.♘f2 ♖d8?** This is too passive. 42...♗h6! offers more resistance, but the compensation is of course still insufficient after 43.♕b2

43.♗c4 ♗c8 44.d6 ♕d7 45.♖e1 ♗b7 46.♘e4 46.♕d3!?+− **46...♗×e4 47.♖×e4 ♘×d6 48.♗×d6 ♗f8**

49.♖d4?! The resulting endgame is won, but 49.♖e6!+− wins directly. **49...♔h7 50.♗×f8 ♕×d4+ 51.♕×d4 ♖×d4 52.♗f1 g5 53.♗a3 ♖d1 54.♔f2 ♔g7 55.♗b4 h4 56.g×h4 ♖d4 57.♗e1 ♖×h4 58.♔g3 ♖d4 59.♗f2 ♖d1 60.♗c4 ♖d6 61.f4 ♔g6 62.f×g5 f×g5 1−0**

Two years later, Botvinnik played in another USSR team championship for Trud, and once again, successfully, scoring 6/8 (+5 −1 =2)! This time, Smyslov, Keres and Spassky fell to the ageless warrior.

(38) Botvinnik – Keres
Moscow 1966
English Opening [A29]

1.c4 ♘f6 2.♘c3 e5 3.♘f3 ♘c6 4.g3 ♗c5 5.♘×e5 Nowadays 5.♗g2 is the main line, but the pseudo-knight sacrifice is also still played. **5...♗×f2+ 6.♔×f2 ♘×e5 7.e4 c5 8.d3 d6 9.h3 h5?!** 9...0-0 is played more often and also scores better. **10.♗e2 ♘h7 11.♔g2 h4 12.g4 ♘g5 13.♗e3 ♗d7 14.♕d2 ♘e6 15.b4 b6 16.♖ab1 ♗c6 17.♖hf1 ♗b7 18.♔g1**

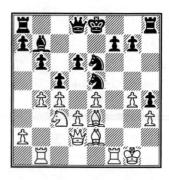

18...♘c6?! This first step in the wrong direction. 18...0-0 is called for. **19.♘d5 ♘cd4?! 20.♗d1 f6?** This weakens the light squares fatally. 20...0-0 was again called for. **21.♔h2?** The direct 21.g5! wins: 21...0-0 22.g×f6 g×f6 23.♔h2. **21...♗c6?** The regrouping 21...0-0 22.♕f2 ♘c6 23.♕×h4 ♘e5 was the last real chance to fight. **22.a4 a5?! 23.b×a5 b×a5 24.♕f2** Again, the direct 24.g5 is even stronger. **24...♖a7?** 24...0-0 was forced, but White just takes the pawn with 25.♕×h4 of course. **25.g5! 0-0 26.g6 f5?!**

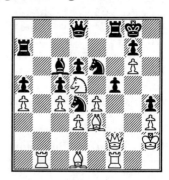

27.♖b8!! The decisive blow. Keres resigned in view of 27...♕×b8 28.♕×h4 ♖c8 29.♕h7+ ♔f8 30.♕h8# **1−0**

Kotov, Alexander Alexandrovich (August 12, 1910, Tula-January 8, 1981, Moscow), international grandmaster (1950), chess author, candidate for the world championship.

When he was young, his father taught him to play checkers. This calculative game of many variations appealed to the youngster, and soon he began to outplay his teacher. In his school years, his friends acquainted him with chess, which immediately engrossed and nurtured Alexander. By 16, he was city champion. After he graduated from the Tula Mechanical Institute, he moved to Moscow. The championship of the capital became his "chess university." Some days, he would study the game 14-16 hours a day! In the Kiev semifinal of the 1938 USSR championship, Kotov fulfilled the master norm and received the right to play in the final, where he played against nearly all of the strongest players of the country, led by the grandmaster duet of Botvinnik and Grigori Levenfish. Unexpectedly for everyone, Kotov turned into a serious challenger to Botvinnik in the fight for first place. And only in the very last round did the winner of Nottingham overcome this upstart debutant, beating him in their individual game. Kotov, taking second place, became the third Soviet grandmaster.

During the war, Alexander worked in the construction bureau, developing the newest mortar systems. In fact, it was he who was responsible for developing the 120-millimeter mortar, for which Kotov was awarded the very highest medal of the time, the Order of Lenin (1944).

After the war, Kotov achieved a number of competitive successes: in the 1948 USSR Championship (first/second

Alexander Kotov

places), international tournaments in Saltsjobaden (1948, fourth place), Stockholm (1952, first place), Venice (1950) and Hastings (1962/63). Botvinnik rated his victory in Sweden (1952) exceptionally highly: "Kotov's greatest triumph was undoubtedly the international tournament at Stockholm. Without losing a single game, he outdistanced his closest competitor by 3 points, although among the competitors were such famous grandmasters as Petrosian, Geller, Gligoric, Taimanov, Averbakh, Szabo, Ståhlberg, and Unzicker. It is notable that in this tournament, the 39-year old Kotov showed himself to be master of a universal style: his opponents could not display their best qualities – the highest sort of mastery in chess!"

In candidates' tournaments, Kotov's successes were less impressive: Budapest (1950, sixth place), Zürich (1953, eighth/ninth). But it was precisely at Zürich that he played his "immortal" game with grandmaster Averbakh, sacrificing a queen for a pawn!

(39) Averbakh – Kotov
Zürich 1953
Old Indian Defense [A55]

1.d4 ♘f6 2.c4 d6 3.♘f3 ♘bd7
4.♘c3 e5 5.e4 ♗e7 6.♗e2 0-0
7.0-0 c6 8.♕c2 ♖e8 9.♖d1 ♗f8
10.♖b1 a5 11.d5 ♘c5 12.♗e3 ♕c7
13.h3 ♗d7 14.♖bc1 g6 15.♘d2
♖ab8 16.♘b3 ♘xb3 17.♕xb3 c5
18.♔h2 ♔h8 19.♕c2 ♘g8 20.♗g4
♘h6 21.♗xd7 ♕xd7 22.♕d2 ♘g8
23.g4 f5

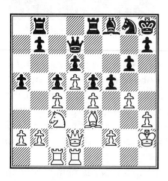

24.f3?! 24.gxf5 gxf5 25.exf5 ♕xf5
26.♖g1 is more in the spirit of the
position as White can play on the kingside
now. 24...♗e7?! 25.♖g1?! ♖f8?!
26.♖cf1?! 26.exf5 gxf5 27.gxf5 ♕xf5
28.♖cf1 ± 26...♖f7?! 26...f4 27.♗f2 ♘f6
limits the damage. 27.gxf5 gxf5
28.♖g2? 28.exf5 ♕xf5 29.♘e4 is much
better for White because of the strong
knight. 28...f4 29.♗f2 ♖f6 30.♘e2?
The prophylactic 30.h4 is called for.

Now one of the most famous king hunt
attacks of all time follows:
30...♕xh3+!! 31.♔xh3 31.♔g1
♖h6-+ **31...♖h6+ 32.♔g4 ♘f6+
33.♔f5 ♘d7 34.♖g5 ♖f8+ 35.♔g4
♘f6+ 36.♔f5 ♘g8+ 37.♔g4 ♘f6+
38.♔f5 ♘xd5+** The d-pawn can be
taken for free. **39.♔g4 ♘f6+ 40.♔f5
♘g8+ 41.♔g4 ♘f6+ 42.♔f5 ♘g8+
43.♔g4** Kotov finally decides to
continue his attack: **43...♗xg5
44.♔xg5**

44...♖f7! and Black's mating threat
cannot be parried without heavy
material losses: **45.♗h4 ♖g6+
46.♔h5 ♖fg7 47.♗g5 ♖xg5+
48.♔h4 ♘f6 49.♘g3 ♖xg3
50.♕xd6 ♖3g6 51.♕b8+ ♖g8 0-1**

Kotov at times was referred to as "the
self-made man from Tula." The talented
young man reached a lot of heights in
chess, as they say, "by himself." He
revealed the secrets of his chess mastery
in a number of books, the most well-
known of which was *Think like a
Grandmaster* (1972), and the one that
came out in Moscow after Kotov's
death, *Train like a Grandmaster* (1985).

Kotov dedicated many years of his life
to the study of the life and creative path
of the fourth world chess champion, his
great countryman Alexander Alekhine.

His fundamental two-volume work, *The Chess Legacy of Alekhine*, was translated into a number of languages, and his novel, *White and Black*, was dedicated to the life of Alekhine. He also wrote a screenplay, *The White Snows of Russia*.

"He spent his last years attentively poring over my work creating an artificial grandmaster," remembered Botvinnik. "He would hurry me, and get angry when the work was delayed... Although his health might have been shaky, the rhythm of his life never weakened. Alexander Kotov managed to accomplish a lot. But his victories over the first (Botvinnik) and second (Euwe) prizewinners at Groningen were remembered by the world of chess."

(40) Botvinnik – Kotov
Groningen 1946
Nimzo-Indian [E25]

1.d4 ♘f6 2.c4 e6 3.♘c3 ♗b4 4.a3 ♗×c3+ 5.b×c3 d5 6.c×d5 e×d5 7.♗g5 c5 8.f3 h6 9.♗×f6 ♕×f6 10.e3 0-0 11.♘e2 ♖e8 12.♔f2 ♕e7 13.♕d2 ♘d7 13...c4!? **14.♘f4 ♘f6**

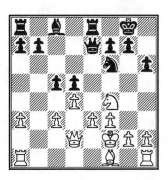

15.♗d3?! The bishop is in the way here. 15.♗b5 ♖d8 16.d×c5 ♕×c5 17.a4 a6 18.♗e2 is called for, when White is not worse. **15...♗d7 16.h3 ♕d6**

17.♖hb1 b6 18.♗f1?! ♖e7?! 18...c4!? **19.a4?!** 19.d×c5 b×c5 (19...♕×c5 20.♕d4) 20.c4 is almost equal in both cases. **19...♖ae8** 19...c4!? **20.♖e1?** White does not have time for this prophylaxis. 20.d×c5 b×c5 21.e4 ♖×e4 22.♘×d5 ♗c6 23.♔g1 ♖4e5 24.♘×f6+ ♕×f6 25.♖d1 limits the damage. **20...c4 21.g4 g5! 22.♘e2 ♖×e3 23.♘g3** 23.♘g1 ♘e4+-+; 23.♔g2 ♖d3 24.♕c1 ♖ee3 25.♘g1 ♖×c3-+; 23.♕×e3 ♕h2+ 24.♗g2 ♖×e3 25.♔×e3 ♕×g2-+

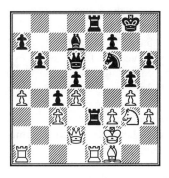

23...♕×g3+! A bolt from the blue. **24.♔×g3 ♘e4+ 0-1**

Books: *International Grandmaster Tournament, Venice 1952*; *International Grandmaster Tournament, Stockholm, 1952*, Moscow 1954 (co-author); *The Soviet School of Chess*, second edition, Moscow 1955 (co-author); *Notes of a Chessplayer*, Moscow 1957; *The Rape of Proserpine*, Moscow 1961; *Selected Games*, Moscow 1962; *Joking, and Seriously*, Moscow 1965; *The Squirrel Cage*, Moscow 1967; *Work, Talent, Victory*, Moscow 1969 (co-author); *Think like a Grandmaster*, Moscow 1970; *Alexander Alekhine*, Moscow 1973; *Mastery*, Moscow 1975; *Chess School*, Moscow 1976 (co-author); *A Ural Semi-precious Stone*, second edition, Moscow 1980; *Alekhine's Chess*

Legacy, second edition, vols. 1 & 2, 1982; *Train like a Grandmaster*, Moscow 1985.
Literature: *Alexander Kotov*, Moscow 1984.

Levenfish, Grigori Yakovlevich (March 9, 1890, Petrokoff, Poland-February 9, 1961, Moscow), international grandmaster (1950), twice USSR champion, defended that title in a match in 1937 with Botvinnik.

He learned chess at six, but only took it seriously after entering the St. Petersburg Technical Institute in 1907. He achieved his first success in chess three years later, becoming champion of St. Petersburg, and in 1911, he made his debut in the strong international tournament in Carlsbad (today, Karlovy Vary), where he played a number of outstanding games. The chess press rated Levenfish's creative achievements highly, noting that he was playing like Chigorin. The subsequent performances at the All-Russian tournaments (1912 and 1913-14) secured a reputation for him as one of the strongest chessplayers in Russia. Levenfish achieved his greatest competitive and creative successes in the 1930s, when he performed successfully in the second and third Moscow international tournaments (1935 and 1936) and won the USSR championships in 1934 and 1937. In 1936, Capablanca wrote about him: "I value master Levenfish very highly. I think that he is the strongest in the USSR, after Botvinnik."

This was also supported by a match between the two for the title of champion of the Soviet Union, which ended in a draw (cf. *Levenfish-*

Grigory Levenfish

Botvinnik match, 1937). Levenfish played with great energy, demonstrating a wonderful skill in playing complicated positions. After the match, as the second-ranking chessplayer in the country, he was awarded the grandmaster title. Characterizing Levenfish as a "universally educated master," Botvinnik wrote: "Elegant combinations came naturally to him: unexpected tactical strokes, and great energy in pursuit of the attack. He plays the ending with exceptional depth..."

(41) Botvinnik – Levenfish
Leningrad 1937
Grünfeld Defense [94]

1.d4 d5 2.c4 c6 3.♘c3 ♘f6 4.e3 g6 5.♘f3 ♗g7 6.♗d3 0-0 7.0-0 e6 8.b3 ♘bd7 9.♕e2 ♖e8 10.♗b2 b6 11.♖ad1 ♗b7 12.♘e5 ♘xe5 13.dxe5 ♘d7 14.f4 ♕e7 15.cxd5 exd5 16.e4?! This plays with fire as White's knight will need time to come back. 16.♗a6 is more solid, e.g., 16...♗xa6 17.♕xa6 f6 18.♕b7 ♕e6 19.e4 d4 20.♖xd4= **16...d4 17.♘b1 c5 18.♘d2**

18...g5!? Black must act to free his pieces on the kingside before White fully consolidates. **19.g3 g×f4 20.g×f4 ♔h8 21.♘c4 ♖g8?** 21...f6 22.♘d6 f×e5 23.♘×e8 ♖×e8 is a better version of the game for Black. **22.♔h1 f6 23.♘d6 f×e5 24.♘×b7 e×f4 25.e5** Of course 25.♖×f4!? ♘e5 26.♗a6 also came into consideration. **25...♗×e5 26.b4?** White does not have time for this. 26.♖de1 ♖af8 27.b4 ♕h4 28.♖f3= is called for. **26...♘f6 27.♕f3 ♘g4! 28.♖d2**

28...♖ab8? Levenfish misses 28...♘e3 which leads to a very strong attack, as White's pieces cannot defend the kingside, e.g., 29.♖c1 ♖g4 30.♗e4 ♕g7 31.b×c5 ♖g8 32.♕f2 f3 33.♗×f3 ♖f4 34.♘d8 ♘g4 35.♕e2 ♘×h2 36.♕×h2 ♖×f3 37.♕×e5 ♕×e5 38.♘f7+ ♖×f7 39.♗×d4 ♕×d4 40.♖×d4 ♖f5–+

29.♗e4 d3 29...♘e3 was again the alternative, but now it only leads to equality. **30.♕×d3 ♖×b7 31.♗×b7 ♕×b7+ 32.♕f3 ♕×f3+ 33.♖×f3 ♗×b2 34.♖×b2 ♘e5 35.♖f1** Of course not 35.♖×f4?? ♘d3–+ **35...♘d3 36.♖g2?** The wrong idea. 36.♖e2 is more or less equal. **36...c4**

37.♖c2! The rook must remain on the board as Black's passed pawns win after 37.♖×g8+? ♔×g8 38.♖f3 b5–+ **37...b5 38.a3?** Activating the rook with 38.♖e2 ♖c8 39.a3 ♔g7 40.♖e6 is called for, as 40...c3? can be met by 41.♖d6= **38...f3 39.♖d2?** Mistakes always seem to come in pairs. 39.♖c3 ♖f8 40.♔g1 limits the damage. **39...♖g2! 40.♖×g2 f×g2+ 41.♔×g2 c3 42.♔f3** desperation as 42.♖f8+ runs into 42...♔g7 43.♖c8 c2 44.♖×c2 ♘e1+–+ **0-1**

Here are two of the comments on this match:

Flohr: "Although the outcome was a draw, it is clear that the hero of the match was Levenfish."

Fine: "Levenfish should unquestionably be considered one of the ten best chess-players in the world."

Levenfish was also a strong theoretician. Working with Pyotr Romanovsky, he wrote a book on the world championship match between Capablanca and Alekhine. Thirty years later, the classic work, *Theory of Rook Endings*, created together with world champion Vassily Smyslov, saw the light of day. Under Levenfish's editorship, on the eve of the war, the first volume of the encyclopedic *Sovremenny Debyut* (1940) was published.

With his activities, Levenfish substantially aided the advance in the USSR of the constellation of candidates for the world championship. Botvinnik called him one of the strongest masters among those "who passed on their experience to young Soviet players," and those who, being very talented themselves, "handled their instructive mission so well." Levenfish successfully combined activities in the area of chess skill with his professional work in the national economy, as a chemical engineer.

Books: *The Chessplayer's First Book*, Leningrad 1926; *Alekhine-Capablanca Match for the World Championship*, Leningrad 1928 (co-author); *IX All-union Chess Championship*, Moscow/Leningrad 1937.

Levenfish – Botvinnik Match, 1937
October 5-November, Moscow – Leningrad. Organized by the All-Union Chess Section at the request of Botvinnik. Not having played in the 10th USSR championship, he challenged Levenfish, the tournament winner, to a match for the title of champion of the Soviet Union. It was played to the first to win six games. Upon reaching a score of 5-5, the match

would be declared drawn, with Levenfish retaining the champion's title. The first eight games were played in Moscow, the rest in Leningrad.

The match was very tense. First Botvinnik led, then Levenfish. The violent nature of the match is confirmed by the extremely low percentage of draws – only 3 out of 13 games (the fourth, fifth and ninth). From time to time, one of the opponents would win several games in a row. The final, 13th game was won by Levenfish, and with the score 6½-6½ (+5 -5 =3), the match was ended.

In the games of the match, along with interesting opening and strategic ideas, and sharp examples of combinative attacks and stubborn defense, we also had episodes of dramatic collapses, brought about by the colossal nervous expenditures of energy in the struggle.

(42) Botvinnik – Levenfish
Leningrad 1937
English Opening [A25]

1.c4 e5 2.♘c3 ♘c6 3.g3 g6 4.♗g2 ♗g7 5.e3 d6 6.♘ge2 ♗e6 7.d4 ♗×c4?! Very risky as the light squares will be very weak. 7...e×d4 8.♘×d4 ♗d7 is more solid. **8.d5 ♘b8 9.♕a4+ b5 10.♘×b5 ♗×b5 11.♕×b5+ ♘d7 12.e4 ♘e7 13.0-0 0-0 14.♘c3 ♖b8 15.♕e2 c5 16.d×c6 ♘×c6 17.♗e3 ♘c5 18.♕d2 ♘e6 19.♖ac1 ♘ed4 20.f4 ♕a5?** 20...♘e7 limits the damage. **21.f5 f6 22.♖f2 ♔h8 23.♕d1** 23.f×g6!? h×g6 24.♕d1 is slightly more precise. **23...♖bd8?** 23...g×f5 24.e×f5 ♘e7 is the lesser evil. **24.f×g6 h×g6 25.♕g4!** Exposing Black's king. The light square are just too weak. **25...♘e7 26.♗f1 d5 27.♘×d5 ♘×d5 28.e×d5 ♘f5 29.♗c5 ♗h6 30.b4 ♕a3**

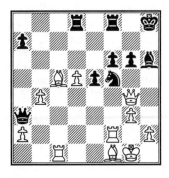

31.♕×g6!? White's attack will be too strong. **31...♕×c1 32.♖×f5 ♗g5 33.h4 ♖g8 34.♕h5+ ♗h6 35.♖×f6 ♔h7 36.♕f5+ ♔h8 37.♕h5 ♔h7 38.♕f5+ ♔h8 39.♕h5 ♔h7** and Black resigned in view of 40.♖×h6+ ♕×h6 41.♗d3+ ♔g7 42.♕×e5+ ♕f6 43.♕c7++− **1-0** In this hopeless position, Black overstepped the time limit.

Savielly Tartakower wrote, in his report on this event: "This match, the winner of which was neither Levenfish, nor Botvinnik, but the whole world of chess, had, in these 13 games, a wealth of exceptionally valuable strategic and technical directions."

Leiden Match-Tournament, 1970, April 18-May 8, This was Botvinnik's last appearance in chess events. The match-tournament was held on the occasion of the 75th anniversary of the Leiden chess club, and was played in four rounds. It included world champion Boris Spassky, the President of the peace conference, Bent Larsen, the champion of Holland, Jan-Hein Donner, and the former world champion, Mikhail Botvinnik. Spassky won the first prize (7/12), going through the entire tournament without a loss; Donner was one point behind; and

Botvinnik and Larsen divided third and fourth places (5½). Victory in a tense game with his "neighbor" in the crosstable might have served as moral consolation to Botvinnik...

(43) Botvinnik – Larsen
Leiden 1970
King's Indian Defense [E81]

1.c4 g6 2.♘c3 ♗g7 3.d4 d6 4.e4 ♘f6 5.f3 0-0 6.♗e3 a6 7.♕d2 c6 8.♗d3 b5 9.♘ge2 ♘bd7 10.0-0 ♖b8 11.c×b5 a×b5 12.b4 ♘b6 13.a4 b×a4 14.♘×a4 ♘×a4 15.♖×a4 ♗d7 16.♖a5 ♕b6 17.♖b1 ♖fc8 18.♘c3 ♕d8 19.♕a2 ♗e6 20.♕a3 d5 21.e5 ♘d7 22.♘a4 ♗f5 23.♗×f5 g×f5 24.♖a6 24.♗g5? runs into 24...♕×a5 25.b×a5 ♖×b1+ 26.♔f2 e6= **24...♖c7 25.♖c1 ♕c8 26.♖a5 e6 27.♗d2 ♗f8**

28.f4 Closing the c1-h6 diagonal is very committal. 28.♖a1 is more flexible. **28...♔h8 29.♘c5 ♘×c5 30.d×c5 ♕d8 31.♕d3 ♕d7 32.♖ca1 ♖cb7 33.♖a8 ♕c8 34.♖×b8 ♕×b8 35.♕a3 ♔g8 36.♕a4** Botvinnik wants to trade queens in the long run according to his solid style. The alternative, 36.h3!?, to eventually play g2-g4, was also interesting. **36...♕c7 37.♖a3 h6 38.♕a8 ♖b8 39.♕a5 ♕c8 40.♕a6 ♗e7** A very difficult decision. Maybe

Larsen should have kept the queens on with 40...♕c7, as in the endgame, Botvinnik can play on for a very long time with no risk. **41.♕×c8+ ♖×c8 42.♔f2 ♔f8 43.♔f3 h5 44.♔e2**

44...♔g7?! This is probably the wrong wing for the king as White always has trumps on the queenside. So 44...♔e8 45.♖h3 h4 was called for. **45.♗e1 ♔g6 46.♖a7 ♗d8 47.♗c3 h4 48.♔d3 h3?!** This rushes things, but good advice is hard to give, as White can make progress in the long run anyway. **49.g×h3 ♗h4 50.♔e2 ♗d8 51.♔f3 ♗h4 52.♔g2 ♖d8 53.♔f3 ♖c8 54.♔e2 ♗d8 55.♗e1 f6 56.♔f3** The computer prefers the direct. 56.♖d7!? **56...f×e5 57.f×e5 ♖c7**

58.♖a8 White must keep his active rook as 58.♖×c7? ♗×c7 is only drawn.

58...♗g5?! 58...♗e7! was necessary to close White's inroads. **59.♖g8+ ♔h5** 59...♔g7 60.♖c8 ♖a7 61.♖×c6 ♔f7 62.b5 ♖a3+ 63.♔g2 ♖a2+ 64.♔f1 ♖a1 65.♔e2 ♖a2+ 66.♔d3 +− **60.h4 ♗h6 61.♖h8?!** The direct 61.♖e8 wins, e.g., 61...♖a7 62.♖×e6 ♖a3+ 63.♔e2 d4 64.♖d6 ♗f4 65.♗g3 ♗×g3 66.h×g3 ♖×g3 67.♖×c6+− **61...♔g6 62.h5+ ♔g7 63.♖a8 ♗g5?!** 63...♔f7 was better. **64.♖a6 ♖c8?!** 64...♔f7 is much more tenacious, but should also not hold in the long run, e.g., 65.b5 c×b5 66.c6 ♗c1 67.♗a5 ♖c8 68.c7 ♗b2 69.♖d6 ♗×e5 70.♖d7+ ♔f6 71.h6 ♔g6 72.h7 ♗×c7 73.♗×c7 ♖h8 74.♖e7+−; 64...♗c1 65.b5 c×b5 66.♗b4+− **65.b5!** The battering ram breaks through. **65...c×b5 66.♖×e6 ♗c1** 66...♖×c5?! 67.♖g6++− **67.♗b4 d4 68.♖g6+ ♔h7 69.♖d6 ♗b2?!** This loses more or less by force, but Black is lost in any case. **70.♖d7+ ♔g8 71.e6 ♗c3**

72.e7! ♖e8 73.♖d8 ♔f7 74.♖×e8 ♔×e8 75.c6 and Larsen resigned because of **75...♗×b4 76.c7 ♔d7 77.e8♕+ ♔×e8 78.c8♕++− 1-0**

"Thus concluded the final tournament game I won in my chess life," wrote Botvinnik.

Leningrad Tournament, 1938
(August 17-31). The international chess stars, the Dutchman Max Euwe, and the Austrian master Hans Kmoch had to test the level of mastery of the young Soviet masters on the eve of the second Moscow International tournament. In all, twelve chessplayers took part – seven Leningraders, three Muscovites, and 2 foreign guests. The event was held in the luxurious environs of the Philharmonic, which was filled on a daily basis with nearly 2,000 people, with many turned away.

In the first round, Botvinnik demonstrated good competitive form, surprising his opponent Vladimir Alatortsev with a novelty on the 10th move, employing a kingside pawn thrust in the Queen's Gambit.

(44) Botvinnik – Alatortsev
Leningrad 1934
Queen's Gambit Declined [D61]

1.d4 e6 2.c4 d5 3.♘f3 ♗e7 4.♘c3 ♘f6 5.♗g5 0-0 6.e3 a6 7.c×d5 e×d5 8.♗d3 c6 9.♕c2 ♘bd7 "After Black's slightly odd sixth move, the game has transposed into the Carlsbad System, identifiable by the pawn structure which occurs after an early exchange on d5. In the 1930s, conventional wisdom left White with one viable option: castle on the kingside and launch a so-called "minority attack" (two pawns against three) on the queenside with b2-b4-b5, intending to create a weakness on c6 or an isolated pawn on d5. In view of this, Alatortsev was sure that an early a7-a6 would not be a waste of time. However, Botvinnik was looking in a different direction!" (Kasparov in the ChessBase Megabase) **10.g4!?**

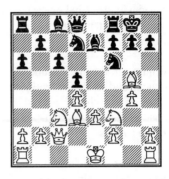

"A shocking blow! No more talk of 'I'll make you a weakness on c6 in ten moves!'" (Kasparov) **10...♘×g4?** 10...♖e8 is more circumspect. **11.♗×h7+ ♔h8 12.♗f4 ♘df6** 12...g6? 13.♗×g6 f×g6 14.♕×g6+− **13.♗d3 ♘h5?** 13...♘e4 14.♘×e4 d×e4 15.♗×e4 ♕a5+ limits the damage. **14.h3 ♘gf6 15.♗e5 ♘g8?!** Too passive and slow. 15...♘d7 16.0-0-0 ♘×e5 17.♘×e5 ♗d6 is more tenacious. **16.0-0-0 ♘h6 17.♖dg1 ♗e6 18.♕e2 ♗f5?!** 18...♘f6 19.♖×g7 ♔×g7 20.♖g1+ ♔h8 21.♘g5 ♖g8 22.♕h5+−; 18...f6 19.♘g5+− **19.♗×f5 ♘×f5 20.♘h4! 1-0**

This game took place on Botvinnik's birthday, when, as praxis showed, he always fought with redoubled energy. (It is enough to recall that on the day of his 25th birthday, he saved a difficult queen ending against Capablanca at Nottingham, while on his 35th birthday, he won a beautiful game at Groningen, against Milan Vidmar). After four rounds, Botvinnik and Euwe had three points, and led the charge in the tournament. The fifth round saw the central game of the event: Botvinnik-Euwe. Botvinnik decided to surprise his opponent by varying his opening repertoire. After 1.d4 in the first round, and 1.c4 in the second, for his game against Euwe he played 1.e4, and continued with the Ruy Lopez. The game continued for 49 tense moves, and ended drawn.

By winning in the sixth round, against Yudovich, and in the seventh, against Chekhover, Botvinnik passed Euwe, who had gained only a half-point from these two rounds.

Botvinnik had competition later from Soviet masters, against whom he drew: in the eighth round, against 42-year old Romanovsky, and in the ninth against the 25-year-old Moscow champion, Ryumin. In the tenth round Botvinnik, unexpectedly for Kmoch, attacked fiercely on the queenside and forced his quick capitulation.

(45) Botvinnik – Kmoch
Leningrad 1934
Caro-Kann Defense [B14]

1.c4 c6 2.e4 d5 3.e×d5 c×d5 4.d4 ♘f6 5.♘c3 ♘c6 6.♗g5 e6 7.c5 ♗e7 8.♗b5 0-0 9.♘f3 ♘e4 10.♗×e7 ♘×e7 11.♖c1 ♘g6 11...b6 is the modern main line. **12.0-0 ♗d7 13.♗d3 f5 14.b4 ♗e8 15.g3 ♖c8 16.♖e1 ♕f6** A bit slow. **17.a3?!** 17.♕e2 a6 18.a4 is quicker. **17...♘e7** The computer suggestion 17...♘h8!? is also interesting. **18.♘e5 ♕h6?!** The start of a misguided plan. 18...♘c6! is almost equal. **19.f3**

Leningrad 1934

		1	2	3	4	5	6	7	8	9	10	11	12	Total
1	Botvinnik	*	½	½	1	½	½	1	1	1	0	½	1	7½
2	Riumin	½	*	½	1	½	1	0	½	½	1	½	1	7
3	Romanovsky	½	½	*	0	½	½	1	1	½	1	½	1	7
4	Rabinovich	0	0	1	*	½	1	½	½	1	½	1	½	6½
5	Kan	½	½	½	½	*	0	1	½	½	1	½	½	6
6	Euwe	½	0	½	0	1	*	½	½	½	½	½	1	5½
7	Kmoch	0	1	0	½	0	½	*	1	0	1	1	0	5
8	Yudovich	0	½	0	½	½	½	0	*	1	½	½	1	5
9	Alatortsev	0	½	½	0	½	½	1	0	*	½	1	0	4½
10	Lisitsin	1	0	0	½	0	½	0	½	½	*	½	1	4½
11	Levenfish	½	½	½	0	½	½	0	½	0	½	*	½	4
12	Chekhover	0	0	0	½	½	0	1	0	1	0	½	*	3½

19...♘f2?! This sacrifice on an empty square in the end just wastes time. 19...♗h5! is the right move. **20.♕e2** 20.♔xf2? ♕xh2+ 21.♔e3 f4+ 22.gxf4 ♕xf4+ 23.♔f2 ♕h2± **20...♘h3+ 21.♔g2 g5?** Black is too slow as White will invade on the queenside very quickly. 21...♖f6 22.♕e3 (22.♘b5 ♘g6) 22...f4 limits the damage. **22.♘b5! ♗xb5 23.♗xb5 ♖f6 24.♗d7 ♖d8 25.b5 ♕h5 26.c6 ♖h6 27.♔h1 1-0**

In his last game of the tournament, Botvinnik drew with Ryumin. The final standings: 1. Botvinnik – 7½ points; 2-3. Romanovsky and Ryumin – 7; 4. Rabinovich – 6½; 5. Kan – 6; 6. Euwe – 5½. What affected Max Euwe's result was a leg injury he suffered while he was swimming.

In the foreword to the game collection, *Masters' Tournament, with Euwe and Kmoch Participating* (1935), chess journalist I. Golubev wrote: "The triumph of Botvinnik in the tournament was hardly expected by anyone. The illness of the USSR champion, which cast his very participation in doubt, could not have aided his success. But, what Soviet toughness! Botvinnik finished the tournament brilliantly and once again (for the eighth time in a row!) took first place.

"What is it that most characterizes Botvinnik's creative output? Above all, he is a sober analyst, with a healthy dose of tactics. He has studied his own play, as an old worker does his machine. More than this: he also studies the works of his opponents, discovering their weak points and making clever use of them. You will not surprise Botvinnik with an opening novelty. On the contrary, he has worked up a whole series of opening variations himself. Botvinnik's steady triumphs are the fruit of ceaseless work. Endurance, and the will to win are the vital characteristics of the tournament fighter, and these are clearly illustrated by Botvinnik. In this tournament, they also helped him to score a number of wins. The accumulation of small advantages (e.g., the game with Rabinovich) and realizing them for the win; a stout defense (with Yudovich and Chekhover) gave him more than one point. Botvinnik's victory says, once again, that in him, the Soviet Union has a world-class chessplayer."

Leningrad Championships, 1926, 1930/31, 1932 Botvinnik, in three of the finals of his native city, scored 31½ points out of 37 games (+27 -2 =9, 85.1%). At the first one, he shared second/third places; he won the last two outright.

1926, June 2-July 9 The young debutant began the tournament, on the eve of his 15th birthday, most auspiciously: 5/5. However, at the end, he nevertheless handed over the victory to the experienced 32-year-old master Ilyin-Zhenevsky, who took 7½/9. Botvinnik and the 35-year-old master I. Rabinovich shared second/third places with seven points. His performance in this tournament placed Botvinnik in the city team for its match with the Stockholm team (cf. *His Youth and Teen Years*).

1930/31, December 3-March 23 Among the 18 players in the next Leningrad championship, one-third of them were masters – Botvinnik, Romanovsky, Kubbel, Model, Wilner, and Ragozin. The games started rather late – at 6:45pm; and went till 11:45pm. The time-control was 2½ hours for 37 moves. From the start, Alatortsev took the lead, with 4½/5. Later, however, he started to play unevenly, winning some and losing some, and ended up in third place, with 11 points, behind Romanovsky, with 11½ points, and Botvinnik, who scored 14 points! Botvinnik played the entire tournament confidently, demonstrating his superiority. For instance, in his sharp encounter with the uncompromising Alatortsev, Botvinnik defended himself brilliantly, and then went over to the counterattack. The outcome of this encounter was decided by an unexpectedly lengthy queen maneuver (d8-a8-h1).

(46) Alatortsev – Botvinnik
Leningrad 1930
Nimzo-Indian Defense [E21]

1.d4 ♘f6 2.c4 e6 3.♘c3 ♗b4 4.♘f3 b6 5.♕b3 ♗×c3+ 6.♕×c3 ♗b7 7.g3 d6 8.♗g2 ♘bd7 9.0-0 0-0 10.b3 a5 11.♗b2 ♖b8 12.♘d2 12.♗h3!? 12...♗×g2 13.♔×g2 ♕e7 14.e4 e5 15.f4 ♖fe8 16.♖ae1 ♖bd8?! 17.h3?! ♔h8?! 17...e×d4 18.♕×d4 ♘c5 19.♖e2 ♕d7 20.♖fe1 b5 is more in the spirit of the position.

18.d×e5? The wrong capture, as Black's gets too much counterplay in the center. After 18.f×e5 d×e5 19.d5, White's space advantage gives him the upper hand. **18...d×e5 19.♘f3 e×f4** 19...♘c5= is the alternative. **20.e5 ♘h5 21.g4 ♘g3 22.e6 f×e6 23.♖×e6 ♕f8** 23...♕×e6?? 24.♕×g7#. **24.♘g5 ♘×f1 25.♕c2?** The wrong square as it exposes the queen. 25.♕d3! draws, e.g., 25...♘f6 26.♖×e8 ♖×e8 27.♗×f6 ♘e3+ 28.♔f3 ♕g8 29.♕d7 ♖f8 30.♗e7 ♖a8 31.♗d8 h6 32.♘f7+ ♔h7 33.♔×f4 ♘g2+ 34.♔g3 ♘e3 35.♔f4= **25...♘f6 26.♔×f1 26.♖×e8 ♖×e8 27.♗×f6 now runs into 27...♘e3+–+ 26.♖d7 27.♘×h7** 27.♖×f6 g×f6–+ **27...♘×h7 28.♖h6 ♕g8 29.g5 ♖e6 30.g6 ♕a8 31.♖×h7+ ♔g8 32.♔f2 ♕h1 0-1**

September 1932 The organizers took pains to ensure conditions for the participants' creativity. The spacious halls of the Leningrad Central House of Physical Culture, where the games were played, were muffled by the quieting rustle of curtains. Demonstration boards stood in the foyer, where the games were displayed and commented upon. 200 to 300 chess aficionados visited the event daily. 12 of the city's strongest players took part in the tournament; among them were Botvinnik, the third place winner Alatortsev, and masters Rabinovich, Ilyin-Zhenevsky, and Ragozin. Botvinnik once again performed confidently, and did not lose a single game. He scored 9/11 games, and placed 2½ points ahead of second-place finisher Alatortsev.

(47) Chekhover – Botvinnik
Leningrad 1932
Queen's Indian Defense [E18]

1.d4 ♘f6 2.c4 e6 3.♘f3 b6 4.g3 ♗b7 5.♗g2 ♗e7 6.0-0 0-0 7.♘c3

d5 8.c×d5 e×d5 9.♗f4 ♘bd7
10.♘b5 10.♖c1 is the modern main
line. 10...♘e8 11.♖c1 c6 12.♘c3
♘d6 13.♕c2 f5 14.♗h3 14.h4!?
14...g6 15.♖fd1 ♘f7 16.♗g2

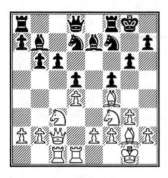

16...g5!? Botvinnik starts his
counterplay on the kingside. 17.♗d2
♘d6 18.♘e1 ♗f6 19.e3 ♕e7
20.♘d3 ♘e4 21.♗e1 ♖ac8
22.♕b3 ♖fe8 23.♗h3 g4 23...♘d6!?
24.♗g2 ♘f8

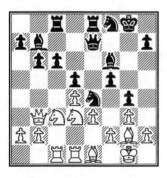

25.♘f4? 25.♘×e4 f×e4 26.♗b4 ♕f7
27.♗×f8 ♖×f8 28.♘f4 was a better way
to execute White's plan, as the black
knight is very strong in the game
continuation. 25...♘e6 26.♘×e6
♕×e6 27.♘e2 ♗g5 28.♕a3?!
28.♘f4 ♗×f4 29.e×f4 ♗a6 30.f3 limits
the damage. 28...a5 29.♕b3 ♗a6!
30.♘c3 ♖b8 31.♕c2 ♖bc8 32.♘e2
♕f7 33.♘f4 ♗×f4 34.g×f4?

Another mistake. But after 34.e×f4 ♕h5
35.♗c3 (or 35.♗d2 ♗e2 36.♖e1 ♗f3)
35...♖e6 36.♖e1 ♖h6 37.h4 g×h3
38.♗×e4 f×e4 39.♖e3, Black should
still win in the long run. 34...♕h5 and
Chekhover resigned in view of 35.♕b3
♖e6 36.♕×b6 ♗e2 37.♕b7 ♘d6
38.♕d7 ♖h6 39.h3 ♗f3 40.♖×c6 ♖×c6
41.♕×c6 ♗×g2-+ 0-1

Lilienthal, Andor (Andre Arnoldovich,
May 5, 1911, Moscow-May 10, 2010,
Budapest), Hungarian chessplayer,
international grandmaster (1950),
participant in the 1950 candidates'
tournament. In 1913, he went to his
homeland and the city of Budapest, with
his mother. Here, he learned a tailor's
trade. The pastime of chess came to him
at the age of 16, and soon he
demonstrated an uncommon talent for
the game.

By age 19, he was playing in
international tournaments, sharing
fourth/fifth places in Paris 1930, and
then in Teplice (Czechoslovakia), he
scored 9/12, ahead of Pirc, Flohr and
other well-known players. In 1933, he
achieved the best individual result at the
"Tournament of Nations" (on reserve
board, 10/13) and shared second/third
places with Alekhine at Hastings
1933/34. In 1934, he won an
international tournament in Ujpest,
scoring 11/15, ahead of Pirc, Flohr,
Grünfeld, Stahlberg, Vidmar,
Tartakower and others. He shared
second/third places in Budapest,
first/third places in Barcelona. The
following year, he shared fifth/sixth
places with Botvinnik at Hastings,
where he scored a sensational victory,
with a queen sacrifice, against
Capablanca.

Andre Lilienthal

(48) Lilienthal – Capablanca
Hastings 1935
Nimzo-Indian Defense [E24]

1.d4 ♘f6 2.c4 e6 3.♘c3 ♗b4 4.a3 ♗×c3+ 5.b×c3 b6 6.f3 d5 7.♗g5 h6 8.♗h4 ♗a6 9.e4

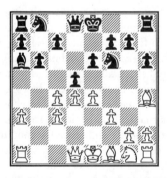

9...♗×c4? Now White's strong center gives him the upper hand. 9...d×e4 10.f×e4 g5 11.♗g3 ♘×e4 is the critical continuation. **10.♗×c4 d×c4 11.♕a4+ ♕d7 12.♕×c4 ♕c6 13.♕d3 ♘bd7 14.♘e2 ♖d8?! 15.0-0 a5?! 16.♕c2** The direct 16.d5!? is even better. **16...♕c4 17.f4 ♖c8 18.f5 e5 19.d×e5 ♕×e4? 19...♘×e5!** limits the damage. **20.e×f6!!** A well

calculated queen sacrifice, as White's far advanced pawn will be a very strong additional trump. **20...♕×c2 21.f×g7 ♖g8 22.♘d4 ♕e4?!** 22...♕d2 23.♖ae1+ ♘e5 24.♖×e5+ ♔d7 25.♖e7+ ♔d6 26.f6 ♔d5 27.♖×f7+– **23.♖ae1 ♘c5 24.♖×e4+ ♘×e4 25.♖e1 ♖×g7 26.♖×e4+ 1-0**

In 1935 and 1936, Lilienthal played in the second and third Moscow International tournaments, where he shared eighth/tenth places, and fourth place, respectively. Commenting on his game with Andre Lilienthal at the 1936 tournament, which earned the first brilliancy prize, Botvinnik wrote: "This was our third encounter. In the first two, at Hastings 1934/35, and in Moscow 1935, I did not find the strongest continuations, and those games ended in draws. This was an appropriate outcome, because the Hungarian's tactical talent and resourcefulness were amazing... In this game, I scored only because the struggle took a positional approach, and my opponent's tactical mastery could not show itself."

Lilienthal made two more successful appearances for the Hungarian team at the "Tournament of Nations" – in 1935 and 1937. In 1939, he went to live in the USSR permanently, as he had gotten married to a Muscovite girl. In 1940, he became Moscow champion, and along with Igor Bondarevsky, won the 12th USSR championship, ahead of Smyslov, Keres, Boleslavsky, and Botvinnik. This victory was to be his highest competitive achievement.

After the championship, Lilienthal, according to Botvinnik, "received the plaudits of all. His style of play was unique. As a rule, modest play at the start of the game, but then he would find his original plans for the middlegame, where he would create more problems for his opponent. I 'suffered' all of this myself. I saved myself more than once, but I also had to endure two heavy losses – at Moscow 1940, and 1941."

Smyslov was of a high opinion about the play of Lilienthal: "As a chessplayer, Andre is distinguished by his amazing intuition and feeling for the position. He is equally dangerous in positional play, as he is in the combinative. His victories over Capablanca and Botvinnik leave a deep artistic impression... His skill as an analyst was of special help to me, when he (along with Vladimir Alatortsev) was my chess trainer."

(49) Lilienthal – Botvinnik
Moscow 1940
Queen's Indian Defense [E19]

1.d4 ♘f6 2.c4 e6 3.♘f3 b6 4.g3 ♗b7 5.♗g2 ♗e7 6.0-0 0-0 7.♘c3 ♘e4 8.♕c2 ♘×c3 9.♕×c3 d6 10.♕c2 f5 11.♘e1 ♘c6?! 11...♗×g2 is the main line and 11...♕c8 the alternative. **12.d5 e×d5 13.c×d5 ♘b4?** 13...♘e5 is more natural. **14.♕d2 a5 15.a3 ♘a6 16.b4 ♗f6 17.♗b2 ♕d7 18.♗×f6 ♖×f6 19.♘d3**

19...a4? Now White is strategically winning as Black has no counterplay. 19...♕b5 is better, but White still keeps his advantage. **20.♖ac1 ♕f7 21.♘f4 ♗c8 22.♖c3 ♗d7 23.♖fc1 h6** 23...g5 24.♘e6+– **24.h4 ♖a7 25.h5 ♖a8 26.♖e3 ♔h7 27.♖cc3 ♖b8 28.♕d3 ♖a8 29.♘g6 ♖×g6 30.h×g6+♔×g6 31.♖e6+!? ♔h7** 31...♗×e6 32.d×e6 ♕×e6 33.♗×a8+– **32.g4 c5 33.b5** The normal 33.♖×d6+– wins as well. **33...♘c7 34.g×f5 ♘×b5 35.f6+ ♔g8 36.♖c4 ♖e8 37.♖g4 g5 38.♖×e8+ ♗×e8 39.♖e4 ♔f8 40.♖e7 ♕g6 41.♗e4 ♕h5** 41...♕×f6 42.♖×e8+ ♔×e8 43.♕×b5+– **42.♗f3 ♕g6 43.♖×e8+ 1-0**

Books: A Life in Chess, Moscow 1969
Bibl: Andre Lilienthal (co-authored w/V. Dvorkovich), Moscow 1989; G. Kasparov, "The Last of the Mohicans" (in *My Great Predecessors*, vol. 4, Moscow 2005)

Matulovic, Milan (b. June 10, 1935, Belgrade), Yugoslav chessplayer, international grandmaster (1965), played in the "Match of the Century" (Belgrade, 1970).

At the age of 24, he achieved his first international success, becoming a prize-winner in the prestigious tournament at Sarajevo (1959; third/fourth places). In 1961, he won three international tournaments (Netanya, Niksic, Skopje) and was awarded the title of International Master.

Twice champion of Yugoslavia (1965 and 1967). As a member of the national team, he participated in five Olympiads (1964-72), where he played 78 games and scored 60 points. Thanks to a series of successes in the second half of the

1960s (he played twice in the interzonal tournaments, in 1967 and 1970, and was a prizewinner, or won outright, in a number of other prestigious events), he was included in the ranks of the world team on eighth board at the "Match of the Century" against the USSR team. Matulovic's opponent was Mikhail Botvinnik, a most uncomfortable opponent for him – Milan had lost all his previous games against him. And he lost in his opening game of the four-round event. However, in the following three games, Matulovic fought hard against the ex-world champion and broke even, though he lost the four-game mini-match (2½-1½). In the third game, he had a "brilliant stalemate" in mid-board!

(50) Matulovic – Botvinnik
Belgrade 1970
Pirc Defense [B08]

1.e4 g6 2.d4 ♗g7 3.♘f3 d6 4.♘c3 ♘f6 5.♗e2 0-0 6.0-0 ♗g4 7.♗g5 ♘c6 8.h3 ♗×f3 9.♗×f3 ♘d7 10.♘e2 h6 11.♗e3 e5 12.c3 ♘b6 13.b3?! 13.d5 ♘e7 14.♕c2 f5 15.c4± **13...d5 14.e×d5 ♘×d5 15.♗×d5 ♕×d5 16.d×e5?!** 16.c4 ♕d6 17.d5 ♘e7 18.♘c3± **16...♕×e5 17.♘d4 ♕d5 18.♕c1 ♔h7 19.♖d1 ♖ad8 20.♕c2 ♖fe8 21.♖d2?!** 21.♘e2= **21...♘×d4 22.♗×d4 ♗×d4 23.♖×d4 ♕e5 24.♖ad1 ♖×d4 25.c×d4 ♕e2 26.♖d2 ♕e1+ 27.♔h2 c6 28.♕c4 ♖e7 29.♖d3 ♔g7 30.♖f3?!** The first step in the wrong direction. 30.♕c5 is necessary. **30...♖d7 31.♕c5 a6 32.♖f4?! ♖d5 33.♕c2?!** (D)

33...♕e6? Botvinnik misses 33...♖×d4! 34.♖×d4 ♕e5+ 35.♔g1 ♕×d4–+ **34.g3 g5 35.♖e4 ♕f6 36.h4** 36.♕b2 to meet 36...c5 with 37.♖e5 is only slightly worse for White.

36...♖×d4 37.h×g5 h×g5 38.♖×d4 ♕×d4 39.♕f5 ♕d5 40.♕c8 c5 41.a4?! 41.♔g1 is better. **♕f6?** 41...b6! 42.a5 b×a5 43.♕×a6 ♕×b3 44.♕×a5 ♕d5 offered very good winning chances.

42.a5 ♕f5 43.♕×b7 ♕×f2+ 44.♔h3 ♕f1+ 45.♔h2 ♕e2+ 46.♔h3 ♕e6+ 47.♔h2 ♕e2+ 48.♔h3 ♔g6 49.♕b6+ ♔h5 50.♕×c5 ♕e6+ 51.♔g2 ♕×b3 52.♕f5 ♕a2+ 53.♔f3 ♕a3+ 54.♔g2 ♕a2+ 55.♔f3 ♕b3+ 56.♔g2 ♕b7+ 57.♔h2 ♕b2+ 58.♔h3 ♔g7 59.♕c5 ♕f6 60.g4+ ♔h6 61.♕b6 ♔g7 62.♔g2 ♕e6 63.♕d4+ f6 64.♕b4 ♕d5+ 65.♔f2 ♔f7 66.♕b6 ♕c4 67.♔g3 ♔e7 68.♔h3 ♕f1+ 69.♔g3 ♕d3+ 70.♔g2 ♕e4+ 71.♔g3 ♕f4+ 72.♔h3 ♕f1+ 73.♔g3 ♕e1+ 74.♔g2 ♕d2+ 75.♔h3 ♕d3+ 76.♔g2 ♕d5+ 77.♔h3 ♕h1+ 78.♔g3 ♕h4+ 79.♔f3 ♕h3+ 80.♔f2 ♕h2+ 81.♔f1 ♕f4+ 82.♔e1 ♕g3+ 83.♔f1 ♕f4+ 84.♔e1 ♕d6 84...♕×g4 85.♕×a6= 85.♕b7+ ♔e6 86.♕b3+ ♔e5 87.♕e3+ ♔d5 88.♕d3+ ♔c5 89.♕a3+ ♔c6 90.♕a4+ ♔d5 91.♕b3+ ♔e4 92.♕c4+ ♔f3 93.♕d3+!? A nice stalemate finish. **½-½**

"What attracts me in chess is the competitive moment, playing to win, for affirmation," was what he said in one

Milan Matulovic

of his interviews. "Chess brings popularity, glory, and travel."

Matulovic considers his greatest creative achievement to have been the following victory over Viktor Korchnoi.

(51) Matulovic-Kortchnoi
Sukhumi 1966
Sicilian Defense [B42]

1.e4 c5 2.♘f3 e6 3.d4 c×d4 4.♘×d4 a6 5.♗d3 ♗c5 6.♘b3 ♗a7 7.♕e2 ♘c6 8.0-0 ♘ge7 9.♗e3 d6 10.c4 0-0 11.♘c3 ♗d7 12.♖fd1 ♕b8 13.♗×a7 ♖×a7 14.♕e3 b6 15.♗e2 ♘c8 16.♘d4 ♖c7 17.♘×c6 ♗×c6 18.a4 a5 19.♖d2 ♖e7 20.f4 ♕b7 21.♗f1 f5 22.e5 d×e5 23.♕×e5 ♕c7 24.♖e1 ♔f7 25.c5 ♖fe8 26.♗c4 ♕×e5 27.♖×e5 ♔f6 28.h4 ♖c7 29.♗a2 ♖ee7 30.♖de2 ♗d7 31.c×b6 ♘×b6 32.♖×a5 ♘c4 33.♖a6 ♔f7 34.♘b5 ♗×b5 35.a×b5 ♖c8 36.b3 1-0

Matches
In all, Botvinnik played 12 matches – seven of them for the world championship. The first was at the age of 23 – against the Czech grandmaster Salo Flohr (6-6), who later obtained Soviet citizenship. He played the last, at the age of 58, against the Yugoslav grandmaster Milan Matulovic (2½-1½), during the historic "Match of the Century." He won five matches, drew four, and lost 3. The game statistics were: 204 games, 51 wins, 47 losses, 106 draws.

Botvinnik became the only world champion in history to play and win two return matches – against Smyslov, in 1958, and Tal, in 1961. By the way, because of the return-match clause, he had to play four matches for the highest title in chess in five years (1957-61). Karpov and Kasparov managed to surpass this record in their famous struggle for the chess Olympus (from 1984 to 1987). It was Botvinnik, himself, who said that "a world championship match takes a year of your life away."

Botvinnik was also successful in the form of struggle called the "match-tournament." He was in three such events: in 1941, in an encounter for the title of Absolute champion of the USSR; in 1948, in the fight for the world championship; and in 1970, in his last tournament in Leiden. In the first two, he scored convincing victories. All seven matches for the world championship took place in Moscow, and twice during the course of one match Botvinnik and his opponent moved from Moscow to Leningrad (against Flohr in 1933, and against Levenfish in 1937). The "Match of the Century" took place in Belgrade in 1970.

With his unyielding and uncompromising character, Botvinnik

was a team fighter, a leader and guide, in the highest degree. He led the USSR team in three matches against the USA team (1945-55). In the years from 1954 to 1964, Botvinnik played in all six Olympiads (four times on board one, and twice on board two). In 1970, the confident play of the veteran of the Soviet team against Matulovic was one of the main links in the victory of the USSR team in the "Match of the Century" (cf. *Olympiads, Team Events*).

In the spring of 1970, Botvinnik wanted to conclude his competitive career with a match against Robert Fischer. The match was supposed to be organized by the chess society of the Dutch city of Leiden to celebrate its 75th anniversary. But Fischer's conditions proved impracticable. Botvinnik wanted to play the match to the best of 16 games, while the American grandmaster wanted it to be played to the first six wins. It looked as though they had finally agreed to play to 18 games, but once again, there followed another caprice from Fischer... The prospect of such an interesting meeting, thus, never took place.

Matches for the World Championship
After taking the title of world champion in the 1948 match-tournament, over the course of twelve years, from 1951 to 1963, Botvinnik had to defend or recover that honorable title seven times, in matches against the finest players in the world: David Bronstein, three times against Vassily Smyslov, twice with Mikhail Tal, and finally, against Tigran Petrosian. All of them were very strong contests of top-class players – candidates for the world championship.

And so this battle epic with these top players elevated Botvinnik's position in world chess. All of his opponents, except for Bronstein, who became a sort of vice-champion, scaled Mt. Olympus of chess as holders of the crown of chess.

Botvinnik – Bronstein, 1951, March 16-May 11 (Moscow, Chaikovsky Hall of Columns). Botvinnik first defended his title of world champion, which he had won three years before in The Hague/Moscow match-tournament. In the candidates' event, the winner was the world's youngest grandmaster, the Muscovite David Bronstein. For the first time in history, the match for the world championship became an "interior matter" for the representatives of a single country. Additionally, it was the first time that the playoff system had been all laid out: Botvinnik had a lot of input in this regard. The world championship was to be contested every three years, regardless of what the world champion himself, or his challenger, might want.

The 1951 match went forward under the new regulations, worked out by FIDE. The players were to play 24 games, with the winner being the one who scored 12½ points. If the final score was 12-12, the world champion would retain his title.

In the previous three decades (1921-51), not one world champion had held on to his title in a match with a challenger (the only exception being Alexander Alekhine, in his contest with Yefim Bogoljubow, who was, however, at that time not the strongest candidate for the world title).

The struggle in this match was very stubborn. At first, the challenger held the initiative, with his brilliant imagination, rich intuition, and delicately tuned psychological nuances of the struggle. However, the world champion showed tenacity and emotional resistance. He responded to his loss in the fifth game with two wins in the sixth and seventh games. In the eleventh game, Bronstein leveled the score, but in the twelfth, he lost again. The ending of the following game is a good example of how tense the struggle was:

(52) Bronstein – Botvinnik
Moscow 1951
French Defense [C100]

1.♘f3 e6 2.g3 d5 3.♗g2 c5 4.0-0 ♘c6 5.d3 g6 6.e4 ♗g7 7.♕e2 ♘ge7 8.e5 ♕c7 9.♖e1 a6 10.c3 ♗d7 11.♘a3 h6 12.♖b1 ♘f5 13.♘c2 ♖c8 14.h4 ♕a5 15.a3 ♕d8 16.♗f4 0-0 17.♘e3 ♘xe3 18.♕xe3 ♔h7 19.♘h2 ♘e7 20.♘g4 ♘g8 21.♕d2 ♗c6 22.d4 cxd4 23.♕xd4 ♗b5 24.b3 a5 25.a4 ♗a6 26.♕d2 ♕e7 27.b4 ♗c4

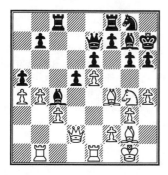

28.bxa5?! 28.♘e3! ♕d7 29.♘xc4 ♖xc4 30.♗f1 ♖c7 31.♗b5 gives White good play on the queenside. **28...♗a6 29.♗f1 ♕c5 30.♗b5 ♕xc3**

31.♕xc3 31.♘h2!? **31...♖xc3** 32.♗xa6 bxa6 33.♖b6 33.♖b7!? **33...♖c4 34.♘h2?!** 34.♖xa6 ♖xa4 35.♘h2= is more precise. **34...♘e7 35.♖xa6 ♘c6 36.♘f3 ♘b4 37.♖b6 ♘d3 38.♖a1 ♘xf4 39.gxf4 ♖xf4 40.♔g2 g5 41.hxg5 hxg5 42.♘xg5+ ♔g6 43.♘f3 ♖g8 44.♖a3 ♗f8 45.♖d3 ♖xa4 46.♔f1 ♖a1+ 47.♔e2 ♖a2+ 48.♖d2 ♖xa5 49.♖b8 ♖h8 50.♘d4 ♗g7 50...♖a3!? 51.♖xh8 ♗xh8 52.f4 ♖a3 53.♖d1 ♖a2+ 54.♔f3 ♖a3+ 55.♔g4 ♗g7 56.♔h4 ♗f8?!** 56...♖a4 is a better practical chance. **57.f5+ exf5 58.♖g1+ ♔h7 59.♘xf5 ♖a6 60.♖g5 ♗h6 61.♖g3 ♖e6 62.♖f3 ♖xe5 63.♘xh6 ♔xh6 64.♖xf7 ♔g6 65.♖f4 ♖f5 66.♔g4 ½-½**

After the 17th game, it was even again; then in the 19th game, the world champion restored the *status quo* and a one-point lead.

Right before the end of the match, in the 21st and 22nd games (cf. *Bronstein*), Botvinnik suffered two misfortunes in a row; but the very next game, he found the strength within himself to strike back. This occurred in the adjourned game, which he analyzed until eight in the morning. Botvinnik exploited the "advantage" of the two bishops over two knights, and scored a victory on the 57th move. Here is the decisive game of the match:

(53) Botvinnik – Bronstein
Moscow 1951
Grünfeld Defense [D71]

1.d4 ♘f6 2.c4 g6 3.g3 c6 4.♗g2 d5 5.cxd5 cxd5 6.♘c3 ♗g7 7.♘h3 ♗xh3 8.♗xh3 ♘c6 9.♗g2 e6 10.e3 0-0 11.♗d2 ♖c8 12.0-0 ♘d7

13.♘e2 ♕b6 14.♗c3 ♖fd8 15.♘f4 ♘f6 16.♕b3 ♘e4 17.♕×b6 a×b6 18.♗e1 ♘a5 19.♘d3 ♗f8 20.f3 ♘d6 21.♗f2 ♗h6 22.♖ac1 ♘ac4 23.♖fe1 ♘a5?! 23...♘f5 is more in the spirit of the position. **24.♔f1 ♗g7 25.g4 ♘c6 26.b3 ♘b5 27.♔e2 ♗f8 28.a4 ♘c7 29.♗g3 ♘a6 30.♗f1 f6 31.♖ed1 ♘a5 32.♖×c8 ♖×c8 33.♖c1** 33.♖b1!? **33...♖×c1 34.♘×c1 ♗a3 35.♔d1 ♗×c1 36.♔×c1 ♘×b3+ 37.♔c2 ♘a5 38.♔c3 ♔f7 39.e4**

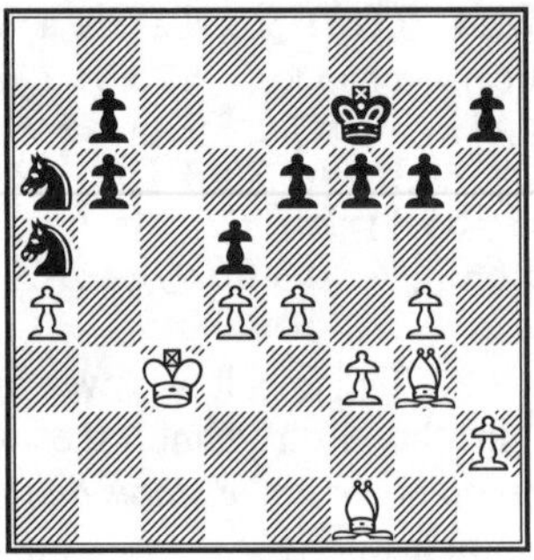

39...f5? This just opens inroads for Botvinnik's bishops. After 39...♘c6, it is more or less equal. **40.g×f5 g×f5 41.♗d3 ♔g6 42.♗d6?!** 42.♗b1 is more precise. **42...♘c6 43.♗b1 ♔f6 44.♗g3!?** This puts Black into *zugzwang*. 44.♗f4?! can be answered by 44...♘e7. **44...f×e4 45.f×e4 h6 46.♗f4 h5 47.e×d5 e×d5 48.h4 ♘ab8 49.♗g5+ ♔f7 50.♗f5** 50.♗d3!? **50...♘a7 51.♗f4 ♘bc6 52.♗d3 ♘c8?** 52...♘e7 (Duncan) is correct. **53.♗e2 ♔g6 54.♗d3+ ♔f6 55.♗e2 ♔g6 56.♗f3 ♘6e7** 56...♘8e7 57.♗c7± (Duncan) **57.♗g5 1-0** and Bronstein resigned. One sample line runs: 57...♘c6 58.♗×d5 ♘d6 59.♗f3 ♔f5 60.♗c1 (Smyslov) 60...b5?! 61.♗×c6 b×c6 62.a5 ♔e6 63.a6 ♘c8 64.♗f4 ♔f5 65.♗h2+– (Zierke, Shirov)

The score was now 11½-11½. The players had one game left to play. On May 11, the Chaikovsky Concert Hall in Moscow was like a fortress under siege. The fans were trying to get into the overflowing hall by hook or by crook.

In this game, Botvinnik was satisfied with a draw, but playing for the draw meant dooming himself to a passive defense, at the risk of finding himself on the verge of defeat. Botvinnik did not know how to play that way; he played to win! Bronstein was also striving for complications, but then "he had met his match!" Botvinnik accepted a pawn sacrifice and defended accurately. After the challenger's position had grown noticeably worse, Botvinnik offered a draw, which was accepted.

The match wound up with the score 12-12 (+5 -5 =14), and the world champion retained his title. This contest emphasized, once again, his unequalled skill as an analyst. As Bronstein acknowledged, "in three out of five games that he won, he triumphed mostly because of his superiority in home analysis."

1951 World Chess Championship

	1	2	3	4	5	6	7	8	9	10	11	12	13	14	15	16	17	18	19	20	21	22	23	24	Total
Bronstein	½	½	½	½	1	0	0	½	½	½	1	0	½	½	½	½	1	½	0	½	1	1	0	½	12
Botvinnik	½	½	½	½	0	1	1	½	½	½	0	1	½	½	½	½	0	½	1	½	0	0	1	½	12

"One should study Botvinnik," wrote the challenger, "to learn how to play inspired chess in the decisive games at the finish, and opening preparation, tournament regime, and the scientific approach to chess." Although Botvinnik's three-year hiatus from chess practice made itself felt – he had been on the verge of losing – on the whole, the match score was well-earned, and the completed match became a notable landmark in the history of chess. In a book, dedicated to this contest and published in England (*The World Chess championship 1951*), its authors, international masters William Winter and Robert Wade, wrote: "In our view, the contest between Botvinnik and Bronstein embodies everything that is good about modern chess, insofar as the game itself, and also insofar as the excellent match organization."

Botvinnik – Smyslov, 1954, March 16-May 12 (Moscow). In his second match for the world championship, as in the next two matches, Botvinnik had to face grandmaster Vassily Smyslov, who had already, starting with 1941, shown himself to be one of the world's strongest players. A year before the match, he had brilliantly won the candidates' tournament in Switzerland, two points ahead of David Bronstein and Paul Keres, who shared second/third places.

The match was played in the same location as the previous match – in the Chaikovsky Concert Hall. Overall, the ebb and flow of the Botvinnik-Smyslov match was approximately reminiscent of the same "swings" as in the match against Bronstein. Except that the amplitude of the rises and falls was a little more engrossing, plus the games

were more decisive. This followed naturally from the difference in the playing style of the candidates, from their temperaments, and their psychological makeup.

In the first four games, the challenger scored only a half-point, while in the seventh through the eleventh games, it was the champion who was stalked by disaster.

In between, there were games that were played excellently by Smyslov – in particular the ninth game, where on the 19th move, he put the crowning touch on his attacking plan with a spectacular queen sacrifice. There were also games notable for Botvinnik's energetic attack, such as, for example, the following double-edged game, which rounded out the first half of the match. He considered it his best game of the match.

(54) Botvinnik – Smyslov
Moscow (m12) 1954
Slav Defense [D18]

1.d4 d5 2.c4 c6 3.♘f3 ♘f6 4.♘c3 d×c4 5.a4 ♗f5 6.e3 e6 7.♗×c4 ♗b4 8.0-0 ♘bd7 9.♘h4 0-0 10.f3 ♗g6 11.e4 e5 12.♘×g6 h×g6 13.♗e3 ♕e7 14.♕e2 14.♘e2 is played more often. **14...e×d4 15.♗×d4 ♗c5 16.♗×c5 ♕×c5+ 17.♔h1 g5 18.g3 ♖ad8 19.♗a2 ♖fe8 20.♖ad1 ♘f8** 20...♕b4!? is more active. **21.♖×d8 ♖×d8 22.e5 ♘d5 23.♘×d5 c×d5 24.♕d2 ♘e6 25.f4 g×f4 26.g×f4 ♕c6?!** 26...♔f8, to meet 27.f5 with 27...♕d4, is favored by the engines. **27.f5 ♘c5?!** The d5-pawn should be protected by 27...♘c7. **28.♕g5 ♖d7?** 28...f6 was forced to limit the damage. **29.♖g1 f6 30.e×f6 ♘e4**

1954 World Chess Championship

	1	2	3	4	5	6	7	8	9	10	11	12	13	14	15	16	17	18	18	20	21	22	23	24	Total
Botvinnik	1	1	½	1	½	½	0	½	0	0	0	1	1	0	1	1	½	½	½	0	½	½	0	½	12
Smyslov	0	0	½	0	½	½	1	½	1	1	1	0	0	1	0	0	½	½	½	1	½	½	1	½	12

31.f7+! The start of a small combination. **31...♖×f7 32.♕d8+ ♚h7 33.♗×d5 ♘f2+ 34.♚g2 ♕f6** 34...♕c2 35.♕h4+ ♚g8 36.♕×f2+– **35.♕×f6 ♖×f6 36.♚×f2 ♖×f5+ 37.♗f3 ♖f4 38.♖g4 1-0** "What a battle of plans – and what consistent play by White! A meaty, modern game (Kasparov)."

By winning the 13th game, Botvinnik forged ahead again. But in the 14th, Smyslov won very nicely and tied the score. Botvinnik won the two succeeding games. At the end, Smyslov just managed to catch his opponent. Not infrequently, however, double-edged play resulted in fighting draws. Such were the conclusions of the 17th, 18th and 19th games.

(55) Botvinnik – Smyslov
Moscow (m18) 1954
King's Indian Defense [E61]

1.d4 ♘f6 2.c4 g6 3.g3 ♗g7 4.♗g2 0-0 5.♘c3 d6 6.e3 ♘bd7 7.♘ge2 a6 8.b3 ♖b8 9.a4 e5 10.♗a3 b6 11.0-0 ♗b7 12.d5 a5 13.e4 ♘c5

14.♕c2 h5 15.♖ae1 h4 16.♗c1 ♗c8 17.♘b5 ♗d7 18.♗g5 h3 19.♗h1 ♗×b5 20.c×b5 ♕d7 21.♗×f6 ♗×f6 22.♘c1 ♗g7 23.♘d3 f5 24.♘×c5 d×c5 25.♗f3 ♕d6 26.g4 26.♚h1!? 26...f4 27.g5 ♚f7 28.♚h1 ♚e7 29.♖g1 ♖h8 30.♖d1 ♖h4 31.♖d3 ♕d7 32.♕e2 ♖bh8?! 32...♕d6 is more precise.

33.♗g4 33.d6+!?, to open inroads on the light squares, was a real alternative, e.g., 33...c×d6 34.♗g4 ♖×g4 35.♖×g4 ♕e6 36.♖d5 ♚d7 37.♖g1 ♗f8 and White increases his edge by 38.b4!? **33...♕d6 34.♕f1 ♗f8 35.♖f3 ♚d8 36.♕d3 ♗e7 37.♗e6 ♖8h5 38.♖×h3 ♖×h3 39.♗×h3 c4** The computer of course prefers 39...♗×g5= **40.b×c4 ♕a3 41.♕×a3 ♗×a3 42.♗f5?** As the resulting rook endgame is just drawn, 42.♗g4 ♖h8 43.h3 offers better practical chances. **42...g×f5 43.g6 ♗f8 44.e×f5 ♗g7 45.f6 ♗×f6 46.g7 ♗×g7 47.♖×g7 f3 48.♖g4 ♖h3 49.♖g3 ♖h4 50.♖×f3 ♖×c4 51.♖a3 ♚d7 52.♚g2 ♚d6 53.♚g3 ♚×d5 54.h3 ♚e6 55.♚f3 ♚f5 56.♚g3 ♚g5 57.♚f3 ♖f4+ 58.♚g3 ½-½**

The contest ended with the score 12-12 (+7 -7 =10), and the world champion held onto his title.

Botvinnik-Smyslov 1957

Three years went by, and once again, Botvinnik was faced with Smyslov at full strength. He had just won the Amsterdam candidates' tournament, and was filled with repressed ambition, and dreaming of finally surmounting the chess Olympus. The first game was already indicative of his excellent competitive form: he won on the 41st move. And although Botvinnik was able to draw two out of the succeeding four games, and even win two of them in a row, his opponent not only did not falter, but won himself, seized the lead, and maintained it until the end.

More than likely, Botvinnik was caught up in a web of evaluations he had made from their previous match, when he explained the sharp vicissitudes in the score by moments of his own weakness, and, for the first time, maybe he underestimated his opponent. In chess, such things are immediately punished. Smyslov prepared himself brilliantly for the contest. Botvinnik did not seem to have an effective answer to 1.e2-e4. The Sicilian and French Defenses he selected led, at best, to draws. Of course, those few victories scored by the world champion were interesting. The following was his third victory, and the last one in this match.

(56) Botvinnik – Smyslov
Moscow (m13) 1957
Nimzo-Indian Defense [E45]

1.c4 ♘f6 2.♘c3 e6 3.d4 ♗b4 4.e3 b6 5.♘ge2 ♗a6 6.a3 ♗×c3+ 7.♘×c3 d5 8.b3 0-0 9.a4 9.♗e2 is the main line. **9...c5 10.♗a3 d×c4 11.b×c4 ♘c6 12.♘b5** 12.d×c5 b×c5 13.♕×d8 ♖f×d8 14.♗×c5 ♘a5 15.♗b4 ♘×c4 16.♗e2 ♖ab8= **12...♗b7 13.♗e2 ♘e4 14.♗f3 ♘g5** 14...♘a5!? 15.♕c2 f5 is the alternative. **15.♗×c6 ♗×c6 16.f3 a6 17.♘c3 f5?!** 17...♕f6 18.0-0 ♖fd8 is much more solid. **18.0-0 ♕f6 19.♕d3 ♖fd8 20.d5 ♘f7 21.e4 e×d5 22.c×d5 ♗d7 23.♗b2 ♘e5 24.♕e2**

24...f4? 24...c4 is more active, as 25.f4?! ♘d3 26.e5 ♕f7 27.e6 can be met by 27...♕e7 28.e×d7 ♕×e2 29.♘×e2 ♘×b2= **25.♘d1 b5 26.♘f2 c4?** White's resulting blockade on the dark squares is very favorable. 26...♕d6 is much more flexible. **27.a×b5 a×b5 28.♕d2 ♖ac8 29.♖fc1 ♖e8 30.♗c3** 30.♖a7!?

1957 World Chess Championship

	1	2	3	4	5	6	7	8	9	10	11	12	13	14	15	16	17	18	19	20	21	22	Total
Smyslov	1	½	½	0	0	1	½	1	½	½	½	1	0	½	½	½	1	½	½	1	½	½	12½
Botvinnik	0	½	½	1	1	0	½	0	½	½	½	0	1	½	½	½	0	½	½	0	½	½	9½

30...♖c7 31.♔h1 ♖b7 32.♖a2 h5?! 33.♖ca1 b4?! Desperation. But good advice is hard to give in any case. 34.♗×b4 ♕b6 35.♗c3 ♕e3 36.♘d1 ♕×d2 37.♖×d2 ♘d3 38.♗d4 ♖eb8 39.♘c3 ♖b3 40.h4 ♖8b7 41.♖a8+ 1-0

This match concluded after 22 games, with the score 12½-9½ (+6 -3 =13) in favor of Smyslov. It is interesting that the number of victories by the two sides is about equal to the number in the Capablanca-Alekhine match. Botvinnik congratulated Smyslov on winning the title of world champion.

Botvinnik – Smyslov, 1958 March 3-May 9 (Moscow, Hotel Sovietskaya, concert/theater hall) The return match was held just one year later – according to the governing rule applicable when the world champion lost that prestigious title. It was a completely different picture in the third match between these two opponents. As Black, Botvinnik chose the Caro-Kann Defense as his weapon against 1.e2-e4. Thus had been the favorite of Capablanca. In the very first game (as well as for the first time in his career), he played this defense.

(57) Smyslov – Botvinnik
Moscow (m1) 1958
Caro-Kann Defense [B11]

1.e4 c6 2.♘c3 d5 3.♘f3 ♗g4 4.h3 ♗×f3 5.♕×f3 ♘f6 6.d3 e6 7.♗e2 ♘bd7 8.♕g3 g6 9.0-0 ♗g7 10.♗f4 ♕b6 11.♖ab1 0-0 11...e5!? 12.♗c7 ♕d4 13.♗f3 e5 14.♗d6?! 14.e×d5 c×d5 15.♘e2 ♕a4 16.c4= 14...♖fe8 15.♗a3 d×e4 16.d×e4 b5 17.♖fd1 ♕b6 18.b3 ♘c5 19.♗c1 ♕c7 19...♘e6!? 20.♗e3 ♘e6 21.a4 a6 22.b4 ♖ad8 23.♗e2 ♕e7 24.a×b5 a×b5 25.♖×d8 ♖×d8 26.♗b6 ♖a8 27.f3 ♖a3 28.♕e1 ♗h6

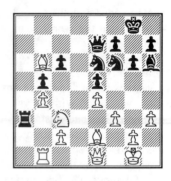

29.♗f1? 29.♗d3 was correct, e.g., 29...♘d4 30.♗c5 ♕c7 31.♖a1 ♗d2 32.♖×a3 ♗×e1 33.♖a8+ ♘e8 34.♖×e8+ ♔g7 35.♗f8+ ♔f6 36.♗e7+ ♔×e7 37.♖×e7 ♔×e7 38.♘a2 and White defends. 29...♘d4! 30.♗c5 ♕e6 31.♗d3 ♘d7 32.♗×d4 e×d4 33.♘e2 ♗e3+ 34.♔h1 ♘e5 35.♕f1 ♕d6 36.f4 ♘×d3 37.c×d3 ♖×d3 38.♕f3 ♖d2 39.♖f1 ♕×b4 40.e5 40.f5 ♕c4 41.f×g6 h×g6-+ 40...♕c4 41.♘g3 ♖c2 42.f5 ♖c1 43.e6 f×e6 44.f×g6 ♖×f1+ 45.♘×f1 h×g6 46.♕f6 b4 47.♔h2 47.♕×g6+ ♔f8 48.♕f6+ ♔e8 49.♕h8+ ♔d7 50.♕g7+ ♔c8 51.♕f8+ ♔b7 52.♕e7+ ♔a6-+ 47...g5 48.♘×e3 d×e3 49.♕×g5+ ♔f7 50.♕×e3 b3

The queen endgame is won as Black's king will always find a hiding place and then the passed b-pawn will decide the day. 51.♕e5 c5 52.♕c7+ ♔g6 53.♕b8 53.♕g3+ ♔f5 54.♕f3+?! ♕f4+ -+ 53...♔f5 54.♕f8+ ♔e4

1958 World Chess Championship

	1	2	3	4	5	6	7	8	9	10	11	12	13	14	15	16	17	18	19	20	21	22	23	Total
Botvinnik	1	1	1	½	0	1	½	½	½	½	0	1	½	1	0	½	½	1	0	½	½	0	½	12½
Smyslov	0	0	0	½	1	0	½	½	½	½	1	0	½	0	1	½	½	0	1	½	½	1	½	10½

**55.♕f6 ♕d5 56.♕f3+ ♔d4
57.♕d1+** After 57.♕f4+ Black's king
escapes with 57...♔d3 58.♕g3+ ♔c2
59.♕f2+ ♔b1 60.♕e1+ ♔b2 61.♕e2+
♔a3 62.♕a6+ ♔b4 63.♕b6+ ♔c3
64.♕a5+ ♔c2−+ **57...♔e5 58.♕e2+
♔d6 59.♕a6+ ♔e7 60.♕a7+ ♔f6
61.♕h7 ♕e5+ 62.♔h1 b2** and in
view of 63.♕h8+ ♔f5 64.g4+ ♔f4
65.♕h6+ ♔g3−+, **0-1**

His opponent was devastated. Smyslov
lost, not only this game, but the next
two games as well.

(58) Botvinnik – Smyslov
Moscow (m2) 1958
King's Indian Defense [E81]

**1.d4 ♘f6 2.c4 g6 3.♘c3 ♗g7 4.e4
d6 5.f3 0-0 6.♗e3 a6 7.♗d3 ♘c6
8.♘ge2 ♖b8 9.a3 ♘d7 10.♗b1
♘a5 11.♗a2 b5 12.c×b5 a×b5
13.b4 ♘c4 14.♗×c4 b×c4 15.0-0
c6 16.♕d2 ♘b6?!** The following
black set-up is too artificial. 16...♘f6 is
more natural. **17.♗h6 ♗×h6
18.♕×h6 f6 19.a4 ♘a8 20.♖fb1 f5
21.♕e3** The direct 21.d5!? is even
stronger. **21...f×e4 22.f×e4 ♘c7
23.d5 c×d5 24.e×d5 ♗b7** 24...♗f5
25.♖b2 e5 26.d×e6 ♘×e6 27.a5±
25.♖f1 ♕d7 26.♕d4?! 26.♕a7!? is
even better. **26...e6 27.d×e6 ♘×e6
28.♕g4 ♖fe8?** 28...♕e7 29.♕×c4
♖×f1+ 30.♖×f1 d5 31.♘×d5 ♗×d5
32.♕×d5 ♖×b4 limits the damage.
29.♘d4! ♕g7 (D)

30.♖ad1? Botvinnik misses the direct
30.♘×e6 ♕×c3 31.♕f4!, when Black has
no real defense, e.g., 31...♗d5 (31...♗f3

32.♖ac1 ♕e5 33.♕×e5 d×e5 34.♖×f3
♖×e6 35.♖×c4+−) 32.♘c7+−
30...♘c7? 30...♘d4 31.♕×d4 ♕×d4+
32.♖×d4 d5 is not completely clear as
Black has counterplay, e.g., 33.b5 ♖e3
34.♘×d5 ♗×d5 35.♖×d5 ♖a3 with
drawing chances. **31.♕f4 ♖e5?**
Mistakes always seem to come in pairs.
31...♕e7 or 31...d5 was better.
32.♘c6!? A small combination to win
the c4-pawn, after which White's passed
pawns will decide the day. **32...♗×c6
33.♕×c4+ d5 34.♕×c6 ♖d8 35.♕b6
♕e7 36.♕d4** 36.b5!? **36...♕d6
37.♖fe1 ♖de8 38.♖×e5 ♖×e5 39.b5
♘e6 40.♕a7 d4?! 41.♘e4** and Black
resigned in view of 41...♖×e4 42.♕a8+
♔f7 43.♕×e4+− **1-0**

In the third game, Botvinnik's "secret
weapon," the Caro-Kann, worked again.
This time Botvinnik, ahead in the
match, did not repeat the mistake he had
made in the first match, and employed
waiting tactics: he played for a draw.
"My opponent would have to play for a
comeback; he would have to lose his
self-control and "slither"; then, [the
important thing is] not to blunder! With

such a fierce opponent as Smyslov was in 1958, this was the only tactic to use," explained Botvinnik later.

Deep, accurate endgame play, a high level of skill in analyzing adjourned games, excellent opening preparation and equanimity – all of this once again distinguished Botvinnik in his brilliant preparation for this new encounter. By the 23rd game, Botvinnik had already secured the victory by the score of 12½-10½ (+7 -5 =11). Thus, for the second time in history, the world champion's title was won back in a return match.

After the match, grandmaster Salo Flohr wrote: "We witnessed a quiet, peaceable Botvinnik, who reminded us of the Botvinnik of 1946-48. Smyslov could not succeed in breaking the resistance of the "old" Botvinnik... The outcome was quite spectacular: on May 9, 1948, Botvinnik became world champion, and on May 9, 1958, he affirmed the title of strongest chessplayer in the world."

After the last match game concluded, Smyslov said: "I felt that I would be playing only against Botvinnik my whole life." And indeed, it was a record, for that time, of two players' opposition to one another for the crown of chess. Previously, no world champion had ever played two matches against the same opponent. We note also that Botvinnik and Smyslov in four years played three matches, 69 games in all. And in 18 years, they had played 91 games! The overall score of those games was 47-44 in favor of Botvinnik.

"I felt that I would be playing only against Botvinnik my whole life," noted Smyslov.

Botvinnik – Tal, 1960 March 11-May 7, Moscow. In accordance with the new regulations for the playoff for the world championship, the person currently holding the crown of chess did not have the moral right to weaken, and to pay no attention to maintaining his creative potential and competitive form. Since every three – or, in the case of a return match, every two years, a challenger would inevitably loom before him, and then he would have to cross swords with him! And so, after his three-round battle against Smyslov, the 48-year old Botvinnik had to face a 23-year-old challenger, Mikhail Tal. Tal's play could not help but impress millions of chess aficionados. In every game, "miracles" were expected of him; and, like an accommodating wizard, he would create these miracles, sometimes "scattering" half his pieces – and would win anyhow.

No one could have predicted the appearance on the chess horizon, after two short years, of such a young and completely unusual chess warrior. And it was only the second time in history – the first was 66 years previously, when Steinitz met Lasker in 1894 – that two opponents who had never previously played each met in a match for the world championship! It was clear that the outcome of their encounter, and even the course of their struggle, would be unpredictable. For the first time, a battle for the world championship was being conducted in a theater – this one named after Pushkin. Both the course of the match, and the character of the battle in it would be distinct from Botvinnik's previous encounters with Bronstein and Smyslov.

Later, in his memoirs, Botvinnik explained the particulars of Tal's play during their first match, which gave the challenger decisive advantages: the creation of such sharp situations in the games, where his pieces would be exceptionally active, and thus give him space to employ his fantasy, the rapid action of his thinking and memory. "I was amazed that my opponent, rather than play "according to the position," would make what appeared to be an illogical move. His logic had a purely practical idea behind it: to set his opponent difficult tasks. We should give Tal his due: when his opponent erred, Tal would find elegant, surprising solutions."

The first game of the match was, in Tal's expression, "transforming." For the challenger won it in the brilliant style so characteristic of him, and

therefore the encounter carried great psychological significance. Tal believed that it would be with exactly this kind of play that he would win the match, and the unpleasant outcome of this game, for Botvinnik, influenced all of his further match tactics. And in spite of his opening erudition (which showed itself, especially in the 8th 17th and 21st games), the depth of his strategic ideas (the 5th, 10th and 12th games), and the excellent way he handled the endgame (the 9th game), on the whole, Tal succeeded in transforming the play into the kind that facilitated his victory.

Both Botvinnik and his opponent called the ninth game among Botvinnik's best in this event. In it, by the eleventh move, White had already launched himself on a dangerous path by sacrificing a piece for two pawns, while Black, by returning a pawn on the 16th move, obtained a sharp, approximately equal position. Then, by trading queens and heavy pieces, Botvinnik transposed into a complex endgame that he played beautifully.

(59) Tal – Botvinnik
Moscow (m9) 1960
Caro-Kann Defense [B18]

1.e4 c6 "The Caro-Kann was Botvinnik's main weapon in three consecutive world championship matches. This resilient defense proved to be very successful in neutralizing Smyslov and Tal's aggressive intentions." (Kasparov) **2.d4 d5 3.♘c3 dxe4 4.♘xe4 ♗f5 5.♘g3 ♗g6 6.♘1e2 ♘f6 7.h4 h6 8.♘f4 ♗h7 9.♗c4 e6 10.0-0 ♗d6**

Game 1 underway

11.♘xe6!? Typical trademark Tal, as in his famous quote: "There are correct sacrifices and then there are mine." **11...fxe6 12.♗xe6 ♕c7 13.♖e1 ♘bd7 14.♗g8+ ♔f8 15.♗xh7 ♖xh7 16.♘f5**

calculation. Botvinnik stood firm in face of this terrible chess twister." (Kasparov) **16...g6! 17.♗xh6+ ♔g8 18.♘xd6 ♕xd6 19.♗g5 ♖e7 20.♕d3 ♔g7**

"The position Tal was heading for. Two pawns is not enough compensation for the sacrificed piece, but if you add permanent problems with the king, the dubious rook on h7, then the practical difficulties of playing this position with Black will become obvious. Such semi-correct sacrifices were a significant element of Tal's phenomenal successes in the late 1950s. His magical energy – and the pressure of the ticking clock – caused his opponents to regularly lose their heads and crack. In Botvinnik's case, Tal was up against an iron character, supported by precise psychological

21.♕g3? "The wrong idea. Tal wanted to prevent a further activation of the black pieces – ♖ae8 would take over the only open file – and to break the especially dangerous trio of queen plus two knights. But the endgame with the mutilated pawn structure offered no chances of escape." (Kasparov) 21.♖xe7+ ♕xe7 22.♗d2 was called for to limit the damage. **21...♖xe1+ 22.♖xe1 ♕xg3 23.fxg3 ♖f8!** "Cutting the white king off from the center." (Kasparov) **24.c4 ♘g4 25.d5?!** "A desperate attempt to remove the blockade. Probably the best option was to stay passive." (Kasparov)

25...c×d5 26.c×d5 ♘df6 27.d6 ♖f7 28.♖c1 ♖d7 29.♖c7 ♔f7 30.♗×f6 ♘×f6 31.♔f2 ♔e6 32.♖×d7 ♔×d7 33.♔f3 ♔×d6 34.♔f4 ♔e6 35.g4 ♘d5+ 36.♔e4 36.♔g5 is met by 36...♔f7 37.h5 ♔g7!–+ (Kasparov) **36...♘f6+ 37.♔f4 ♘d5+ 38.♔e4 ♘b4 39.a3 ♘c6 40.h5 g5**

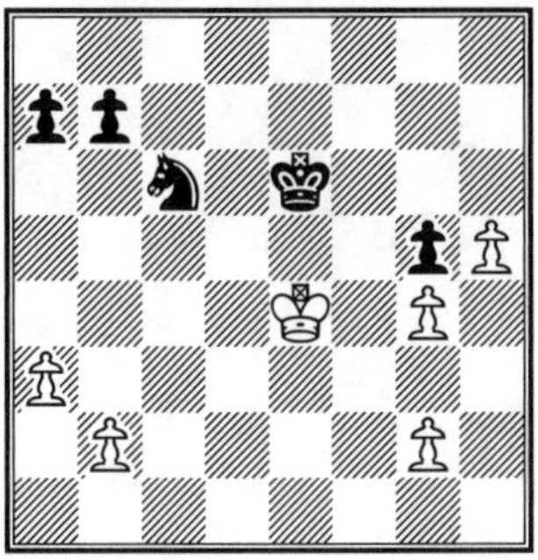

Black will win now as he has pawns on both wings: **41.h6 ♔f6 42.♔d5 ♔g6 43.♔e6 ♘a5 44.a4 ♘b3 45.♔d6 a5 46.♔d5 ♔×h6 47.♔c4 ♘c1 48.♔b5 ♘d3 49.b3 ♘c1 50.♔×a5 ♘×b3+ 51.♔b4 ♘c1 52.♔c3 ♔g6 53.♔c2 ♘e2 54.♔d3 ♘c1+ 55.♔c2 ♘e2 56.♔d3 ♘f4+ 57.♔c4 ♔f6 58.g3 ♘e2 0-1** Now 59.♔b5 would be met by 59...♘×g3 60.♔b6 ♘e4 61.a5 ♘d6. As Tal wrote in his book on the match, "The ninth game was without doubt one of the most interesting of the match, and faultlessly played by Botvinnik."

Botvinnik wrote that, "Although after this game the score was minimally in Tal's favor (5-4, or +3 -2 =4), as the match proceeded, either he was dominant, or I failed to exploit the chances that came my way. Tal won deservedly; in this match, clearly he was much stronger than his opponent."

The upshot was, Botvinnik lost this match after the 21st game by a score of 8½-12½ (+2 -6 =13), and Tal was crowned the eighth world chess champion.

Botvinnik – Tal, 1961 March 15-May 12 (Moscow). The return-match. The event took place at the Variety Theater. Botvinnik's brilliant victory in his first return-match against Smyslov had shaken the whole world of chess: such a practice could extend for many years to come, and not one new champion would be able to "stay" upon his throne the "legal" three years. At the FIDE Congress in Luxembourg (1959), it was decided to do away with the right to a return match with the next three-year cycle – that is, starting with 1963. As the British magazine *Chess* wrote, an "anti-Botvinnik decision" was taken. "Personally, I was glad to hear of this decision," Botvinnik later acknowledged. "How many decades can one live in suspense? So I had no objection to losing the right of a return-match."

But while the rule still existed, Botvinnik was determined to exploit it again. He analyzed in detail all the games of the match he had just finished and concluded that work must be done

1960 World Chess Championship

	1	2	3	4	5	6	7	8	9	10	11	12	13	14	15	16	17	18	19	20	21	Total
Tal	1	½	½	½	½	1	1	½	½	½	1	½	½	½	½	½	1	½	1	½	½	12½
Botvinnik	0	½	½	½	½	0	0	1	1	½	0	½	½	½	½	½	0	½	0	½	½	8½

in two directions: (1) Learn from Tal, and make oneself a good, clever practitioner; and (2) Prepare such openings and associated middlegame plans, so that the struggle would take on a closed character, the board would be split into separate segments, and the pieces be almost immobile. Let your position become, perhaps, a bit inferior to your opponent's – at least, that way, he would have no chance to use his "quick-acting" abilities and memory so effectively.

This would be the fifth world championship match in ten years that the citizens of Moscow would witness. As in all of the previous ones, on one side of the table sat Mikhail Botvinnik, drawn up just as severely as ever – only the hair betrayed a touch of gray.

On the other side was the world champion – the genius Mikhail Tal. But this time, Tal was not in his best physical shape: he was often sick, and could not endure a tense struggle in the fifth hour of play. At the same time, Botvinnik, making use of his own kind of "doping" (he always brought along a thermos of coffee), felt just fine...

But the main reason for Botvinnik's victory was, of course, something different – he had stubbornly prepared himself for the match, studying both the strong and the weak points of his opponent, fleshing out his opening repertoire, and the strategy he would use in transitioning from the opening to the middlegame.

In basketball and soccer there is a saying, "full-court press." when the players of one team literally give their

"Two Mikhails"

opponents no time to look around, and attack them even before they themselves get the ball.

All of Tal's pieces were subjected to an original sort of press, and just could not get space to operate in. In those cases where he was able to do so, Botvinnik would meet him fully armed. The spectators marveled: Botvinnik was giving Tal no ground for combinative complications. After the return-match ended, the chief arbiter, grandmaster Gideon Ståhlberg, wrote: "I think that, for this match, the outcome of the third and seventh games had great significance. And not just because they were won by Botvinnik, but because Botvinnik met Tal's aggressive play with the same sort of thing."

(60) Botvinnik – Tal
Moscow (m7) 1961
Nimzo-Indian Defense [E24]

1.c4 ♘f6 2.♘c3 e6 3.d4 ♗b4 4.a3 ♗×c3+ 5.b×c3 b6 6.f3 ♗a6 7.e4 d5 8.c×d5 ♗×f1 9.♔×f1 e×d5 10.♗g5 10.e5!? **10...h6 11.♕a4+ c6 12.♗h4 d×e4 13.♖e1 g5 14.♗f2 ♕e7**

15.♘e2 b5 16.♕c2 ♕×a3?! This pawn grab is extremely risky. 16...♘bd7 is more natural. **17.h4 g×h4?** This just opens White's attacking roads. 17...g4 keeps the position more closed. **18.♗×h4 ♘bd7 19.♘g3 0-0-0 20.♘×e4**

20...♖he8? 20...♘×e4 21.♕×e4 ♕×c3 22.♗×d8 ♖×d8 23.♖×h6 ♘b8 was the last chance to fight. **21.♔f2 ♘×e4+ 22.f×e4 f6 23.♖a1 ♕e7 24.♖×a7 ♕×e4 25.♕×e4 ♖×e4 26.♖a8+ ♘b8** 26...♔c7 27.♗g3+ +− **27.♗g3 ♔b7 28.♖ha1 ♖c8 29.♖8a7+ ♔b6 30.♗×b8 b4** 30...♖×b8?! 31.♖1a6# **31.♗d6 b×c3 32.♗c5+ ♔b5 33.♖1a4 1-0**

"For the first time in my life, I have been knocked out in the opening!," wrote Tal.

"An excellent game, showing how this match was different from the first. This time, Botvinnik acted much more confidently, not avoiding complexities and the calculation of "dangerous" variations," wrote Kasparov.

The number of games won or lost in this match was unusually high – 71.4%, while in their previous one it was 38%. And Botvinnik won ten of them, which set a record for all previous 24-game title matches.

Botvinnik's defensive play was at the highest level: sharp-witted and stubborn, foresight and accuracy in calculation characterized his play. Thus, an unexpected temporary piece sacrifice to settle the game peacefully in the fourteenth game of the match.

(61) Tal – Botvinnik
Moscow (m14) 1961
Caro-Kann Defense [B12]

1.e4 c6 2.d4 d5 3.e5 ♗f5 4.h4 h5 5.♘e2 e6 6.♘g3 g6 7.♘×f5 g×f5 8.c4 c5?! 8...d×c4 9.♗×c4 ♘d7 is more solid. **9.c×d5?!** 9.♗g5!? is more dangerous. **9...♕×d5 10.♘c3 ♕×d4**

11.♕f3? This sacrifice is typical Tal, but it oversteps the mark. 11.♕×d4 c×d4 12.♘b5 is better and more or less equal.

1961 World Chess Championship

	1	2	3	4	5	6	7	8	9	10	11	12	13	14	15	16	17	18	19	20	21	Total
Botvinnik	1	0	1	½	½	½	1	0	1	1	1	1	0	1	½	1	½	0	1	0	½	1	13
Tal	0	1	0	½	½	½	0	1	0	0	0	1	0	½	0	½	1	0	1	½	0	8

11...♘c6 12.♗b5 ♘ge7 13.♗g5 ♕xe5+ 14.♔f1 ♗h6 14...♕c7!? **15.♖e1 ♕d4 16.♗xe7 ♔xe7 17.♕xf5 ♖ad8?** This allows Tal time to consolidate. 17...♗d2 18.♖e2 ♕d6 19.♕e4 ♗xc3 20.bxc3 ♖ag8 21.♖h3 ♖g4 gives Black a dangerous initiative. **18.♖h3! ♕d2 19.♕xc5+** 19.♕e4!? **19...♕d6 20.♕c4?!** 20.♕f5!? ♘d4 21.♕e4 ♘xb5 22.♘xb5 ♕c5 23.♘c3 ♗d2 24.♖d1 ♕b6 25.♕c2 applies slightly more pressure. **20...♕b4 21.♕e2 ♕g4?!** 21...♗d2 22.♗xc6 bxc6 23.♖d1 ♗xc3 24.bxc3 ♕g4= is more precise. **22.♗xc6 ♕xe2+ 23.♘xe2 bxc6 24.♖a3 ♖d7 25.♖a6?!** 25.♘g3!? **25...♖b8 26.♘g3** With 26.b3!?, White can play on.

26...♖xb2!? This more or less forces the draw. But 26...♗d2 27.♖d1 ♖xb2 28.♘e4 f5 29.♘xd2 ♖bxd2 30.♖xd2 ♖xd2 31.♖xa7+ is also equal. **27.♘f5+ ♔f6 28.♘xh6 ♖dd2 29.♔g1 ♖xf2 30.♖f1 ♖xf1+ 31.♔xf1 ♔g7 32.♖xa7 ♔xh6 33.♖xf7 ½-½**

As Black, Botvinnik showed elegant play in the queen endgame of the 16th game which ended in a draw on the 91st move. And in the 20th game, which was a complex rook endgame in which he was a pawn down, he finally forced a draw on the 122nd (!) move after 14½ hours of play. Such extended struggles

had never before been seen in a match for the world championship.

Overall, Botvinnik won the match by the convincing score of 13-8 (+10 -5 =6), and for the second time won back the respected title of champion in a return match. The chess world rated his fighting qualities very highly, as well as his skill in preparing for a specific opponent, forcing upon him an unpleasant battle strategy. "How many times have we seen in a return-match," wrote grandmaster Alexander Kotov in his article, "Convincing Victory for Chess Logic" (*Match Bulletin*, 12/1961) "how he categorically refused to examine even favorable variations which were fraught with unclear complications. Several times, he would return even extra pawns, if he could avoid stirring up unnecessary aggravation on the board. Botvinnik skillfully forced his opponent into the kind of fight that he liked least, and this skill would be useful for our young chessplayers to learn from the games of this return-match."

Folke Rogard, President of FIDE, in his telegram wrote: "I wish to give world champion Mikhail Botvinnik my congratulations. The entire world of chess is delighted with his notable result, based on strength of mind and self-control, and his high competitive spirit, which again makes Botvinnik a wonderful example for all chessplayers."

At the festive conclusion of the event, Mikhail Botvinnik gave his opponent his due, considering that the chief reason that he lost was his lighthearted approach to this repeat encounter: "I think that Tal did not 'program' himself especially for this match, and that was the basis for his misfortune. The importance of preparation, in my view, is the chief conclusion one may draw from this return match. Nevertheless, one must acknowledge that Tal's appearance on the chess firmament has already played, and no doubt will play, a great role."

At the press-conference dedicated to the results of the event, Botvinnik, considering the possible opponents for a match against him in 1963, in the first place named some of the Soviet grandmasters who took part in the candidates' tournament, and the talented American Fischer and the experienced Yugoslav, Gligoric.

Botvinnik was more forthcoming with one of the authors. Upon meeting the world champion in the lobby of the USSR Central Chess Club, and congratulating him on the victory he had just won, Isaak Linder noted in passing, "Mikhail Moiseevich, is it likely that you will have a match in two years, again with the same opponent?"

"I'm not sure. Look at Petrosian's games. He is very strong. He senses the approach of danger like nobody else, and skillfully wards it off. One may expect great things of him."

These words were, most naturally, not for print. But they were prophetic. Whereas, in the spring of 1958, after he won the return-match with Smyslov, it was still too early to imagine that his next challenger two years hence would be Tal, what he was saying in 1961 was symptomatic. More than that, one could sense in it a certain danger, bordering on an understanding of how

complicated it would be to fight against another opponent for the world crown.

And now, after his brilliant victory in the 1962 candidates' tournament, on the island of Curaçao, Botvinnik's next opponent was to be Tigran Petrosian.

Botvinnik – Petrosian, 1963 March 23-May 20 (Moscow, Variety Theater). Botvinnik won the first game; after a string of draws, and a win for each side, the score was level. In the next game, Petrosian seized the initiative, and held on to it until the end of the match. The world champion wound up with only two wins. Here is the second of these.

(62) Botvinnik – Petrosian
Moscow (m14) 1963
Queen's Gambit Declined [D31]

1.d4 d5 2.c4 e6 3.♘c3 ♗e7 4.cxd5 exd5 5.♗f4 c6 6.e3 ♗f5 7.g4!

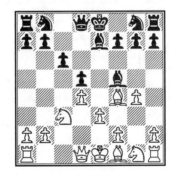

"Botvinnik suddenly causes inconvenience in the black ranks." (Kasparov) **7...♗e6 8.h3 ♘f6 9.♗d3 c5 10.♘f3 ♘c6 11.♔f1 0-0 12.♔g2** "White's accomplishments look small, but in modern chess, to limit the opponent's chances for active counterplay counts for something." (Kasparov) **12...cxd4 13.♘xd4 ♘xd4 14.exd4 ♘d7 15.♕c2 ♘f6**

16.f3 ♖c8 **17.♗e5** ♗d6 **18.♖ae1**
♗×e5 **19.♖×e5** g6 **20.♕f2** ♘d7
21.♖e2 ♘b6 **22.♖he1** ♘c4
23.♗×c4 ♖×c4 **24.♖d2** 24.f4!?
24...♖e8 25.♖e3 a6 **26.b3** ♖c6
27.♘a4 b6 **28.♘b2** a5 **29.♘d3** f6
30.h4 ♗f7 **31.♖×e8+** ♗×e8
32.♕e3 ♗f7 **33.g5** ♗e6 **34.♘f4**
♗f7 **35.♘d3** ♗e6 **36.g×f6** ♕×f6
37.♕g5 ♕×g5+ **38.h×g5** a4?!
38...♖c3 is more circumspect.

39.b×a4 The intermediate move
39.♘e5!? was also interesting, e.g.,
39...♖c3 40.b×a4 ♖a3 41.♖b2 ♖×a4
42.♖×b6 ♗f5 43.♖b8+ ♔g7 44.♖b7+
♔f8 45.♘c6 ♖×a2+ 46.♔g3 ♖c2
47.♖b6 ♗d7 48.♘e5 ♗f5 49.♖b5 and
White can continue to play for a win.
39...♖c4 40.a5 b×a5 41.♘c5 ♗f5
42.♔g3 a4 43.♔f4 a3 44.♔e5 ♖b4
45.♘d3 45.♔×d5? ♖b2= **45...♖b5**
46.♔d6 ♔f7 47.♔c6 ♗×d3?
47...♖b1 gives Black more counterplay.
48.♖×d3 ♖b2 49.♖×a3 ♖g2
50.♔×d5? The very deep 50.♖b3
♖×a2 51.♔d6 ♖a6+ 52.♔e5 ♖a7
53.♖b5 wins according to the computer.
50...♖×g5+ 51.♔c6 h5 52.d5 ♖g2
53.d6 ♖c2+ 54.♔d7 h4 55.f4

55...♖f2? Black does not have time for
this. 55...♔f6! should still draw, e.g.,
56.♖h3 ♖×a2 57.♖×h4 ♔f5= **56.♔c8**
♖×f4 57.♖a7+ 1-0

Among several stirring draws, an
especially notable on was the 11th
match game, where in the adjourned
position, many observers predicted a
win for Botvinnik; but analysis showed
that a drawn outcome to that game was
unavoidable.

(63) Petrosian – Botvinnik
Moscow (m11) 1963
Queen's Gambit Declined [D32]

**1.c4 c5 2.♘f3 ♘f6 3.♘c3 e6 4.e3
d5 5.d4 ♘c6 6.c×d5 e×d5 7.♗b5
♗d6 8.d×c5 ♗×c5 9.0-0 0-0 10.b3
♗e6 11.♗b2 ♕e7 12.♘e2 ♖ac8
13.a3 ♖fd8 14.♘ed4** 14.♘f4!?
14...♗g4 15.♗e2 ♘e4 16.♕d3?!
16.b4 ♗×d4 17.♘×d4 is more natural.
16...♗d6 17.g3 ♘c5 18.♕b1 ♘e4
18...♘×d4!? 19.♗×d4 ♘e4 20.♕b2 f6
was also interesting. **19.♕d3 ♘c5
20.♕d1?!** 20.♘×c6 b×c6 21.♕d4 f5

1963 World Chess Championship

	1	2	3	4	5	6	7	8	9	10	11	12	13	14	15	16	17	18	19	20	21	22	Total
Petrosian	0	½	½	½	1	½	1	½	½	½	½	½	½	½	0	1	½	½	1	1	½	½	12½
Botvinnik	1	½	½	½	0	½	0	½	½	½	½	½	½	½	1	0	½	½	0	0	½	½	9½

22.♕d1= **20...♘e6** The computer prefers 20...♗h3!? 21.♖e1 ♘e4 with good play for Black. **21.♖e1 ♗c5 22.♘×c6 b×c6 23.b4 ♗b6 24.♕a4 ♕e8 25.♖ad1 f6 26.♖d2 ♕h5 27.♕d1 c5 28.♘d4?!** 28.b×c5 ♘×c5 29.♘d4= is more precise. **28...♗×e2 29.♕×e2 ♕×e2 30.♘×e2 ♘g5?!** 30...c×b4 31.a×b4 ♖c4 makes more pressure. **31.♔g2 ♘e4 32.♖dd1 c×b4 33.a×b4 ♖c2** 33...♖c4!? **34.♗d4 ♗×d4 35.♖×d4 ♖b2 36.h4 ♖c8 37.♖×d5 ♖cc2 38.♔f3 ♘d2+ 39.♔g2 ♘e4 40.♔f3 ♘d2+ 41.♔g2 ♘c4 ½-½**

In all, 22 games were played in this match, and with the score 12½-9½ (+5 -2 =15) in Petrosian's favor, it was ended. Explaining the reason for his loss and the transfer of the chess crown to Tigran Petrosian, Botvinnik wrote, "...the new champion is distinguished, in his style, from other grandmasters. It is not easy to accustom oneself to his play. No other chessplayer has ever been like him. If I may say, Petrosian underscores defensive values very highly... And this somewhat unusual manner of play by Petrosian may have knocked me off my feet, deprived me of my famed "creative harmony"... At any event, I played with excessive nervousness and hesitancy."

After this match, the 52-year-old Mikhail Botvinnik decided to end his battle for the world champion's title, and therefore did not enter the next three-year cycle of candidates' events. This was not because of the diminution of his strength – in his next few appearances at the USSR Team championship, he beat the world champion Petrosian, Smyslov and Stein. And at the Dutch tournament, he

beat Larsen. He justified this decision with his disagreement with FIDE over eliminating the return-match clause, and his desire to dedicate himself to researching the problems of creating an electronic chessplaying program. And since in the new candidates cycle the drawing put Botvinnik in a match with Smyslov, he "gave the baton" to the first alternate for that match, grandmaster Yefim Geller.

Match-Tournament for the World Championship, 1948, March 1-May 16 (The Hague/Moscow)

After world champion Alexander Alekhine died in March 1946, the chess throne was vacant. By a decision of The Hague FIDE Congress in 1947, it was decided to hold a match-tournament with the six strongest chessplayers in the world, and designate the winner the world champion. These included Mikhail Botvinnik, Paul Keres and Vassily Smyslov (USSR), Samuel Reshevsky and Reuben Fine (USA), and former world champion Max Euwe (Netherlands). At the last minute, Fine declined his invitation, motivated by the fact that his time was entirely taken up by his chief occupation. It was then decided to hold a five-round tournament for the other five players. The first two rounds would be held at The Hague, the remaining rounds would be in Moscow. Each week, three games would be played. The time-control was 2½ hours for the first 40 moves, and an hour for each 16 moves thereafter. Grandmaster Milan Vidmar of Yugoslavia was designated chief arbiter, and his assistants would be representatives of three countries of the tournament participants.

The Hague/Moscow 1948. Left to right: Paul Keres, Vassily Smyslov, Sam Reshevsky, Max Euwe, Mikhail Botvinnik.

Before the match-tournament began, there was no shortage of predictions. The majority of spectators and chess authorities predicted a victory for Botvinnik. His appearances in recent years had been the most stable. Botvinnik's wins in the postwar tournaments of Hastings 1946, and Moscow 1947 convinced the entire world that it was precisely he who was the most worthy candidate for the top spot in chess. He also enjoyed the best statistics in his previous encounters with his soon-to-be opposition. Botvinnik had won 10, lost 3, and drawn 18 games. His overall percentage in these encounters was 61%, with second and third places shared by Keres and Euwe, at 52%. Thus, Botvinnik started this tournament as the favorite, Euwe with pleasant memories, Smyslov having youth on his side, Keres being in the very flower of his creative abilities, and Reshevsky never doubting his success, as he was considered one

of the strongest chessplayers in the world.

Botvinnik's first game was with Max Euwe. The score of their previous encounters was +2 -0 =4 in Euwe's favor. Having White, Botvinnik was in an aggressive mood. Obtaining a positional advantage, he exploited it for the win, thus, overcoming a psychological barrier.

(64) Botvinnik – Euwe
The Hague/Moscow 1948
Semi-Slav Defense [D46]

1.d4 d5 2.c4 e6 3.♘f3 ♘f6 4.♘c3 c6 5.e3 ♘bd7 6.♗d3 ♗b4 7.a3 ♗a5 8.♕c2 ♕e7 9.♗d2 d×c4 10.♗×c4 e5 11.0-0 0-0 12.♖ae1 12.♗a2!? is the modern main line. **12...♗c7 13.♘e4 ♘×e4 14.♕×e4 a5 15.♗a2 ♘f6 16.♕h4 e4 17.♘e5 ♗×e5?!** 17...♗e6 18.♗b1 ♖fe8 is more natural. **18.d×e5 ♕×e5 19.♗c3 ♕e7 20.f3**

1948 Match-Tournament for the World Chess Championship

		1	2	3	4	5	Total
1	Botvinnik	*****	½½1½½	1½011	11110	1½1½½	14
2	Smyslov	½½0½½	*****	½½1½½	00½1½	11011	11
3	Reshevsky	0½100	½½0½½	*****	1½01½	1½½11	10½
4	Keres	11½0½	11½0½	0½10½	*****	1½111	10½
5	Euwe	0½0½½	00100	0½½00	0½000	*****	4

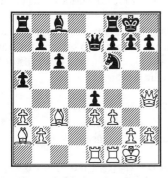

20...♘d5? White's initiative in the resulting ending is very strong. 20...♗e6 21.f×e4 ♗×a2 22.♖×f6 ♖fe8 23.♕g3 ♕f8 24.♖f4 ♖e6 was the lesser evil. **21.♕×e7 ♘×e7 22.f×e4 b6?!** **23.♖d1 ♘g6?!** 23...♗g4 24.♖d6 ♖ae8 is more tenacious. **24.♖d6 ♗a6 25.♖f2 ♗b5 26.e5 ♘e7 27.e4** 27.♖d7!? ♖ae8 28.e6 f6 29.♖fd2 ♔h8 30.♖b7+− **27...c5?!** **28.e6 f6 29.♖×b6 ♗c6?!** **30.♖×c6 ♘×c6 31.e7+ ♖f7 32.♗d5 1-0**

After drawing with Smyslov, Botvinnik next faced Reshevsky. The American grandmaster was subject to a chronic "chess disease" – almost every one of his games ended in fierce time-pressure. Nor did his game with Botvinnik prove an exception. With a good position, Reshevsky fell into deep thought and into time-pressure. Afterwards, he said, "I was proud that the tournament leader was in even greater time-pressure. True,

he played excellently in his time-pressure, and the struggle did not end in my favor."

Botvinnik concluded the first round with a victory over Keres on the 59th move, and became the sole leader. In the second round, he once again beat Euwe and Keres, while against Reshevsky and Smyslov, his games ended in draws. His game against Keres this time lasted just 23 moves, and faced with the threat of mate, his opponent resigned.

(65) Botvinnik – Keres
The Hague/Moscow 1948
Nimzo-Indian Defense [E28]

1.d4 ♘f6 2.c4 e6 3.♘c3 ♗b4 4.e3 0-0 5.a3 ♗×c3+ 6.b×c3 ♖e8 7.♘e2 e5 8.♘g3 d6 9.♗e2 ♘bd7 10.0-0 c5 11.f3 c×d4? Opening the position plays into White's hand. 11...♘f8 is called for. **12.c×d4 ♘b6 13.♗b2** 13.e4!? **13...e×d4 14.e4 ♗e6 15.♖c1 ♖e7?! 16.♕×d4 ♕c7?** Black must try to keep the position more closed with 16...♘a4 **17.c5! d×c5 18.♖×c5 ♕f4?!** **19.♗c1?!** 19.♗b5!+− **19...♕b8?** 19...♖d7! 20.♕a1 ♕d6 21.♗e3± **20.♖g5 ♘bd7** (D)

21.♖×g7+!! A mighty blow. **21...♔×g7 22.♘h5+ ♔g6 23.♕e3 1-0**

In the second round, Botvinnik added 2½ points to his 3½ points from the first round and returned to Moscow with 6/8, leading Reshevsky, in second place, by 1½ points. Keres and Smyslov had just four points each. Former world champion Euwe had had an unfortunate start to the tournament, and was in last place.

Soviet master Pyotr Romanovsky called Botvinnik's victories over Keres and Euwe in the first half of the tournament "a genuine gift to the art of chess." In his article, reviewing the results of the Hague half of the match, Romanovsky wrote, "The content of these victories, and their creative character, speak to the fact that, if Botvinnik can maintain, in the following rounds, his competitive form, the question of the next world champion will have been decided..."

As in The Hague, Botvinnik played his first game in Moscow against Max Euwe. This encounter was interesting, not only in a competitive sense, but also from a theoretical standpoint. Both players were considered experts in the Meran Variation of the Slav Defense, and Botvinnik enjoyed playing it as both White and Black. Later, he recalled that as far back as 1941, he had found the proper plan of play precisely in the system which Euwe unexpectedly chose

for this game. Afterwards, Botvinnik considered it his best game played in the tournament.

And in fact, despite the small amount of material remaining on the board, White skillfully created threats against the black king, which was unable to hide, sacrificed the pride of his position (the centralized knight), and his heavy pieces broke into the enemy camp. Euwe was forced to give up his queen for a rook, but this only put off defeat for a little while.

(66) Botvinnik – Euwe
The Hague/Moscow 1948
Semi-Slav Defense [D49]

1.d4 d5 2.♘f3 ♘f6 3.c4 e6 4.♘c3 c6 5.e3 ♘bd7 6.♗d3 d×c4 7.♗×c4 b5 8.♗d3 a6 9.e4 c5 10.e5 c×d4 11.♘×b5 a×b5 12.e×f6 ♕b6?! 12...g×f6!? is played more often and scores much better. **13.f×g7 ♗×g7 14.0-0 ♘c5** 14...0-0 is the alternative. **15.♗f4 ♗b7 16.♖e1**

16...♖d8? 16...♘×d3 17.♕×d3 ♗×f3 18.♕×f3 0-0 19.♕g4 (Kasparov) with the initiative. **17.♖c1 ♖d5 18.♗e5 ♗×e5** 18...0-0 19.♗×g7 (19.♗×h7+!?) 19...♔×g7 20.♘e5 ♘×d3 21.♕×d3 (Kasparov) is also very dangerous for Black. **19.♖×e5 ♖×e5?** Now Black's king will never be safe. 19...♘xd3 20.♕xd3 ♕d6 21.♖xd5 ♕xd5 22.♕xd4 0-0 to evacuate it was correct. **20.♘xe5 ♘xd3 21.♕xd3 f6?!** 21...♖g8? 22.♕xh7 ♖xg2+ 23.♔f1 +− (Kasparov) **22.♕g3! fxe5 23.♕g7 ♖f8 24.♖c7 ♕xc7** 24...♕d6 25.♖xb7 d3 26.♖a7 ♕d8 27.♕xh7 +− (Kasparov) **25.♕xc7 ♗d5 26.♕xe5 d3 27.♕e3 ♗c4 28.b3 ♖f7 29.f3!** "Botvinnik did not like to waste time calculating variations like 29.bxc4 ♖d7 30.♕xe6+ ♔d8 if there was a crystal-clear route to victory." (Kasparov) 31.♔f1 bxc4 32.♕g8+ ♔e7 33.♕xh7+ ♔d6 34.♕xd7+ ♔xd7 35.h4 c3 36.♔e1 +− 29...♖d7 30.♕d2 e5 31.bxc4 bxc4 32.♔f2 ♕f7 32...c3 33.♕xc3 d2 34.♕c8+ ♔e7 35.♕xd7+ ♔xd7 36.♔e2 +− (Kasparov) **33.♔e3 ♔e6 34.♕b4 ♖c7 35.♔d2 ♖c6 36.a4 1-0**

The following round saw another game played: Smyslov-Botvinnik. (Reshevsky fell ill, and his game with Keres was postponed; Euwe had the bye.) The spectators were understandably disappointed, for many of them supposed that, as in The Hague, the players would go their ways in peace. But already, the opening selected by Botvinnik – the Sicilian Defense – showed that his mood was hardly a peaceful one. In any event, as early as move 23 it was obvious that Black had the upper hand, with the two bishops, an open file, and the attack. Commenting on the further course of battle in this game, Keres wrote, in his book of the tournament: "Botvinnik played very strongly. White's pieces were soon forced on the defensive, while Black's pieces controlled almost the entire board. After losing the exchange, Smyslov's resistance proved useless."

(67) Smyslov – Botvinnik
The Hague/Moscow 1948
Sicilian Defense [B62]

1.e4 c5 2.♘f3 ♘c6 3.d4 cxd4 4.♘xd4 ♘f6 5.♘c3 d6 6.♗g5 e6 7.♗e2 ♗e7 8.0-0 0-0 9.♘db5?! 9.♔h1 is the modern main line. **9...a6 10.♗xf6 gxf6 11.♘d4 ♔h8 12.♔h1 ♖g8 13.f4 ♗d7 14.♗f3 ♖c8 15.♘xc6 bxc6 16.♘e2 d5 17.f5?!** 17.♕d2 ♕c7 18.♖ad1 is more natural. **17...♕c7 18.c4?!** Opening the position like this plays into the hand of Botvinnik's bishops. 18.c3 is favored by the computer. **18...dxc4 19.♕d4 c5 20.♕xc4 ♗d6 21.g3 ♗b5 22.♕c2 exf5 23.exf5 ♖ce8 24.♖f2 ♖e3 25.♗g2?** Now Black pressure on the e-file gets too strong too quickly. 25.♖d1 is a better defense, when White can continue the fight. **25...♕e7 26.♘g1 ♗d3 27.♕d2 c4 28.♖f3 ♖e8 29.♖d1?! ♗c5?!** 29...♖e1 −+ **30.b3?!** Now Black's attack crashes through. 30.♖xe3 ♗xe3 31.♕c3 reduces the potential, but Black should win in the long run anyway. **30...♖e1 31.bxc4 ♗xc4 32.♗f1 ♖xd1 33.♕xd1 ♖d8 34.♕c2 ♗d5 35.♕c3**

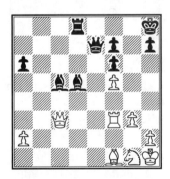

A winning *petite combinaison* follows: **35...♗d4!? 36.♕d3** 36.♕xd4 ♗xf3+ 37.♘xf3 ♖xd4 38.♘xd4 ♕e4+ −+

36...♕e3 37.♕×e3 ♗×e3 38.♗g2
♗×f3 39.♗×f3 ♖d2 40.♘e2 ♖×a2
41.♔g2 0-1

Among the games played in Moscow,
there were three against Reshevsky, of
which Botvinnik lost one and won two.
The last one, played in the fifth round,
was especially noteworthy.

(68) Botvinnik – Reshevsky
The Hague/Moscow 1948
Four Knights' Game [C49]

**1.e4 e5 2.♘f3 ♘c6 3.♘c3 ♘f6
4.♗b5 ♗b4 5.0-0 0-0 6.d3 ♗×c3
7.b×c3 d6 8.♗g5 ♕e7 9.♖e1 ♘d8
10.d4 ♘e6 11.♗c1 ♖d8 12.♗f1**
♘f8?! 12...c5 is the main line. **13.♘h4
♘g4 14.g3 ♕f6 15.f3 ♘h6 16.♗e3
♖e8 17.♕d2?!** 17.♗c4 ♘g6 18.♘g2 is
easier. **17...♘g6 18.♘g2**

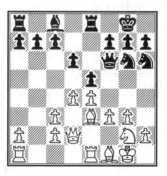

18...♗h3? Now White is just better
because of the bishops and the space
advantage. After 18...♕×f3 19.♗e2 ♕f6
20.♗c4 e×d4 21.c×d4 ♕e7, White is
also better, but things are not that clear.
**19.♗e2 ♗×g2 20.♔×g2 d5 21.e×d5
e×d4 22.c×d4** 22.♗×d4!? ♕d6 23.c4
♘f5 24.♗f2+− **22...♘f5 23.♗f2
♖ed8 24.c4 h5 25.h4 b5 26.♕g5**
26.♖ac1!? **26...♕×g5 27.h×g5 h4
28.♗d3 h×g3 29.♗×g3**

29...♘×d4? Now Botvinnik's bishops
will reign supreme. 29...♘×g3 30.♔×g3
b×c4 31.♗×c4 ♖ab8 was the last chance
to fight. **30.♖ad1 c5 31.d×c6 ♘×c6
32.♗e4 ♖ac8 33.♖×d8+ ♘×d8
34.♗f5!?** ♖a8 34...♖×c4 35.♖e8+
♔h7 36.♖×d8+− **35.♖e8+ ♔h7
36.c×b5 f6 37.♗c7 ♘e6 38.♖×a8
♘×c7 39.♖×a7 ♘×b5 40.♖d7 f×g5
41.a4 1-0**

Botvinnik secured the title of world
champion three rounds before the end of
the event. He won the mini-matches
against all of his opponents, and
outstripped Smyslov, who placed second,
by three full points; the latter played the
third and fourth cycles of the tournament
very powerfully. Third/fourth places
were shared by Keres and Reshevsky.
Euwe was unable to raise himself higher
than fifth place.

It was May 9, 1948. The columns of the
hall of the House of Unions in Moscow
is filled to capacity. The people stand
in the hallways, crowd into the
vestibule, and throng in the streets. The
succeeding games are played in the
match-tournament for the world
championship. The attention of chess-
lovers is fixed on the encounter between
Botvinnik and Euwe. The Soviet
grandmaster has only to draw the game,

Milan Vidmar, the match-tournament's chief arbiter, congratulates Botvinnik on his victory.

when his tournament will be over and the highest of goals attained. A rumble starts in the hall. The chief arbiter of the match goes out to center stage a few times and raises his hands, meaning: "Quiet, please!"

But now Botvinnik and Euwe, exchanging handshakes, have agreed to a draw, and the Dutch grandmaster is the first to congratulate his opponent with the world champion's title.

A little girl bearing flowers scurries onto the stage. It is Vidmar's daughter, who congratulates the new world champion. The chief judge is once again at center stage. He smiles, and raises his hands over his head, but finds it just as hard to stem the hurricane of applause...

After the match-tournament concludes, all of its participants were of the same opinion: Botvinnik fully deserved his victory: he was truly the strongest of chessplayers. Here is the opinion of former world champion Max Euwe:

"Botvinnik showed himself to be a great master, and expert in every phase of the game, not revealing a single weakness. If Botvinnik maintains such competitive form, then he will be very hard to beat; I think that he will prove to be world champion for many years."

At the ceremony celebrating the naming of the new world champion, Alexander Rueb (Netherlands, 1882-1959, one of the founders and the first president of FIDE (1924-49) and honorary president of FIDE (since 1949) said, turning to the newly crowned Mikhail Botvinnik, "Now you enter the ranks of famous persons with a well-deserved triumph and authority, acknowledged by the chess world, united by numerous chess organizations. This world acknowledges your superiority and your right to defend that title."

Match-Tournament for the Title of Absolute Champion of the USSR, 1941 (March 23-April 29). The only such event in the history of national championships. It was a four-round tournament with the participation of the first six prize-winners of the 12th USSR Championship in 1940. The first and second rounds took place in Leningrad; the third and fourth, in Moscow. The participants were Mikhail Botvinnik, Andre Lilienthal, Paul Keres, Igor Bondarevsky, Isaak Boleslavsky, and Vassily Smyslov.

More than a thousand spectators gathered daily in the spacious Uritsky Hall. The hall was radio-equipped, and at the fans' service was the detailed commentary of grandmaster Grigory Levenfish. In the first round, Botvinnik did not have to play (his opponent, Boleslavsky, was ill), and in the second round, he won from Lilienthal. In the third, he met with what the commentator considered his main rival, Paul Keres, who had won his first two games. The *Izvestia* special correspondent wrote: "Botvinnik came to the table, as always, sheathed outwardly in calm. He had White. A variation of the Nimzo-Indian Defense was played, which seemed to have been worked out thoroughly by the players..." Unexpectedly for everyone, the game became the shortest game of the round. Botvinnik employed an improvement on Simagin's opening continuation, and by a violent queenside attack, decided the outcome of the struggle in a mere 22 moves.

(69) Keres – Botvinnik
Leningrad/Moscow 1941
Nimzo-Indian Defense [E35]

1.d4 ♘f6 2.c4 e6 3.♘c3 ♗b4 4.♕c2 d5 5.c×d5 e×d5 6.♗g5 h6 7.♗h4 c5 8.0-0-0? White's king is not safe on the queenside. 8.d×c5 is the main line. **8...♗×c3 9.♕×c3 g5 10.♗g3 c×d4 11.♕×d4?! ♘c6 12.♕a4 ♗f5 13.e3 ♖c8 14.♗d3?!** "The decisive error. 14.♘e2 a6 15. ♕a3! b5 16.♔d2 a5 17.♖c1 ♘e4+ 18.♔d1, with an inferior, but wholly defensible position. Here, it turns out that it is safer to keep the king, not in the corner, but in the center" – Kasparov. **14...♕d7 15.♔b1 ♗×d3+ 16.♖×d3 ♕f5 17.e4 ♘×e4 18.♔a1 0-0 19.♖d1** (D)

19...b5!! The start of Botvinnik's beautiful final attack. **20.♕×b5 ♘d4 21.♕d3** 21.♖×d4 ♖c1# **21...♘c2+**

22.♔b1 ♘b4 and **0-1** in view of 23.♕f3 ♘d2+ 24.♔a1 ♘c2#

Commenting on this encounter many years later, Botvinnik wrote: "I have always been underestimated as an attacking master. Keres clearly also shared this widely held opinion, considering that in sharp situations, my chess shortcomings would be revealed..."

Finally, in the fourth round, Boleslavsky began the tournament, playing his game with Smyslov in his hotel. That day, Botvinnik began his long-suffering game against Bondarevsky. The advantage passed "from hand to hand"; the encounter was adjourned twice, and ended in victory for the player from Rostov-on-Don. This was Botvinnik's only loss in the first half of the tournament.

Then the tournament's chief contender fell victim to a cold, and into second place behind Boleslavsky. Having played ten rounds, the participants took their places on the Leningrad-Moscow train. April 11, in the Union House Hall of Columns, the tournament continued. By this time, the actual position of most of the players was unclear, because of the number of unplayed and unfinished games. The only thing that was clear was that Botvinnik was in the lead: 1. Botvinnik had 6/9, with one unfinished game, in which he had the better position; 2. Keres, 5½/10; 3. Smyslov, 4½/10; 4. Boleslavsky, 3½/7; 5. Lilienthal, 3½/9; and Bondarevsky, 3/7.

In Moscow, Botvinnik methodically increased his lead over his pursuers. As in Leningrad, he lost only one game – this one to Lilienthal. One of the most striking victories in this tournament was the one he achieved in the last round against Bondarevsky. Curiously, once again – as in the game with Keres – Botvinnik had Black, and once again the opening featured the name of Nimzovich – this time, with his variation in the French Defense.

(70) Bondarevsky – Botvinnik C02
Leningrad/Moscow 1941
French Defense [C02]

1.e4 e6 2.d4 d5 3.e5 c5 4.♘f3 ♘c6 5.♗d3?! 5.c3 transposes to the main line. **5...c×d4 6.0-0 ♗c5 7.a3 ♘ge7 8.♘bd2 ♘g6 9.♘b3 ♗b6 10.♖e1 ♗d7 11.g3 f6 12.♗×g6+ h×g6 13.♕d3?! ♔f7** The computer prefers 13...0-0!? **14.h4**

14...♕g8!? The start of an original maneuver to activate Black's queen. **15.♗d2 ♕h7 16.♗b4?** The bishop just hits air. 16.a4 is more in the spirit of the position, but Black is better in any case. **16...g5!?** Botvinnik breaks White's blockade forcefully. **17.♕×h7 ♖×h7 18.e×f6?!** 18.h×g5 f×e5 19.♖×e5 ♖ah8 20.♖ae1 was a better practical chance. **18...g×f6 19.h×g5 e5 20.g×f6 ♔×f6 21.♗d6 ♖e8 21...e4!?–+ 22.♘h4?! ♖g8 23.♔h2 ♗f5 24.♖e2 d3 25.♖d2 d×c2 26.f4 ♗e3 27.♗×e5+ ♘×e5 28.f×e5+ ♔e7 29.♖f1 c1♕ 0-1**

Botvinnik recalled, "Immediately after the game, Ragozin came to me and asked, "Misha, how did the move 29...c2-c1♕ enter your head?"

In the end, Botvinnik won all his matches from his opponents, and, with 13½ points, confidently took first place. Second, with 11 points, was Keres, and Smyslov was in third place, with 10 points. Commenting on this new success of Botvinnik in *Pravda*, grandmaster Alexander Kotov wrote: "Botvinnik's games are distinguished by their clarity of thought, accuracy in carrying out plans, forcefulness in attack, resourcefulness and stubbornness in defense. All sides of the chess struggle, all the stages of the game of chess are developed to the same extent in Botvinnik's play. The Soviet champion knows how to parcel out his strength so that he plays the same at the beginning of the tournament as he does at the end. This is one of the main reasons for Botvinnik's always elevated achievements in chess events.

Botvinnik knows when to play sharply, specifically for the win, and he knows how to accept defeat quietly. And these characteristics of the fighter determine success."

Monte Carlo, 1968 (April 3-17). One of the last tournament appearances by Mikhail Botvinnik. 14 chessplayers took part, 11 international grandmasters among them. The chief struggle for first prize was among five of them: 33-year old Bent Larsen, 24-year old Vlastimil Hort, 30-year old Robert Byrne, and the old rivals, 47-year old Vassily Smyslov and 56-year old Mikhail Botvinnik. Lajos Portisch, who observed his 31st birthday on the second day of the tournament, attempted to give them a run for their money, but suffered a loss in the seventh round to Botvinnik, and was relegated to the crosstable's rear-guard (cf. *Attack*). Botvinnik not only punished his opponents mercilessly for their mistakes – destroying, for example, the Bulgarian grandmaster Nikola Padevsky in 30 moves – but also defended outstandingly as, for example, in his game against the American grandmaster, Pal Benko.

(71) Botvinnik – Padevsky
Monte Carlo 1968
Queen's Indian [E17]

1.♘f3 ♘f6 2.c4 e6 3.g3 d5 4.♗g2 ♗e7 5.0-0 0-0 6.d4 ♘bd7 7.b3 b6 8.♗b2 ♗b7 9.c×d5 e×d5 10.♘c3 ♖e8 11.♘e5 ♗d6 12.f4 ♘e4 13.♘×e4 d×e4 14.e3 ♘f6 15.a3 c5 16.♕e2 c×d4 17.♗×d4 ♕e7 18.b4 a5 19.b5 ♗×e5 20.♗×e5 ♘d7 21.♗d4 ♘c5 22.f5

22...♘d7? 22...f6! keeps the position more closed. **23.f6!** Botvinnik's battering ram drives a wedge into Black's position. **23...♕e6?** 23...♘×f6? 24.♖×f6 g×f6 25.♕g4+ ♔f8 26.♕h4 ♕d6 27.♕h6+ ♔e7 28.♖f1 ♗d5 29.♗h3 ♗e6 30.♗×f6+ ♔d7 31.♕h5+−; 23...♕d6 is forced, but 24.♕g4 g6 25.♕g5 ♔h8 26.♖ac1 is still very good for White. **24.♕h5 ♘e5 25.♖f5 ♘g6** 25...g6 26.♕h6+− **26.f×g7 ♖ad8 27.♕×h7+ 1-0** 27...♔×h7 28.♖h5+ ♔g8 29.♖h8+ ♘×h8 30.g×h8♕#

(72) Benko – Botvinnik
Monte Carlo 1968
English Opening [A26]

1.c4 g6 2.g3 ♗g7 3.♗g2 e5 4.♘c3 ♘e7 5.e4 d6 6.♘ge2 ♘bc6 7.d3 f5 8.♘d5 0-0 9.♗e3 ♗e6 10.♕d2 ♕d7 11.0-0 ♖f7 12.♖ae1 12.♖ac1 is played more often. **12...♖af8 13.f4 f×e4 14.d×e4 ♘c8 15.c5** 15.b3!? is the main line. **15...♗h3 16.b4 ♗×g2 17.♔×g2 e×f4 18.g×f4 ♖e8?!** It is better to challenge White's mighty d5-knight with 18...♘e7 **19.♘g3 h5?** This invites White to attack with the battering ram f4-f5. 19...d×c5 20.b×c5 ♔h8 is more solid. **20.b5?** 20.f5+− is the right way to start White's attack. **20...♘6e7 21.f5 h4 22.f×g6?!** 22.c6! b×c6 23.b×c6 ♕×c6 24.f6 makes more pressure. **22...♖×f1 23.♖×f1 h×g3 24.♖f7 ♗e5! 25.♗d4 ♕g4**

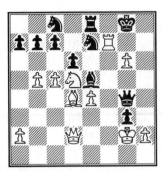

26.♖f4? A miscalculation. 26.♗xe5 gxh2+ 27.♗g3 ♕xe4+ 28.♔xh2 ♕xg6 29.♘xe7+ ♖xe7 30.♖xe7 ♘xe7 31.cxd6= is more or less forced. **26...♕h5 27.♗xe5 ♕xh2+ 28.♔f3 ♕xd2 29.♘f6+ ♔g7 30.♘xe8+ ♔xg6 31.♖f6+ ♔h7 32.♗xg3 ♕d3+ 33.♔f2 ♕xb5 34.cxd6 ♕xe8 0-1**

"The veteran experiences a 'second childhood,'" wrote a magazine, commenting on Botvinnik's play. The outcome of first prize was decided at the finish. Larsen took first place, with 9½ points; Botvinnik was just a half-point behind him, with 9; Hort and Smyslov had 8½ points, Byrne had 8, and in sixth/eighth places were Benko, Gheorghiu, and Portisch, with 7½.

Moscow Championship, 1943/44 (December 5-January 1) Botvinnik played *hors de concours*. In addition, grandmasters Smyslov and Kotov were invited. Through a system of qualifying events, masters Alatortsev, Lisitsyn, Mikenas, Panov, Ravinsky, Ragozin, Tolush and Yudovich were included. In addition, as the newspaper *Vechernaya Moskva* wrote, there were "brought forward young master-candidates, the undergraduate student Averbakh, the woodworker Simagin, Ljublinski the second-class foreman, and other winners of the semi-final tournaments..."

The tournament was held in the Actors' Hall and Officers' Club of the Narcomat of the Wartime Fleet. The chief arbiter of the event was Pyotr Romanovsky. Botvinnik truly outclassed the field. He scored 13½/16, losing only one game (to Smyslov), while drawing three (Alatortsev, Yudovich and Averbakh), winning all the rest. Smyslov finished two points behind him, while Alatortsev and Lisitsyn were 2½ points behind.

(73) Zhivtsov – Botvinnik
Moscow Championship, 1943
Semi-Slav Defense [d44]

1.d4 d5 2.c4 e6 3.♘c3 c6 4.♘f3 ♘f6 5.♗g5 dxc4 6.e4 b5 7.e5 h6 8.♗h4 g5 9.♘xg5 hxg5 "I started to analyze this system with 9...hg after the game Szabo-Euwe, Hastings 1938/39," wrote Botvinnik, "in which White obtained a small advantage: 10. ♗xg5 ♘bd7 11.♕f3 ♗b7 12. ♗e2 ♖g8 13.♗xf6. Later, this same variation occurred in van Scheltinga-Grünfeld (1940), and Black did not achieve anything special after 10...♗e7. Nonetheless, I decided to try all of this out, since I believed in the positional sense of Ernst Grünfeld, the well-known theoretician, although the move 10...♗e7 seemed too passive to me..." **10.♗xg5 ♘bd7 11.♕f3?!** 11.exf6 and 11.g3 are the modern main lines. **11...♗b7 12.exf6 ♕b6 13.♕e3 0-0-0 14.0-0-0 ♕a5 15.♔b1 ♘b6 16.h4 b4 17.♘e4 c5 18.f3?** 18.♗e2 is called for. **18...c3 19.♗e2?** Mistakes always seem to come in pairs. 19.bxc3 bxc3 20.♔a1 ♗d5 21.♕e2 limits the damage. **19...♗d5 20.a3 ♘a4** 20...♗b3 −+ is even better. **21.dxc5 ♗xc5 22.♘xc5 ♘xc5 23.bxc3?** This just opens the way for Black's attack. 23.♖d4 is correct, but Black is for choice after 23...bxa3

24.♕×c3 a2+ 25.♔a1 ♕×c3 26.b×c3 ♘b3+ **23...b×c3 24.♖d3 ♕b6+ 25.♔c1 ♕b2+ 26.♔d1 ♘×d3 27.♗×d3 ♗b3+** and White overstepped the time limit. **0-1**

Later, Botvinnik was able to play the opening this way more than once. He wrote that "My opponents saw my newly prepared opening, and, based upon the usual positional considerations, thought that this system was incorrect, and went willingly into the variations offered, like... moths to a flame!"

Moscow Tournaments, 1935 & 1936

Botvinnik was twice one of the main heroes of a grandiose chess spectacle, the "Moscow International Tournament."

1935, February 15-March 15 The second Moscow International Tournament was held in the spacious halls of the Museum of Fine Arts (today it is called the A. S. Pushkin Museum), In addition to the twelve best Soviet masters, eight foreign grandmasters and masters participated. Among them were former world champions, Emanuel Lasker and José-Raúl Capablanca along with Rudolf Spielmann, Andre Lilienthal, Salo Flohr, and the women's world champion, Vera Menchik.

From the start, Flohr and Botvinnik, recent match opponents, forged ahead. They were pursued by those "perpetual opponents" in the strong international tournaments held in the USSR in the 1920s and 1930s, Lasker and Capablanca. Despite the fierce competition and lively struggle for the top places, immediately after the conclusion of each round, the Soviet participants huddled with the ex-world champions, showing them their games. Both Lasker and Capablanca always enthusiastically took part in those evening analyses and friendly conversations.

In his memoirs, Botvinnik wrote: "After the round, the young participants would usually show their games to Lasker or Capablanca in the restaurant. At the start of the tournament, I won almost all my games, and when my game with Alatortsev ended in a draw, I begged Lasker, 'Where did White miss the win?' Lasker patiently listened to my complaints; finally, he said, 'What – so you must necessarily win every game?'"

Of course, winning every game would be impossible. More so, in that the nine games Botvinnik ended up winning (more than any of the other participants) out of 11 games, turned out to be enough to share first place with Flohr, who, by the way, won two games fewer than he did. The tournament winners each scored 13 points. A half-point behind were Lasker and Capablanca. The former world champions felt that Botvinnik had already attained grandmaster strength, and that he should be awarded that honorable title.

Characterizing this tournament, Capablanca noted that the victory of Flohr and Botvinnik was "wholly deserved, since both played very well. Botvinnik showed greater resourcefulness, and Flohr greater steadiness."

Seven prizes were awarded for the best games of the tournament, of which the first and second prizes were shared equally between Botvinnik, for his

Moscow 1935

		1	2	3	4	5	6	7	8	9	10	11	12	13	14	15	16	17	18	19	20	Total
1	Flohr	*	½	½	½	½	½	½	½	½	1	1	½	½	1	1	1	1	1	½	½	13
2	Botvinnik	½	*	½	½	1	0	1	½	1	1	½	1	½	1	½	0	1	½	1	1	13
3	Lasker	½	½	*	1	½	1	½	½	½	½	½	½	½	1	½	½	½	1	1	1	12½
4	Capablanca	½	½	0	*	½	1	1	½	1	½	½	0	1	½	1	½	½	½	1	1	12
5	Spielmann	½	0	½	½	*	½	½	½	0	1	0	½	1	½	½	½	1	1	1	1	11
6	Kan	½	1	0	0	½	*	½	0	1	0	1	1	½	½	0	1	1	½	½	1	10½
7	Levenfish,	½	0	½	0	½	½	*	½	½	½	0	1	1	½	1	1	1	½	0	1	10½
8	Lilienthal	½	½	½	½	½	1	½	*	0	½	0	1	½	½	½	½	0	1	1	½	10
9	Ragozin	½	0	½	0	1	0	½	1	*	0	½	1	0	½	½	½	1	1	½	1	10
10	Romanovsky	0	0	½	½	0	1	½	½	1	*	1	0	½	½	½	½	1	0	1	1	10
11	Rabinovich	0	½	½	½	1	0	1	1	½	0	*	0	1	½	0	½	0	½	1	1	9½
12	Riumin	½	0	½	1	½	0	0	0	0	1	1	*	0	½	0	1	1	1	½	1	9½
13	Alatortsev	½	½	½	0	0	½	0	½	1	½	0	1	*	0	1	½	½	½	1	1	9½
14	Goglidze	0	0	0	½	½	½	½	½	½	½	½	½	1	*	½	½	0	1	1	1	9½
15	Lisitsin	0	½	½	0	½	1	0	½	½	½	1	1	0	½	*	0	½	½	½	1	9
16	Bohatirchuk	0	1	½	½	½	0	0	½	½	½	½	0	½	½	1	*	½	½	0	½	8
17	Stahlberg	0	0	½	½	0	0	0	1	0	0	1	0	½	1	½	½	*	½	1	1	8
18	Pirc	0	½	0	½	0	½	½	0	0	1	½	0	½	0	½	½	½	*	1	1	7½
19	Chekhover	½	0	0	0	0	½	1	0	½	0	0	½	0	0	½	1	0	0	*	1	5½
20	Menchik	½	0	0	0	0	0	0	½	0	0	0	0	0	0	0	½	0	0	0	*	1½

game against Ryumin, and Lasker, for his game against Capablanca.

(74) Ryumin – Botvinnik
Moscow 1935
Ruy Lopez [C86]

1.e4 e5 2.♘f3 ♘c6 3.♗b5 a6 4.♗a4 ♘f6 5.0–0 ♗e7 6.♕e2 b5 7.♗b3 d6 8.c3 0–0 9.d4 ♗g4 10.♖d1 e×d4 11.c×d4 d5 12.e5 ♘e4 13.h3 ♗h5 14.a4 14.♘c3 is the main line. **14...b4 15.a5 ♔h8 16.g4?! ♗g6 17.♘h2?!** very artificial. 17.♘bd2 is more natural. **17...♗h4 18.♗e3 f5** 18...f6!? **19.f4 ♗g3?!** 19...f×g4!? 20.h×g4 ♗g3 21.f5 ♕h4 22.♘d2 ♗×f5 23.g×f5 ♘f2 forces White to give up the queen with 24.♕×f2 ♗×f2+ 25.♗×f2 ♕g5+ 26.♔h1 ♖×f5, when Black is for choice. **20.g5?!** Too ambitious. 20.♘d2!? is more natural. **20...h6**

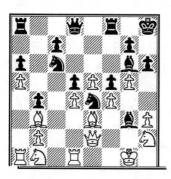

21.g×h6? This opens inroads for Black's attack. The computer prefers 21.h4 ♗×h4 22.♘f3 ♗h5 23.♘bd2 h×g5 24.♕h2 to limit the damage. **21...g×h6 22.♘d2 ♘e7?** The direct 22...♖g8–+ gives Black a strong attack. **23.♔h1 ♕e8 24.♖g1** 24.♕g2!? **24...♗h5 25.♘hf3 ♖g8 26.♘f1?** Disrupting the harmony in White's position. 26.♖g2 with equality was correct. **26...♕f7 27.♗d1 ♖g7 28.♖c1?** 28.♘1d2 was forced.

28...c6? The direct 28...♖ag8 just wins. **29.♖c2?** Now Botvinnik's attack crashes through. 29.♘1d2 was the last chance to fight, albeit for a lost cause. **29...♖ag8 30.♖g2**

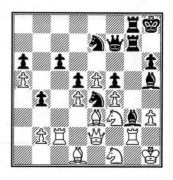

30...♗×f4! The point of Black's attack. **31.♕×a6** 31.♖×g7 ♕×g7 32.♗×f4?! ♗×f3+ 33.♕×f3 ♕g1#. **31...♖×g2 32.♖×g2 ♖×g2 33.♔×g2 ♕g6+ 34.♔h1 ♗×e3 35.♘×e3 ♘f2+ 36.♔h2 ♘×d1 0–1**

1936, May 14-June 8
The third Moscow International Tournament was held in the Hall of Columns of the House of Soviets, featuring five foreign players and an equal number of Soviet players: Lasker, Capablanca, Flohr, Lilienthal, Eliskases, Botvinnik, Levenfish, Rjumin, Ragozin and Kan.

The tournament was a double round-robin. In the foreign press, it was called a " grandmaster tournament," although only Botvinnik held that title among the Soviet masters. But this was essentially true, since all the Soviet players demonstrated a genuinely grandmasterly level of play. The battle for first place, in the main, was between Botvinnik and Capablanca, re-establishing his competitive fighting form and playing excellently throughout. Defeating Botvinnik in their encounter, the Cuban grandmaster amassed 6½ points by the end of the first cycle, and led his closest competitors by 1½ points. The decisive game was played in the seventh round, when the leaders met for the first time, with identical scores of 4/6. Here is what Botvinnik wrote of this memorable encounter: "I obtained a winning position against Capablanca, and on move 28, I could have achieved an overwhelming advantage but I "flew" into time-pressure, and Capablanca punished me, according to all the laws of the art of chess..."

It is interesting, how the outcome of this important encounter influenced Botvinnik. "Upset, I went from here to the Moscow Academic Art Theater for a performance of "The Marriage of Figaro." Androvskaya, Zawadsky and Prudkin were brilliant. I was rolling with laughter; my cares were forgotten. During the entr'acte, behind my back I heard a man's voice saying, "Botvinnik is sitting in front of you." And the answer: "But he lost yesterday – how could he go to the theater?" came from some schoolgirl.

But in the second cycle, Botvinnik played better than anyone, scoring 7/8, beating Flohr, Ragozin, Lasker, Kan and Ryumin.

But even so brilliant a finish only meant that he reduced his distance from the leader by a half-point. Capablanca repeated the result of his first round, and ended up winning the tournament, with 13/18. In fact, this was the first time in his entire tournament career that he

Lasker-Botvinnik – always the game of the round! (Moscow, 1936)

finished ahead of Lasker. Botvinnik took second place with 12 points (+7 -1 =10). Flohr took third place, with 2½ points less. Fourth was Lilienthal, with 9; Ragozin was fifth with 8½; Lasker, sixth with 8; and seventh/tenth were Levenfish, Kan, Ryumin, and Eliskases, with 7½.

For both top prizewinners, Capablanca and Botvinnik, the event was a "prelude" to the next powerful tournament of that year, at Nottingham.

Prizes for the best games were awarded: first to Botvinnik, for the game he won as White against Lilienthal; second to Levenfish, for his win against Flohr; and third to Capablanca, for his win over Lilienthal.

(75) Botvinnik – Lilienthal
Moscow 1936
Queen's Indian Defense [A30]

1.♘f3 ♘f6 2.c4 b6 3.g3 ♗b7 4.♗g2 c5 5.0-0 g6 6.d4 c×d4 7.♘×d4 ♗×g2 8.♚×g2 ♗g7 9.♘c3 0-0 10.e4 ♘c6 11.♗e3 ♕c8 12.b3 ♕b7 13.f3 ♖fd8 14.♖c1 ♖ac8 15.♕d2 a6 16.♖fd1 ♘×d4 17.♗×d4 d6 18.a4 ♘e8 19.♘d5 ♖c6 20.♗×g7 ♘×g7 21.h4 ♖e8 22.♖c3 ♘h5 23.♕d4 A typical centralizing move. The computer prefers the direct attack with 23.g4 ♞g7 (23...♞f6 24.♞xf6+ exf6 25.♖d3 ♖e6 26.♖d5) 24.f4 b5 25.f5 which might be even better.

23...b5? Opening the queenside backfires completely. Retreating the knight with 23...♞g7 is correct. **24.cxb5 axb5 25.♖dc1!** Botvinnik wins the fight for the c-file. **25...♖xc3 26.♖xc3 bxa4 27.♖c7 ♛b5** 27...♛xb3? 28.♞xe7+ ♖xe7 29.♖c8+ ♖e8 30.♖xe8# **28.bxa4 ♛e2+ 29.♛f2 ♛xf2+ 30.♔xf2 e6 31.♞b6 ♞f6 32.a5 ♖b8 33.♖c8+ ♖xc8 34.♞xc8 ♞e8 35.a6 ♞c7 36.a7 ♞a8 37.♞xd6 ♔f8 38.e5 ♔e7 39.♔e3 f6 40.♔f4 h6 41.♞c8+ ♔f7 42.♔e4 ♔g7 43.♔d4 ♞c7 44.♔c5 1-0**

Najdorf, Miguel (April 17, 1910, Warsaw-July 6, 1997, Malaga), Argentine grandmaster (1950). Candidate for the world championship in the 1950s.

Najdorf's original creative talent was developed, starting from his earliest years, under the influence of grandmaster Savielly Tartakower, his first teacher. At 22, he achieved his first major success, drawing two exhibition games with world champion Alexander Alekhine. Three years later, Najdorf won a match from Tartakower (+2 -1 =2) and was included in the Polish team for the "Tournament of Nations" in 1935, 1937 and 1939. During the last of these, which was held in Buenos Aires, the Second World War began, and Najdorf made the decision to remain behind in South America. During the war, Najdorf's entire family died, and he did not return to his native land, becoming one of Argentina's most popular sportsmen. In this, he was aided by his joviality and kindliness, his great talent, and unceasing activity for the benefit of chess. "Miguel el Grande" was what the Argentines began to call their hero. Najdorf was one of the initiators and organizers of the tournaments in Mar del Plata, where he was victorious more than 10 times. In 1947, in the Brazilian city of Saõ Paolo. Miguel set a world record for blindfold play. In 24 hours, he played 45 chessplayers, with the phenomenal score of +39 -2 =4.

Miguel Najdorf

Najdorf was not only the strongest Argentine player (he won the national championship seven times, from the 1950s to the 1970s). After winning a memorable game at the Groningen International, he went on to try to obtain a match with Botvinnik for the highest title.

(76) Najdorf – Botvinnik
Groningen 1946
Nimzo-Indian Defense [E35]

1.d4 e6 2.c4 ♘f6 3.♘c3 ♗b4 4.♕c2 d5 5.c×d5 e×d5 6.a3 ♗×c3+ 7.b×c3 c5 8.♘f3 ♕a5 9.♘d2 ♗d7 10.♘b3 ♕a4 11.♕b2 ♘a6 12.e3 c4 13.♘d2 0-0 14.♗e2 b5?! 14...♗f5 is more active. **15.♗d1 ♕a5 16.♗c2 ♖fe8 17.0-0 ♖ab8 18.♘f3 ♕c7 19.♘e5 ♗e6 20.f3 ♘c5 21.♗d2 ♘a4 22.♕b1 ♖b6 23.♕e1** 23.e4!? **23...♘d7 24.♕h4 ♘f8 25.e4 f6 26.♘g4 ♘g6 27.♕h5 ♕f7?! 28.♖ae1?!** 28.e×d5!? ♗×d5 29.♖fe1 applies more pressure.

28...♖bb8?! 28...d×e4 29.f×e4 ♘e5 30.♕×f7+ ♘×f7 reduces the pressure by exchanges. **29.♘e3 ♘e7?! 30.♕h4 f5?** Black should wait with 30...♘g6 31.♕g3 ♘e7 **31.g4 f4?** Now White's attack wins, but good advice is hard to give. **32.e×d5 ♘g6** 32...♘×d5 33.♕×h7+ ♔f8 34.♘×d5 ♗×d5 35.♗g6+–; 32...f×e3 33.d×e6 ♕×e6 34.♕×h7+ ♔f8 35.♖×e3 ♕g8 36.♕h4

♘b6 37.♖e5 ♘bd5 38.♗g5 ♕f7 39.♗×e7+ ♘×e7 40.♖fe1 +– **33.d×e6 ♖×e6 34.♗×g6 h×g6 35.♘g2 ♖be8 36.♖×e6 ♖×e6 37.♘×f4 ♖f6 38.♕g5 ♘×c3 39.♗×c3 ♖×f4 40.♔g2 1-0**

Early in the 1950s, Najdorf earned the right to play in the candidates' tournaments in Budapest 1950 and Zürich 1953, where he took fifth and sixth/seventh places, respectively. For many years, he showed consistent, high results in the strongest international tournaments. At 52, he won the Capablanca Memorial in Havana, 1962, ahead of Spassky, Smyslov, Polugaevsky, Gligoric, and Ivkov. Among his most memorable victories, Najdorf mentioned his win over Fischer in the 1966 Piatigorsky Cup. At 60, he played in the "Match of the Century" for the world team, drawing his match 2-2 against Mikhail Tal.

(77) Najdorf – Fischer
Santa Monica 1966
Modern Benoni Defense [A72]

1.d4 ♘f6 2.c4 g6 3.♘c3 ♗g7 4.e4 d6 5.♗e2 0-0 6.♗g5 c5 7.d5 e6 8.♘f3 h6 9.♗h4 e×d5 10.c×d5 g5 11.♗g3 b5? Too optimistic. A better way to exploit the weakened light squares in White's camp is 11...♘h5, as Fischer played against Larsen in the 15th round. **12.♘d2 a6 13.0-0 ♖e8 14.♕c2 ♕e7 15.♖ae1 ♘bd7 16.a4 b4 17.♘d1 ♘e5 18.♘e3 ♘g6 19.♘ec4 ♘f4 20.♗×f4 g×f4** (D)

21.e5!! this strong breakthrough opens roads into Black's camp which cannot be closed again. It is quite typical that the decisive breakthrough occurs on squares of the other color complex. **21...d×e5 22.♗f3 ♕f8 23.♘×e5**

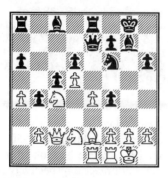

♗b7 24.♘dc4 ♖ad8 25.♘c6 ♖×e1 26.♖×e1 ♖e8 27.♖d1 ♖c8 28.h3 ♘e8?! A better try to muddy the waters is 28...♘xd5 29.♘6a5 ♘e3 30.f×e3 ♗×f3 31.g×f3 f×e3 32.♘×e3 ♗d4 33.♘ac4 ♖e8 but White wins nevertheless. **29.♘6a5 ♖b8 30.♕f5 ♘d6 31.♘×d6** and Fischer resigned in view of 31...♕×d6 32.♘×b7 ♖×b7 33.♕c8+ +− **1-0**

Miguel Najdorf is the author of a string of theoretical discoveries, among them the popular system of development in the Sicilian Defense that opens with 1.e4 c5 2.♘f3 d6 3.d4 cd 4.♘×d4 ♘f6 5.♘c3 a6 6.♗g5 e6 7.f4 ♗e7 8.♕f3 ♕c7 9.0-0-0 ♘bd7 10.g4. This system corresponds quite well with the spirit of the Argentine grandmaster.

Books: Kasparov, G., Don Miguel: Najdorf (from his *My Great Predecessors*, v. 4. Fischer and the Stars of the West, Moscow 2005); Lissowski, T., Mikhachisin, A., Najdorf, M.: *Life and Games*, Leningrad 2005; Najdorf, L.: *Najdorf x Najdorf*, Milford 2016.

Noordwijk, 1965 (February 21-28). The 25th tournament, dedicated to the memory of the untimely death of the

Dutch master Daniel Noteboom (1910-32), for whom Alexander Alekhine forecast a great future. It was also timed for another jubilee − the 70th anniversary of the Leiden Chess Club, located not far from Noordwijk. Among the participants were Botvinnik and Flohr, as well as Larsen (Denmark), Trifunovic (Yugoslavia), Bobotsov (Bulgaria), Donner (Holland), van den Berg, and the champion of Leiden, Kort.

In the very first round, Botvinnik beat Larsen, who had played in the candidates' matches, sacrificing his knight on the 26th move.

(78) Botvinnik – Larsen
Noordwijk 1965
Queen's Gambit Declined [D36]

1.c4 e6 2.♘c3 d5 3.d4 ♘f6 4.c×d5 e×d5 5.♗g5 c6 6.e3 ♗e7 7.♕c2 0-0 8.♗d3 ♘bd7 9.♘ge2 h6 10.♗h4 ♖e8 11.f3 c5 12.0-0 a6 13.♖ad1 b5 14.♗f2 14.d×c5 ♗×c5 15.♘d4 is the alternative, as 15...♖×e3? runs into 16.♘×d5 ♗×d4 7.♗h7+ ♘×h7 18.♖×d4 ♕e8 19.♘c7 ♕e5 20.♖d5 ♖e2 21.♖×e5 ♖×c2 22.♖e8+ ♘df8 23.♘×a8+ − **14...c4 15.♗f5 ♘b6 16.♘g3 ♗f8** 16...♗×f5 17.♘×f5 b4 18.♘e2 ♗f8 was the alternative. **17.a3 ♗b7 18.e4 g6 19.♗h3**

19...a5? Black's queenside counterplay is too slow. 19...♘h7, to meet 20.e5 with 20...♘g5, makes it more difficult for White to develop his play on the kingside. **20.e5 b4 21.♘ce2 ♘h7 22.f4** The battering ram starts advancing. **22...♗c6 23.♖a1 ♗a4 24.♕b1 f5 25.a×b4 a×b4 26.♘×f5!** Botvinnik opens the floodgates. **26...g×f5 27.♗×f5 ♕e7?!** 27...♕c7 is correct. **28.♘g3?** 28.♗g6 ♖eb8 29.f5 +− mobilizes White's forces quicker. **28...♗d7?** Now White's queen can invade quickly. 28...♗b5 offers more resistance. **29.♗×d7 ♘×d7 30.♕g6+ ♕g7 31.♕c6 ♖×a1 32.♖×a1 ♕f7 33.♖a7**

33...♘×e5? The resulting endgame is lost because of White's passed kingside pawns. 33...♘b8! was the last chance to fight as 34.♖×f7? runs into 34...♘×c6 35.♖c7 c3 36.b×c3 b3 and Black is better. **34.d×e5 ♕e6 35.♕×e6+ ♖×e6 36.♘f5** 36.♖c7!? +− is easier. **36...♖c6 37.♔f1 c3 38.b×c3 b×c3 39.♗e3 ♗c5 40.♗×c5 ♖×c5 41.♖a1 ♘f8 42.♔e2 ♘e6 43.g3 h5 44.♔d3 d4 45.♘d6 ♖c7 46.♘e4 ♔h7 47.f5 ♘d8** 47...♘c5+ 48.♘×c5 ♖×c5 49.♔×d4 +− **48.♘f6+ ♔h6 49.♘d5 ♖b7 50.e6 ♘c6 51.♖a6 ♘e5+ 52.♔×d4 1-0** 52...c2 53.e7+ ♔g5 54.e8♕ c1♕ 55.♖g6+ ♔×f5 56.♕e6# **1-0**

In the next round, Botvinnik won from Trifunovic, and climbed into the lead.

(79) Botvinnik – Donner
Noordwijk 1965
Queen's Gambit Declined [D32]

1.c4 ♘f6 2.♘c3 e6 3.♘f3 d5 4.e3 c5 5.c×d5 e×d5 6.d4 ♘c6 7.♗e2 c×d4 8.♘×d4 ♗d6 9.0-0 0-0 10.b3 a6?! 10...♗e5 is the main line. **11.♗b2 ♖e8 12.♖c1 ♗d7 13.♗f3 ♘×d4?!** 13...♕a5 is more natural as Black does not want to exchange pieces. **14.♕×d4 ♗e5 15.♕d2 ♗g4 16.♖fd1** 16.♗×g4!? ♘×g4 17.h3 ♘f6 18.♖fd1 was the alternative. **16...♗×f3 17.g×f3 ♕d7 18.♔g2 ♕f5?!** It was better to get rid of the isolated pawn with 18...d4 19.♘e2 (19.e×d4? ♖ad8 20.♖e1 ♘h5 is dangerous for White) 19...d×e3 20.♕×d7 ♘×d7 21.♗×e5 ♘×e5 22.f×e3 ♖ad8 and the endgame is almost equal. **19.♘e2 ♗×b2 20.♕×b2 ♖ac8 21.♘d4 ♕e5**

22.♖c2!? Botvinnik wins the fight for the c-file in typical fashion. **22...♘d7 23.♖dc1 ♖b8 24.♕c3 ♘f8 25.♕c7 ♕f6 26.♕g3 ♘e6 27.♘×e6 f×e6 28.♖c7 ♖ed8 29.h4 e5 30.♖1c5 h6 31.h5 ♖d6 32.♕g4 d4 33.e×d4 ♖×d4 34.♕g3 ♖f4 35.♖c4?!** 35.♖d5 applies more pressure. **35...♖f8 36.♖×f4 e×f4 37.♕g4 b6 38.♖b7 ♖f7 39.♖×f7**

39...♔×f7? This loses precious time. 39...♕×f7! draws, e.g., 40.♕c8+ ♔h7 41.♕×a6 ♕×h5 42.♕×b6 ♕g5+ 43.♔f1 ♕d5 44.♔e2 ♕e5+ 45.♔d3 h5= **40.♕d7+ ♔g8** 40...♕e7 is met by 41.♕d5+ **41.♕c8+ ♔h7 42.♕×a6 ♕g5+ 43.♔f1 ♕×h5 44.♕d3+ ♔g8?!** 44...♔h8 is more precise, but White is much better in any case. **45.a4 ♕h1+ 46.♔e2 h5 47.♕d5+ ♔h7 48.♕d1! ♕h2?!** 48...♕h3 offers more resistance. Of course not 48...♕×d1+? 49.♔×d1 h4 50.♔e2 h3 51.♔f1 ♔g6 52.b4 ♔f6 53.a5+− **49.b4 h4?!** **50.♕f1!** Now Black's queen is imprisoned. **50...g5 51.a5 b×a5 52.b×a5 g4 53.a6 1-0** in view of 53...g3 54.a7 g2 55.♕b1+ ♔g7 56.a8♕ g1♘+ 57.♔d1 +−

Botvinnik's result: 6/7 (+5 =2) and a confident first place, outdistancing second-place Trifunovic by 1½ points. Third place was taken by the peaceable Flohr – (+1 =6) but what a win – over Larsen!

Nottingham, 1936 (August 10-28) Botvinnik received an invitation to the "tournament of champions" in the spring of 1935. After his success in the second Moscow International tournament of 1935, Krylenko, the president of the All-Union chess section

had no doubts: "He must go!" Following the advice of Emanuel Lasker, who was at that time living in Moscow, Botvinnik and his wife left early, to allow to for acclimatization. For the first time since Hastings 1895, the English had once again managed to gather the world's greatest chessplayers together: the four world champions – Euwe, Alekhine, Capablanca, and Lasker; four young Candidates – Botvinnik, Flohr, Fine and Reshevsky; Bogoljubow, who had played two matches for the world championship; and four "host players" from their own country – Tylor, Alexander, Thomas and Winter.

The atmosphere of the tournament was an unusual one: the inimitable coloration of "good old England" – as was described by the correspondent of the magazine *Shakhmaty v SSSR*, Pyotr Mussuri: "In the evening, after dinner, the players studied the tournament schedule. It was upsetting to them to have to play off adjourned games on the same day. Capablanca conversed peaceably with Tartakower. Alekhine reads the Parisian magazines. Bogoljubow (acknowledging his excessive corpulence, they used to call him "the doubled pawn") plays Vidmar and two others at bridge. Someone asks Bogoljubow why he looks so "poorly." "Don't you know," Vidmar answers for him, "that he escaped from a labor camp?"

First round, a test of strengths. A red curtain separates the spectators from the players. The participants can pass through it. There are about 150 spectators. 150 smoking cigars... Soon, you cannot breathe there. Opocensky,

Nottingham 1936

		1	2	3	4	5	6	7	8	9	10	11	12	13	14	15	Total
1	Capablanca	*	½	½	1	½	1	0	½	1	½	½	1	1	1	1	10
2	Botvinnik	½	*	½	½	½	½	½	½	1	1	1	1	1	1	½	10
3	Fine	½	½	*	½	½	½	½	1	½	½	1	1	1	½	1	9½
4	Reshevsky	0	½	½	*	0	1	½	1	1	½	1	1	1	1	½	9½
5	Euwe	½	½	½	1	*	0	½	0	1	1	½	1	1	1	1	9½
6	Alekhine	0	½	½	0	1	*	1	½	½	1	1	½	1	½	1	9
7	Flohr	1	½	½	½	½	0	*	1	1	½	1	0	0	1	1	8½
8	Lasker	½	½	0	0	1	½	0	*	½	½	1	1	1	1	1	8½
9	Vidmar	0	0	½	0	0	½	0	½	*	½	1	½	1	½	1	6
10	Tartakower	½	0	½	½	0	0	½	½	½	*	½	0	0	1	1	5½
11	Bogoljubow	½	0	0	0	½	0	0	0	0	½	*	1	1	1	1	5½
12	Tylor	0	0	0	0	0	½	1	0	½	1	0	*	½	½	½	4½
13	Alexander	0	0	0	0	0	0	1	0	0	1	0	½	*	½	½	3½
14	Thomas	0	0	½	0	0	½	0	0	½	0	0	½	½	*	½	3
15	Winter	0	½	0	½	0	0	0	0	0	0	0	½	½	½	*	2½

who was once a chess correspondent himself, calms us: "They were specially invited to the launch; tomorrow, they'll be gone."

Botvinnik got off to a good start. In his first game, he won with Black against Alexander in 35 moves, using the Sicilian Defense. In the second round, playing White in a very sharp struggle against Fine, he agreed to the draw after 34 moves; in round three, he again won with Black, against Bogoljubow, in 25 moves!

The only one who had a better start was world champion Max Euwe – 3 points out of 3! In the fourth round, Botvinnik played his best game of the tournament, destroying Savielly Tartakower (cf. *Combinations*). This game was adjudged the most beautiful one of the tournament. For his next encounter, the leader would face Alexander Alekhine himself. Commenting on the first three moves in the "Nottingham" games

collection, Akekhine wrote: "1.e4 c5 2.♘f3 d6 3.d4. Under other circumstances, I should probably have played 3.b4 – a sacrifice for which White, in this concrete situation, would, in my view, have sufficient strategic basis. However, meeting the Soviet champion for the first time over the board, for whose play I have always had the highest opinion, I did not want to be accused of excessive self-regard or unjustified courage (all of this, regardless of the outcome) or such things as "underestimation," "braggadocio," etc."

And here is how Botvinnik remembered this memorable encounter: "In one of the variations of the Sicilian Defense, Alekhine had prepared a very dangerous continuation... Alekhine was a fine psychologist – he knew how important it was to exert a sort of moral pressure on the opponent. So right up to the critical moment, he played with lightning speed, circling the table (and

155

his sacrifice), sitting down only to make his move quickly – he had to convince his opponent that everything had been worked out to the end in the quiet of the study, and that therefore resistance was futile."

But this time, Alekhine's "homework" did not work.

"I thought for 20 minutes," wrote Botvinnik, "and found the saving move. True, I had to sacrifice both my knights, but it guaranteed a repetition of moves..."

(80) Alekhine – Botvinnik
Nottingham 1936
Sicilian Defense [B72]

1.e4 c5 2.♘f3 d6 3.d4 c×d4 4.♘×d4 ♘f6 5.♘c3 g6 6.♗e2 ♗g7 7.♗e3 ♘c6 8.♘b3 ♗e6 9.f4 0-0 10.g4 d5 10...♘a5 and 10...♖c8 are the alternatives. **11.f5** "I first saw this interesting move in a game by the talented Czech master Foltys, at a recent tournament in Podebrady, but I did not know that it had already been played in a Moscow tournament. As this game shows, the move allows White to force a quick draw – but no more than that" (Alekhine). **11...♗c8 12.e×d5 ♘b4**

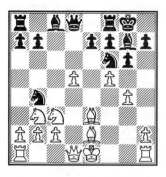

13.d6 This leads more or less by force to a draw. 13.♗f3! is the critical continuation. **13...♕×d6 14.♗c5 ♕f4 15.♖f1 ♕×h2 16.♗×b4 ♘×g4 17.♗×g4 ♕g3+** 17...g×f5? 18.♕e2 ♕g3+ 19.♕f2± **18.♖f2 ♕g1+ 19.♖f1 ♕g3+ 20.♖f2 ♕g1+ ½-½**

After the draw with Flohr, the Soviet champion withstood Capablanca's assault in the next round. On that day, Botvinnik turned 25. Learning of this after the game was over, Capablanca congratulated his opponent.

Suffering not a single loss in so strong a tournament, Botvinnik finished even with Capablanca, who nevertheless lost one game, to Flohr; but in compensation, he did beat Alekhine. The winners scored 10/14, outdistancing Euwe, Fine and Reshevsky by a half-point.

One more example of Botvinnik's work at the "tournament of the century" was his game against the professor from Ljubljana, Milan Vidmar, hailed as the best game of the 13th round.

(81) Botvinnik – Vidmar
Nottingham 1936
Queen's Gambit Declined [D40]

1.c4 e6 2.♘f3 d5 3.d4 ♘f6 4.♗g5 ♗e7 5.♘c3 0-0 6.e3 ♘bd7 7.♗d3 c5 8.0-0 c×d4 9.e×d4 d×c4 10.♗×c4 ♘b6 11.♗b3 ♗d7 12.♕d3 ♘bd5 13.♘e5 ♗c6 14.♖ad1 ♘b4 15.♕h3 ♗d5 16.♘×d5 (D)

16...♘b×d5? The wrong knight captures, which leads to a knightmare for Black. 16...♘f×d5 17.♗×e7 ♕×e7 18.f4 ♖ad8 19.f5 e×f5 20.♕×f5 ♘c6 reduces

the pressure by exchanges and is close to equality. **17.f4** The battering ram moves forward. **17...♖c8?!** 17...♕b6 is correct. **18.f5 exf5?!** 18...♕d6 19.♖de1 exf5 20.♖xf5 ♖cd8 is called for, but it is highly unlikely that Black can defend in the long run, as all White's pieces are attacking. **19.♖xf5 ♕d6?!** 19...♖c7 is more tenacious, but loses as well. The computer gives the amazing 20.♖df1 ♘b6 21.♗h6+− Now the time to strike has come: **20.♘xf7! ♖xf7 21.♗xf6 ♗xf6** 21...♘xf6 22.♖xf6 gxf6 23.♕xc8+ +− +− **22.♖xd5 ♕c6 23.♖d6 ♕e8 24.♖d7 1-0**

"Botvinnik," wrote Alekhine after the conclusion of the Nottingham tournament, "has the best chances to become world champion in the coming years. He has all of the qualities needed: coolness, self-control, and most of all, a deep positional understanding."

Botvinnik's triumph at Nottingham received great publicity in the homeland, where in conformity with the times, its political meaning was also noted! Summing up the outcome of the tournament, the newspaper *Pravda* wrote: "The young Soviet chessplayer, electrical engineer and graduate student of one of the Leningrad laboratories of the Narcomtyazhprom, Komsomolets Mikhail Botvinnik was the winner of the international chess tournament in Nottingham. Affairs were unchanged by the fact that, at the last minute, Botvinnik was caught by the ex-world champion, the virtuoso of chess technique, José Raúl Capablanca, with whom the USSR champion share first and second prizes. Prizes are not the important thing here. What is important is that Botvinnik, from the start of the tournament to its finish, showed the highest mastery, self-control, stubbornness, and will to win. He showed the kind of strength that the combination of theoretical knowledge and a complete mastery of technique gives. Botvinnik was the real tournament leader – he carried through with great brilliance and without losing a single game."

Palma de Mallorca, 1967 For the third year in a row, an international tournament was held on the island of Palma de Mallorca. Every year, the number of players had been increased – in 1965, there were 10 players; in 1966, there were 16; and in 1967, there were 18. And every year, it grew more and more impressive: in 1965, the winners were Darga, O'Kelly and Pomar; in 1966, it was won by Tal.

"The organizers, following the example of the Dutch (AVRO 1938), decided to run a 'tournament on wheels.' The participants were subjected to many exhausting journeys throughout the entire Balearic Isles," as Botvinnik told later at a lecture in the Central Chess Club. "The playing regime was difficult: rounds from four until eight in the evening , a two-hour meal, and then adjournments from eleven until one in the morning. If the game was adjourned again, another session after that, in the morning, from nine until eleven. Ten hours of play in one day!"

In the first 13 rounds, the Dane, Bent Larsen, who was the main favorite of the tournament, had an exceptionally high score: 11½ points, but he was still unable to break away from Botvinnik (who defeated him in their individual encounter) and Smyslov, both of whom were right behind him. Everything was decided in the last round, in which Larsen had White versus the Spanish master Diez del Corral, while the Soviet grandmasters had Black – Smyslov versus Gligoric and Botvinnik against Ivkov. Only Larsen managed to beat his opponent. With 13 points, he led the tournament table, followed by Botvinnik and Smyslov, with 12½. Fourth was Portisch, with 11½ and fifth was Gligoric with 10½.

(82) Gligoric – Botvinnik
Palma de Mallorca 1967
Nimzo-Indian Defense [E43]

1.d4 ♘f6 2.c4 e6 3.♘c3 ♗b4 4.e3 c5 5.♗d3 b6 6.♘f3 ♗b7 7.♗d2 0-0 8.a3 ♗×c3 9.♗×c3 d6 10.d×c5 b×c5 11.0-0 ♘bd7 12.b4 ♕c7 13.♖c1 ♘e4 In fact, this move decided the game," wrote Botvinnik, in his comments to the game. "The base of the pawn chain, c5-d6-e5, the d6-pawn, is securely defended; the black queen brings itself to the king's wing, and White does not succeed in bringing his knight back to defend the castled position." **14.♗×e4?!** There is no reason to give up the bishop pair as 14.♗b2 is playable. **14...♗×e4**

15.♘d2 ♗g6 16.♘b3 ♖ad8 17.♘a5 ♘b6 18.♕g4 e5 19.b5?! 19.♕e2 is more circumspect. **19...f5** 19...♗d3!? **20.♕e2 f4 21.e×f4 ♖×f4 22.♖fd1 ♖df8 23.♗e1 ♘c8 24.♘b3?** 24.♕d2 ♕f7 25.f3 ♖d4 26.♕e2 is a much better more active set up and almost equal. **24...♕f7 25.♘d2 e4**

26.♘f1? 26.f3 e×f3 27.♘×f3 ♖e8 28.♕f1 ♗e4 29.♖c3 limits the damage. **26...♗h5! 27.♕c2 ♗×d1 28.♖×d1 ♘e7 29.♘e3** 29.♖×d6 ♘f5 30.♖d1 e3-+ **29...♘f5 30.♘×f5 ♕×f5 31.♖×d6 e3 32.♕×f5 e×f2+ 33.♗×f2 ♖8×f5 34.♖d2 ♖×c4 35.h3 h5 36.h4 ♖a4 37.♖d8+ ♔h7 38.♖d3 ♖a5 39.♖b3 c4 40.♖c3 ♖f×b5 41.♖×c4 ♖×a3 42.♗d4 a5 0-1**

Petrosian, Tigran Vartanovich (June 17, 1929, Tbilisi-August 13, 1984, Moscow) ninth world champion, 1963-1969.

Petrosian was far from being fortune's favorite: his childhood came during the severe years of the war. He lost his parents at an early age. And only chess, which he occupied himself with starting at 12 years of age, and which he rapidly showed a talent for, helped him to forget about his troubles.

Palma de Mallorca 1967

		1	2	3	4	5	6	7	8	9	10	11	12	13	14	15	16	17	18	Total
1	Larsen	*	0	½	1	1	1	½	½	1	½	1	1	0	1	1	1	1	1	13
2	Botvinnik	1	*	½	½	1	½	1	1	½	1	1	½	1	0	½	1	½	1	12½
3	Smyslov	½	½	*	½	½	½	1	1	1	0	½	1	1	1	1	½	1	1	12½
4	Portisch	0	½	½	*	½	½	½	1	½	½	1	½	1	1	½	1	1	1	11½
5	Gligoric	0	0	½	½	*	½	1	½	½	½	½	½	1	1	1	½	1	1	10½
6	Ivkov	0	½	½	½	½	*	½	1	1	½	½	½	½	1	1	½	½	½	10
7	Matulovic	½	0	0	½	0	½	*	0	½	½	1	½	0	1	1	1	1	1	9
8	Toran	½	0	0	0	½	0	1	*	½	1	1	1	½	½	½	½	½	½	8½
9	Lehmann	0	½	0	½	½	0	½	½	*	½	½	½	1	½	1	1	½	½	8½
10	Donner	½	0	1	½	½	½	½	0	½	*	½	1	1	½	½	0	0	½	8
11	Diez del Corral	0	0	½	0	½	½	0	0	½	½	*	0	1	1	1	½	1	1	8
12	O'Kelly	0	½	0	½	½	½	½	0	½	0	1	*	½	½	1	½	0	0	6½
13	Medina	1	0	0	0	0	½	1	½	0	0	0	½	*	½	½	½	1	½	6½
14	Damjanovic	0	1	0	0	0	0	0	½	½	½	0	½	½	*	½	1	1	0	6
15	Tatai	0	½	0	½	0	0	0	½	0	½	0	0	½	½	*	1	1	1	6
16	Bednarski	0	0	½	0	½	½	0	½	0	1	½	½	½	0	0	*	0	1	5½
17	Calvo	0	½	0	0	0	½	0	½	½	1	0	1	0	0	0	1	*	½	5½
18	Jimenez	0	0	0	0	0	½	0	½	½	½	0	1	½	1	0	0	½	*	5

His first teacher, A. Ebralidze, drew attention to the boy's logical play: he would not try for the piece sacrifices or combinations, so characteristic of young chessplayers, but would defend stubbornly and resourcefully; he would evaluate the position deeply and rationally, as he took part in the USSR junior championship of 1946. Petrosian did not lose a single game, although at that time he was just 17-years old. Dus-Chotimirsky, the veteran of Russian chess, was amazed: "What sort of youngster does not lose a single game?" For his further development, Petrosian moved to Moscow. There he began working a great deal on his style of play, trying to render it universal, and on chess theory.

Slowly and unswervingly, Tigran's successes mounted. In 1951, he became a prizewinner in the USSR championship, and won the right to play in the Interzonal tournament. Over a period of ten years, he improved his results in tournaments for the world championship. Finally, in 1962, the 33-year-old Petrosian achieved a brilliant success in the candidates' tournament on the island of Curaçao in the Caribbean, winning with a score of 17½/27. He won his mini-matches against five of his competitors: Fischer, Korchnoi, Benko, Tal, and Filip – and drew against only two of them – Geller and Keres. Thus, he became Candidate Number One for the match with world champion Botvinnik, and began his strong preparation for the event. His analyses of Botvinnik's previous matches, with Smyslov and Tal, proved invaluable to him. He had been the one who commented on those games in the pages of the newspaper *Sovietsky Sport*.

Tigran Petrosian

"I learned from Botvinnik's games when I was twenty-years old," Petrosian said after the match, "and I still learn from them today."

In 1963, Tigran Petrosian met Mikhail Botvinnik (cf. *World Championship Matches*: Botvinnik-Petrosian, 1963). The match, played to the best of 24 games, ended in victory for him after 22 games, with the score 12½-9½ (+5 -2 =15). Petrosian thus became the ninth world chess champion.

The fifth game of the match was especially memorable for Petrosian, as it was his first victory over Botvinnik. Petrosian came up with original plan involving a regrouping of his forces, which led to a weakening of his opponent's position. The march of the white king and its maneuvers in the enemy camp are beautiful.

(83) Petrosian – Botvinnik
Moscow (m5) 1963
Grünfeld Defense [D94]

1.c4 g6 2.d4 ♘f6 3.♘c3 d5 4.♘f3 ♗g7 5.e3 0-0 6.♗e2 dxc4 7.♗xc4

c5 8.d5 e6 9.d×e6 ♕×d1+ 10.♔×d1 ♗×e6 11.♗×e6 f×e6 12.♔e2 ♘c6 13.♖d1 ♖ad8?! 13...h6 is more circumspect. 14.♖×d8 ♖×d8 15.♘g5 ♖e8 16.♘ge4 ♘×e4 17.♘×e4 b6 18.♖b1 ♘b4 19.♗d2 ♘d5 19...♘×a2? 20.♖a1 ♘b4 21.♗×b4 c×b4 22.♖×a7 ♗×b2 23.♖b7± **20.a4 ♖c8 21.b3 ♗f8 22.♖c1 ♗e7 23.b4 c4** 23...♔f7 24.b×c5 b×c5 25.♖b1 ♘b4 is the alternative. **24.b5 ♔f7 25.♗c3 ♗a3?** The first step in the wrong direction. 25...g5 26.♘d2 g4 is a better defensive set up. **26.♖c2 ♘×c3+ 27.♖×c3 ♗b4 28.♖c2 ♔e7 29.♘d2 c3 30.♘e4 ♗a5 31.♔d3 ♖d8+ 32.♔c4 ♖d1** 32...♖d2!? **33.♘×c3**

33...♖h1? 33...♗×c3 34.♔×c3 g5 was the last chance to fight. **34.♘e4! ♖×h2 35.♔d4** The king starts a long march right into the heart of Black's position. **35...♔d7 36.g3** 36.♘f6+ ♔d6 37.♖c6+ ♔e7 38.♔e5 ♖×g2 39.♖c7+ ♔d8 40.♖×h7 ♖c3+ 41.♔×e6 ♗×f6 42.♔×f6 ♖f2+ 43.♔e5+− **36...♗b4 37.♔e5 ♖h5+ 38.♔f6 ♗e7+ 39.♔g7 e5?!** 40.♖c6 ♖h1 41.♔f7 ♖a1 42.♖e6 ♗d8 43.♖d6+ ♔c8 44.♔e8 44.♔e6!?+− **44...♗c7 45.♖c6 ♖d1** 45...♖×a4 46.♘c3 ♖a5 47.♘d5 ♖×b5 48.♖×c7+ ♔b8 49.e4+− **46.♘g5 ♖d8+ 47.♔f7 ♖d7+ 48.♔g8 1-0** in view of 48...h5 49.♖×g6 ♖d2 50.♖c6 ♔b7 51.♘e4+−

"What do you think is your opponent's [main] strength?" Answering this question, Botvinnik noted Petrosian's elevated technique, his positional mastery, and in conclusion emphasized: "His strength lies primarily in defense." However, this characteristic did not take into account Petrosian's other potential skills. Already, in the match against Boris Spassky in 1966, the spectators witnessed a Petrosian "unknown to them." As it turned out, he knew not only how to defend, but also to attack − and brilliantly. Here is the tenth game of that match, where Petrosian achieved a spectacular victory, by means of the sacrifice of both knights, and then his queen.

(84) Petrosian − Spassky
Moscow (m/10) 1966
King's Indian Defense [E66]

1.♘f3 ♘f6 2.g3 g6 3.c4 ♗g7 4.♗g2 0-0 5.0-0 ♘c6 6.♘c3 d6 7.d4 a6 8.d5 ♘a5 9.♘d2 c5 10.♕c2 e5 11.b3 ♘g4 12.e4 f5 13.e×f5 g×f5

14.♘d1!? A retreat in typical Petrosian style. Spassky is probably lured into the following premature attack. **14...b5 15.f3 e4 16.♗b2 e×f3 17.♗×f3 ♗×b2 18.♕×b2 ♘e5 19.♗e2 f4?**

Spassky follows his style and starts a direct attack. But he is not ready for it. 19...♗d7 20.♘e3 ♛f6 is called for. **20.g×f4?** Exchanging Black's active rook with 20.♖×f4 ♖×f4 21.g×f4 is even stronger: 21...♘g6 22.♘e4 ♘×f4 23.♔h1 ♗f5 24.♘df2± **20...♗h3** 20...♖×f4 does also not neutralize White's initiative completely, e.g., 21.♖×f4 ♛g5+ 22.♔h1 ♛×f4 23.♘c3 ♛d4 24.♖f1 **21.♘e3!**

21...♗×f1? too greedy. Spassky most probably has difficulties switching over to defense. Black had to try to exchange as many pieces as possible with 21...♖×f4 22.♖×f4 ♛g5+ 23.♖g4 ♘×g4 24.♘×g4 ♗×g4 25.♗×g4 ♛×g4+ 26.♔h1 ♛d4 27.♖g1+ ♔h8 28.♛×d4+ c×d4 29.♘e4 ♘b7 and the limited material gives Black practical drawing chances according to Kasparov. **22.♖×f1 ♘g6 23.♗g4!** The last critical moment has arisen. **23...♘×f4?** This runs into a thunderous attack. 23...♛f6! was the last chance to fight, e.g., 24.♗e6+ ♔g7 (24...♔h8 25.♛×f6+ ♖×f6 26.f5 ♘e5 27.♘e4!± Kasparov) 25.♘f5+ ♔h8 26.♛×f6+ ♖×f6 27.c×b5 ♘f8 28.♘e4± **24.♖×f4! ♖×f4 25.♗e6+ ♖f7 26.♘e4 ♛h4** 26...♖aa7 27.♘f5 ♛f8 28.♛f6+– **27.♘×d6 ♛g5+ 28.♛h1 ♖aa7**

28...♛×e3 29.♗×f7+ ♔f8 30.♛h8+ ♔e7 31.♘f5+ ♔d7 (31...♔×f7 32.♛g7+ ♔e8 33.♘e3+–) 32.♗e6+ ♔c7 33.♛×h7++– **29.♗×f7+ ♖×f7 30.♛h8+! 1-0** A beautiful finish in the style of this masterpiece!. The annotations are from *The Chess Puzzle Book 3* by Müller and van Delft.

After the match, an amazed Spassky acknowledged to grandmaster Gligoric: "Above all, Tigran is an astonishing tactician!" When Petrosian was asked why he had not released his "secret weapon" before, he answered: "Each man plays according to the gifts nature has given him. By nature, I am a careful man. I do not generally like situations that involve risk. But I was never accused of being weak at spotting a combination. It was precisely my tactical mastery that led me to decide not to go in for number of combinations, since I had found refutations for my opponent..."

For six years, Petrosian wore the crown of the king of chess. In those years, he was victorious in such incredibly strong tournaments as Los Angeles 1963, and Buenos Aires 1964. As the head of the Soviet team at the Tel Aviv Olympiad in 1964 and Lugano in 1968, he turned in the best result on first board.

And it was only in 1969 that, meeting Spassky once again, Petrosian lost this match by the score of 12½-10½ (+4 -6 =13). But even as a former world champion, Petrosian continued to play in the world championship cycle, remaining one of the strongest chessplayers. He won tournaments in San Antonio 1972, Las Palmas,1973, Lone Pine 1976, Tallinn 1979, and Bar 1980. And in his match against Fischer (1971), Petrosian handed the future world champion his only loss in his candidate's matches.

Petrosian was a man of wide-ranging interests and abilities. He was known as a chess theoretician and journalist. For a number of years, he was chief editor of *Shakhmatnaya Moskva* magazine, and then of the weekly *64*. He traveled all over the country, lecturing, giving simultaneous exhibitions, and leading a school for young players in the club "Spartak," and did some teaching. At Yerevan University, he defended his candidate's dissertation in philosophy on the theme, "Some problems of logic in chess thinking." In all of his works, including literary, pedagogical and social activities, Tigran Petrosian, the ninth world champion, helped increase the popularity of chess culture.

Works: Chess and Philosophy, Yerevan, 1968 (in Armenian); *Safe Strategy*, Moscow 1985; *Chess Lectures*, Moscow 1989; *T. Petrosian, 350 Partien*, Hamburg, 1963.

Books: Vasiliev, V., *Life of a Chessplayer*, Yerevan, 1969; Boleslavsky, I. and Bondarevsky, I., *Petrosian-Spassky 1969*, Moscow 1970; Vasiliev, V., *The Mystery of Tal:*

The Second "I" in Petrosian, Moscow 1973; A. Suetin, A. and Petrosian, Tigran, *Die Kariere eines Schachgenies*, Berlin 1997; Botvinnik, M., *Portraits*, Moscow 2000 (edited by I. Botvinnik); Linder, Isaak and Vladimir, *Tigran Petrosian* (in the book, *Kings of the Chess World*, Moscow 2001); Kasparov, G. (working with D. Plisetsky), *Tigran the Ninth* (in the book *My Great Predecessors*, volume 3, Moscow 2004); Voronkov, C. and Plisetsky, D. *The Russians versus Fischer*, Moscow 2004; Botvinnik, I., *Botvinnik-Petrosian, Moscow 1963*, Moscow 2005.

Ragozin – Botvinnik, Match 1940 (May 2-29, Leningrad) This 12-game contest was considered a training event, and was organized by the sporting society "Central Building" in the Leningrad club of masters of sport by V. V. Ragozin.

After a tense struggle – played at three games per week – the match was concluded with the score 8½-3½ (+5 0 =7) in Botvinnik's favor. In a lecture on the result of this contest, he noted: "Despite the unfortunate outcome of the match, Ragozin showed good form, on the whole. In all 12 games, he only made a few errors; but those errors were of such a nature that at the end, Ragozin was unable to bring even one game to victory."

In support of this, Botvinnik presented a number of positions from the second, fourth and ninth games, in which his opponent achieved, respectively, a "significant advantage," "in a roughly equal position found a most elegant pawn sacrifice," and "by out-standing play adjourned the game in a winning position." But in all his, Ragozin was unable to exploit the situation, which had become good for him. In some cases, he underestimated the opponent; in others, he refused the draw, without any justification and... lost. Knowing when to agree to a draw at the right time is a great skill!" concluded Botvinnik.

Another interesting thing about the match was the variety in the openings: Queen's Gambit, English Opening, Dutch Defense, Nimzo-Indian Defense, French Defense, Ruy Lopez, Grünfeld Defense. Eight openings in twelve games – hard to find a similar example in a match!

(85) Botvinnik – Ragozin
Leningrad 1940
English Opening [A32]

1.c4 e5 2.♘c3 ♘f6 3.♘f3 ♘c6 4.d4 e4 5.♘d2 ♗b4 6.e3 0-0 7.♗e2 ♖e8 8.0-0 ♗×c3 9.b×c3 d6 10.f3 e×f3 11.♗×f3 ♖×e3 12.♘b3 12.♘b1!? **12...♖e8?!** 12...♖×c3 13.♗×c6 (or 13.♗g5 ♖×c4 14.♕d2 d5) 13...b×c6 14.♗g5 ♕e8 is probably critical. **13.♗g5** The pin is very annoying. **13...♘e7 14.♕d2 c6 15.♖ae1 ♗f5 16.♗×f6 g×f6 17.h4 d5 18.c×d5 c×d5 19.♗d1** 19.♗e2!? **19...♗e4?** 19...b6 **20.♘c1 ♗e4 21.♖×f6 ♘g6** slows White's attack down a bit. **20.♖×f6?!** 20.♘c5 +– is more precise. **20...♘g6?** Now White's attack crashes through. 20...♘f5 is more tenacious, e.g., 21.♕g5+ ♔h8 22.♖×e4 ♖×e4 23.♖×f5 ♕×g5 24.h×g5 ♖e1+ 25.♖f1 ♖×f1+ 26.♔×f1 ♖c8 with chances to fight in a technical endgame. **21.♕f2 ♖e6 22.♖×e6 f×e6 23.h5 ♘f8 24.♕g3+ ♔f7 25.♖f1+ ♗f5 26.♕f4 ♘d7 27.♗c2 ♕b8 28.♕h6 ♕g8 29.♗×f5 e×f5 30.♖×f5+ ♔e7**

31.♖g5 ♕e6 32.♖g7+ 1-0 with 32...♔d6 3.♖×d7+ ♔×d7 34.♘c5+ +– to follow.

"After Black's acceptance of the sacrificed pawn, White's pressure increased slowly, but irresistibly." (Botvinnik)

Reshevsky, Samuel (November 26, 1911, Ozerkow, Poland-April 4, 1992, Spring Valley, New York), American chessplayer, international grandmaster, candidate for the world championship, participant in the 1948 match-tournament for the world championship.

Sammy could have been titled the "world champion" among wunderkinder. The world had never seen anything like him – a 6-year-old boy, dressed in a sailor suit, conducting a simultaneous exhibition against the members of the Vienna Chess Club, winning game after game. Chessplayers wise in their experience and white of hair were astonished by what was happening. For this event, they had no rational explanation. And Reshevsky would recall later: "For me, chess had already become a normal human function, like breathing. It never required conscious effort. I made my moves the same way other people breathed in and out."

He had not yet reached the age of eleven, when he first took part in a master tourney. Edward Lasker, Osip Bernstein, Dawid Janowsky – such were the chiefs he met in 1922 in New York. His game against Janowsky was remembered his whole life.

"The little boy knows no more about chess than I do of rope-dancing! Look

Sam Reshevsky

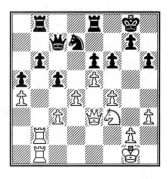

at his position! Soon he will not be able to move! Complete paralysis!" – exclaimed Janowsky to Ed. Lasker after 12 moves. Gradually, his attack grew stronger, but his opponent defended himself with amazing tenacity.

(86) Janowsky – Reshevsky
New York 1922
Queen's Gambit Declined [D53]

1.d4 ♘f6 2.♘f3 d5 3.c4 e6 4.♘c3 ♘bd7 5.♗g5 ♗e7 6.e3 c6 7.♗d3 a6 8.0-0 d×c4 9.♗×c4 ♘b6?! 9...b5 is the main line. **10.♗d3 ♘fd5 11.♗×e7 ♕×e7 12.♕d2 ♘×c3 13.b×c3 c5 14.♖ab1 ♘d7 15.a4 0-0 16.♕c2 h6 17.♖fe1?!** 17.a5 Fixing the queenside was more principled and also better. **17...b6 18.♖b2 ♖b8** 18...♗b7!? **19.♖eb1 ♕d6 20.♕e2 a5 21.♗b5 ♖d8?! 22.h3?!** 22.e4!? **22...♕c7 23.e4 ♘f8** 23...♘f6 is more natural. **24.♕e3** 24.♘e5!? **24...♗d7 25.♘e5 ♗e8 26.♗×e8 ♖×e8 27.f4** Very committal. 27.♖c1 is more flexible. **27...f6 28.♘f3 ♘d7 29.e5**

29...f5? Black does not have time for this pawn move. 29...c×d4 30.c×d4 ♕c6 is more active. **30.g4** 30.d5!? e×d5 31.♘h4 ♖f8 32.♕f3± **30...g6?** 30...♖f8 limits the damage. **31.g×f5 g×f5 32.d5 ♘f8 33.♖g2+ ♔h7 34.c4 ♕f7 35.♔h2?!** 35.♘h4!?+– **35...♘g6** 35...e×d5 36.c×d5 ♕×d5 37.♘h4 ♘e6 38.♘×f5+– **36.♖bg1 ♖g8 37.d6 ♕b7 38.h4?!** 38.♘g5+!? h×g5 39.♖×g5+– **38...♕c6?! 39.h5** 39.♘g5+ wins as well, e.g., 39...h×g5 40.♖×g5 ♕e8 41.♕f3+– **39...♘h8**

40.♘g5+? This only leads to a draw. 40.♘h4 wins, e.g., 40...♖×g2+ 41.♖×g2 ♖g8 42.♖×g8 ♔×g8 43.♕g3+ ♔h7 44.♘g6 ♕e8 45.♕g2 ♔g8 46.♘×h8+ ♔×h8 47.♕g6+– **40...h×g5 41.f×g5 ♘g6 42.♖g3 ♔g7 43.♖h3 ♖h8 44.h×g6 ♖×h3+ 45.♔×h3?** 45.♕×h3 ♖h8 46.♕h6+ ♔g8 47.g7 ♔h7 48.♕g3 ♖×h6 49.g×h6 ♕e4 50.d7 ♕×e5+

165

51.♔f3= **45...♖h8+ 46.♔g3 ♕×a4 47.♕f3 f4+ 48.♔g4** 48.♕×f4 ♕b3+ 49.♔f2 ♖f8-+ **48...♕c2 49.♕×f4 ♕e2+ 50.♔g3 ♕d3+ 51.♔g2 ♕e2+ 52.♔g3 ♕h2+?** The direct 52...♖f8! wins: 53.♕f6+ ♖×f6 54.g×f6+ ♔f8 55.g7+ ♔g8 56.♔h3 ♕h5+ 57.♔g2 ♕×e5 58.d7 ♕g5+ 59.♔h1 ♕×f6-+ **53.♔f3 ♖f8** 53...♖h3+ 54.♖g3 ♕h1+ 55.♔e3 ♕c1 ± **54.♕f6+ ♔g8 55.d7 ♖×f6+ 56.g×f6** 56.e×f6 ♕d2 57.♖h1 draws as well and is probably easier. **56...♕d2**

57.♖h1? 57.f7+ ♔g7 58.♖h1 still saves the day, e.g., 58...♕d3+ 59.♔f4 ♕f5+ 60.♔e3 ♕×e5+ 61.♔d2 ♕d6+ 62.♔c2 ♕b8 (62...♕×d7? 63.f8♕+ ♔×f8 64.♖h8++−) 63.♖d1 ♕d8 64.♖f1 ♕f8 65.♖d1 ♕d8= **57...♕d3+ 58.♔g2 ♕×g6+ 59.♔f2 ♕f5+ 60.♔g2 ♕g4+ 61.♔h2 ♕e2+ 62.♔h3 ♕d3+ 63.♔h4 ♕×d7 64.♖g1+ ♔f8 65.♔g5 ♕d4 0-1**

"I beat a great master!," exclaimed the happy Sammy, and threw his arms around his father's neck.

Thirteen years later Reshevsky, already a two-time U.S. champion, went to Europe, and confidently won at Margate (1935), ahead of Capablanca, whom he defeated in their individual game.

(87) Reshevsky – Capablanca
Margate 1935
Queen's Gambit Declined [D62]

1.d4 ♘f6 2.c4 e6 3.♘c3 d5 4.♗g5 ♘bd7 5.c×d5 e×d5 6.e3 ♗e7 7.♗d3 0-0 8.♕c2 c5 9.♘f3 c4 10.♗f5 ♖e8 11.0-0 g6 12.♗h3 ♘f8 13.♗×c8 ♖×c8 14.♗×f6 14.♘e5!? **14...♗×f6 15.b3 ♕a5 16.b4 ♕d8 17.♕a4 a6 18.b5 ♖e6?!** 18...♘e6, to meet 19.b×a6 b×a6 20.♕×a6 with 20...♘c5, is the computer's suggestion. **19.♖ab1 ♖b8 20.♖b2 ♗e7 21.b×a6 ♖×a6 22.♕c2 ♘e6?!** The pawn sacrifice 22...b5 23.♘×b5 ♕a5 is more active. **23.♖fb1 ♖a7 24.a4 ♘c7 25.♘e5 ♕e8**

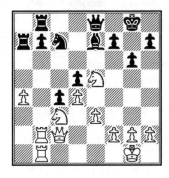

26.f4? The resulting structure is too rigid. White can choose between the flexible 26.♕e2 and the direct 26.e4, in both cases with a clear advantage. **26...f6 27.♘g4 ♕d7 28.h3 ♔g7 29.♘f2 ♗a3 30.♖a2 ♗d6 31.♘fd1 f5 32.♘b5 ♖a5 33.♘×c7 ♗×c7 34.♘c3 ♕d6?** 34...b6= is called for. **35.♕f2?** Reshevsky misses the moment to increase the pressure with 35.♖ab2! b6 36.♖b5± **35...b6 36.♕f3 ♖d8 37.♖ab2 ♕e7 38.♖b4 ♖d7 39.♔h1 ♗d8 40.g4 f×g4?!** 40...♕f8 is equal, as 41.♖b5?! can be met by 41...♕a3 **41.h×g4 ♕d6**

42.♔g1 ♗c7 43.♔f2 ♖f7 44.g5?!
The direct 44.♖b5 ♕a3 45.♘×d5 ♖×b5
46.♖×b5 applies more pressure.
44...♗d8 45.♔e2 ♗×g5? This
exchange plays into White's hands as
his rooks have inroads now. 45...♕e6
46.♖b5 ♖×b5 47.♖×b5 ♕f5 48.♖×d5
♕c2+ 49.♔f1 ♗×g5 50.♖×g5 ♕×c3=
**46.♖×b6 ♕a3 47.♔d2 ♗e7
48.♖b7 48.♕h1!?**

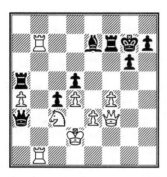

48...♖×a4? White's queen will reign
supreme now. After 48...♖f5!, White is
better, but Black's fortress is not so easy
to breach. **49.♕×d5 ♖a5 50.♕×c4
♖h5 51.♔d3** 51.♖d7!? +− **51...♕a8?**
51...♖hf5 offers more resistance, but
Black is fighting for a lost cause.
**52.♕e6 ♕a3 53.♖d7 ♖hf5 54.♖b3
♕a1 55.♖×e7 ♕f1+ 56.♔d2 1-0**

After this victory, the master Pyotr
Romanovsky wrote: "Undoubtedly, the
chess world has acquired a prodigious
thinker in the person of Reshevsky, who
has every chance of making a future
challenge for the world championship."

And this forecast came true. In 1948,
Reshevsky was a participant in the
match-tournament for the world
championship, and together with Paul
Keres, shared third/fourth places. He
remained a candidate also at 42 (when

he shared second through fourth places
at Zürich 1953), and at 57 (when he lost
a quarterfinal match to Korchnoi), and
at 62, when for the last time, me
appeared in an Interzonal tournament,
at Petropolis 1973.

Besides Capablanca, Reshevsky
managed to score victories over other
world champions – Lasker, Alekhine,
and Euwe. In the 1948 match-
tournament, he managed to win a game
from the eventual world champion,
Botvinnik. However, the final score of
their mini-match ended in Botvinnik's
favor (+3 -1 =1) – as did their mutual
score in other years. Nevertheless, the
final game between the two of them
ended in victory for Reshevsky. Here is
this interesting game.

(88) Reshevsky – Botvinnik
Moscow 1955
Queen's Gambit Declined [D49]

**1.d4 d5 2.c4 e6 3.♘c3 c6 4.♘f3
♘f6 5.e3 ♘bd7 6.♗d3 d×c4
7.♗×c4 b5 8.♗d3 a6 9.e4 c5 10.e5
c×d4 11.♘×b5 ♘×e5 12.♘×e5
a×b5 13.♕f3** 13.♗×b5+ and 13.0-0
are played much more often nowadays.
**13...♕a5+ 14.♔e2 ♗d6 15.♕c6+
♔e7 16.♗d2 b4 17.♕×d6+ ♔×d6
18.♘c4+ ♔d7 19.♘×a5 ♖×a5
20.♖hc1** 20.♗×b4 ♖e5+ 21.♔d2 is the
alternative. **20...♗a6 21.♗×a6 ♖×a6
22.♖c4 ♘d5 23.♖×d4 ♖b8
24.♔d3 h5 25.♔c4 b3 26.a4 ♖c6+
27.♔d3 ♖c2 28.♖b1 ♖bc8 29.a5
♖8c6?!** 29...♔d6!? **30.♔e2 ♖d6
31.♔e1 ♘c7 32.♖×d6+ ♔×d6
33.♗c3 f6 34.♖a1** (D)

34...♘a6? 34...♔c5! defends as 35.a6?
runs into 35...♘×a6 36.♖×a6? ♖×c3
37.b×c3? b2−+ **35.♖a3 ♔c7** 35...♘c5

36.a6 ♘d3+ 37.♔f1 ♖c1+ 38.♔e2 ♖xc3 39.a7 ♘f4+ 40.♔d1 ♖c8 41.a8♕ ♖xa8 42.♖xa8 ♘xg2 43.♖a3± **36.♖xb3 ♘c5 37.♖b5 ♘a4?!** 37...♔c6 38.♖b6+ ♔c7 39.♗d4 ♘d3+ 40.♔d1 ♖c4 41.♗e3 ♖a4 42.a6 ♘b4 43.♖xe6 ♘c6 44.♗c5± **38.♗d4 e5 39.♔d1 ♖c4 40.♗e3 ♔c6 41.♖b8** 41.♖b3!?+− **41...♔c7 1-0** After 42. ♖b3 ♖c6 43. ♖b5, Black would be in *zugzwang*)

"A good game by Reshevsky," wrote Botvinnik. They had first met over the board two decades earlier – at Nottingham and at the AVRO tournament.

"On the whole, what do you think of Botvinnik; what about his overall place in chess?" That was the question, among many others, that was put to Reshevsky, when he gave a wide-ranging interview to *64 – Chess Review* magazine in 1991.

"Everybody knows that he is one of the greatest chessplayers, acknowledged the world over... As a champion, he had great influence on the chess world."

By the way, Reshevsky arrived in Moscow that year to participate in events marking the 70th birthday of Vassily Smyslov. Short in stature, in a colorful little cap, 80-year-old Samuel sat at the chessboard as though charged with energy from the game. In the Veterans' World Cup of quick chess, Reshevsky was matched with Smyslov. Losing the first two games, he then fought back, winning the next two games in a row, and drew the match! The ovations and gratitude of chessplayers were for him the best reward. Garry Kasparov, who witnessed this finale, said: "Reshevsky showed fantastic technique."

"Struggle and resistance – that's what attracts me about chess," said Reshevsky. He could not live without chess, but he also could not live by chess alone. In order to raise a family, he had to work as an accountant; but he would always return to "the Hearth and Home of the Kingdom of Chess."

Reshevsky died at 81. In an article about him, Botvinnik ranked the grandmaster on the same level as the most famous leaders of North America: "In the last 150 years, the USA has given the world a whole constellation of great masters: Morphy, Pillsbury, Marshall, Fine, Reshevsky, Fischer. In our day, alas, that country has no worthy successors. But when some talents appear once again, they can follow the example of that deep and uncompromising chess battler, Samuel Reshevsky."

Lit: Reshevsky On Chess, New York 1948; *Zo schaakt Reshevsky*, Lochem 1950; *Meine Schachkarriere*, Berlin 1957; *How Chess Games Are Won*, New York 1962; *Great Chess Upsets*, New York 1976.

Books: Kagan, B., *Samuel Rzeschewski, das Schachwunderkind,* 1920; *De Amerikaansche Schackmeeste Reshevsky* Rotterdam, The Haag, 1937; Kasparov, G., "Olimpiiskuu dolgozhitel" Reshevsky (in *My Great Predecessors,* Book 4, Moscow 2005).

Romanovsky, Pyotr Arsenievich (July 29, 1892, St. Petersburg-March 1, 1964, Moscow), one of the strongest of Soviet chessplayers in the 1920s, Botvinnik's opponent early in his career. Chess teacher, theoretician, historian and author, international arbiter.

He was a poet, who knew Blok personally, whose verses were venerated, and who much admired Bagritsky. He was musical, a virtuoso of folk instruments – the balalaika and the harmonica, and appeared on stage on occasion, performing Beethoven and Liszt. His passion for chess overrode all others, and it was to that he dedicated his entire life. He first drew attention to himself as a 17-year old, playing in the All-Russian amateur tournament of 1909, where he was the only one to win against the first-prizewinner, Alexander Alekhine, who was the same age.

(89) Alekhine – Romanovsky
St Petersburg 1909
Giuoco Piano [C27]

1.e4 e5 2.♘c3 ♘f6 3.♗c4 ♗c5 4.d3 h6?! 5.f4 d6 6.f5 ♘c6 7.a3 ♘d4 8.♘a4? This plays into Black's hand as White development is much too slow now. 8.♘f3 is the main move. **8...b5! 9.♘×c5 b×c4 10.♘a4 ♕d7?!** 10...c×d3!? 11.c×d3 ♘×e4 was very strong. **11.♘c3 ♗b7 12.♘f3 ♘b5 13.0-0 ♘×c3 14.b×c3 ♕c6 15.♕e1?!** The start of a misguided plan

as Black will play on the kingside later. 15.♗e3 was called for. **15...♗a6 16.♕g3 ♖g8 17.d4 ♘×e4 18.♕h4 ♗b7 19.♖e1?! g5! 20.f×g6 ♖×g6 21.d×e5?** 21.♔f1 is forced.

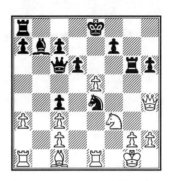

21...d×e5? Romanovsky misses the hammer 21...♘d2!! 22.e×d6+ ♔f8 23.♗×d2 ♖×g2+−+ **22.♖e2?** 22.♔f1 is forced and defends at least for the moment. **22...♔f8?!** 22...♖d8 is even better, e.g., 23.♕e1 ♕f6−+ **23.♗×h6+?** 23.♕h3! limits the damage. **23...♖×h6 24.♕e1 ♖d8 25.♖b1 ♗a8 26.♔h1 ♕d5 27.a4 f6 28.a5 ♔f7 29.a6 ♖g8 30.♖e3 ♘g5 31.♕f1 ♘×f3 32.♖×f3 ♕d2 33.♕×c4+ ♗d5 34.♕×c7+ ♔e6 35.♖b6+ a×b6 36.♕×b6+ ♔f7 37.♕c7+ ♔f8 38.♕d8+ ♔g7 39.♖g3+ ♖g6 40.♕d7+ ♔h8 41.♖h3+ ♖h6 0- 42.♖×h6+ 0-1** There would follow 42...×h6 43.♕×d5 ♕c1+ 44.♔d1 ♕×d1 ♯

In the years that followed, the paths of Romanovsky and Alekhine would cross more than once. Within five years, they were both playing in tournament of the German Chess Congress in Mannheim: Alekhine – in the main event (where he took first place) and Romanovsky – in the ancillary one (second/fourth places). Both of them were interned when the First World War started. In 1920, they

Pyotr Romanovsky

took part in the All-Russian Olympiad – the first championship of Soviet Russia, where Romanovsky took second place, while Alekhine was first.

In 1921, Romanovsky was one of the founders of the first chess periodical in Soviet Russia – *Listok shakhmatnovo kruzhka Petrogubkommuni*, and prophetically wrote: "Not too far in the future, the time will come when the art of chess in Russia, raised up by the single-minded labor of all its students and their teachers, will occupy an honorable place in the arena of global contests, in the creation of rich chess thought, so beautiful in its depth of content."

In that same year, Alekhine left for the West to storm the chess Olympus; and within two years, in 1923, Romanovsky would become champion of the Russian Federation. At the Moscow International Tournament of 1925, he finished the best of all the Soviet participants, sharing seventh/eighth places with Réti.

In spring 1928, preparing for the USSR championship, the six best players in Leningrad held a match-tournament. First place, ceding just two draws, was taken by Pyotr Arsenievich. After a sharp fight, his victory was sealed by a win in this encounter with the young Botvinnik.

(90) Romanovsky – Botvinnik
Leningrad 1927
Réti Opening [A04]

1.♘f3 d5 2.c4 d4 3.b4 g6 4.♗b2 ♗g7 5.g3 b6 6.♗g2 ♗b7 7.0-0 e5 8.d3 ♘e7 9.♘bd2 0-0 10.♘b3 ♘d7 11.c5? White is not ready for this advance yet. 11.a4 c5 12.♗a3 is more circumspect. **11...a5! 12.b×a5 b×a5 13.a4 ♗d5 14.♗a3 ♘c6 15.♘fd2 ♘f6 16.♕c2 ♖e8** 16...♗×g2!? 17.♔×g2 ♘d5 was the alternative. **17.♘e4 ♖b8 18.♘bd2 ♘×e4 19.♘×e4 f5?**

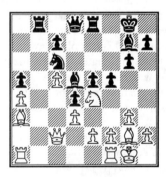

This runs into a powerful blow. Black is slightly better after 19...♘b4 or 19...♗b3. **20.♘d6! ♗b3** 20...♗×g2?? 21.♕c4+ ♔h8 22.♘f7+ ♔g8 23.♘h6+ ♔h8 24.♕g8+ ♖×g8 25.♘f7 **#** **21.♕c1 c×d6?** 21...♘b4 22.♘×e8 ♕×e8 23.♗×b4 ♖×b4 offers much more resistance. **22.♗×c6 ♖e6 23.c×d6 ♗f8** 23...♖×d6 24.♗×d6 ♕×d6

25.♗b5+– 24.d7 ♗h6 25.♛c5 ♗f8 26.♛×f8+ ♛×f8 27.♗×f8 ♚×f8 28.♖fc1 ♖d6 29.♖ab1 ♖b4 29...♚e7 30.♖c5+– 30.♗b5 ♚e7 31.♖c8 ♖×d7 32.♗×d7 ♚×d7 33.♖a8 ♗c2 34.♖×b4 a×b4 35.a5 ♚c7

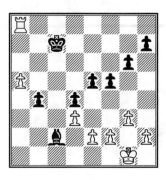

36.a6? White misses the deadly *zwischenschach* 36.♖a7+! ♚c6 (36...♚b8 37.♖a6+–) 37.a6 ♚b5 38.♖b7+ ♚×a6 39.♖×b4+– **36...b3 37.a7 ♚b7 38.♖b8+ ♚×a7 39.♖b4 e4?** Black does not have time for this. The king must be activated immediately with 39...♚a6 40.♚f1 ♚a5 41.♖b8 ♚a4 42.♚e1 ♚a3 43.♚d2 ♚b2= **40.♚f1?!** 40.d×e4 f×e4 41.♚f1 ♚a6 42.e3 ♚a5 43.♖b7 ♚a4 44.♚e1 ♚a3 45.♚d2 ♗d3 46.♚c1+– **40...e×d3** Black's king is quite passive now. But it is also not likely that 40...♚a6 defends in view of 41.♚e1 ♚a5 42.♖b8 ♚a4 43.♚d2 ♚a3 44.d×e4 ♗×e4 45.f3 ♗c6 46.♖b6 ♗a4 47.♚c1± **41.e×d3 ♗×d3+ 42.♚e1 ♗c2 43.♚d2 d3 44.♚c3 ♚a6 45.h4 ♚a7 46.♖b5 h5 47.♖b4 ♚a6 48.♖b8 ♚a5 49.♖g8 d2 50.♚×d2 f4 51.g×f4 ♚b4 52.♖b8+ ♚c4 53.♖c8+ ♚d4 54.f3 ♗f5 55.♖b8 ♚c4 56.♖b7 ♗c2 57.♖c7+ ♚d4 58.♖a7 ♚c4 59.♖a4+ ♚b5 60.♖e4 ♚c5** 60...♗×e4 61.f×e4 ♚b4 62.♚c1 ♚a3 63.♚b1+– **61.♚c3 ♚c6?!** 61...♚d6 62.♖e5 ♚d7 63.f5 g×f5 64.♖d5+ ♚e6 65.♖d4 ♚e5 66.f4+ ♚e6 67.♖d8 ♚e7 68.♖h8 ♗d1 69.♚d2 ♗f3 70.♖b8 ♗d5 71.♖b6 ♚d7

72.♚c3+– **62.♖d4 ♚c5 63.♖d2 ♚b5 64.♖×c2 b×c2 65.♚×c2 ♚c6 66.♚d3 ♚d7 67.♚e4 ♚e6**

68.f5+ Romanovsky forces open the gates to Botvinnik's position. **68...g×f5+ 69.♚d4 1-0**

In the same year, Romanovsky once again became national champion. For the first time, Mikhail Botvinnik took part in the USSR championship, and shared fifth/sixth places.

In the 1920s, Romanovsky already showed himself to be a talented teacher, conducting lessons in the chess circle of the "Sovtorgcluzhaschikh" club. Among his students were the talented masters Vladimir Alatortsev, Vitaly Chekhover, Grigory Ravinsky, and others.

At the start of the 1930s, Romanovsky and his student Alatortsev were the chief opponents of the young chess giant Botvinnik in all of the Leningrad tournaments.

Heart disease, which afflicted Romanovsky in 1939, made him quit competitive appearances for a while. He lived with his four daughters, aged 5 to 17. His wife had died giving birth to his

Fortunate was the childhood, and tragic was the fate of the daughters of Pyotr Romanovsky.

youngest daughter Anechka. When war began, he was named director of the Central Chess Club of Leningrad. The terrible blockade of winter 1942 took the lives of all his daughters. They were only able to save the sick and helpless Romanovsky. Chess helped him not to lose his strength and live through it. Thinking about the necessity to finish his work, once begun, would not leave him for one second. Again and again, he would sit with his chess notebook... "Life and chess skill have flowed together harmoniously in my worldview," wrote Romanovsky. A clear propagandist of Chigorin's kind of ideas, a foe of routine and dogmatism in the art of chess, Romanovsky won special popularity as a journalist, as a literary man, and as a chess historian, pedagogue, and reader, especially among the young. His wonderful work in chess in the middlegame and the history of chess became common tableside works for many generations of Soviet chessplayers.

Works: Alekhine-Capablanca, Match for the World Championship, Leningrad 1928 (co-author); *Middlegame. Combination and Planning in Chess,* Leningrad 1929; *What Everyone Should Know about the Opening,* Leningrad 1929; *Chess Ideas In Practice,* Moscow-Leningrad 1930; *Paths to Chess Creativity,* Moscow-Leningrad 1933; *Questions of Chess Methodology – Various Programs for Chess Schools,* Moscow-Leningrad, 1938; *Selected Games,* Moscow 1959; *Romanticism in the Art of Chess,* Moscow 1959; *Middlegame Planning,* Moscow 1960; *Middlegame Combinations,* Moscow 1963; *Chess in Russia: The Players and Their Games,* London 1946 (published by Soviet News).

Books: Romanov, Pyotr Romanovsky, Moscow 1984

Ryumin, Nikolai Nikolaevich (September 5, 1908, Moscow-November 17, 1942, Omsk), Russian chess master, notable for his activity in the Soviet chess movement. In 1935, former world champion Emanuel Lasker gave notice that he was ready to work with "a group of the most gifted chessplayers, led by Ryumin..."

Nikolai learned chess relatively late – at 16-years of age. But just four years later, in the championship of Moscow, he showed himself to be one of the strongest chessplayers in the capital. In 1931, he won the master's title by beating the famous theoretician N. Grigoriev in a match, by the score of +6 -1 =1.

The same year, he became the champion of Moscow. What distinguished his play was his striving for a complex struggle, original treatment of positions, tactical sharpness, and beautiful combinations.

In the mid-1930s, Ryumin showed himself to be one of the strongest players in the USSR. He played successfully in three USSR championships; in the seventh, he took second place behind Botvinnik. He shared second/third places in a tournament in Leningrad with Euwe and Kmoch. He took part in the second and third Moscow International tournaments. His resumé featured wins over Botvinnik, Euwe, Ståhlberg and other grandmasters. Capablanca suffered a sensational loss to him in the very first round of the 1935 Moscow tournament.

(91) Ryumin – Capablanca
Moscow 1935
Nimzo-Indian Defense [E37]

1.d4 ♘f6 2.c4 e6 3.♘c3 ♗b4 4.♕c2 d5 5.a3 ♗×c3+ 6.♕×c3 ♘e4

Nikolai Ryumin

7.♕c2 c5 8.d×c5 ♘c6 9.e3 ♕a5+ 10.♗d2 ♕×c5 11.b4 ♕e7 12.♗c1 a5?! 13.b5 ♘e5 14.♗b2 ♘g4 15.♘h3 ♕h4?!

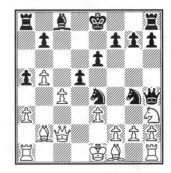

16.g3? Now Black can seize the initiative. The direct 16.♗×g7! ♘e3 (16...♖g8 17.g3) 17.♕d3 ♘×f1 18.♗×h8 is critical and better for White. **16...♕h6 17.♕e2 ♘gf6?** This retreat is too passive. Now White's bishops will reign supreme. 17...e5! is more in the spirit of the position, e.g., 18.f3 ♘×e3 19.f×e4 ♗g4 20.♕d3 d4, with good compensation. **18.♘f4 0-0 19.♗g2 d×c4?! 20.♕×c4 ♘d6 21.♕d3 ♖d8 22.♖d1 ♘fe8 23.0-0 a4 24.♘e2?** After 24.♗e5+–, Black is unable to untangle. **24...♗d7 25.♘c3 ♖a5?** 25...♕h5 limits the damage. **26.♕d4 ♕g5?** 26...♗×b5 27.♕b4 ♖da8 was the lesser evil, but Black's position still looks lost. **27.♕b4 b6 28.♖d2 ♗×b5 29.♖fd1 h6** and in this lost position Capablanca overstepped the time limit. **1-0**

(92) Ryumin – Botvinnik
Leningrad 1934
English Opening [A34]

1.c4 ♘f6 2.♘c3 d5 3.c×d5 ♘×d5 4.♘f3 ♘×c3 5.b×c3 g6 6.g3 ♗g7 7.♗g2 0-0 8.0-0 c5 9.♕a4 ♗d7 10.♕a3 ♘a6 11.♖b1 ♗c6 12.d3 ♕c8 13.♗e3 b6 14.d4 ♗e4 15.♖bc1 ♖d8 16.♖fe1 ♕b7 17.♕b3 e6 18.♖ed1 ♖ac8 19.♕b2 ♗f8 20.♗g5 ♖e8 21.♘e1 ♗×g2 22.♘×g2 h6 23.♗e3 ♖ed8 24.f3 ♗g7 25.♗f2 c×d4 26.c×d4 ♘b8 27.♖×c8 ♖×c8 28.e4 ♕c7 29.♕e2 ♕c2 30.♖d2 ♕b1+ 31.♘e1 ♕b4 32.♔g2 ♖d8 33.♘c2?! 33.♖c2 ♕a4 34.♖c4 ♕e8 35.♕b2 ♘c6 36.♘c2 is more harmonious. **33...♕a4 34.a3 ♗f8 35.♕d3 ♘c6 36.d5 e×d5 37.e×d5 ♘e7** 37...♘e5!? **38.♕e4 ♕×e4 39.f×e4 f5! 40.♔f3 f×e4+ 41.♔×e4 ♘f5 42.a4 ♘d6+ 43.♔d3 ♘b7 44.♔c4 ♘d6+ 45.♔d3 ♖c8 46.♘a3 ♖c1 ½-½**

Books: Kan, I., *The Chessplayer A. Ryumin*, Moscow 1968.

Szabo, Laszlo (March 19, 1917, Budapest-August 8, 1998, Budapest), Hungarian grandmaster and chess author; candidate for the world championship in the 1950s.

His father taught him to play chess at the age of 6. At 14, he started playing in tournaments, and three years later became a master and the champion of Hungary (1935). In the 1930s, he twice won at Hastings (1938/39), and also played twice for his national team in the "Tournament of Nations" (1935 and 1937).

At the close of the 1940s and in the 1950s, Szabo showed himself to be one of the strongest players in the world. In the period from 1947 to 1964, he played in zonal tournaments ten times, and three times in candidates' tournaments – Budapest 1950, Zürich 1953, and Amsterdam 1956. In the last of these, Szabo came closest to scaling the chess Olympus, sharing third/seventh places with Bronstein, Geller, Petrosian and Spassky, allowing only Smyslov and Keres ahead of him. "A sharp, interesting chessplayer," Botvinnik wrote about him. Beginning in 1952, Szabo played nine times in the Olympiads and seven times in the European Team championships.

In the years 1946 through 1979, he took part in 88 international tournaments, winning first prize 21 times, and 30 times finishing in either second or third place. Szabo was three times victorious in the New Year's tournaments in Hastings (1947/48, 1949/50, and 1973/74), twice in Budapest (1948 and 1965), and Paris (1964 and 1966), took first prize in strong tournaments in Valencia (1949), Zagreb (1964), Sarajevo (1972), Hilversum (1973), Kapfenberg (1976), and Helsinki (1979).

Szabo's playing style was aggressive and combinational – he was always striving for the initiative and the attack. Here are games that he played at the XIV Olympiad, and in the finals of the European team championship.

Laszlo Szabo

(93) Szabo – Ståhlberg
Leipzig 1960
King's Indian Defense [E70]

1.d4 ♘f6 2.c4 g6 3.♘c3 ♗g7 4.e4 d6 5.♗g5 h6 6.♗h4 c6?! 7.f4 ♕b6 8.♕d2 ♘a6 9.♗e2 ♘c7?! Black's set up is too passive. **10.e5 d×e5 11.f×e5 ♘d7 12.♘f3 c5 13.♗f2 0-0 14.d×c5 ♕a5 15.0-0 ♘e6 16.♖ab1 ♘×e5 17.♘×e5 ♗×e5 18.♕×h6** 18.b4 ♕d8 19.♘d5 is also very strong. **18...♘f4?! 19.♗f3 ♕c7?!**

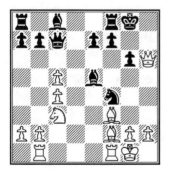

20.♖be1? 20.♘b5 is even better: 20...♕b8 21.♗g3 ♗e6 22.♖fe1 ♗×c4 23.♘c3+– **20...♗g7 21.♕h4 ♗f6 22.♕g3** 22.♘b5!? **22...♗×c3**

23.b×c3 e5 24.♗d5 ♖d8? Black must bring in another defender with 24...♗e6 with chances to defend. **25.♗d4! ♘×d5** 25...e×d4 26.♖×f4 ♗f5 27.c×d4+– **26.♖×e5 ♘×c3 27.♗×c3 1-0**

(94) Botvinnik – Szabo
Hamburg 1965
King's Indian Defense [E85]

1.c4 g6 2.d4 ♘f6 3.♘c3 ♗g7 4.e4 d6 5.f3 0-0 6.♗e3 ♘c6 7.♘ge2 e5 8.d5 ♘e7 9.♕d2 ♘d7 10.g3 f5 11.♗g2 f×e4 12.f×e4 a6 13.h3 ♖b8 14.♗a7 ♖a8 15.♗f2 h6 16.0-0 ♘f6 17.♗e3 ♔h7 18.c5 ♗d7 19.b4 g5 20.a4 ♕e8 21.♕e1 ♕g6 22.♖b1 ♘h5 23.g4 ♘f4 24.♘g3 ♕f6 25.♖f2 ♘eg6 26.♗f1 ♘h4 27.♕d1 ♕e7 28.♖bb2 ♖f7 29.♘f5?! White is too impatient. The preparatory 29.♔h1 is better. **29...♗×f5 30.g×f5 h5?** 30...♗f6 31.♔h1 ♖g7 followed by ...g4 is a better attacking set up as also the second rook can quickly join via g8. **31.♖h2 ♗h6 32.♔h1 ♖g8 33.♗f2 ♖fg7 34.♘e2 g4 35.h×g4 ♖×g4 36.♘g1?** Too passive. The active solution 36.♖b3 ♕g5 37.♖c3 is better for White. **36...♕g7?!** 36...♕g5!? **37.♗h3?** 37.♗c4 ♕g5 38.♕f1= coordinates the defense in a better way. **37...♘×h3 38.♖×h3 ♘g2?** 38...♕g5 39.♖bb3 ♖×e4 is more precise.

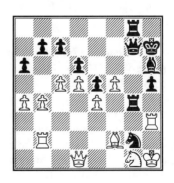

175

39.♖×h5? Now Black's attack allows a very good transformation of advantages. The rooks had to be activated with 39.c×d6 ♘f4 40.♖c3 c×d6 41.♖bc2 ♕f6 42.♖c7+ ♔h8 43.♖c8= **39...♘f4 40.♖h4 ♘d3** Szabo simplifies into a very favorable endgame. **41.♖×g4** 41.♕×d3? ♖×h4+ 42.♗×h4 ♕×g1♯ **41...♕×g4 42.♕×g4 ♖×g4 43.♖c2 ♘×f2+ 44.♖×f2 ♖×e4 45.♖b2?!** The active 45.♖c2 is preferable. **45...♖c4 46.♘e2 ♔g7 47.♔g2?!** 47.c×d6 c×d6 48.a5 offers better chances, but it is not likely that White can defend in view of Black's activity. **47...♔f6 48.♔f3 e4+ 49.♔g4 e3+ 50.♔f3 ♔×f5 51.c×d6 c×d6 52.♖b1 ♗g5 53.a5 ♔e5 54.♖g1 ♗f6 55.♖b1 ♔×d5 56.♔×e3** 56.b5 ♖c5–+ **56...♔c6 57.♔d3 ♔b5 58.♖f1 ♗e5 59.♖f7 ♖×b4 60.♖×b7+ ♔×a5 61.♖a7 ♔b6 62.♖a8 ♔b7 63.♖f8 a5 64.♖f7+ ♔a6 65.♖f8 ♔a7 66.♖c8 ♔b7 67.♖f8 ♖b3+ 68.♔c2 ♖h3 69.♘c1 a4 70.♘d3 ♖h2+ 71.♔b1 ♗c3 72.♖f3** 72.♖f4 ♖d2–+ **72...♔b6 73.♘f4 ♗d4 74.♖d3 ♗e5 75.♘g6 ♔c5 76.♖e3 ♗d4 77.♖f3 ♔c4 0-1**

Szabo's societal and literary activity greatly aided the popularization and development of chess in Hungary. He edited chess columns in periodicals, and wrote books, the most famous of which was *50 Years – 100,000 Moves!* (Budapest, 1981).

Book: 50 Years – 100,000 Moves!, Budapest, 1981; *Meine besten partien*, Budapest, 1990.

Sverdlovsk, 1943 (April 20-May 16). A double-round training event with the participation of eight chessplayers became the first strong tournament since the start World War II. In spite of his two-year absence from practical play (since the match-tournament of 1941), Botvinnik showed that he was in excellent competitive form. In fourteen games, he scored seven victories and seven draws.

(95) Botvinnik – Konstantinopolsky
Sverdlovsk 1943
Caro-Kann Defense [B14]

1.e4 c6 2.d4 d5 3.e×d5 c×d5 4.c4 ♘f6 5.♘c3 e6 6.♘f3 ♗e7 7.♗g5 0-0 8.♖c1 ♘c6 9.c5 ♘e4 10.♗×e7 ♕×e7 11.♗e2 ♗d7 12.a3 f5 13.♗b5 ♘g5 14.♗×c6 ♘×f3+ 15.♕×f3 b×c6 16.♕f4 ♖ae8 17.0-0 e5 18.♕×e5 ♕×e5 19.d×e5 ♖×e5 20.f4 ♖e7 21.♖fe1 ♖fe8 22.♖×e7 ♖×e7 23.♔f2 ♔f7 24.♖d1 ♖e8 25.♖d2 h6 26.♖e2

26...♖b8! Black keeps the rook for counterplay. **27.♔e3 ♖b3?!** 27...♗c8 28.♔d4 ♗a6 29.♖d2 ♗c4= **28.♔d4 ♔f6 29.♘a2 ♖b8?!** 29...a5 30.♘c1 ♖b8 31.♘d3 ♖b3 is a better defensive set up. **30.b4 g5 31.g3 g×f4 32.g×f4 a6 33.♘c3** 33.♘c1!? **33...♖g8 34.a4 ♖g4 35.♖f2** (D)

35...♗e6? 35...♔f7 36.b5 c×b5 37.a×b5 a×b5 38.♘×d5 ♖g1 was the last chance to fight. **36.b5 a×b5 37.a×b5 c×b5 38.♘×b5 ♖g1 39.♘c3 ♔f7 40.♖b2 ♖f1 41.♘e2 ♖e1** 41...♖f2 42.♔e5 ♗c8 43.♖a2 ♖×h2 44.♖a7+

♔g6 45.♘d4+– **42.♔e5** 42.c6!?+–
42...d4 43.♔×d4 ♔g6?! 44.♘c3
44.c6!?+– **44...♔h5 45.♖e2 ♖×e2**
46.♘×e2 ♔g4 47.♔e5 ♗c8
48.♘d4 h5 49.♘×f5 ♗d7 50.♘g7
♗a4 51.f5 ♔g5 52.♘e6+ 1-0

Smyslov, Vassily Vassilievich (March 24, 1921, Moscow-March 27, 2010 Moscow), Russian chessplayer, international grandmaster (1950); seventh world champion (1957-58); chess theoretician and composer.

At the age of six, Vasya was taught chess by his father, a strong Moscow player. "The first chess book I read," Smyslov tells us, "was Dufresne's *Chess Self-Teacher*, published with a supplement: Emanuel Lasker's lecture series, *Common Sense In Chess*. Through it, I became familiar with the romantic games of the old masters, and with gambit style of play." Soon, *My Best Games* by Alekhine, *Chess Fundamentals* by Capablanca, *Contemporary Chess* by Tarrasch, and *My System* by Nimzovich became his favorite books. The first of these was given to him by his uncles, with the inscription, "To A Future champion."

In his first school championships, his opponents of the same age felt that an exceptionally gifted player had

Vassily Smyslov

appeared among them. At 17, Vassily Smyslov became a master and Moscow champion; and two years later, in his first appearance in the USSR championship, he took third place, ahead of Keres, Botvinnik, and other well-known players.

In the USSR-USA match of 1945, Smyslov beat Reshevsky in both their games; and a year later, in 1946, his score at the international tournament of Groningen was good enough for third place, and he became a candidate for the world championship. Ossip Bernstein, the tournament's oldest participant, said at the time: "The world of chess has, in the person of Smyslov, a great talent, who awaits great creative and competitive successes."

This was confirmed by the match-tournament of 1948. Smyslov was successful, taking second place. And in doing so, he lost to the future world champion, Botvinnik, and the USSR champion, Keres, by scores of 3-2 in each mini-match. His performances against Reshevsky and Euwe ended in his favor. He defeated the former Dutch world champion by the score of 4-1. Euwe heartily exclaimed: "Yes, Smyslov is an amazing player, a friendly and pleasant person – but to play with him is very dangerous!"

"The Number Two Chessplayer in the World" – such was the way they started to write about Smyslov after this tournament. But Vassily firmly decided that he was going to become first. And he completed his mastery in tournaments – he deepened his understanding in openings and endgames. Soon he achieved the long-awaited success: he was the winner of the candidates' tournament at Zürich, 1953, which gave him the right to meet Botvinnik in a match for the world championship.

There were, of course, many differences between the challenger and the challenged: a decade's difference in ages, the fact that their opening tastes did not converge, and their different ways of preparing themselves for these events. But they had a lot in common, as well. Both of them would fight, without compromise, in every game, and looked on chess, in the first instance, as an art. So their match struggle was tense and interesting. Here is the shortest, and also the most spectacular game of this entire event, in which Smyslov sacrificed his queen as early as the 19th move.

(96) Smyslov – Botvinnik
Moscow (m9) 1954
French Defense [C18]

1.e4 e6 2.d4 d5 3.♘c3 ♗b4 4.e5 c5 5.a3 ♗a5 6.b4 c×d4 7.♕g4 ♘e7 8.b×a5 d×c3 9.♕×g7 ♖g8 10.♕×h7 ♘d7 11.♘f3 ♘f8? Too passive.

11...♕c7 is the main move. **12.♕d3** 12.♕h5!? **12...♕×a5 13.h4 ♗d7 14.♗g5** 14.♖b1!? **14...♖c8 15.♘d4 ♘f5 16.♖b1 ♖c4?** 16...b6 17.♘b5 ♖×g5 18.h×g5 ♖c4 19.♘d6+ ♘×d6 20.e×d6 ♕×a3 limits the damage. **17.♘×f5 e×f5 18.♖×b7 ♖e4+**

19.♕×e4!! d×e4 20.♖b8+ ♗c8 21.♗b5+ ♕×b5 22.♖×b5 ♘e6 23.♗f6 ♖×g2 24.h5 ♗a6 25.h6 1-0

The match ended drawn, 12-12. This was the third drawn outcome in the history of world championship matches. Previously the matches Lasker-Schlechter 1910 and Botvinnik-Bronstein 1951 had also been drawn.

After this encounter, a moment occurred in Smyslov's life when he had to make a choice between chess and his singing talent. Having inherited a well-tempered baritone from his father, a good deal of Vassily's spare time was devoted to music. Vassily was one of 50 students from all corners of the nation excused from school. He successfully passed through the first round, and ... did not prepare as he should have for the second, because of an upcoming tournament. "I chose chess, and I don't regret it," Smyslov said. His mastery of both music and chess did not go unnoticed. During his chess appearances, he gave solo concerts in both New York and Amsterdam...

After winning the candidates' tournament in Amsterdam, 1956, Smyslov beat Botvinnik by a score of 12½-9½, and became the seventh world champion. "Smyslov's chief strength in chess," wrote his defeated opponent, "is the fact that he is very astute. He has a talent that is universal and exceptional. He can play very delicately in the opening, withdraw into a deep defense or attack fiercely, or finally maneuver coolly; and more cannot be said of his endgame talent – this is his element."

(97) Smyslov – Botvinnik
Moscow (m6) 1957
Grünfeld Defense [D98]

1.d4 ♘f6 2.c4 g6 3.♘c3 d5 4.♘f3 ♗g7 5.♕b3 d×c4 6.♕×c4 0-0 7.e4 ♗g4 8.♗e3 ♘fd7 9.0-0-0 ♘c6 10.h3 ♗×f3 11.g×f3 ♘b6 12.♕c5 f5 13.♘e2 13.♗c4+!? ♔h8 14.♘e2± **13...♕d6 14.e5 ♕×c5+?** 14...♕e6 15.♕b1 f4 16.♗c1 ♕f5+ 17.♔a1 ♕f7 is more active. **15.d×c5 ♘c4 16.f4 ♖fd8 17.♗g2 ♘×e3?!** 17...♘b4 18.♘d4 ♔f7 19.♗×b7 ♖ab8 gives better practical chances as Black has more counterplay. **18.f×e3 ♘b4 19.♗×b7 ♖ab8 20.c6** 20.♖×d8+!? ♖×d8 21.♘d4± **20...♔f7** 20...♘d5!? **21.♘d4** 21.♖d7!? **21...e6?!** 21...♘d5 22.♖he1± **22.♘b5 ♘d5?!**

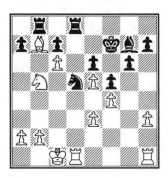

23.♖×d5! e×d5 24.♘×c7 ♖dc8 25.♗×c8 ♖×c8 26.♘×d5 ♖×c6+ 27.♔d2 ♕e6 28.♘c3 1-0

In a conversation with one of this book's authors, Smyslov had this to say about his creative credo: "If I were to answer this question in one word, it would be the search for 'harmony.' It shows itself most clearly in many areas of creativity: mathematics, music, or chess... The amazing world of chess ideas and beauty is revealed in logical thought, in the dialectic of constantly changing relationships, in the richness of its composition. The last, in turn, finds expression, both in combinative play with spectacular sacrifices, and in positions that appear at first sight to be simple. A chessplayer's genuine talent as an artist consists in the constant pursuit of harmony, the ability to have an intuitive feeling for the coordination of the pieces. I get particular esthetic satisfaction whenever I can execute an idea in clear relief."

And Smyslov succeeds in this, not just in his practical appearances, but in composition also, which he has enriched with a number of beautiful studies, and in the theory of openings and endgames. One could name a number of openings in which he has added something new: in the Spanish Game, Sicilian and French Defenses, the English Opening, King's Indian Defense, as well as entire systems bearing Smyslov's name.

"Not one year without a tournament!" – this would be Smyslov's motto. Over the course of the three decades which passed since his third match with Botvinnik, he has won a number of the strongest international tournaments – in Moscow, Leningrad, Hastings, Havana, Amsterdam, Monte Carlo, Skopje, Zagreb, Polanica Zdroj, Reykjavik, Palma de Mallorca, Mar del Plata, Las Palmas, Buenos Aires, Saõ Paulo, and many other cities. In many tournaments, Smyslov has played a number of beautiful games. Here we have a game with an exceptionally beautiful ending, played in the 55th national championship against grandmaster Vyacheslav Eingorn. In the final position, Black had to resign, although he was a rook ahead, because of a most unusual *zugzwang*!

(98) Smyslov – Eingorn
USSR 1988
Sicilian Defense [B42]

1.e4 c5 2.♘f3 e6 3.d4 c×d4 4.♘×d4 a6 5.♗d3 ♘f6 6.0-0 ♕c7 7.♕e2 ♗c5 8.♘b3 ♗a7 9.♔h1 d6 10.c4 ♘c6 11.♗g5 ♗d7 12.♘c3 ♘d4 13.♘×d4 ♗×d4 14.♖ac1 ♕c5 15.♗d2 ♕h5?! Black's plan is very provocative. 15...0-0 is more natural. **16.f3 ♗e5?! 17.g4 ♕h4 18.♕g2 g5 19.♗e1** 19.♘e2!? **19...♕h6 20.♗g3 ♕g7**

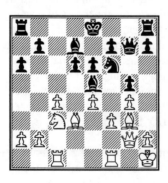

21.c5!? Smyslov undermines Black's center and opens inroads. **21...♗c6** 21...♗×g3 22.♕×g3 d×c5 23.e5 ♘d5 24.♘×d5 e×d5 25.♖×c5 is also better for White. **22.c×d6 ♘d7 23.f4?** This gives Black a strong blockade on the dark squares. 23.♗e2 ♗×g3 24.♕×g3 h5 25.g×h5 ♘f6 26.♖g1 applies more pressure. **23...g×f4** 23...♗×d6 24.f×g5 ♗×g3 25.♕×g3 ♕×g5= is also playable. **24.♗×f4 0-0 25.♗×e5?! ♕×e5 26.♕g3 ♖ad8 27.♖cd1 ♔g7?!** 27...♕×g3 28.h×g3 b5 29.a3 ♘e5= **28.♔g2 f6?! 29.♗c2?!** 29.♖f2!? **29...♖g8 30.h3 h5 31.♕×e5 ♘×e5 32.g×h5 ♔f7+ 33.♔f2 ♖h8 34.♘e2**

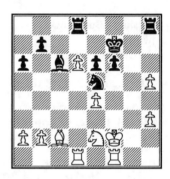

34...♖×h5? White's knight is very strong now. It should be exchanged with 34...♗b5! 35.♖g1 ♗×e2 36.♔×e2 ♖×h5= **35.♘f4! ♖h4 36.♔g3 ♖hh8 37.♗b3 ♖de8 38.♖d4?!** 38.♖c1!?± **38...♘d7?** 38...♗d7 39.♖d2 ♖c8 is a better set up. **39.♖c1 ♖hg8+ 40.♔f2 ♖g5 41.♖dc4 a5?** 41...♖e5 42.♗d1 ♖h8 43.♗g4 f5 44.e×f5 e×f5 45.♗f3± **42.♖×c6! b×c6 43.♖×c6 ♖e5 44.♖c7 ♖d8** (D)

45.♘×e6!? ♖×e6 46.h4 1-0 Black is in fatal *zugzwang*.

Smyslov is one chessplayer with a lengthy competitive lifespan. He continued to perform successfully in

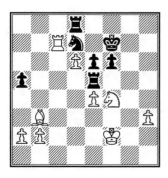

tournaments, even after he observed his 70th birthday.

At the start of the 21st century, Smyslov, owing to his deteriorating eyesight, preferred to busy himself with composing studies, which grew to over one hundred in number and became a noteworthy direction for his chess creativity.

In 1988, the Italian Chessplayers' Association awarded their international prize in honor of the well-known Italian Gioacchino Greco, emblazoned "Chess Is Life." And the first chessplayer on the planet to receive this award was Vassily Smyslov. In their congratulatory words, the association said that he had, thanks to "his notable competitive longevity, achieved the very highest level of mastery and creative successes," and brought "a considerable contribution to the development of the game as a gifted teacher and author."

Books: *Guide for Beginning Chessplayers*, 1949 , Kaluga, 1951 (co-authored); *Selected Games*, Moscow 1952; *International Chess Tournament in Switzerland (Impressions of a Participant)*, Moscow 1954; *Sixth Board, The Smyslov-Reshevsky Match*, Moscow 1971; *Theory of Rook Endgames*, 1957, 3rd ed., Moscow 1986 (co-authored with G. Levenfish); *In Search of Harmony*, Moscow 1979; *A Chronicle of Chess Creativity*, Moscow 1995; *My Studies*, 2nd ed., Moscow 2005.

Lit.: Alatortsev, V., Stepanov, A., *Botvinnik-Smyslov – Match for the World Championship*, Moscow 1954; Botvinnik, M., *Smyslov-Botvinnik Return Match*, Moscow 1960; Linder, V., Linder, I., "Vassily Smyslov" (in the book *Kings of the Chess World*, Moscow 2001); Kasparov, G., with Plisetsky, D., "Vassily the Seventh" (in the book, *My Great Predecessors*, vol. 2, Moscow 2003; *The Three Botvinnik-Smyslov Matches*, Moscow 2004 (composed by I. Botvinnik); Voronkov, C., Plisetsky, D., *The Russians vs. Fischer*, Moscow 2004.

USSR Championships

Mikhail Botvinnik played in 12 national championships. Of these, he took part in 10 finals, and won six of them; in the rest, he was one of the top six. His first was the fifth championship (in 1927) at 16-years of age; he concluded playing in the championships with the 22nd (in 1955), at age 43. In all, he played 181 games in these championships, winning 95, drawing 65 and losing 21 – that is, he amassed 127½ points (70.4%) in all! In addition, Botvinnik won the match-tournament of 1941 for the title of absolute champion of the USSR. Therefore, he is considered a seven-time champion of the USSR. No other Russian chessplayer achieved that kind of success.

1927, September 36-October 25, Moscow At the opening ceremony of the 5th USSR championship, which was to be held in the Hall of Unions, the poet Alexander Bezimensky read his poem, *Chess*, which began with the words:

"Do not be forty-degree men.
Worker! Get drunk on chess!"

And, in that autumn of 1927, when a tournament of the strongest chessplayers in the country was being held in Moscow, there was a match between the strongest chessplayers on the planet taking place in Buenos Aires, Capablanca and Alekhine. Millions of enthusiasts of this ancient game could indeed "drink up" chess.

The 16-year old Leningrader, Mikhail Botvinnik, had an auspicious debut. He shared fifth/sixth places with Vladimir Makogonov, and had already fulfilled the master norm by the 17th round (that is, three rounds before the end). The results of the first six prizewinners: 1-2. Romanovsky, Bohatyrchuk – 14½/20; 3-4. Dus Chotimirsky, Model – 13; Botvinnik, Makogonov – 12½. Characterizing Botvinnik's play, *Shakhmatny Listok* (21/1927) wrote: "Great restraint and deep understanding of various types of positions assure him of outstanding success. The drawback of his creativity is a somewhat routine evaluation of positions, as a consequence of which, he sometimes misses the strongest continuations, contenting himself with realizing advantages that are sometimes insufficient to win."

1931, October 10-November 11, Moscow 50 years later, the magazine *Shakhmaty v SSSR* (10/1981) noted that there were many things in this 7th USSR championship which occurred for the first time:

(a) Youth offered determined resistance to experienced masters... and confidently assumed the upper hand. 20-year old Mikhail Botvinnik, a student from Leningrad, became champion. Second place was taken by the Muscovite, Nikolai Ryumin, who was then 23-years old. And the Leningrader Vladimir Alatortsev and the Muscovite Mikhail Yudovich also secured top prizes; (b) The creative content of this final and the semifinal events were presented in the tournament book, issued in 1933 under the general editorship of Botvinnik, Wainstein and Nenarokov; (c) A special bulletin was issued; and (d) Radio coverage was set up for the championship's events. This encounter between the leaders was what decided the victor of the tournament:

(99) Botvinnik – Ryumin
Moscow 1931
Semi-Slav Defense [D30]

1.d4 d5 2.c4 c6 3.♘f3 ♘f6 4.e3 e6 5.♗d3 ♘bd7 6.0-0 ♗d6 7.♘bd2 e5 8.e4 0-0 9.c×d5 c×d5 10.e×d5 e×d4 11.♘e4 ♘×e4 12.♗×e4 ♘c5 12...♘f6 is the main line. **13.♗c2 ♗g4 14.♕×d4 ♗×f3 15.g×f3 ♖e8 16.♖d1 ♖e2** 16...♘d7!? **17.♗f5 g6 18.♗h3 ♘d7?!** 18...♕b6 19.♗f1 ♗e5 20.♕h4 ♖c2 is more active. **19.♗e3 ♗e5 20.♕c4?** 20.♕e4 ♗d6 21.b3± **20...♖×b2 21.♖ac1?!** 21.d6!? ♖b6 22.♖ab1 ♖×b1 23.♖×b1 ♘b6 24.♗×b6 a×b6 25.d7 ♔g7± **21...♘b6 22.♕e4** (D)

22...♕d6? The wrong blockading piece as now the d-pawn will advance

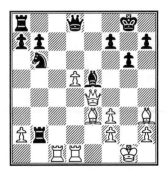

very soon. After 22...♗d6, Black is by no means worse. **23.f4 ♗g7 24.♗c5 ♕d8 25.♗e7 ♕e8 26.d6 ♕b5 27.d7 ♘×d7 28.♗×d7 ♕b6 29.♕e3 ♕×e3 30.f×e3 ♖×a2 31.♗c8 h5 32.♖d8+ ♔h7 1-0**

1933, August 16-September 9, Leningrad 20 chessplayers took part in the 8th USSR championship. A particular competition for first place developed among four of the Leningraders: 22-year old Mikhail Botvinnik, 24-year old Vladimir Alatortsev, the experienced 44-year old Grigory Levenfish and 42-year old Ilya Rabinovich. Botvinnik and Alatortsev scored an identical number of wins – eleven; but Botvinnik only lost two games, while his chief rival lost four. And this was what decided the tournament outcome. Among Botvinnik's best games in this competition, his game Vsevolod Rauzer was awarded the brilliancy prize (cf. *Famous Games*) and his game with Mikhail Yudovich, winding up in a terrific mating attack. There was also an interesting opening in his game against Alatortsev, and interesting endgames against Kirillov and Levenfish.

(100) Botvinnik– Yudovich,
Leningrad 1933
Grünfeld Defense [D96]

1.c4 ♘f6 2.d4 g6 3.♘c3 d5 4.♘f3 ♗g7 5.♕b3 c6 6.c×d5 ♘×d5 7.♗d2 7.e4 is the main line. **7...0-0 8.e4 ♘b6 9.♖d1 ♘8d7?!** 9...♗e6 10.♕c2 ♗g4 is more active. **10.a4 a5 11.♗e3 ♕c7 12.♗e2 ♕d6 13.♘a2 e6 14.0-0 h6?! 15.♖c1 f5 16.♘c3** 16.♘e5!? **16...♔h7?!** **17.♖fd1** 17.♕c2!? **17...f×e4?!** 17...f4 18.♗d2 e5 keeps the position more closed. 17...♕b4 is also interesting. **18.♘×e4 ♕b4?!** 18...♕e7 19.♗d2 ♘d5 20.♖e1± **19.♕c2 ♕×a4?! 20.b3 ♕a3 21.♘h4 ♕e7?!**

22.♘×g6! ♔×g6 23.♗h5+ 1-0 There follows 23...♔×h5 (23...♔h7 24.♘g5+ ♔g8 25.♕h7#) 24.♘g3+ ♔g4 25.♕e4+ ♖f4 26.♕×f4#

1939, April 15-May 16, Leningrad The theme of the 11th USSR championship was reminiscent of a good detective story in which the *denouement* is only revealed on the very last page. Throughout the entire tournament, Mikhail Botvinnik, the tournament favorite, was in the lead, while Alexander Kotov, the upstart

Leningrad 1939

		1	2	3	4	5	6	7	8	9	10	11	12	13	14	15	16	17	18	Total
1	Botvinnik	*	1	½	½	½	½	½	½	1	½	1	1	½	1	1	1	1	½	12½
2	Kotov	0	*	½	1	0	½	1	0	1	1	½	½	1	1	1	1	1	½	11½
3	Belavenets	½	½	*	½	1	½	1	1	½	1	0	½	½	½	½	1	½	1	11
4	Makogonov	½	0	½	*	1	½	½	1	½	½	½	½	1	1	½	½	½	1	10½
5	Chekhover	½	1	0	0	*	1	½	½	½	0	½	1	½	1	1	1	½	1	10½
6	Bondarevsky	½	½	½	½	0	*	0	0	½	1	1	½	½	½	1	1	1	1	10
7	Lisitsin	½	0	0	½	½	1	*	1	½	0	½	½	½	1	½	½	1	½	9
8	Levenfish	½	1	0	0	½	1	0	*	½	1	½	1	0	½	0	0	1	1	8½
9	Dubinin	0	0	½	½	½	½	½	½	*	½	½	1	0	½	½	1	1	½	8½
10	Ragozin	½	0	0	½	1	0	1	0	½	*	1	0	0	½	1	1	½	1	8½
11	Panov	0	½	1	½	½	0	½	½	½	0	*	½	½	½	½	1	1	1	8
12	Rabinovich	0	½	½	½	0	½	½	0	0	1	½	*	½	1	1	0	½	1	8
13	Yudovich	½	0	½	0	½	½	½	1	1	1	½	½	*	½	0	0	0	½	7½
14	Kan	0	0	½	1	0	½	0	½	½	½	1	0	½	*	1	1	½	1	7½
15	Tolush	0	0	½	½	0	0	½	1	½	0	½	0	1	0	*	1	0	1	6½
16	Pogrebissky	0	0	0	½	0	0	½	1	0	0	½	1	1	0	0	*	1	1	6½
17	Chistiakov	0	0	½	½	½	0	0	0	0	½	0	½	1	½	1	0	*	0	5
18	Romanovsky	½	½	0	0	0	0	½	0	½	0	0	0	½	0	0	0	1	*	3½

debutant, had several adjourned games. When he had played off all of them, it became clear that he had become, in fact, Botvinnik's chief rival. Before the final round, they both had the same number of points, and neither one could be caught by any of the others.

The luck of the draw determined that the fate of first place rested on the battle between the two leaders. "The tension surrounding that game was at a high point," Botvinnik recalled later, "the onrush of the spectators was comparable to any of the post-war world championship matches. Behind the demonstration board set up on the balcony of the House of Physiculture, one could see a crowd on both banks of the Moika. It was not just the transportation that was blocked, but the pedestrian traffic too.

"...I spent a long time on the eve of that game, and also the morning before the round, solving the puzzle of what to play as Black against an opponent, who at that time had not had much experience. I selected the Nimzo-Indian Defense – the general opinion was, that it was alright for Black, but contained some positional subtleties. More than likely, I thought, the young master (who would find it very tempting indeed to become champion himself!) would strive energetically for the win, not paying sufficient attention to the strict observance of positional principles. Such were my hopes of success."

His hopes came true. Botvinnik won, and for the third time, became USSR champion. His total score was 8 wins and 9 draws, and not a single loss!

(101) Kotov – Botvinnik
Leningrad 1939
Nimzo-Indian Defense [E33]

1.d4 ♘f6 2.c4 e6 3.♘c3 ♗b4 4.♕c2 ♘c6 5.♘f3 d5 6.e3 0-0 7.a3 ♗×c3+ 8.♕×c3 ♗d7 9.b3 a5 10.♗d3 a4 11.♘d2? 11.b4 is more natural and also played more often. **11...♖e8 12.0-0 e5 13.d×e5 ♘×e5 14.♗b2 a×b3 15.♘×b3 ♘e4 16.♕c2 ♘×c4 17.♗×c4 d×c4 18.♕×c4 ♕g5** 18...♘d6!? **19.f4?** 19.h4 with the idea 19...♕×h4 20.♕d4 ♕f6 21.♕×e4 is called for. **19...♕g6 20.♖fd1?** 20.♕×c7 looks more risky, but in fact is correct, e.g., 20...♗h3 21.♕c2 ♖ac8 22.♕e2 and Black is better, but matters are not clear, e.g., 22...♗e6 23.f5 **20...♘d6 21.♕d3 ♗f5 22.♕c3**

22...♗e4? Botvinnik misses the direct 22...♗h3! 23.♕×g7+ (23.♖d2 ♘e4–+) 23...♕×g7 24.♗×g7 ♗e6–+ **23.♖d2 ♗c6 24.♕d3 ♘f5 25.♗e5 f6 26.♗×c7?** 26.♘d4 f×e5 27.♘×f5 limits the damage by reducing the attacking potential, but Black is still much better. **26...♖×e3?** The pawn is not as important as the speed of the attack: 26...♗e4 27.♕c4+ ♔h8 28.♗b6 ♘h4 29.♕f1 ♘f3+–+ **27.♕c4+ ♔h8 28.♗b6 ♖ee8** 28...♘d6!? **29.♕f1 h5 30.♘d4?!** 30.♕d3 is correct. **30...♘×d4!?** Botvinnik continues his attack with opposite-color bishops. The alternative, 30...♘e3 31.♕d3 ♕×d3 32.♖×d3 ♘×g2 33.♘×c6 ♘×f4 34.♖d4 ♘e2+ 35.♔f2 ♘×d4 36.♘×d4 ♖a4, is also better for Black, but not as practical as Botvinnik's choice. **31.♗×d4 ♖e4** 31...♕f5!? **32.♖e1?** On principal it is good if the defender exchanges attacking pieces but here the price is too high. White should keep the position with 32.♗c5 or 32.♗b6 **32...♖×e1 33.♕×e1 ♖×a3 34.♔h1?! ♖a8?!** The immediate 34...♖f3–+ is stronger. **35.♖e2?! ♔h7** 35...♖a4!? **36.h3?** 36.♕c3 is more tenacious.

36...♖e8? Black needs his rooks for the attack. The double attack 36...♕d3! wins a pawn first and the game later. **37.♕f2?** This runs into a powerful shot. 37.♕d2 ♖×e2 38.♕×e2 was called for with chances to defend. **37...♕×g2+ 38.♕×g2 ♖×e2 0-1**

(102) Dubinin – Botvinnik
Leningrad 1939
Ruy Lopez [C90]

1.e4 e5 2.♘f3 ♘c6 3.♗b5 a6 4.♗a4 ♘f6 5.0-0 ♗e7 6.♖e1 b5 7.♗b3 d6 8.c3 0-0 9.d3 ♘a5 10.♗c2 c5 11.♘bd2 ♕c7 12.♘f1 h6 13.h3 ♗e6 14.♘e3 ♖ad8 15.♘f5? 15.♕e2 is less committal. **15...♗×f5 16.e×f5 ♘c6 17.d4?** 17.♘h2 is more circumspect. **17...e×d4 18.c×d4 d5 19.♗e3 ♖fe8** 19...c4!?

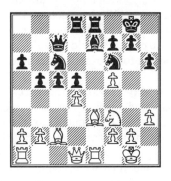

20.♖c1? The resulting structure is very good for Black because of his space advantage on the queenside. 20.♕c1 was better as 20...c4?! can now be met by 21.♗×h6 g×h6 22.♕×h6= **20...c4! 21.g4 ♘e4 22.♗b1 ♗d6 23.♘h4?! ♗f4 24.♕f3?! ♗g5 25.♘g2 ♗×e3** 25...♘d2!?–+ **26.♕×e3 ♖e7 27.♕f4 ♘×d4 28.♕×c7?!** Dubinin allows a beautiful mate: **28...♘f3+ 29.♔f1** 29.♔h1 ♘×f2# **29...♘ed2# 0-1**

1940, September 5-October 3, Moscow The 12th USSR championship was held in the Great Hall of the Conservatory. Botvinnik considered it to be unsuitable for chess tournaments.

After losing in the first round to Bondarevsky, he went on to set a scorching pace, and by the tenth round, was in the lead. However, at the close, his play no longer appeared fresh. He lost two games, and wound up sharing fifth/sixth places with Boleslavsky (with 11½/19), while Bondarevsky and Lilienthal became the winners of the championship (with 13½). The young Muscovite, Vassily Smyslov, was third with 13 points, and fourth was Paul Keres, with 12. Soon after the close of the tournament, it was decided to hold a match-tournament for the title of absolute USSR champion of 1941, in order finally to determine who of the Soviet players would make a worthy opponent for Alexander Alekhine.

1944, May 21-June 17, Moscow The final thunderings of war had not quite ended when the capital saw the next USSR championship, the 13th. Many of the players who played in the semi-finals and final were coming directly from the front, by special orders. The general conditions of that tournament were noted by one of the arbiters of the event, Yudovich: "I recall the verve with which every participant played, how joyful we were that peaceable chess had returned to us, if only for a moment. For every round, the October Hall was filled to capacity. The majority of those in attendance were in uniform: many wore medals, and bandages over their wounds. They all paid serious attention to the boards."

Many telegrams were received by the tournament, and published in a special bulletin. "I greet the masters, who are bringing creativity and daring to the most ancient game in the world. Ilya Erenburg." Both the composer Sergei Prokofiev and the violinist David Oistrakh, longtime practitioners of the chess art, sent their greetings also.

The battle for the championship was waged between Botvinnik and Smyslov, who was making great strides toward Olympus. Botvinnik, by scoring a convincing victory in their individual encounter, dotted the final "I." The game was awarded a special money prize, as one of the finest of the tournament.

(103) Smyslov – Botvinnik
Moscow 1944
French Defense [C19]

1.e4 e6 2.d4 d5 3.♘c3 ♗b4 4.e5 c5 5.a3 ♗×c3+ 6.b×c3 ♘e7 7.a4 ♘bc6 8.♘f3 ♕a5 9.♗d2 c4 "An important strategic decision. Botvinnik closes the queenside and prepares to annex the white a-pawn ... He judges that White's initiative on the kingside is not sufficient compensation for the pawn." (Taulbut) **10.♘g5?!** 10.g3 is the main line. **10...h6 11.♘h3 ♘g6 12.♕f3?! ♗d7 13.♘f4 ♘×f4 14.♕×f4 ♘e7!**

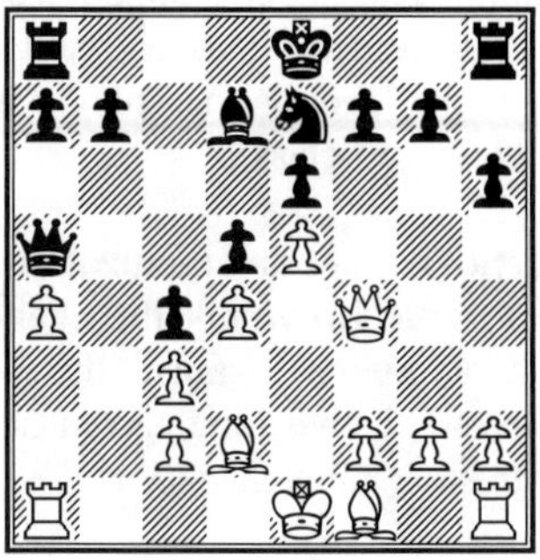

"The result of the opening can be summarized as not favorable to White. He must lose his a-pawn. True, he can launch a pawn attack on the kingside, but Black has sufficient defensive resources." (Botvinnik) **15.h4 ♗×a4! 16.h5 ♕b5 17.♔d1 ♖c8 18.♗c1** 18.♗e2 ♖c6 19.g4? ♗×c2+ 20.♔×c2 ♕b3+ 21.♔c1 ♖b6−+ (Ftacnik) **18...♖c6 19.♗e2 ♖a6 20.♔d2** "A great achievement for Black! Now the c1-h6 diagonal is closed to White's bishop." (Botvinnik) **20...0-0 21.g4** 21.♗a3? ♗×c2! 22.♗×e7? ♕b2!−+ (Botvinnik) **21...f6 22.e×f6 ♖×f6 23.♕c7 ♖f7 24.♕d8+ ♔h7 25.f4! ♕a5?!** 25...♕d7 26.♕×d7 ♗×d7 27.♖×a6 b×a6 28.♔e3 ♗b5= (Botvinnik) **26.♕b8** 26.♕×a5!? ♖×a5 27.♗a3 was a very interesting alternative. **26...♘c6 27.♕e8 ♖e7?!**

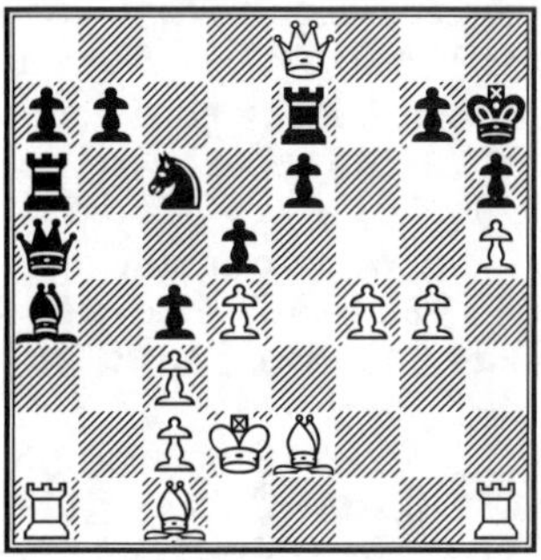

The computer prefers 27...♕c7, for example: 28.g5 h×g5 29.f×g5 ♕f4+ 30.♔d1 ♗×c2+ 31.♔×c2 ♕e4+ 32.♔d2 ♕f4+= **28.♕g6+?** 28.♕f8! ♕d8 29.♕×d8 ♘×d8 30.g5 (Botvinnik) gives White a strong initiative in the endgame. **28...♔g8 29.♗a3** 29.g5!? ♘×d4 30.g×h6 ♘×e2 31.♔×e2 ♕×c3−+ **29...e5?** 29...♕c7! 30.♖hf1 ♘b4! 31.♗×b4 ♗e8!∓ (Ftacnik) **30.f×e5?** 30.d×e5 (Botvinnik) is forced and leads to a dynamic balance, e.g., 30...♘d4 31.♗b4 ♕b5 32.♗×e7 ♖×g6 33.♖hb1

Moscow 1944

		1	2	3	4	5	6	7	8	9	10	11	12	13	14	15	16	17	Total
1	Botvinnik	*	1	1	1	1	½	0	1	½	1	½	1	1	1	0	1	1	12½
2	Smyslov	**0**	*****	**0**	**½**	**1**	**1**	**1**	**0**	**½**	**1**	**1**	**1**	**½**	**1**	**½**	**½**	**1**	10½
3	Boleslavsky	0	1	*	½	½	½	1	1	0	½	½	1	1	1	½	½	½	10
4	Flohr	0	½	½	*	½	½	1	½	½	½	0	½	1	1	1	½	1	9½
5	Mikenas	0	0	½	½	*	½	1	0	1	½	1	1	1	0	1	0	1	9
6	Makogonov	½	0	½	½	½	*	0	0	1	0	1	½	1	1	½	1	1	9
7	Tolush	1	0	0	0	0	1	*	½	1	1	1	1	0	0	0	1	1	8½
8	Lilienthal	0	1	0	½	1	1	½	*	½	½	0	0	1	½	0	½	½	7½
9	Sokolsky	½	½	1	½	0	0	0	½	*	0	0	½	1	1	1	1	0	7½
10	Veresov	0	0	½	½	½	1	0	½	1	*	1	0	0	0	1	1	½	7½
11	Ragozin	½	0	½	1	0	0	0	1	1	0	*	0	1	½	0	½	1	7
12	Kotov	0	0	0	½	0	½	0	1	½	1	1	*	0	½	1	1	0	7
13	Khavin	0	½	0	0	0	0	1	0	0	1	0	1	*	1	1	1	½	7
14	Lisitsin	0	0	0	0	1	0	1	½	0	1	½	½	0	*	½	1	1	7
15	Bronstein	1	½	½	0	0	½	1	1	0	0	1	0	0	½	*	0	½	6½
16	Alatortsev	0	½	½	½	1	0	0	½	0	0	½	0	0	0	1	*	1	5½
17	Ravinsky	0	0	½	0	0	0	0	½	1	½	0	1	½	0	½	0	*	4½

♕d7 34.c×d4 c3+ 35.♔×c3 ♖c6+ 36.♗c5 b6 37.♖×a4 ♖×c5+ 38.d×c5 ♕×a4 39.c×b6 a×b6 40.♖f1= **30...♘×d4!** 30...♘×e5? 31.♕f5 ♖f6 32.♕×f6 g×f6 33.♗×e7± **31.♗b4 ♕d8?** 31...♕b5 32.♗×e7 ♖×g6 33.h×g6 ♕b2−+ **32.♕×a6?** 32.c×d4! is more or less forced, e.g., 32...♖×g6?! (but 32...c3+!? 33.♗c3 ♖×g6 34.h×g6 ♗e8 35.♖×a7 ♖c7 looks good for Black) 33.h×g6 ♗e8 34.♗×e7 ♕×e7 35.♗f3 ♕g5+ 36.♔e2 ♗×g6 37.♗×d5+ ♔h7 (Fine) and White can still fight with 38.♔f3 **32...b×a6 33.c×d4 ♖b7! 34.♖×a4 ♕g5+ 35.♔d1?! a5?!** 35...c3! 36.♔e1 ♕d2+ 37.♔f2 ♖f7+ 38.♔g3 ♕×e2−+ (Bromberg) **36.♗f3 ♖×b4 37.♗×d5+ ♔f8 38.♖f1+ ♔e8 39.♗c6+ ♔e7 40.♖×b4 ♕×g4+** Annotations in this game follow Ftacnik's notes in ChessBase Megabase. **0-1**

1945, June 1-July 3, Moscow Summing up the results of the 14th USSR championship in the pages of the magazine *Shakhmaty v USSR* (3/1945), grandmaster Alexander Kotov wrote in his article, "Botvinnik's 14th Symphony":

"The entire tournament was under the banner of the absolute dominance of Botvinnik over all the other participants. In only two or three games did Botvinnik obtain dubious positions, but his solid, stubborn defense enabled him to avoid a loss. In the end, the national champion scored only four draws, while winning thirteen games. He also scored a 14th win over Flohr, which was not counted. An overall result unheard of in the USSR championships.

"What happened? Is it possible the other players played too weakly? I do not

think so. One fact is beyond doubt: the war years widened the gap in playing strength between Botvinnik and the rest of the Soviet players. The Soviet champion has never stopped working on completing his mastery, and these days, is the leading chessplayer of the worldwide top-class...

"The Soviet chess organization will have to give Botvinnik the chance to obtain a match against the world champion – he has long ago earned the right to such a match."

(104) Lilienthal – Botvinnik
Moscow 1945
Semi-Slav Defense [D35]

1.d4 d5 2.c4 e6 3.♘c3 c6 4.♘f3 ♘f6 5.c×d5 e×d5 6.♗g5 h6 7.♗×f6 ♕×f6 8.♕b3?! 8.e3 is the main move. **8...♗d6 9.e3 ♘d7 10.♗d3 ♕e7 11.0-0-0?! ♘f6 12.♖he1 ♗e6 13.♕c2 0-0-0 14.♘e5 ♔b8 15.f4 c5 16.♔b1 c4 17.♗f5?** 17.♗e2 to meet 17...g6 with 18.♔a1 ♗f5 (18...♗b4 19.g4) 19.e4 is the lesser evil. **17...♗×f5 18.♕×f5 ♗b4 19.♕c2?! ♖d6 20.♖e2 ♗×c3 21.b×c3 ♘e4 22.♕a1 ♖a6 23.♕c1 ♖d8** 23...♕c7!? **24.♖c2 ♖dd6 25.♘g4 ♖g6 26.h3 h5 27.♘e5 ♖gb6 28.♘f3 ♕a3 29.♘g5**

Moscow 1945

		1	2	3	4	5	6	7	8	9	10	11	12	13	14	15	16	17	18	Total
1	Botvinnik	*	1	½	½	1	1	1	½	1	1	1	½	1	1	1	1	1	1	15
2	Boleslavskyk	0	*	½	1	1	½	½	0	1	1	1	½	1	½	1	½	1	1	12
3	Bronstein	½	½	*	0	0	½	½	0	1	½	½	1	0	1	1	1	1	1	10
4	Kotov	½	0	1	*	1	½	0	1	0	½	1	½	0	½	1	½	½	1	9½
5	Bondarevsky	0	0	1	0	*	½	½	1	½	½	½	½	1	½	1	½	1	½	9½
6	Konstantinopolsky	0	½	½	½	½	*	0	½	0	½	1	1	1	½	½	1	½	1	9½
7	Lilienthal	0	½	½	1	½	1	*	1	0	0	½	0	1	1	½	1	0	½	9
8	Ragozin	½	1	1	0	0	½	0	*	0	½	1	1	0	0	1	½	1	1	9
9	Rudakovsky	0	0	0	1	½	1	1	1	*	½	0	½	1	0	½	0	1	1	9
10	Chekhover	0	0	½	½	½	½	1	½	½	*	1	½	0	½	1	½	1	0	8½
11	Smyslov	0	0	½	0	½	0	½	0	1	0	*	½	1	½	1	1	1	1	8½
12	Alatortsev	½	½	0	½	½	0	1	0	½	½	½	*	1	0	0	1	½	½	7½
13	Tolush	0	0	1	1	0	0	0	1	0	1	0	0	*	1	½	1	0	1	7½
14	Koblencs	0	½	0	½	½	½	0	1	1	½	½	1	0	*	0	½	½	0	7
15	Romanovsky	0	0	0	0	0	½	½	0	½	0	0	1	½	1	*	1	1	½	6½
16	Ratner	0	½	0	½	½	0	0	½	1	½	0	0	0	½	0	*	1	1	6
17	Kan	0	0	0	½	0	½	1	0	0	0	0	½	1	½	0	0	*	1	5
18	Goldberg	0	0	0	0	½	0	½	0	0	1	0	½	0	1	½	0	0	*	4

29...♘×c3! 30.♕×a3 ♖×a3 31.♖dc1 ♘b5 32.♘×f7 ♖×e3 33.♘e5 ♔c7 34.g4 ♘×d4 35.♖d2 ♘e2 36.♖e1 ♘c3 37.♖c1 37.♖×e3?! ♖b1# **0-1**

(105) Tolush – Botvinnik
Moscow 1945
Caro-Kann Defense [C19]

1.e4 e6 2.d4 d5 3.♘c3 ♗b4 4.e5 c5 5.a3 ♗×c3+ 6.b×c3 ♘e7 7.♘f3 ♕a5 8.♗d2 c4 9.a4 ♘d7 10.♗e2?! "White's opening plan is too slow." (Botvinnik) 10.♘g5! is the main move, and scores much better. **10...♘b6 11.0-0?! ♘×a4 12.♘h4?!** "An unfortunate sally for White. As the result of the exchange of knights, Black's h-pawn is transferred to g6, and the break-through f4-f5 becomes practically impossible." (Botvinnik) **12...♘g6 13.♘×g6 h×g6 14.♖e1 ♗d7 15.♗f1 b5! 16.♕f3 ♖b8 17.♖eb1 ♕c7 18.♗c1 a5! 19.♗a3 ♖b6!?** Black prepares to sacrifice the exchange. "Without his good Bishop, White cannot prevent the exploitation of Black's pawn superiority on the queenside." (Botvinnik) **20.♕g3 ♕d8 21.♗d6?!** 21.h3 (Fine) is better. **21...♖×d6!? 22.e×d6 ♗c6 23.h3 ♔d7 24.♖e1 ♕h4! 25.♕e5 ♕f6 26.♕g3** 26.f4!? **26...♖h4!?**

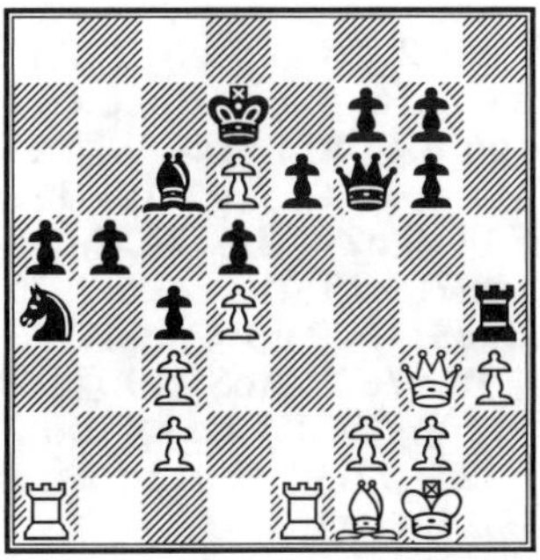

"With this maneuver, Black parries the transfer of the White Rook to f3. In addition, he prepares to advance his pawn to b4, which, in conjunction with the attack on the d-pawn, becomes decisive." (Botvinnik) **27.♖e3 ♖f4 28.♗e2?!** 28.♖e5 ♔×d6 29.♕e3 ♔e7 30.♗e2 ♔f8 31.♗g4= **28...♕h4 29.♗f3 b4 30.♕×h4?** 30.♗g4! ♕×g3 31.f×g3 ♖×g4 32.h×g4 ♘×c3 33.♖×c3 b×c3 34.♖×a5= **30...♖×h4 31.g3?!** 31.c×b4 a×b4 32.♖b1 ♖×d4 33.♖×b4 (Botvinnik) **31...♖h8!** 31...♖×h3? 32.c×b4 a×b4 33.♖b1= **32.c×b4 a×b4 33.♖b1 ♖b8 34.h4 ♖b7 35.♔h2**

♔×d6 **36.g4?!** The prophylactic 36.♗g4 is more tenacious. **36...♘c3 37.♖a1** 37.♖b2 f6 38.g5 e5–+ **37...♘b5! 38.♖d1 ♖a7 39.h5 g5 40.♔g2 ♖a2 41.♗e2** "The sealed move, although Tolush resigned without resuming play." (Ftacnik). Annotations in this game follow Ftacnik's notes in ChessBase Megabase. **0-1**

The following game was one of Botvinnik's best. In his opinion, "Probably the most elegant game I played in this tournament."

(106) Botvinnik – Boleslavsky
Moscow 1945
Ruy Lopez [C79]

1.e4 e5 2.♘f3 ♘c6 3.♗b5 a6 4.♗a4 ♘f6 5.0-0 d6 6.c3 ♗d7 7.d4 g6 8.♘bd2 ♕e7 9.♖e1 ♗g7 10.♘f1 0-0 11.♗g5 h6 12.♗h4 ♕e8 13.♗c2 ♘h5 14.♘e3 ♘e7 15.d×e5?! 15.♗b3 ♘f4 16.♗g3 **15...d×e5 16.♗g3 ♘×g3 17.h×g3 ♖d8 18.♕e2 ♘c8 19.♖ad1 c6 20.♖d2 ♕e7 21.♖ed1 ♘b6 22.b4 ♗e6 23.♗b3 ♖×d2 24.♕×d2 ♗×b3 25.a×b3**

25...♕e6? 25...♖e8 26.c4 ♘c8 27.♕d7 ♔f8 is called for. **26.c4 ♗f6?** Mistakes always seem to come in pairs. 26...♘c8

27.♕d7 ♕×d7 28.♖×d7 b5± limits the damage. **27.c5 ♘c8 28.♕d7 ♕×b3 29.♕×b7 ♗g5 30.♘×g5 h×g5 31.♕×a6 ♘e7 32.♕b7 ♖e8 33.♕d7 ♔f8 34.♕d6 ♕×b4 35.♘g4 ♖a8 36.♕×e5 ♕b3 37.♖d7 ♘g8 38.♕d6+ ♔g7 39.♕d4+ ♔h7 40.♘f6+?!** 40.♔h2!? +– **40...♘×f6 41.♕×f6 ♔g8 42.♔h2 ♖f8 43.♕×c6 43.♖d6!? 43...♔g7 44.♕d5 ♕b1?!** 44...♖h8+ 45.♔g1 ♕b1+ 46.♕d1 ♖b8 47.f3 +– **45.♕d4+ ♔h7 46.c6 1-0**

1951, November 11-December 14, Moscow
The 19th USSR championship was, at the same time, a FIDE Zonal tournament, selecting players for the right to go to the interzonal tournament. Botvinnik had just recently defended his title in a match with Bronstein (cf. *Botvinnik – Bronstein, 1951 Match*); and although he was leading at first, he did not withstand the tension, and at the end of another lengthy contest, took fifth place.

The results were: 1. P. Keres – 12/17; 2-3. Geller, Petrosian – 11½; 4. Smyslov – 11; 5. Botvinnik – 10; 6-8. Averbakh, Bronstein, Taimanov – 9½; 9-10. Aronin, Flohr – 9; Kopylov – 8½; 12-13. Bondarevsky, Kotov – 8; 14, Simagin – 7½; 15-16. Lipnitsky, Moiseev – 6½; 17. Novotyelnov – 3; 18. Terpugov – 2½.

(107) Botvinnik – Moisieev
Moscow 1951
Nimzo-Indian Defense [E45]

1.d4 ♘f6 2.c4 e6 3.♘c3 ♗b4 4.e3 b6 5.♘ge2 ♗a6 6.a3 ♗e7 7.♘f4 0-0 8.b4 d5 9.b5 ♗b7 10.c×d5 e×d5 11.♗b2 c5 12.♗e2 c4 13.0-0 a6 14.a4 ♗b4 15.♕c2 ♕d7 16.♖fb1 ♖e8 17.♗a3 ♗×a3

18.罝×a3 豐d6 19.罝a2 a5 20.豐c1?! 20.豐f5 is more natural. **20...公bd7 21.豐a3 豐×a3 22.罝×a3 公f8 23.h4 罝ad8 24.皇f3 公e6 25.公h5 公×h5 26.皇×h5 g6 27.皇f3 f5 28.罝a2 曾g7 29.曾f1 h6 30.g3 曾f6?!** It is better to clarify matters on the kingside with 30...g5!? before White finishes his regrouping. **31.曾g2 罝h8 32.罝h1 罝he8 33.罝d2 罝e7 34.罝e2 罝ee8 35.曾f1 罝h8 36.曾e1 罝he8 37.曾d2 罝e7 38.罝ee1 罝ee8?!** 38...h5!? **39.公e2 39.g4!? 39...罝h8?** 39...h5! is correct.

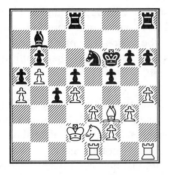

40.g4!? A good moment to open the kingside. **40...罝hg8 41.罝eg1 f×g4?!** This opens the floodgates. But good advice is already hard to give. One suggestion is 41...罝df8!? 42.罝g2 f4 but White is also much better here. **42.皇×g4 罝df8** 42...罝d6 43.罝h3 曾f7 44.罝f3+ 曾e7 45.罝fg3 公f8 46.公f4+– **43.皇×e6** 43.罝h3!?+– **43...曾×e6 44.公f4+ 曾d6** 44...曾f7 45.罝h3+– **45.罝h2 罝f6 46.罝hg2 皇c8 47.罝×g6 罝g×g6 48.罝×g6 罝×g6 49.公×g6 皇f5 50.公e5 皇b1 51.曾c3 皇a2?!** 52.e4 d×e4 **53.公×c4+ 皇×c4 54.曾×c4 h5 55.d5 曾e5 56.d6 曾×d6 57.曾d4 1-0**

1952, November 19-December 29, Moscow For the first time, in the 20th USSR championship, agreeing to a draw was prohibited before the 30th

move. From the start, the lead was taken by 26-year-old grandmaster Mark Taimanov, one of the first of Botvinnik's Leningrad pupils. It was only thanks to a finishing spurt (three wins in a row!) that Botvinnik managed to catch his opponent. The victors scored 13½/19, and outdistanced the third place finisher, Geller, by 1½ points. Afterwards, a match for the champion's title brought victory to Botvinnik – 3½-2½ (+2 -1 =3) (cf. *Taimanov – Botvinnik match, 1953*). This seventh victory was to be Botvinnik's last, but it was a record in national championships.

One of the most principled encounters in this championship was the game between Bronstein and Botvinnik – recent opponents in a match for the world championship. True to his principles, Bronstein employed the King's Gambit! Botvinnik accepted his challenge!

(108) Bronstein – Botvinnik
Moscow 1952
King's Gambit Accepted [C36]

1.e4 e5 2.f4 e×f4 3.公f3 d5 4.e×d5 公f6 5.皇b5+ c6 6.d×c6 b×c6 7.皇c4 公d5 8.d4 皇d6 9.0-0 0-0 10.公c3 公×c3 11.b×c3 皇g4 12.豐d3 公d7 13.g3 公b6 13...f×g3? 14.公g5+– **14.皇b3 c5 15.c4?** Too creative. The simple 15.皇×f4 is better. **15...豐f6** The computer prefers 15...f×g3!?, for example 16.公g5 f5 17.h3 皇h5 18.皇e3 公d7 and Black is better. **16.公e5 皇×e5 17.d×e5 豐×e5 18.皇×f4 豐h5 19.罝fe1 罝fe8?!** **20.a4?** 20.罝e3 罝×e3 21.豐×e3 f6 22.罝e1 is more natural. **20...皇e2 21.豐c3 公d7** 21...a5!? to lock the b3-bishop in, looks very attractive. **22.a5 公f6 23.皇a4**

23...♖e6 The computer suggests the amazing 23...♘e4!? 24.♕b3 ♘f2, but of course over the board this cannot be played. **24.♔g2?** 24.♕d2! is forced and Black is only slightly better. **24...♘e4 25.♕a3 g5 0-1**

1955, February 11-March 15, Moscow The 22nd USSR championship was the last time the 43-year-old Botvinnik would participate. He sensed that the competition from the new generation was becoming fiercer and stronger. To maintain his position at the summit, it would be necessary to have not only strength, but also research work in chess. "My chess was not clear this time, either," recalled Botvinnik. "I think that my three-year absence from chess (1948-51) was still a factor – my nervous system had a lot of inertia."

Even before the last round, Botvinnik retained chances of gaining his eighth title; but "apparently, somehow, I angered the chess goddess Caissa: my helpless play in the game with Keres knocked me out of first place." A mere half-point separated him from Geller and Smyslov, who shared first/second places with 12/19. Botvinnik shared third/sixth places with Ilivitsky and two

future world champions – Tigran Petrosian and Boris Spassky (11½). Notable company!

In the second volume of his game collection, *Analytical and Critical Works 1942-1956*, he presented his five best games of this tournament. Botvinnik surprisingly focused on the longest games, the ones with Antoshin (49 moves), Kotov (65 moves), Kan (75 moves), Averbakh (65 moves), and Borisenko (61 moves). It becomes clear, that it was these fierce struggles, and not the goddess Caissa, that were to blame for the decisive misfortune of Mikhail Botvinnik, her faithful servant.

Taimanov, Mark Yevgenievich (February 7, 1926, Kharkov-November 28, 2016, St. Petersburg) Russian grandmaster, world championship candidate, chess author, musician and pianist.

At 11, Mark was twice blessed, in that he was invited to be a part of the Leningrad chess circle, and was also invited to appear in the film, *A Beethoven Concert*. Since that time, in his life, chess went hand in hand with music. "I have been a devoted servant of two masters my entire life," wrote Taimanov, an acknowledged pianist and a talented grandmaster. He played in the USSR championships 23 times, and was among the prizewinners seven times. In 1953, he lost the title to Botvinnik in a match by a score of 3½-2½, and in 1956, became national champion by winning a subsequent match-tournament over Averbakh and Spassky.

Moscow 1952

		1	2	3	4	5	6	7	8	9	10	11	12	13	14	15	16	17	18	19	20	Total
1	Botvinnik	*	0	1	½	½	½	1	½	1	1	1	½	½	½	1	1	½	1	½	1	13½
2	Taimanov	1	*	0	½	0	1	1	½	½	0	½	1	1	1	1	1	1	½	1	1	13½
3	Geller	0	1	*	1	1	½	½	0	0	½	1	½	1	1	1	½	½	1	½	½	12
4	Tolush	½	½	0	*	1	½	0	1	1	½	½	0	1	0	½	1	1	½	1	1	11½
5	Boleslavsky	½	1	0	0	*	½	½	1	½	1	½	0	0	1	½	½	1	1	1	1	11½
6	Korchnoi	½	0	½	½	½	*	0	1	½	0	0	1	1	½	1	0	1	1	1	1	11
7	Bronstein	0	0	½	1	½	1	*	½	1	½	½	1	1	½	½	½	½	½	0	½	10½
8	Smyslov	½	½	1	0	0	0	½	*	½	1	1	½	0	1	1	½	½	½	½	1	10½
9	Moisieev	0	½	1	0	½	½	0	½	*	0	½	½	1	1	½	1	1	½	1	½	10½
10	Suetin	0	1	½	½	0	1	½	0	1	*	0	½	1	½	½	0	0	1	1	½	9½
11	Keres	0	½	0	½	½	1	½	0	½	1	*	½	0	½	½	1	0	1	½	1	9½
12	Aronin	½	0	½	1	1	0	0	½	½	½	½	*	½	½	0	1	½	½	½	½	9
13	Byvshev	½	0	0	0	1	0	0	1	0	0	1	½	*	0	1	0	1	1	1	1	9
14	Simagin	½	0	0	1	0	½	½	0	0	½	½	½	1	*	0	1	½	½	½	1	8½
15	Ilivitzki	0	0	0	½	½	0	½	0	½	½	½	1	0	1	*	1	½	½	1	½	8½
16	Konstantinopolsky	0	0	½	0	½	1	½	½	0	1	0	0	1	0	0	*	1	½	½	½	7½
17	Lipnitsky	½	0	½	0	0	0	½	½	0	1	1	½	0	½	½	0	*	1	½	0	7
18	Kan	0	½	0	½	0	0	½	½	½	0	0	½	0	½	½	½	0	*	1	1	6½
19	Kasparian	½	0	½	0	0	0	1	½	0	0	½	½	0	½	0	½	½	0	*	½	5½
20	Goldenov	0	0	½	0	0	0	½	0	½	½	0	½	0	0	½	½	1	0	½	*	5

Mark Taimanov, pianist

(109) Taimanov – Botvinnik
Moscow (m5) 1952
Nimzo-Indian Defense [E58]

1.d4 ♘f6 2.c4 e6 3.♘c3 ♗b4 4.♘f3 c5 5.e3 0-0 6.♗d3 d5 7.0-0 ♘c6 8.a3 ♗xc3 9.bxc3 b6 10.cxd5 exd5 11.a4 c4 12.♗c2 ♗g4 13.♕e1 ♖e8 14.♘h4 ♗h5? 14...♘a5 15.f3 ♗c8 16.♗a3 ♘b3 from Taimanov-Bondarevsky, Leningrad 1952 is correct. **15.f3 ♗g6?! 16.♘xg6 hxg6 17.e4 dxe4 18.fxe4 ♕d7** 18...♘xe4? 19.♗xe4 f5? 20.♗xc6 ♖xe1 21.♖xe1 +– **19.♗g5 ♘h7 20.♗e3 ♘e7 21.♖f3 f5 22.e5 ♘f8 23.h4 ♘e6 24.♖d1 ♕d5**

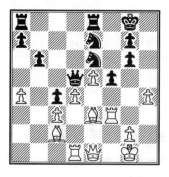

25.♗c1! A strong regrouping. **25...♖f8 26.♗a3 ♖ae8 27.♕g3 g5 28.♗xe7 ♖xe7 29.♖xf5 ♖xf5 30.♗xf5 ♘f4 31.♕xg5 ♖xe5 32.dxe5 ♕xd1+ 33.♔h2 ♕d2 34.♗e6+ ♔h7 35.♗xc4 g6 36.♗e6 1-0**

For 20 years (1952-71), Taimanov was a participant in tournaments for the world championship. After competing successfully in the Interzonals of Stockholm 1952, and Palma de Mallorca 1970, he went on to the candidates' events. But after the "roses" came the "thorns" – at Zürich 1953, he only shared eighth/ninth places. And his match with Bobby Fischer ended in his defeat by a score of 6-0. This outcome brought the 45-year-old grandmaster more than just moral sufferings: in Moscow, the sport committee's leadership decided to "punish this chessplayer" for allowing himself to be so thoroughly trounced by his opponent, who was threatening to rob the Soviet Union of the champion's crown. Taimanov lost his title of "Honored USSR Master of Sport" (later restored), taken off the roster of the USSR team; and, for a while, lost his "foreign travel" privileges.

"I don't know how things would have gone," Taimanov later wrote, "had not support come to me from a totally unexpected source. Thanks go to my colleague, Bent Larsen, who lost to Fischer after I did by the same 6-0 score, the hot heads of my persecutors were cooled somewhat. Certainly, the Danish grandmaster could not have been accused of being in collusion with the imperialists!"

Time, music and chess slowly healed the wounds of his soul. Taimanov once again began to make successful appearances in strong events. To his great store of earlier victories (in all, he won, or was among the prizewinners, in over 40 international tournaments) he added new trophies. Among the best results of his lengthy competitive career were: Liverpool 1952, first/second places; Reykjavik (1956 and 1958), second/third and first/second places; Moscow 1956 – third; Dresden 1959 and Santa Fe 1960 – first/second; Leningrad 1960, Dortmund and Rostov-on-Don 1961, Mar del Plata 1962, Luxemburg 1963 – first; Havana (1964 and 1967) – third and second; Budapest and Copenhagen 1965 – first/third; Helsinki 1966 – first; Zalaegerszeg 1969 and Wijk aan Zee 1970 – first; Skopje 1970 – first/second; Bucharest 1973 – first; Vrnjacka Banja 1974, Decin 1975 and Bucharest 1979 – first/second; and Lisbon 1985 – first place.

In many games Taimanov performed like a true artist, showing a fine positional understanding; he executed deeply planned and effective combinations.

(110) Taimanov – Hort
Tallinn 1975
English Opening [A25]

1.c4 e5 2.♘c3 ♘c6 3.g3 ♘f6 4.♗g2 ♗c5 5.e3 d6 6.a3 ♗e6 7.b4 ♗b6 8.d3 ♕d7 9.h3 0-0 10.♘ge2 ♘d8 10...a5!? **11.♘a4 c6 12.♘×b6 a×b6 13.♗b2 ♘e8 14.f4 f6 15.g4 ♚h8?!**

Very slow and passive. 15...e×f4 16.♘×f4 (16.e×f4 f5 17.g5 d5) 16...♘c7 17.0-0 ♗f7 is more active. **16.0-0 ♕e7 17.♕e1 ♗f7 18.♘g3 ♗g6?! 19.♖d1 ♘c7 20.♕f2** 20.d4!? **20...b5?**

20...h6 21.d4 ♘f7 is more tenacious. **21.c5!** A strong undermining. **21...e×f4** 21...d×c5 22.f×e5 ♘e8 23.b×c5 +- **22.e×f4 h6 23.♗e4 ♗×e4** 23...♗h7 24.♖fe1 ♕d7 25.c×d6 ♕×d6 26.♗×h7 ♚×h7 27.♘f5 ♕d5 28.♖e7 ♖f7 29.♖de1 +- **24.c×d6 ♕×d6 25.d×e4 ♕e6 26.e5 f×e5 27.♗×e5 ♘d5 28.♕b2 ♕f7 29.♘h5 ♖g8 30.f5 b6 31.♖fe1 ♘b7 32.♕c1 ♚h7 33.♕×c6 1-0**

There are Taimanov variations in a number of openings. And a number of books have flowed from his pen.

Books: *Over-the-border Encounters*, Leningrad 1958; *Nimzo-Indian Defense*, 3rd ed., Moscow 1985; *World Championship Match Karpov-Kasparov*, Moscow 1986 (co-author); *I Was Fischer's Victim*, St. Petersburg. 1993.

About: Voronkov, S., Plisetsky, D., *The Russians against Fischer*, Moscow 2004.

Taimanov – Botvinnik Match, 1953 (February 1-16, Moscow) After sharing first/second places in the 20th USSR championship (cf. *USSR Championships*), Botvinnik and Taimanov, according to the rules of the tournament, needed to play a match for first prize. It took place in Moscow two months after the close of the championship, and concluded in victory for Botvinnik, by a score of 3½-2½ (+2 -1 =3), resulting in Botvinnik's seventh championship win.

In both games that Botvinnik won – the first and fourth – he ended up winning in the endgame.

(111) Taimanov – Botvinnik
Moscow (m1) 1952
Semi-Slav Defense [D45]

1.d4 ♘f6 2.c4 c6 3.♘c3 d5 4.♘f3 e6 5.e3 ♘bd7 6.♕c2 ♗d6 7.♗d2 0-0 8.0-0-0?! c5! 9.c×d5 e×d5 10.♔b1 a6 11.♗c1 c4 12.g4 ♘b6 12...♘×g4 13.♘×d5 b5 14.e4 ♗b7 is also playable, but Black wants to keep the roads on the kingside closed. **13.h3 ♖e8 14.♗g2 ♗b4 15.♘e5 ♗×c3 16.♕×c3 ♘e4 17.♕c2** 17.♗×e4 d×e4 18.♘×c4 ♘d5 19.♕a3 is the alternative. **17...♘d6 18.♗d2 a5 19.♗e1 f6 20.♘f3 ♗d7 21.♖c1 ♗a4 22.♕e2 ♗b5 23.♗c3 ♘a4 24.g5 ♗d7 25.g×f6 ♗f5+ 25...♕×f6!? 26.♔a1 ♗d3 27.♕d1 ♘×c3 28.b×c3 g×f6?** 28...♕×f6 29.♘e5 ♗e4 30.f3 ♗f5 31.e4 ♗e6= (D)

29.♘e1? The active realization of the idea with 29.♘h4! is much better: 29...♘f5 (29...♗e4? 30.♕h5+−) 30.♘×f5 ♗×f5 31.♕h5 ♗e6 32.♖b1± **29...♗e4 30.♗×e4 ♘×e4 31.♖c2 ♔h8 32.♘g2 ♖g8** 32...b5!? **33.♘f4**

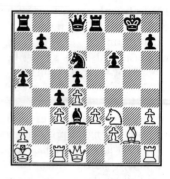

♕d7 34.f3 ♘g5 35.♖b2 b5 36.♖e1?! 36.♕b1! is called for and White is not worse. **36...♖ae8?!** The computer prefers 36...b4 37.c×b4 c3 38.♖f2 a×b4 39.♕b3 ♖gb8 40.♘×d5 ♖a3 41.♕c4 ♕e6 and Black is better. **37.h4 ♘e6 38.♘×e6 ♖×e6 39.e4 ♖ge8 40.♖be2 b4 41.♕d2 ♔e7 42.e5 b×c3 43.♕×c3 ♕b4 44.♕b2?** 44.♕×b4 a×b4 45.f4 is a better version of the rook endgame. **44...f×e5 45.♕×b4 a×b4 46.♖×e5?** 46.d×e5 is the last chance to fight. **46...♖×e5 47.♖×e5 ♖×e5 48.d×e5**

48...d4! Botvinnik has calculated that he wins by *zugzwang* in the end. **49.e6 ♔g7 50.f4 ♔f6 51.f5 d3 52.♔b1** 52.♔b2 h5 53.a4 b×a3+ 54.♔×a3 d2−+ **52...h5 0-1** in view of 53.♔b2 ♔e7 54.♔c1 b3 55.a×b3 c×b3 56.♔d2 b2−+

(112) Botvinnik – Taimanov
Moscow (m4) 1952
Nimzo-Indian Defense [E40]

**1.d4 ♘f6 2.c4 e6 3.♘c3 ♗b4 4.e3
♘c6 5.♘ge2 d5 6.a3 ♗e7 7.c×d5
e×d5 8.♘f4 0-0 9.♗e2 ♗f5?!** Very
provocative. 9...♘a5 is probably
preferable. **10.g4! ♗e6 11.♘×e6
f×e6 12.0-0 ♕d7 13.f4 ♘d8
14.♗d3 ♘f7 15.b4 a5?!** 15...♘d6!?
**16.b5 ♘d6 17.♕f3 a4 18.♖a2 c6
19.b×c6 ♕×c6 20.♖c2 ♕d7 21.g5
♘fe8?** 21...♘fe4 is forced.

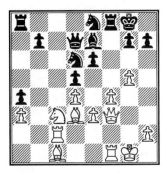

22.♗×h7+!! A very strong sacrifice as
White can bring in new attackers
quickly. **22...♔×h7 23.♕h3+ ♔g8**
23...♔g6 24.♘×d5 ♖a6 25.♘b4 ♘f5
26.♘d3± **24.♘×d5 ♗d8 25.g6 ♘f6**
26.♘×f6+ g×f6 27.g7? The pawn can
be taken, so 27.♖g2! was better, and
White's attack is very dangerous, e.g.,
27...♖e8 28.g7 ♘f7 29.♖f3 ♖c8
30.♗b2 ♖c7 31.♕h4+− **27...♖e8?**
27...♔×g7 28.♖g2+ (28.♕h5 ♖f7-+)
28...♔f7 29.♗d2 ♔e8-+ **28.♕h8+
♔f7 29.♕h5+ ♔g8 30.♖g2 ♘f7
31.♖f3 ♖a5 32.♕h4 e5 33.♖h3**
33.f5!?+− **33...♕×h3 34.♕×h3 e×f4
35.e×f4 ♗b6 36.♗b2 ♖b5 37.♔f1
♗a5 38.♖c2 ♖b3 39.♕d7 ♖be3
40.♕×a4 ♖e1+ 41.♔f2 ♗c7
42.♕×e8+ 1-0**

Tal, Mikhail Nehemovich (November
9, 1936, Riga-June 28, 1992, Moscow),
Latvian grandmaster, the eighth world
chess champion (1960-1961).

At the age of 10, Misha was attracted to
the game of chess, and it defined his
life's path. At 17, Tal became champion
of Riga and won the master title; at 20,
he became a grandmaster. That year,
Tal's talent really showed itself in the
24th USSR championship. All the
strongest Soviet grandmasters took part,
with the exception of Smyslov and
Botvinnik. The hall was filled beyond
capacity with spectators right from the
start of the event. The fans were "with
Tal," who showed an amazing ability to
stir up a whirlwind of combinative
complications with a piece sacrifice, or
a whole cascade of sacrifices, in
seemingly simple positions.

Within a year, in 1957, Tal again became
USSR champion. In 1958, he entered the
fight for the championship of the world.
In his first appearance in the interzonal
tournament, Tal took first place, leaving
behind Petrosian, Gligotic, Fischer,
Olafsson... And in September 1959, Tal
won the candidates' tournament in Bled
(Yugoslavia) just as brilliantly. This
time, the tournament was played in four
cycles. Tal lost just one mini-match – to
the second place finisher Paul Keres, and
played one of them to a draw –
Petrosian. But then, he won against
Gligoric, Olafsson, and Benko, taking
3½/4 from each of them; and he won all
four games against Fischer. Tal had
become the challenger for the world
championship.

The following game won the prize for
the most beautiful game of the
tournament.

(113) Tal – Smyslov
Belgrade 1959
Caro-Kann Defense [B10]

1.e4 c6 2.d3 d5 3.♘d2 e5 4.♘gf3 ♘d7 5.d4 d×e4?! 6.♘×e4 e×d4 7.♛×d4 ♘gf6 8.♗g5 ♗e7 9.0-0-0 ♘d6+!? 9...0-0 10.♘d6 ♛a5 11.♗c4 b5 12.♗d2 ♛a6 13.♘f5 ♗d8 14.♛h4 b×c4 15.♛g5

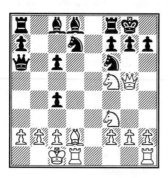

Mikhail Tal

15...♘h5 15...g6 16.♗c3 (16.♘h6+ ♔g7 17.♗c3 ♛b5! 18.h4=; 16.♛h6 g×f5 17.♗c3 ♖e8 18.♖×d7 ♗×d7 19.♛g5+ ♔h8 20.♖d1 ♛×a2 21.♗×f6+ ♗×f6 22.♛×f6+ ♔g8 23.♛g5+ ♔f8 24.♛h6±) 16...♛a2! (16...♖e8? 17.♖he1 ♖×e1 18.♖×e1 ♛×a2 19.♖e8+ ♘×e8 20.♛×d8 g×f5 21.♛×e8+ ♘f8 22.♛e5+−) 17.♘h6+ ♔g7 18.♖he1 was Tal's plan over the board "with an attack." (Kasparov gives 18.♘g4 winning, but Black has a fantastic resource: 18...♘e5!! 19.♛×e5 [19.♖×d8? is met by 19...♘e×g4 20.♖×f8 ♔×f8; 19.♗×e5? ♗×g4 20.♖×d8 ♛a1+ 21.♔d2 ♖f×d8+ 22.♘d4 ♛×h1 23.♗×f6+ ♔g8 24.♛h6 ♛d1+ 25.♔c3 ♛e1+−+] 19...♗×g4 20.♖d6 ♗e6 21.♘d2 ♖e8 22.♖×d8 ♖a×d8 23.♛×f6+ ♔f8 24.♗b4+ ♔g8 25.♗c3=) 18...♛a1+ (18...♖b8 19.♘h4 ♛a1+ [19...♖b5? 20.♘4f5+ ♖×f5 21.♘×f5+ ♔g8 22.♛h6 g×f5 23.♖e3 f4 24.♛×f4+−] 20.♔d2 ♛a5 21.♘4f5+

♔h8 22.♔c1=) 19.♔d2 ♛a4 20.♘h4 ♘b6 21.♘4f5+ (21.♖e7 ♘bd5=) 21...♗×f5 22.♘×f5+ ♔g8 23.♖e7 ♘e4+ 24.♔e3 ♘d5+ 25.♖×d5 ♗b6+ 26.♔f4 ♘×c3 27.♘h6+ ♔g7 28.♘f5±; 15...♘e8? 16.♛×d8 ♛×a2 17.♗c3 ♘df6 (17...♘ef6? 18.♖×d7 ♗×d7 19.♘h6+ ♔h8 20.♛×f6+− Tal) 18.♛a5 ♛×a5 19.♘e7+ ♔h8 20.♗×a5± **16.♘h6+ ♔h8 17.♛×h5 ♛×a2** 17...g×h6? 18.♗c3+ f6 19.♛×h6 ♖g8 20.♘g5 ♖g7 21.♖he1+−; Tal's suggestion, 17...♗f6?, is met by 18.♘×f7+ (over the board, Tal had planned 18.♗c3? but this is refuted by 18...♗×c3 19.♘g5 ♗×b2+ 20.♔×b2 ♛b5+ 21.♔c1 g×h6 22.♛×h6 ♛f5−+ Kasparov) 18...♔g8 19.♘7g5 h6 20.♘e4 ♛×a2 21.♘×f6+ ♘×f6 22.♛a5 ♛×a5 23.♗×a5−+ **18.♗c3**

18...♘f6? Smyslov cracks under the pressure. The d8-bishop had to move: 18...♗f6 19.♘g5!? ♗xg5+ 20.♕xg5 f6 21.♕g3 ♘c5 22.♘f7‡; 18...♗c7 19.g3 (19.♘xf7+ ♔g8 20.♘h6+ ♔h8 21.♘f7+ also draws.) 19...♘f6 20.♕h4 ♗g4 21.♕xf6 (21.♗xf6 ♕a1+ 22.♔d2 ♕a5+ 23.♔c1 ♕a1‡; 21.♘xg4?? ♘e4−+) 21...♕a1+ 22.♔d2 ♖ad8+ 23.♔e3 ♖de8+ (23...♖fe8+? runs into the amazing 24.♕e5!!+−) 24.Kd2= **19.♕xf7 ♕a1+** 19...♖xf7? 20.♖xd8+ ♖f8 21.♖xf8+ ♔g8 22.♘f7‡; 19...♖e8? 20.♕g8+ ♘xg8 21.♘f7‡ **20.♔d2 ♖xf7 21.♘xf7+ ♔g8 22.♖xa1 ♔xf7 23.♘e5+ ♔e6 24.♘xc6 ♘e4+ 25.♔e3 ♗b6+ 26.♗d4** The notes are based on Müller and Stolze, *The Magic Tactics of Mikhail Tal*, New in Chess 2012. **1-0**

The following year, millions of chess aficionados avidly followed the "Two Mikhails' Match" between Botvinnik and Tal (cf. *World Championship Matches*), This encounter was underscored because their styles of play differed so sharply, because Tal had reached the foot of Olympus on his first attempt, and finally because neither one had ever played the other.

The first game, on March 15, 1960, was won by the challenger. And in the sharp struggle that followed, he never relinquished the initiative.

(114) Botvinnik – Tal
Moscow (m6) 1960
King's Indian Defense [E69]

1.c4 ♘f6 2.♘f3 g6 3.g3 ♗g7 4.♗g2 0-0 5.d4 d6 6.♘c3 ♘bd7 7.0-0 e5 8.e4 c6 9.h3 ♕b6 10.d5 cxd5 11.cxd5 ♘c5 12.♘e1 ♗d7 13.♘d3 ♘xd3 14.♕xd3 ♖fc8 15.♖b1 ♘h5 16.♗e3 ♕b4 17.♕e2 ♖c4 18.♖fc1 ♖ac8 19.♔h2 f5 20.exf5 ♗xf5 21.♖a1

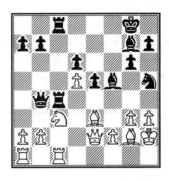

One of Tal's most famous sacrifices follows. But it is not correct according to Tal's famous motto: "There are correct sacrifices and then there are my sacrifices." Over the board, White's defensive task is next to impossible to solve of course. **21...♘f4!?** 21...♘f6 was better as per the objective computer evaluation. But Tal's sacrifice gives much better practical chances. **22.gxf4 exf4 23.♗d2?** The refutation is well hidden: 23.a3 ♕b3 24.♗xa7 ♗e5 25.f3 b6 26.a4!! To help the bishop in this way was missed by both players. (26.♕d1? ♕xb2 27.♖a2 ♖xc3 28.♖xb2 ♖xc1 29.♕d2 ♗xb2 30.♕xb2 ♖b1 31.♕f6 ♖c2=) Tal only gives the forcing 26...♕b4 (26...♖b4 27.♘d1 ♖xc1 28.♖xc1 ♕xa4 29.♖c7±; 26...♗xc3? 27.bxc3 ♖xc3 28.♖xc3 ♕xc3 29.♖e1 ♕a5 30.♕e7 ♖a8 31.♕b7+− Ragozin) 27.a5 bxa5 28.♗f2± (Kasparov) **23...♕xb2?** 23...♗e5 24.f3 ♕xb2 25.♘d1

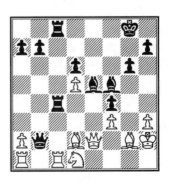

25...♛×a1! (25...♛d4?! 26.♖×c4 ♖×c4 27.♖c1 ♖×c1 28.♗×c1 ♛×d5 29.♘f2 with a slight white advantage, but also here Black's initiative does count for something.) Kasparov gives 26.♖×a1 ♗×a1 27.♛e7 ♗e5 28.♛×b7 ♖d4 29.♛b2 a5 and Black's initiative is worth the sacrificed material and perhaps even more. **24.♖ab1 f3 25.♖×b2?** Botvinnik had to shift to the attack now: 25.♗×f3 ♗×b1 26.♖×b1 ♛c2 27.♗e4!! (Flohr): 27...♖×e4 (27...♗e5+ 28.♔g2 ♖×e4 29.♘×e4 ♛×b1 30.♘×d6 ♗×d6 31.♛e6+ ♔g7 32.♛d7++−) 28.♘×e4 ♛×b1 29.♘×d6 ♖f8 30.♛e6+ ♔h8 31.♘f7+ ♖×f7 32.♛×f7+− **25...f×e2 26.♖b3 ♖d4 27.♗e1 ♗e5+ 28.♔g1 ♗f4?!** Tal misses the beautiful and deadly 28...♖×c3!! 29.♖b×c3 ♖d1 30.♖c4 ♗b2−+ (Tal) **29.♘×e2 ♖×c1 30.♘×d4 ♖×e1+ 31.♗f1 ♗e4 32.♘e2 ♗e5 33.f4 ♗f6 34.♖×b7 ♗×d5 35.♖c7 ♗×a2 36.♖×a7 ♗c4 37.♖a8+ ♔f7 38.♖a7+ ♔e6 39.♖a3 d5 40.♔f2 ♗h4+ 41.♔g2 ♔d6 42.♘g3 ♗×g3 43.♗×c4 d×c4 44.♔×g3 ♔d5 45.♖a7 c3 46.♖c7 ♔d4** The notes are based on Müller and Stolze, *The Magic Tactics of Mikhail Tal* (New in Chess 2012). **0–1**

"Way to go! A typical Tal way of relying on psychology − it turned out that Botvinnik would find it hard to resist his 'wild' play. Not for nothing did he attempt, until the end of his life, to create a chess supercomputer: it seemed as if only a machine could withstand the Tal's inscrutable combinations..." wrote Kasparov.

Winning the match by a score of 12½-8½, Tal became the eighth world champion.

Like the young prince in the fairytale "Sleeping Beauty" by Charles Perreault, awakening the kingdom from slumber, at the end of the 1950s, the young graduate of the University of Riga, Mikhail Tal, brought life back into chess. Breaking down the usual canons of struggle, smashing authority in his way, he won tournament after tournament and rose to Olympus in an hour! No one had ever seen such a story before: Alekhine was 35, when he beat Capablanca; Botvinnik was crowned with the laurel wreath at 37, Smyslov − at 36. And now, here was this 23-year-old grandmaster occupying the chess throne!

Tal's play impressed millions of fantasy-lovers, those striving for attack and spectacular combinations. Arguments over the "Tal Phenomenon," and the style of his play never abated. Nor did the hypotheses about the his secret, supernatural strength. "It is impossible to play with him − he hypnotizes us," said the American grandmaster, Pal Benko, and came to his next game against Tal in the 1959 candidates' tournament wearing dark glasses. It did not help − he resigned on the 30th move.

The secret of Tal's victories, of course, is not in his creative method of play itself, which was in complete accordance with his credo: "At its root, the beauty of logic, in my view, retreats before the effect of paradox." This was exactly the way that Tal responded to the question, "How do you understand chess beauty?," that Isaak Linder posed to him, while preparing his book, *Chess Esthetics* for print.

Tal regarded the future with optimism; he believed that new victories awaited him. And with that, he repeated the mistake of the seventh world champion, Vassily Smyslov, forgetting his vanquished opponent, who, deciding to make use of his right to a return-match and prepared intensely for the same. Botvinnik, great strategist and psychologist that he was, during the return-match of 1961, would create such positions during the games that the young grandmaster's combinative gifts could not show themselves with the same power and brilliance as they had in their previous encounter. In the end, Botvinnik won by a score of 13-8.

The prefix "ex" made Tal years smarter, more experienced, and more calculating. His creativity underwent an evolution in favor of "solidity," and a classical basis for his combinations. Less and less frequently would he "overbear" the position, and would sacrifice pieces mainly when circumstances favored him, and when he could beautifully conclude the game with their aid.

Tal was able to participate in candidates' events for the world championship more than once after that, as well as in chess Olympiads, and in strong international tournaments, where he would often take first prize.

(115) Tal – Larsen
Bled (m10) 1965
Sicilian Defense [B82]

1.e4 c5 2.♘f3 ♘c6 3.d4 c×d4 4.♘×d4 e6 5.♘c3 d6 6.♗e3 ♘f6 7.f4 ♗e7 8.♕f3 0-0 9.0-0-0 ♕c7 10.♘db5 ♕b8 11.g4 a6 12.♘d4 ♘×d4 13.♗×d4 b5 14.g5 ♘d7

15.♗d3 b4 16.♘d5?! A typical Tal sacrifice. It is not correct, but very dangerous. Objectively, 16.♘e2 is better. **16...e×d5 17.e×d5**

17...f5? The computer gives 17...g6! and Black is better, e.g., 18.♖he1 ♗d8 19.♕h3 ♘e5 20.♕h6 ♗b6 21.f5 ♗×f5 22.♗×f5 ♖e8 **18.♖de1** 18.g×f6 was the alternative, e.g., 18...♘×f6 19.♖hg1 ♖f7 20.♖de1 ♕b7 21.♗×f6 ♖×f6 22.♕e4 g6 23.♕×e7 ♕×e7 24.♖×e7 ♖×f4 25.h4 **18...♖f7?** The computer's main line runs: 18...♗d8 19.♕h5 ♘c5 20.♗×g7 ♘×d3+ 21.♔b1 ♕c7 22.♗×f8 ♘×e1 23.♖×e1 ♕f7 24.♕×f7+ ♔×f7 25.♗×d6 a5= **19.h4 ♗b7 20.♗×f5** 20.h5!?+− **20...♖×f5** 20...♘f8? 21.♗×h7+ (21.♕e4+−) 21...♔×h7 22.h5 ♗g5 23.♕e4+ ♔g8 24.f×g5 ♕d8 25.g6+− **21.♖×e7 ♘e5 22.♕e4 ♕f8 23.f×e5 ♖f4?!** 23...♕×e7 24.♕×f5 ♗×d5± is a slightly better version of the game. **24.♕e3 ♖f3 25.♕e2 ♕×e7 26.♕×f3 d×e5 27.♖e1 ♖d8?! 28.♖×e5 ♕d6?** 28...♕f7 was the last chance to fight. **29.♕f4 ♖f8** 29...♗×d5 30.♖e8+ ■ **30.♕e4 b3 31.a×b3 ♖f1+ 32.♔d2 ♕b4+ 33.c3 ♕d6 34.♗c5 ♕×c5 35.♖e8+ ♖f8 36.♕e6+ ♔h8 37.♕f7 1-0**

In 1988, with a victory in the World Blitz Championship, Tal again was pronounced strongest in the world. For the first time, this tournament was held with 32 grandmasters participating, among them Kasparov and Karpov.

"Chess is many-faceted," the 51-year old Tal said after his victory, "and there's no need to squeeze it into the procrustean bed of traditional rules. Rapid chess is entertaining, dynamic, and scenic."

His brilliant blitz play once again underscored a feature of Tal's character: his courage and fearlessness. And more than once, he displayed these characteristics in his life, too. At a tournament in Spain, in 1966, the organizers suggested that the grandmasters could try out the role of toreador. Although the *corrida* was a bit easier (the "bullfighters" would face only calves), there were only three takers – Tal among them. Witnesses said that, dressed in his red cape, performed with his "muleta" elegantly, which drew shouts of approval from the stands.

Another example. In 1958, at Portoroz, on one of his free days, Tal came to see how athletes were training to dive. He was approached by a Yugoslav journalist. who began to nag him, saying, "Yesterday, you were so brave over the board, and now you're afraid to jump..." And Tal dove in. "Of course, the dive was not very elegant," Mikhail admitted later, "and I understood that diving was not my 'element'..."

His element was chess. His great love for the game and his equally great courage are shown by the fact that, when he was already gravely ill, he took a day out of the hospital to play in a prestigious blitz-tournament, and took third place in it, behind only Kasparov and Bareev.

His creativity inspired *aficionados* and chessplayers alike – world champions among them! In a letter to one of the present book's authors, Euwe wrote: "I very much enjoy the games of Mikhail Tal. The kind of combinations he executes are difficult to calculate beforehand; he is able to prepare them, thanks to his incomparable intuition and fantasy." The opinion of Smyslov on Tal was similar: "When he made his appearance in the upper reaches of chess, he had the effect of an exploding bomb, since the style of his game was so different: an unusual combinative brilliance. The pieces seemed to come alive in his hands; everything fell into place for him. And he, and only he, could create and play "his" seemingly irrational positions. And now, that sharp-witted, life-affirming person is no longer with us. But what remains to us are his creations."

Books: *Tal-Botvinnik 1960: Match for the World Championship*, Riga 1961; *In the Fires of the Attack*, Moscow 1978 (co-author, Ya. Damsky); *When the Pieces Come Alive*, Moscow 1983.

,

Khalifman, A., *Mikhail Tal. Games 1949-1992*, Soevier 1994-96; Laudau, S., *Elegy for Mikhail Tal*, Moscow 1998; Botvinnik, M., *Portraits* (composed by I.Yu.Botvinnik), Moscow 2000; Linder, V. I., Linder, I. M., "Mikhail Tal" (in the book *Kings of the Chess World*, Moscow 2001); Kasparov, G., "Mikhail the Eighth" (in the book *My Great Predecessors*, vol. 2, Moscow 2003); Voronkov, S., Plisetsky, D., *The Russians vs. Fischer*, Moscow 2004

Tournaments In 59 tournaments, among them twelve USSR championships and fourteen international, Mikhail Botvinnik was a participant – from the championship of the metallurgists' society (Leningrad 1927/28) to the highest-level events: Nottingham 1936, the 1938 AVRO tournament, Groningen 1946, the Hague-Moscow 1948. In 35 of these, he took first place. and only six times was he outside the top three finishers. He played in six Olympiads and in dozens of other team events; in them, he scored over 70%. He never distinguished these events by their order of importance, but gave completely of himself, showing absolutely selfless sacrifice in all of them, whether it was the championship semi-final of Leningrad or the USSR Championship.

In Botvinnik's competitive career, we can distinguish two of the clear tournament periods in which he showed "super-class." The first was, beginning with the tournament of the masters of Leningrad in 1930, up to and including the tournament of masters with the participation of Euwe and Kmoch in 1934. Botvinnik played nine tournaments at that time – in seven of them, he took first place. In one he shared first/second places, and once he was in sole second place. The second period was even more unique. From the match-tournament for the title of Absolute Champion of the USSR in 1941, and up to and including the match-tournament of 1948, Botvinnik played in eight events (among them, the tournament at Sverdlovsk 1943, the Moscow championship of 1943/44, two USSR championships, 1944 and 1945, and the tournaments at Groningen 1946

and the Chigorin Memorial of 1947) and in every one of them, he confidently took first place! In these eight tournaments, he played 137 games, and in them, he scored 104½ points (winning 83 games and losing only 11), for a score of 76.3%.

Like Lasker in his day, Botvinnik prepared not only for every tournament, but also for every one of his opponents. By the close of the 20th century, every self-respecting grandmaster operated according to this "Botvinnik's Rule." But about those who have personal computers with an information base exceeding the book-based home libraries, we shall speak later.

Flohr, Salomon (October 21, 1908, Gorodenka, Ukraine-June 18, 1983, Moscow), grandmaster, world championship candidate. During the First World War, Salo's family left the Ukraine and moved to Prague. He turned to chess relatively late – at 14. Trying to outstrip his older brother, to whom he often lost, Salo began to study chess literature.

At the close of the1920s, witty chess reporting started appearing in the press, followed by the signature of Salo Flohr. Soon, his name also flashed among the participants in international events, and among the prizewinners. Making his debut at the tournament of Rogaska-Slatina 1929, the 21-year old Flohr took second place, behind Rubinstein. Then followed victories at Brno 1931, Hastings 1931/32, 1932/33, 1933/34, Slanchev 1932, Moscow 1935, Podebrady 1936. In the years 1931-1933 he played four matches, winning two of them – from Stoltz (in 1931), and

Mir Sultan-Khan (in 1932), and drawing two, against Euwe (1932) and Botvinnik (1933) (cf. *Flohr-Botvinnik, match*). The last two drew great interest in the USSR as well as abroad, because it was seen as the first trial of two gifted young players of the West and the Soviet Union. In it, Flohr demonstrated great mastery in the accumulation and exploitation of a minimal advantage, especially in the endgame. A particularly clear example of this was the following game.

(116) Flohr – Botvinnik
Leningrad 1933
Nimzo-Indian [E38]

1.d4 ♘f6 2.c4 e6 3.♘c3 ♗b4 4.♕c2 c5 5.d×c5 ♘a6 6.a3 ♗×c3+ 7.♕×c3 ♘×c5 8.f3 d6 9.e4 e5 10.♗e3 ♕c7 11.♘e2 ♗e6 12.♕c2 0-0 13.♘c3 ♖fc8 14.♗e2 a6 15.♖c1 ♘cd7 16.♕d2 ♕b8 17.♘d5 ♗×d5 18.c×d5 ♖×c1+ 19.♕×c1 ♕d8 20.0-0 ♖c8 21.♕d2 ♕c7 22.♖c1 22.♕b4!? **22...♕×c1+ 23.♕×c1 ♖×c1+ 24.♗×c1 ♔f8**

The endgame which has arisen is quite famous and is given in many textbooks. It is still an open question whether White can win against best defense, but over the board, Black's task is next to impossible. **25.♔f2 ♔e7 26.♗e3**

♔d8 27.♔e1 ♔c7 28.♔d2 ♘c5 29.b4 ♘cd7 30.g3 ♘b6 31.♔c2 ♘bd7 32.a4 ♘b6 33.a5 ♘bd7 34.♗c1 ♔d8 35.♗b2 ♘e8 36.♔d2 ♘c7 37.♔e3 ♔e7 38.♗f1 ♘b5 39.h4 ♘c7 40.♗h3 ♘e8 41.f4 f6 42.♗f5 g6 43.♗h3 h6 44.♗c1 ♘g7 45.f×e5 d×e5 46.♔f3 h5 47.♗e3 47.♗f1!? **47...♔d6 48.♗h6** 48.g4!? **48...♘e8 49.g4 h×g4+ 50.♗×g4**

50...♘c7? 50...♔e7 51.♗e3 ♘d6 was a better set up and the last chance to fight. **51.♗e3 ♘b5 52.♔e2 ♘c7 53.♔d3 f5** 53...♘b5 54.♗e6 ♔e7 55.♗c5+± **54.e×f5 g×f5 55.♗×f5 ♘×d5 56.♗d2 ♘7f6 57.♔c4 ♔c6 58.♗g6** 58.♗g5!? **58...b5+ 59.♔d3 ♘e7 60.♗e4+ ♘ed5 61.♗g5 ♘h5 62.♗f3 ♘g3 63.♗d2 ♔d6 64.♗g4 ♘f6?!** 64...♘f1 65.♗e1 ♘fe3 66.♗h3 ♘c4 67.♔e4 ♘f6+ 68.♔f5 +- **65.♗c8 ♔c6 66.♗e1** 66.♗×a6!? +- **66...e4+?!** 66...♘ge4 is more tenacious, but after 67.♗×a6 ♘d6 68.♗f2, White should win as well in the long run. **67.♔d4 ♘gh5 68.♗f5 ♔d6 69.♗d2 1-0**

The strength of Flohr's game can be seen from his tournament wins over Capablanca, Euwe, Emanuel Lasker, and also over Spielmann, Ståhlberg, Bogoljubow, Vidmar, and other chieftains. Many of these wins were garnered in the endgame, where he showed himself to be a true virtuoso.

(117) Flohr – Vidmar
Nottingham 1936
Queen's Gambit Declined [D62]

1.c4 e6 2.♘c3 d5 3.d4 ♘f6 4.♗g5
♗e7 5.e3 0-0 6.♘f3 ♘bd7 7.♕c2
c5 8.c×d5 ♘×d5 9.♗×e7 ♕×e7
10.♘×d5 e×d5 11.♗d3 g6 12.d×c5
♘×c5 13.0-0 ♗g4 14.♘d4 ♖ac8
15.♕d2 a6 16.♗c2 ♕g5?! 16...♘e4!?
17.f3 ♗d7 18.♖fe1 ♖fd8 19.♖ad1
♕f6 20.♗b3 ♗a4 21.♗×a4 ♘×a4
22.♖c1 ♘c5 23.♖ed1 ♕b6 24.♘e2
♘d7 25.♕d4 25.♖c3!? 25...♕×d4
26.♘×d4 ♘e5 27.b3 ♔f8 28.♔f1
♖×c1 29.♖×c1 ♘c6 30.♘×c6 ♖c8
31.♖c5 b×c6 32.♔e2 ♔e7 33.♔d3
♔d6 34.♖a5 ♖a8 35.♔d4 f5 36.b4

36...♖b8? Mark Dvoretsky's
suggestion to change the role of the
defenders with 36...♔c7 37.♔c5 ♔b7
38.♔d6 ♖e8 39.♖a3 g5= is better.
37.a3 ♖a8 38.e4 Flohr opens a second
front. **38...f×e4 39.f×e4 d×e4
40.♔×e4 ♖a7 41.♔f4 h6 42.h4
♔e6 43.♔g4 ♖a8 44.h5 g5?** This
was the very last chance to activate the
rook with 44...♖g8! **45.g3 ♖a7
46.♔f3 ♖a8 47.♔e4 ♖a7 48.♔d4
♔d6 49.♔e4 ♔e6 50.♖e5+** The
decisive check, as now White' king will
penetrate on one of the wings.
**50...♔d6 51.♖e8 c5 52.♖d8+ ♔c6
53.♖c8+ ♔b6 54.♖×c5 ♖h7
55.♖e5 ♔c6 56.♖e6+ ♔b5 57.♔f5
♖f7+ 58.♖f6 1-0**

Flohr was one of Euwe's trainers in his
world championship match against
Alekhine in 1935. And two years later,
in December 1937, he himself challenged
Alekhine, who had regained the title of
champion in his return match with Euwe.
After a short exchange of letters,
Alekhine arrived in Prague. And as Flohr
wrote in the pages of *64* magazine
(October 7, 1938), "On May 30, we
signed a formal agreement for a match.
It will be in autumn 1939, in the Czech
Republic, with the same conditions as in
the Alekhine-Euwe match. The only
point that will be changed, is in the
matter of seconds. As opposed to the
latter match, our seconds will no longer
be chess masters." And here a
photograph was presented, in which
Alekhine and Flohr were shown seated
around a table, signing the agreement.

But the war upset all their plans. Flohr
moved to Moscow, and entered actively
into the chess life of the country, In
post-war years. Flohr no longer showed
the strength which had allowed him to
make a serious attempt at the highest
title. The "ex-president" became the
"world champion" in chess journalism.
Here he achieved indubitable success.
His articles, reportage, and sketches were
filled with humor and irony, historical
excursions and sharp, laconic portraits of
the chess chieftains. From time to time,
he would remind his readers that he,
himself, was once an outstanding
chessplayer, having participated in the
16th USSR championship, in an
interzonal tournament in 1948, in the
1950 candidates' tournament, in the
international tournaments at Göteborg
1958 (first place), Beverwijk 1960,
fourth/fifth places, Stockholm 1962,
third place, and Amsterdam 1966, third
place.

Books: *The Clocks Aren't Stopped,* Moscow 1984; *Through the Prism of a Half-Century,* Moscow 1986; *Sowjetisches Schach,* 1917-1955, Hamburg, 1960 (co-author); *Petrosjan bleibt Weltmeister,* Arnst., 1967; *Spassky – Weltmeister,* Amsterdam 1971.

About: Grossmeister Flohr (composed by V. D. Baturinsky), Moscow 1985.

Flohr – Botvinnik Match, 1933 (November 28-December 19, Moscow/Leningrad) Played in twelve games, on the initiative of Czech grandmaster Salo Flohr, who started negotiations with Botvinnik through an intermediary, Ilyin-Zhenevsky, who was at the time an adviser to the USSR consul in Prague.

Was Mikhail Botvinnik, the champion of the USSR, ready to meet successfully with the best foreign masters? This question was disturbing Soviet chess society then. Many experienced chessplayers were inclined to be pessimistic. But the chairman of the All-Union chess section, N. V. Krylenko (1885-1938) was sure: "The match will take place; we have to find out our genuine strength." And Botvinnik started to prepare himself. This would be his first international match – and against a most serious opponent. At the start of the 1930s, Flohr, who had won a number of strong international tournaments, was already considered a candidate for the world's championship.

After analyzing over a hundred of Flohr's games, Botvinnik concluded that the man he was about to face was a fine strategist, who would be wonderfully at home in the endgame, and that the characteristic of his play had altered in recent years: not so long ago, he had been a combinative-style chessplayer, but now he was starting to aim for a more positional kind of struggle – to the resolution of problems by pure technique. His opening repertoire was somewhat limited – as White, he primarily used the Queen's Gambit; with Black, he mostly answered 1.d4 with the Queen's Gambit Accepted, and 1.e4 with the Caro-Kann Defense. Finally, he realized that Flohr was not always psychologically stable in the face of his very occasional losses. This led him to draw the necessary conclusions.

Nevertheless, the match – the first six games of which were played in Moscow, in the Hall of Columns of the Home of Unions – began badly for Botvinnik. In the very first game Flohr, with Black, found an elegant endgame combination to force his opponent's resignation on the 41st move. Overall, in the match's first half, Botvinnik drew four games and lost two. And in the sixth game, as in the first, Flohr exploited his advantage of "the two bishops over the two knights" very accurately, and increased his lead...

The second half of the match was in Leningrad. Almost no one believed any longer that Botvinnik could pull things out – that is, bring the match to a drawn conclusion. "Winning two out of six games from the 'impregnable' Flohr would be utopia," said observers.

But they did not know Botvinnik. Besides being among his old friends, he was in familiar surroundings where, as they say, "the very walls help out." Soon, there was not a trace left of that bitter taste of defeat. For him, it was as though the battle was joined anew. It was a sort of revenge-match for the defeats he had suffered in Moscow. And his strength in such a situation had already been demonstrated brilliantly.

Careful analysis of the first game let Botvinnik find the resources to improve his play in the opening. And he appeared "fully armed" for the ninth game. Flohr quietly met his opponent's plans halfway, repeating the variation from their tenth game up to the tenth move. The more so, in that two draws in the preceding games – the seventh and the eighth – created the illusion that his opponent had made his peace with the match's unfortunate outcome, and that no storm was to be anticipated.

This time, Botvinnik played the entire game confidently, from beginning to end, and Flohr, "falling out of the boat," sank to the bottom... Thus was the gap shortened between them.

(118) Botvinnik – Flohr
Leningrad 1933
Caro-Kann Defense [B13]

1.e4 c6 2.d4 d5 3.e×d5 c×d5 4.c4 ♘f6 5.♘c3 ♘c6 6.♗g5 d×c4 7.d5 ♘e5 7...♘a5!? **8.♕d4 ♘d3+ 9.♗×d3 c×d3 10.♘f3 g6 11.♗×f6 e×f6 12.0-0 ♕b6?** Black does not have time for this. 12...♗e7 was called for. **13.♖fe1+ ♔d8 14.♕h4!? g5 15.♕h5 ♗d6 16.♕×f7 ♖f8 17.♕×h7 g4?! 18.♘d2 ♕c7 19.♕h6 ♕f7 20.♘c4 ♗e5 21.♘×e5 f×e5**

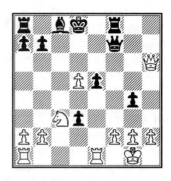

22.♕g5+?! The direct 22.♘e4! wins, e.g., 22...♗f5 23.♕d6+ ♗d7 24.♘c5 ♕×f2+ 25.♔h1 +− **22...♕e7 23.♕×e5 ♕×e5 24.♖×e5 ♗f5 25.♖f1 ♔d7 26.f3 b5 27.f×g4 ♗×g4 28.h3 b4 29.♘e4 ♖×f1+ 30.♔×f1 ♖f8+ 31.♔e1 ♗f5 32.g4 ♗g6 33.♖e6** "This game showed me that I was capable of beating Flohr and I make no bones about admitting that this game encouraged me a lot." (Botvinnik in *The Flohr-Botvinnik Match*, Moscow 1934) **1-0**

And success in the following, tenth, game was made possible by pre-match preparation. Botvinnik took note of the fact that in the Dutch Defense, Flohr had never yet encountered the "Stonewall Variation" – so he played it, and undertook a kingside assault. Flohr could not cope with the finesses of this unfamiliar position, played passively, and by the 31st move was forced to capitulate.

The Leningraders were overjoyed at the success of their countryman. The last two games were drawn, so the final score of the match was 6-6 (+2 -2 =8). Thus, the first trial of the new Soviet champion ended successfully. Clearly, he had already reached the level of the strongest chessplayers in the world.

Chigorin Memorial, 1947 (November 25-December 23, Moscow) This tournament was organized by the Committee for Physiculture and Sport with the Soviet of Ministers of the RSFSR and held in the Hall of Columns of the Central House of the Red Army, named after M. V. Frunze. 20 Soviet chessplayers participated with these six foreign players: Trifunovich and Gligorich (Yugoslavia), Pachman and Kottnauer (Czechoslovakia), Plater (Poland) and Tsvetkov (Bulgaria).

After a dull start (in the first four rounds, Botvinnik won just one game and drew three), he went on to win five games in a row, and maintained his lead until the end of the event. Botvinnik ended up winning the tournament with a score of +7 -1 =6. The only game that he lost was against Pachman. His friend and trainer Ragozin was only a half-point behind. The same interval separated him from the third/fourth place finishers, Boleslavsky and Smyslov.

In many of the games that Botvinnik won, the finish came in the endgame. For example, the curious ending of his game against Plater shows that, in analogous positions, the bishop's superiority over the knight has, as Botvinnik wrote, only "academic significance."

Black's fine play to restrict the knight's mobility led to the win of a queenside pawn. White had to drag all his main forces (that is, king and knight) there, and thus leave his kingside unprotected...

(119) Plater – Botvinnik
Moscow 1947
Sicilian Defense [B20]

1.e4 c5 2.♘e2 ♘f6 3.♘bc3 d5 4.e×d5 ♘×d5 5.♘×d5 ♕×d5 6.♘c3 ♕d8 7.♗c4 ♘c6 8.d3 e6 9.0-0 ♗e7 10.f4?! Too committal. 10...0-0 11.♘e4 ♘a5! 12.♗b3 ♕d4+ 13.♔h1 c4! 14.c3 ♕×d3 15.♕×d3 c×d3 16.♘f2 ♖d8 17.♖d1 ♗c5 18.♖×d3 ♗d7 19.♗e3 ♗×e3 20.♖×e3 ♗b5 21.♘e4 h6 22.♖ae1 ♘×b3 23.a×b3 a5 24.h3 ♖ac8 25.♔g1 ♔f8 26.♔h2 ♖c7 27.♔g3 b6 28.♔h2?! ♖cd7 29.♔g1 ♖d1 30.c4?! 30.♔f2 is more tenacious. 30...♗c6 31.♘c3 ♖×e1+ 32.♖×e1 ♔e7 33.♖e2 f6 34.♔f2 ♖d3 35.h4 h5 36.♖e3?! ♖d2+?! There was nothing wrong with 36...♖×e3!? 37.♔×e3 ♗×g2 38.♘a4 ♔d6 39.♔d4 e5+ 40.f×e5+ f×e5+ 41.♔e3 ♔c6–+ 37.♖e2 ♖d3 38.♖e3?! ♖d2+?! 39.♖e2 ♖×e2+ 40.♘×e2 ♔d6 41.♘d4 g6?! 41...♗e4!? 42.g3 e5 is more precise. 42.g3 e5 43.f×e5+ f×e5

44.♘c2? 44.♘e2 ♔c5 45.♔e3 ♔b4 46.♘c1 was the last chance to fight. 44...♗e4 45.♘e1 ♔c5 46.♔e3 ♗f5 47.♘f3 ♔b4 48.♘d2 ♗c2 49.♔f3 ♗×b3 50.♔e4 ♗×c4 51.♔×e5 ♗d3 52.♔d4 ♗f5 53.♘c4 b5 54.♘d2 a4 55.♔d5 ♗h3 56.♔d4 ♗g2 57.♔d3

*The five top prizewinners of the Chigorin Memorial (1947): Left to right:
Botvinnik, Kotov, Ragozin, Smyslov, Boleslavsky*

♔c5 58.♔c3 b4+ 59.♔d3 ♗d5
60.♘b1 ♗e6 61.♘d2 ♗f5+
62.♔e3 ♗c2 0-1

(120) Botvinnik – Kottnauer
Moscow 1947
Slav Defense [D13]

1.♘f3 d5 2.d4 ♘f6 3.c4 c6 4.c×d5
c×d5 5.♘c3 ♘c6 6.♗f4 e6 7.e3
♗d6 8.♗d3 0-0 9.0-0 b6 10.♖c1
♗b7 11.a3 ♖c8 12.♕e2 ♗×f4
13.e×f4 ♘a5 14.♖c2 ♘c4 15.♖fc1
a6 16.♘b1 b5 17.b3 ♘d6 18.♖×c8
♗×c8 19.♘e5 ♗d7 20.g4 g6
21.♔g2?! 21.♘c3!? 21...♘fe8
22.♕e3 f6 23.♘f3 ♘g7 24.h3 ♕b6
25.♖c5 ♘b7 26.♖c2 ♖c8 27.♖×c8+
♗×c8 28.g5 ♕c7? 28...♕d8 limits the
damage. **29.g×f6 ♘h5**

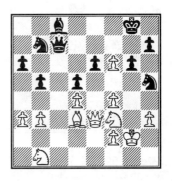

30.♘e5? Now Black can consolidate.
The battering ram 30.f5!!+− decides.
30...♘×f6 31.♕d2 ♘d6 32.♕c2
♕×c2 **33.♗×c2 ♘f7 34.♘c3**
♘×e5?! 34...♘d6!? is more or less
completely equal. **35.f×e5 ♘e8
36.♔f3 ♘c7 37.♔e3 ♔f7 38.♘e2
♔e7 39.♘f4 a5 40.♘d3 ♘a6**

Moscow 1947

		1	2	3	4	5	6	7	8	9	10	11	12	13	14	15	16	Total
1	Botvinnik	*	1	½	½	½	1	1	0	½	½	½	1	1	1	1	1	11
2	Ragozin	0	*	0	½	½	1	½	½	1	1	1	1	½	1	1	1	10½
3	Boleslavsky	½	1	*	½	½	0	½	½	1	½	1	1	½	½	1	1	10
4	Smyslov	½	½	½	*	0	½	½	1	½	½	1	½	1	1	1	1	10
5	Kotov	½	½	½	1	*	0	1	½	½	1	0	½	½	1	1	1	9½
6	Keres	0	0	1	½	1	*	0	½	½	½	½	1	1	½	1	1	9
7	Novotelnov	0	½	½	½	0	1	*	½	0	1	½	1	1	1	½	1	9
8	Pachman	1	½	½	0	½	½	½	*	0	1	½	1	0	½	1	1	8½
9	Trifunovic	½	0	0	½	½	½	1	1	*	½	½	½	½	½	1	½	8
10	Gligoric	½	0	½	½	0	½	0	0	½	*	½	1	1	1	½	1	7½
11	Bondarevsky	½	0	0	0	1	½	½	½	½	½	*	0	½	1	0	1	6½
12	Kholmov	0	0	0	½	½	0	0	0	½	0	1	*	½	1	½	1	5½
13	Kottnauer	0	½	½	0	½	0	0	1	½	0	½	½	*	0	½	½	5
14	Plater	0	0	½	0	0	½	0	½	½	0	0	0	1	*	½	½	4
15	Sokolsky	0	0	0	0	0	0	½	0	0	½	1	½	½	½	*	½	4
16	Tsvetkov	0	0	0	0	0	0	0	0	½	0	0	0	½	½	½	*	2

41.b4 a×b4 42.a×b4 ♘b8 43.♔d2 ♘c6 44.♔c3 ♘d8 45.h4 ♘f7 46.♘f4 ♗d7 47.♔d2 ♗e8 48.♗d3 ♘h6 49.h5 ♘f5 50.h×g6 h×g6 51.♔c3 ♔f7 52.♗e2 ♗d7 53.♘d3 ♔e7 54.♘c5 ♗e8 55.♘a6 ♔d8 56.♗g4 ♗d7 57.♘c5 ♔e7 58.♔d3 ♗c8 59.♗h3

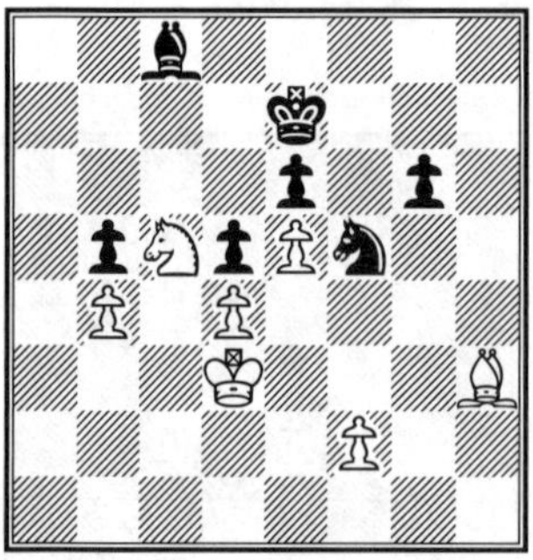

59...♔e8? 59...♘h6 defends, e.g., 60.♔e3 g5 61.♗f1 ♘f5+ 62.♔d3 ♗d7 63.♗h3 ♘h4 64.♗g4 ♘f5= **60.♔c3 1-0** 60...♗d7 61.♗f1 ♘h6 62.♘×d7 ♔×d7 63.♗×b5+ ♔c7 64.♗e8 g5 65.b5 ♘f5 66.♗f7 ♘g7 67.♔b4 ♔b6 68.♗g6+−

Six-way Tournament, 1927 This double-round tournament, with six strong chessplayers, was held in Leningrad, at the end of the summer of 1927, and became, for the 16-year-old Botvinnik, one of the "stages on the great journey." "For me, the event had great significance, since in the autumn of 1927, the fifth USSR championship, the next in line, was due to take place. In the event of my successful performance in this match-tournament, I could be included on the "list of candidates for participation in the championship," recalled Botvinnik. "I played the tournament with great enthusiasm, losing only a match with Pyotr Arsenievich Romanovsky, and winning the rest. I felt fine. I lived in a dacha in Sestroretsk (I was on the beach the whole time), traveled to Leningrad twice a week, my physical shape was great, my head was clear."

(121) Botvinnik – Ragozin
Leningrad 1927
French Defense [C01]

1.e4 e6 2.d4 d5 3.♘c3 ♗b4 4.e5 f6?! 5.♘f3 c5 6.a3 ♗a5 7.b4 c×b4 8.♘b5 ♘c6 9.a×b4 ♗c7 10.c3

10.♞xc7+!?± **10...♞ge7 11.exf6 gxf6 12.♝d3 0-0 13.0-0 ♝d7 14.♝a3?! ♖f7?! 15.♕d2?!** 15.♞xc7± **15...e5?** This opens the position for White. 15...♝b8 is called for. **16.dxe5 ♞xe5 17.♞xe5 fxe5 18.♞xc7 ♕xc7 19.♕g5+?!** 19.b5± **19...♚h8 20.♕h5**

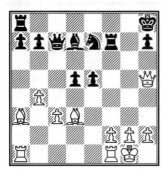

20...♝e6? Black's set up is not really stable. 20...♖g7 21.♝b2 ♖f8 offers more resistance. **21.♖ae1 e4 22.c4 ♖f5?!** 22...♕f4 23.♝b2+ ♚g8 24.♝b1± **23.♕e2?!** 23.♝b2+ ♚g8 24.♕g4+ ♞g6 25.cxd5+− **23...♕e5?** 23...♞g6 24.cxd5 exd3 25.♕xe6 ♕f7± limits the damage. **24.♝c1** 24.♝b2 d4 25.♕xe4+− **24...♕d6 25.cxd5 exd3 26.♝b2+ ♚g8 27.♕g4+ ♞g6 28.♖xe6 ♕xd5 29.♖xg6+ hxg6 30.♕xg6+ ♚f8 31.♕g7+ ♚e8 32.♖e1+ ♚d8 33.♕e7+ ♚c8 34.♖c1+ 1-0**

Ståhlberg, Andera Gideon Tom (January 26, 1908, near Göteborg-May 26, 1967, Leningrad), Swedish international grandmaster, world champion candidate, chess author, international arbiter.

From 1957 to 1962, Gideon Ståhlberg was chief arbiter for five world championship matches involving Mikhail Botvinnik.

Gideon was not yet 20-years old when he won the Swedish championship together with the talented Gosta Stoltz (1904-1963), another eventual grandmaster. In 1929, he won the tournament of the North Countries, and an international tournament at Dieren. In one of his articles, Emanuel Lasker, naming Ståhlberg one of the most qualified representatives of the younger generation of those years, wrote: "This generation grew up in that difficult era; it does not believe in rules, such as those believed by Steinitz and Rubinstein. It is not romantic, like Chigorin or Alekhine; it does not strive to follow logical paths to the same extent as did Capablanca. But it is endowed with a deep sense of what is real and significant. This generation does not dream, it struggles – manfully and fearlessly..."

In 1931, Gideon performed brilliantly at the "Tournament of Nations," demonstrating the fifth-best result on first board (11½/18): he finished ahead of Flohr, Grunfeld, Rubinstein, and Vidmar. In total, in almost 40 years (1928-1964), Ståhlberg was on the national team for the Olympiad twelve times. At the start of the 1930s. Ståhlberg won two matches against gifted grandmasters: Rudolf Spielmann (1933, +3 -1 =4), and Nimzovich (1934, +4 -2 =2). After his match, Nimzovich wrote, "I like Ståhlberg's style because of its new synthesis of positional maneuvering and lively combinative play. I was also impressed by his manner of inducing complications; it is rare that he misses the strongest move; his attacks are always distinguished by spectacular effects. All this taken together compels me to acknowledge him as our new grandmaster."

The following game of the match, which was won nicely by Ståhlberg, made the rounds of the international chess press.

(122) Ståhlberg – Nimzowitsch
Göteborg 1934
Nimzo-Indian [E22]

1.d4 ♘f6 2.c4 e6 3.♘c3 ♗b4 4.♕b3 c5 5.d×c5 ♘c6 6.♘f3 ♘e4 7.♗d2 ♘×c5 8.♕c2 0-0 9.a3 ♗×c3 10.♗×c3 a5 11.g3 a4 12.♗g2 b6 13.0-0 ♗b7 14.♖ad1 ♘a5 15.♗b4 ♗e4 16.♕c3 ♘ab3 17.♘d4 ♗×g2 18.♔×g2 ♖e8?! 18...♘×d4 19.♖×d4 ♕c7 20.♖fd1 ♖fd8 **19.♘×b3 ♘×b3 20.♖d6 ♕c7 21.♖fd1 ♖ed8 22.♕f3 ♖ab8 23.♕g4 f6 24.♗c3 ♔h8 25.♕h4?!** The battering ram should come: 25.h4 ♘c5 26.h5 ♖g8 27.h6± **25...e5?**

25...♔g8 is correct. **26.♖×f6!! g×f6?** 26...d6 is forced. **27.♕×f6+ ♔g8 28.♖d6 ♖f8 29.♕×e5 ♖×f2+ 30.♔g1 ♔f7 31.♖f6+ 1-0** 31...♖×f6 32.♕×c7 ♖e8 33.♗×f6 ♔×f6 34.♕×b6++– follows.

Ståhlberg drew against Capablanca, at the Moscow International Tournament of 1935, with Alekhine at the Erebro tournament of 1935, and with Botvinnik at the Maróczy Memorial tournament of

Gideon Ståhlberg

1952, and defeated Emanuel Lasker at Zürich 1934.

(123) Ståhlberg – Em.Lasker
Zürich 1934
Queen's Gambit Declined [D41]

1.d4 d5 2.c4 e6 3.♘f3 ♘f6 4.♘c3 c5 5.c×d5 ♘×d5 6.e4 ♘×c3 7.b×c3 c×d4 8.c×d4 ♘c6 9.♗e2 ♗b4+ 10.♗d2 ♕a5 11.♖b1 ♗×d2+ 12.♕×d2 0-0 13.♗b5 ♕×d2+ 14.♔×d2 ♘a5 15.♖hc1 b6 16.♘e5 ♗b7 17.f3 ♖fd8 18.♔e3

18...♖ac8? 18...f6 19.♘c4 ♘c6 20.♘×b6 a×b6 21.♗×c6 ♗×c6 22.♖×c6 ♖a3+ 23.♖b3 ♖×a2 limits the damage.

19.♗d7 ♘c4+ 19...♖a8 20.♖c7±
20.♔e2! ♖×d7 21.♘×d7 ♗a6
22.♔f2 f6 23.♖b4 ♖d8 24.♖a4
♘b2 25.♖×a6 ♘d3+ 26.♔e3 ♘×c1
27.♖×a7 ♘×a2 28.♘×f6+ g×f6
29.♖×a2 ♔f7 29...♖b8 30.♔d3 b5
31.♖a7± 30.♖a7+ ♔g6 31.♖b7
♖d6 32.♖c7 b5 33.♖b7 ♖a6 34.d5
♖a3+ 35.♔d4 e×d5 36.e×d5 ♖a2
37.g4 ♖×h2 38.d6 h5 39.g×h5+
♖×h5 40.d7 ♖h1 41.♔d5 41.d8♕??
♖d1± 41...♖d1+ 42.♔e6 ♖e1+
43.♔d6 ♖d1+ 44.♔c7 ♖c1+
45.♔b8 1-0

"A game characteristic of the technique of masters of the younger generation," wrote Alekhine.

After the "Tournament of Nations" in 1939, Ståhlberg stayed in Argentina, and after 10 years in Buenos Aires, returned to his homeland. At the start of the 1950s, Ståhlberg played in world championship events – in the candidates' tournament of 1953 and in four interzonals. He played with particular success in the first interzonal, in 1948, in which he led for a number of rounds, and ended up sharing sixth/ninth places. Among Ståhlberg's best appearances were: Kemeri 1939 – second/third places; Buenos Aires 1941 – first/second places; Mar del Plata 1941 – first place; 1943 and 1947 – second place; Trnava, 1949 – first place; Amsterdam 1950 – third place; Göteborg 1957/59 and Beverwijk 1958 – first place.

Works: Schack och Schackmastare, Stockholm 1937; *El gambito de dama*, Buenos Aires 1942; *Interzonala Schackturneringen Saltsjobaden 1948*, Stockholm 1959; *Varldsmastarmatschen*, Moscow 1948; *Varldsmastarmatchen Moskva 1954*, Stockholm 1954 (co-auth.); *Chess and Chessmasters*, New York 1955.

Books: Grahn, L., Westberg, I., *Stormastere Gideon Ståhlberg, Gosta Stoltz, Ulf Andersson*, Stockholm 1979.

Chapter Three

His Chess Career –
Games, Discoveries and Trainers

Attack The struggle for the initiative from the very opening was a characteristic of Botvinnik's style. And if, in the middlegame, the situation turned out favorably for him, then he would play a strategically exact attack, as straightforward as it was inspired. In his chess legacy, we can find dozens of games in which the struggle ended somewhere in the neighborhood of the 20th or 30th move, under the threat of great material loss or mate. As a rule, the onslaught was accompanied by combinative strokes, with sacrifices and mating threats, affording genuine esthetic satisfaction to those watching the game. Here are just a few examples. In the first, we make use of the commentaries both of the winner and Garry Kasparov.

(124) Denker – Botvinnik
USA-USSR Radio Match 1945
Semi-Slav Defense [D44]

1.d4 d5 2.c4 e6 3.♘c3 c6 4.♘f3 ♘f6 5.♗g5 d×c4 6.e4 b5 7.e5 h6 8.♗h4 g5 9.♘×g5 h×g5 10.♗×g5 ♘bd7 11.e×f6 ♗b7 12.♗e2?! 12.g3 is the modern main line. **12...♕b6 13.0-0 0-0-0 14.a4 b4 15.♘e4 c5 16.♕b1?!** 16.♘d2 is favored by the

computer but Black is still much better. **16...♕c7 17.♘g3?!** 17.h3 ♗h6 18.♕c1 ♗×e4 19.♗×h6 ♖dg8 20.♗g4 ♘×f6 21.♗f4 ♕c6 22.f3 ♗d3∓ **17...c×d4 18.♗×c4 ♕c6 19.f3 d3 20.♕c1 ♗c5+**

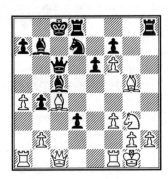

21.♔h1? 21.♗e3 d2 22.♕×d2 was forced, when White can still fight, e.g., 22...♘e5 23.♕f2 ♘g4 24.♗×c5 ♘×f2 25.♗×f2 ♔b8 26.b3∓ **21...♕d6 22.♕f4 ♖×h2+** The final combination. **23.♔×h2 ♖h8+ 24.♕h4 ♖×h4+ 25.♗×h4 ♕f4 0-1**

Not infrequently, it was precisely against attacking-style players that Botvinnik would play the game in the same style. Here we have the final, 21st game of the Tal-Botvinnik return match, 1961.

(125) Botvinnik – Tal
Moscow (m21) 1961
King's Indian Defense [E87]

1.d4 ♘f6 2.c4 g6 3.♘c3 ♗g7 4.e4 d6 5.f3 ♘bd7 6.♗e3 e5 7.♘ge2 0-0 8.d5 ♘h5 9.♕d2 f5 10.0-0-0 a6 11.♔b1 11.exf5 gxf5 12.g4 was the alternative. **11...♘df6 12.exf5 gxf5 13.♘g3 ♕e8 14.♗d3 ♘xg3?!** The computer favors 14...f4 15.♘xh5 ♕xh5 16.♗f2 ♗f5 **15.hxg3 c5?** Now White's attack will clearly come first. 15...h5 was a better chance to fight. **16.♗h6 ♕g6 17.g4 b5 18.♗xg7 ♔xg7 19.♖h4 bxc4 20.♗c2** 20.♖dh1!?+- **20...h6 21.♖dh1 ♕g5 22.♕xg5+ hxg5 23.♖h6 fxg4 24.fxg4 ♗xg4?!** 24...♖f7 25.♘e4 ♘xe4 26.♗xe4 ♔f8 27.♖xd6 ♖f4 28.♖h8+ ♔e7 29.♖dh6 ♖xe4 30.d6+ ♔f7 31.d7+- **25.♖g6+ ♔f7 26.♖f1 ♔e7 27.♖g7+ ♔e8 28.♘e4 ♘d7 29.♘xd6+ ♔d8 30.♖xf8+ ♘xf8 31.♘xc4 ♗d7 32.♖f7 ♔c7 33.d6+ 1-0**

In his last active years, Botvinnik would demonstrate more than once the power and beauty of his attacks.

(126) Botvinnik – Portisch
Monte Carlo 1968
English Opening [A29]

1.c4 e5 2.♘c3 ♘f6 3.g3 d5 4.cxd5 ♘xd5 5.♗g2 ♗e6 6.♘f3 ♘c6 7.0-0 ♘b6 8.d3 ♗e7 9.a3 a5 10.♗e3 0-0 11.♘a4 ♘xa4 12.♕xa4 ♗d5 13.♖fc1 ♖e8 14.♖c2 ♗f8 15.♖ac1 ♘b8?? Too artificial. 15...h6 is called for. **16.♖xc7! ♗c6?!** (D)

17.♖1xc6! The start of a wonderful combination: **17...bxc6** 17...♘xc6 18.♖xf7+- **18.♖xf7! h6** 18...♔xf7 19.♕c4+ ♔g6 20.♕g4+ ♔f7 21.♘g5+ ♔g8 22.♕c4++- **19.♖b7 ♕c8 20.♕c4+ ♔h8 21.♘h4 ♕xb7**

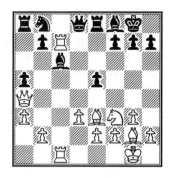

22.♘g6+ ♔h7 23.♗e4 ♗d6 24.♘xe5+ g6 25.♗xg6+ ♔g7 26.♗xh6+ 1-0

An inspiring concluding attack by Botvinnik, against an upper-class grandmaster in the style of representatives of chess romanticism in the 19th century.

Aphorisms and Thoughts on Chess
It is well-known, that the one who achieves success is usually he who, other things being equal, better knows what he is doing. And that chessplayer, seeking to attain great heights, must study chess. He must study the creations of masters present and future, his own games and others' as well. He must study, not just his opposition, but also himself – his own character.

Working out analytical habits, developing an affinity for researches in chess goes a long way toward defining the lifelong philosophy of the chessplayer – his purposefulness.

Of course, one should not think that it is enough to occupy oneself seriously with research for great competitive successes to follow. One also needs a talent for chess and a competitive character. One must have good health and a hardy nervous system. Research, for the chessplayer, is no substitute for talent; but it is absolutely necessary, in order to achieve the highest, continuous competitive results.

The best ages for achievements in chess are the 20s and 30s.

In order to win, one must be an artist as well as a competitor... One cannot achieve competitive successes without a solid creative base; nor can you create worthy chess games without good competitive preparation.

Every style is good if it leads to victory. But the more multi-faceted a chessplayer, the more winning chances he will have.

In order to set yourself apart from other masters, you must learn to analyze well, to annotate games so as to criticize your own mistakes and achievements. It is necessary to teach yourself to work at home at the chessboard, to work on studies, chess history, the development of chess theory, and chess culture.

In order to capture the world championship, perhaps the first thing you need is a strong character, the ability for deep self-criticism and intense creative work.

Chess is composed of typically inexact tasks, like the ones people constantly have to resolve in their daily lives... Probably, I have a definite predilection for the definite solution of indefinite tasks...

Strictness, conclusiveness and the power of the logical constructions included in various substantive games induce a sense of the beauty of chess: those emotions which are known to every chessplayer.

The essential part of a master's strength lies in his positional evaluation.

How many tremendous talents (in chess) have been wasted, for the simple reason that those who possessed them were small-minded.

Thinking is my profession.

I don't feel I deserve to have lived through this planet's seventy orbits of the sun.

The system of determining the world champion we have at present appears to me to be the most reasonable one. If a chessplayer is acknowledged to be the strongest on the planet, then he must show it, by engaging the one who wins the right to single combat with him. In a match system, there are no additional factors, like other participants, who could influence the determination of the stronger player in the struggle.

I am sure that three great players – Lasker, Capablanca, and Alekhine – were on the same level as our current champions.

The international language of chess, that apparently abstract intellectual game, is understandable to everyone... Here, you need no interpreter, no explainer. In this regard, chess may compete with any other skill, such as music or art.

In our era, television has entered into every realm of human activity, so a connection between chess and the blue screen is absolutely necessary. With the blue screen's help, chess can reach even greater heights of popularity.

Research into the connection between the game of chess and learning is not only interesting, but also necessary, because they could lead to very useful results.

With the foundational work of Shannon (1949), the story of the artificial chessplayer begins.

The understanding (and acceptance) of the chess master's method raises chess to an unusual height. If, 200 years ago, Franklin showed that chess could aid in the establishment of a human personality, then now many years' labor by chess masters has taken on a different significance – the results of their creative activity may be turned towards the good of society as a whole.

Since the computer has immeasurably greater resources than a human, the artificial chessplayer can outstrip the living one. And when this happens, the computer will not play either active chess or blitz, but will play real, serious chess, demonstrating its depth, its logical beauty – this is what the artificial chessplayer will have been created for. Then what will the grandmasters do? They will have to compete with opponents worthy of them – computers – and go back to serious chess. Apparently, this is our hope for a return to the better in the future of chess. And it might be that that fierce lady, our goddess Caissa, will bring about order in the world of chess.

In Koltushy [a suburb of Leningrad], where the well-known physicist Pavlov carried out his experiments on four-legged creatures, there is a memorial to a dog. In front of the teaching center where the work on the creation of the artificial grandmaster will be successfully completed, they should place another memorial: a chess knight.

Opening Discoveries
Basic to Botvinnik's amazing tournament and match successes was his scientific attitude toward the opening stage of the game. He succeeded in working out a number of new systems, the characteristic design of which was their organic ties to the entire succeeding struggle in the middlegame and endgame, the striving for initiative with the white pieces and for active counterplay with the black pieces. This also defined Botvinnik's creativity in his searches and the working-out of original lines of play in many of openings, chiefly the closed and semi-closed games.

Although earlier both Alekhine and Euwe tried to set up their openings while considering their plans for the middle game, in Kasparov's opinion, Botvinnik "was the first to work out well-thought-out opening systems, aimed at luring his opponents into positions that he had carefully analyzed at home. Intuition, and accurate understanding of the many nuances gave him superiority in complications. This method was even more effective when he had black. Botvinnik's punctuality, and his unusual systems, made his opponents panic. They were not used to risking too much as White, while Botvinnik would boldly fight for the initiative."

Botvinnik's opening repertoire was rather broad. Both in his research and his notes to the games, however, closed games would predominate.

Above all, it would be the Queen's Gambit Declined. And in one of its popular "branches," Slav Defense, the very sharp, strategically and tactically most interesting continuation, the Botvinnik Variation, gained fame. Here is its starting position:

1.d4 d5 2.c4 c6 3.♘f3 ♘f6 4.♘c3 e6 5 ♗g5 d×c4

With this continuation, Black shows that he intends to hold on to the c4-pawn, so that, by allowing his kingside pawn structure to be ruined, he can force a weakening of his opponent's center and begin a counterattack of his own after queenside castling.

Botvinnik employed this system for the first time at the Moscow championship, 1943/44, against Zhivkov, and two

years later, in the USA-USSR radio-match against Denker (cf. *Attack*), where, after eleven moves (1.d4 d5 2.c4 e6 3.♘c3 c6 4.♘f3 ♘f6 5.♗g5 d×c4 6.e4 b5 7.e5 h6 8.♗h4 g5 9.♘×g5 h×g5 10.♗×g5 ♘bd7 11. e×f ♗b7), a position arose, which Kasparov, in his essay, "The Diamond in Botvinnik's Crown" (1999), commented:

"Black's position appears to be destroyed, but Botvinnik saw great dynamic potential in it, giving him the opportunity to organize rapid and dangerous central counterplay, also exploiting the kingside open lines. Not surprisingly, Botvinnik was not to be caught up in his own analytical jungles and, even many years after he quit playing serious chess, we professionals are still researching his unreachable blank spots on the opening map. The contemporary analysis of variations reaches a long way – 30 moves deep. It would seem that only now, after much terrible suffering, White has finally uncovered a few weak spots in this super-dangerous system. Undoubtedly, Botvinnik's futuristic method was fatal to his unprepared opponents. But even now, one can hardly find an authoritative voice that can say with certainty that he has found its final refutation."

In our day, the analysis of the Botvinnik System is characterized by an exceptionally wide-ranging palette of sharp combinative solutions. Many of these are presented in a book by Kondratiev, *The Slav Defense* (Moscow 1985). In this monograph, the author came to the conclusion that "Summing up the analysis of the Botvinnik System, one may assert that, despite all of its apparent extravagancies, it is still a correct opening. It is true that practical employment of the Botvinnik System requires courage and resourcefulness."

Botvinnik also introduced original ideas when he played the Queen's Gambit Declined as White. His advance of the g-pawn to the fourth rank, the idea being to drive away the main piece defending the king and controlling the center squares – the knight on f6 – so as to achieve a long-term strategic initiative on the kingside, was a complete surprise to his opponents. For example, this was the way Botvinnik played in 1934 against Alatortsev, three decades later in his 14th match game with Petrosian, and in his last tournament, at Leiden, 1970, against Spassky. In the first of these, the battlefield picture after White's 10th move appeared as follows:

1.d4 e6 2.c4 d5 3.♘f3 ♗e7 4.♘c3 ♘f6 5.♗g5 0-0 6.e3 a6 7.c×d5 e×d5 8.♗d3 c6 9.♕c2 ♘bd7 10.g4!

Here, Black recklessly "took the pawn, and thereby opened the floodgates" for a rapid, crushing attack by his opponent (cf. *Leningrad Tournament 1934).*

The move g4 was also unexpected for Petrosian, after **1.d4 d5 2.c4 e6 3.♘c3 ♗e7 4.c×d5 e×d5 5.♗f4 c6 6.e3 ♗f5 7.g4! ♗e6 8.h3**

That game continued: **8...♘f6 9.♗d3 c5 10.♘f3 ♘c6 11.♔f1 0-0 12.♔g2 c×d4 13.♘×d4 ♘×d4 14.e×d4 ♘d7 15.♕c2 ♘f6 16.f3 ♖c8 17.♗e4 ♗d6 18.♖e1**

And here Black experienced difficulty defending himself, and went on to lose on the 57th move. In his game with

Spassky, Botvinnik played even more energetically: **8.h4,** and after **8...♘d7 9.h5 ♕b6 10.♖b1 ♘gf6 11.f3 h6 12.♗d3 ♕a5 13 ♘ge2 b5 14.♘c1! ♕d8 15.♘b3 0-0 16.♘e2 a5,** the following position arose:

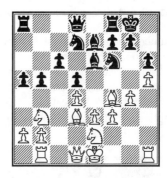

Here, Botvinnik played 17.♘g3, and the players soon agreed to a draw. Afterwards, they also examined another natural continuation, which would have led to a White win: 17.♖c1 a4 18.♘c5 ♘×c5 19.d×c5 ♘d7 20.♗b1! ♘×c5 21.♖×c5 ♗×c5 22.♕c2.

Botvinnik enriched both the theory and the practice of the Queen's Gambit Accepted with new ideas. As Black, he did not play the opening; but as White, instead of the usual queen maneuver, (7.♕e2), he used Rubinstein's move, 7.a4, which, in his opinion, led to "a difficult game for Black." This opening occurred seven times in the 1963 Botvinnik-Petrosian 1963. Among a number of ideas that Black introduced in this line (causing Neistadt, the author of the monograph, *The Queen's Gambit Accepted* (1965), to call it the Rubinstein-Botvinnik Variation), White's surprising center-pawn push on the 13th move is of particular interest, as it gave White a lengthy initiative. An example of this was the 10th game of the Botvinnik-Petrosian match:

1.d4 d5 2. c4 d×c4 3.♘f6 ♘f6 4.e3 e6 5.♗×c4 c5 6.0-0 a6 7.a4 ♘c6 8.♕e2 c×d4 9.♖d1 ♗e7 10.e×d4 0-0 11.♘c3 ♘b4 12.♗g5 ♗d7 13 d5!

Commenting on this game. Smyslov wrote, about this 13th move: "An interesting idea. White breaks up his opponent's defensive buildup in the most fortified location. Now complications arise, requiring accurate defense by Black."

The game continued: **13...e×d5 14.♘×d5 ♘b×d5 15.♗×d5 ♘×d5 16. ♖×d5 ♗×g5 17.♘×g5 h6 18.♕d2 h×g5 19.♖×d7 ♕f6 20.♖×b7 ♖ad8 21.♕a5 ♖d6 22.♕b4 ♖fd8 23.♖f1 ♖d4 24.♕b3 ♖d3 25.♕c2 ♖d2 26.♕c7 ♕f4** Only the highest level of skillful defense by Petrosian allowed Black to obtain a draw in the rook endgame on the 43rd move.

Botvinnik showed great interest in the Grünfeld Defense, giving lectures on it and in 1940 publishing an article on it in the magazine *Shakhmaty v SSSR*. In it, the possibility for Black to exploit the instability of the white center is emphasized. His successful

employment of the defense in practice led to one of the lines being called the Botvinnik Variation.

1.d4 ♘f6 2.c4 g6 3.♘c3 d5 4.c×d5 ♘×d5 5.e4 ♘×c3 6.b×c3 ♗g7 7.♗c4 c5 8.♘e2 0-0 9.0-0 ♘bd7

The Grünfeld Defense, a 1979 book by Botvinnik and Estrin (Moscow 1979), gives the following evaluation of this position: "The knight's development on d7, without the exchange of central pawns, is a peculiarity, characteristic of the Botvinnik Variation.. Black tries to ward off his opponent's attack with ♘d7-b6 and f7-f5, and secure the powerful support point d5 for his knight. The shortcoming of this most flexible variation is its sluggishness, and also the knight's passive placement on d7."

An effective riposte to the Botvinnik Variation was found in the 1950s by Furman – 10.♗g5! So Botvinnik's idea was modernized: the queen's knight came out, not to d7, but to c6, where it is more actively placed.

Botvinnik also worked out new strategic plans in the Nimzo-Indian Defense. As early as his game against Capablanca, (AVRO tournament, under *Famous Games*), he countered Black's queenside pawn advance by creating central counterplay with f2-f3 and e3-e4, and a dangerous attack against the enemy king. And he executed a similar plan in the 1946 USSR-Great Britain radio-match, against Alexander (cf. *Combinations*) and in the game against Keres in the 20th USSR championship, 1952 (cf. *Middlegame*). But if, in those games, the main point was the advance of the e- and f-pawns, in other circumstances, it was an attack by the g-pawn. This wing attack in the Nimzo-Indian Defense (as also in similar situations in the Slav Defense) was employed spectacularly by Botvinnik in his second match game with Smyslov (1954), and a year earlier in the fourth game of his match for the title of USSR champion against Taimanov. The opening battle in the former is notable:

1.d4 ♘f6 2.c4 e6 3.♘c3 ♗b4 4.e3 b6 5.♘ge2 ♗a6 6.a3 ♗e7 7.♘f4 d5 8.c×d5 ♗×f1 9.♔×f1 e×d5 10.g4!

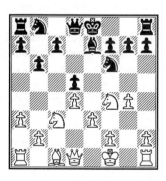

As a result of Black's inexact reply, **10...c6** (10...g6 was better), Botvinnik's strategy was triumphant: **11.g5 ♘fd7**, etc.

The g2-g4 attack introduced by Botvinnik became a typical method of fighting for the initiative. Several times

Botvinnik played the Dutch Defense with Black and gained an advantage in the Stonewall Variation: **1.d4 e6 2.c4 f5 3.g3 ♘f6 4.♗g2 ♗e7 5.♘f3 c6 6.0-0 d5**

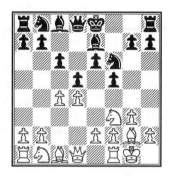

Kasparov: "From the viewpoint of classical understanding, the gaping hole on e5 renders Black's position hideous; but in many games, Botvinnik successfully neutralized White's apparent advantages, and went on to demonstrate a kingside initiative, thanks to his knight on e4." One example of this was the 10th game of the 1933 Flohr-Botvinnik match, in which already after 14 moves, Black's advantage was obvious.

1.d4 e6 2.c4 f5 3.g3 ♘f6 4.♗g2 ♗e7 5.♘f3 c6 6.0-0 d5 7.♘c3 0-0 8.b3 ♕e8 9.♗b2 ♘bd7 10.♕d3 ♕h5 11.cd ed 12.♘d2 ♘e4 13.f3 ♘×c3 14. ♗×c3 f4! The further course of the game is chiefly interesting as an example of the strategically effective exploitation of the advantages achieved in the opening.

From time to time, Botvinnik managed to carry out this idea of setting up a "Stonewall" formation for Black in other openings, sometimes in the Queen's Indian Defense. An interesting game in this line was his game against Bogoljubow at Nottingham 1936:

1.d4 ♘f6 2. ♘f3 b6 3.e3 c5 4.c4 ♗b7 5.♘c3 c×d4 6.e×d4 e6 7.♗d3 ♗e7 8.0-0 0-0 9.b3 d5 10.♗e3 ♘e4 11.♖c1 ♘d7 12.♕e2 ♖c8 13.♖fd1 f5 14. ♗f4 g5!

Most often, Botvinnik met 1.e2-e4, with semi-open defenses, the Caro-Kann or the French Defense. Occasionally, he would employ the Sicilian Defense. In the French Defense, he would generally cede White the advantage of the two bishops, and dark-square domination, while in the way of compensation, he chiefly exploited his kingside chances:

1.e4 e6 2.d4 d5 3.♘c3 ♗b4 4.e5 c5 5.a3 ♗:c3+ 6.b×c3 ♘e7

Botvinnik would also play 6...♕c7, but Black's strategic plan would not alter. In any case, even many very well-known and impressive opponents often found it beyond their abilities to combat, in Kasparov's words, his "signature method." As the noted theoretician and researcher of the sixth world champion's creations, Suetin, wrote: "This French Defense system was for a long time one of the main strategic weapons in Botvinnik's arsenal." To support this, he presented as examples

his game against Pogrebissky from the 11th USSR championship (1939), Smyslov from the 13th USSR championship (1944), and Tolush from the 14th USSR championship (1945). In his game against Pogrebissky (White), the game reached this position:

Botvinnik wrote, in evaluating this position: "Black has a positionally won game. The only question is where he should make the breakthrough. Most likely, on the queenside, since there the break will be aided by the poor placement of the white pawns. However, these considerations have only theoretical significance, because Black soon commits a positional blunder..." And the theater of battle moved over to the kingside, where Black's decisive onslaught occurred, concluding in a win for him on the 37th move.

The attack developed along different lines in the French Defense played against Smyslov. Here Black won the opening struggle according to all the rules, obtaining an overwhelming position on the queenside, which is where the outcome of the game was decided in his favor. Here is the first phase of the battle, after which the course of the game took on a forcing character:

1.e4 e6 2.d4 d5 3.♘c3 ♗b4 4.e5 c5
5.a3 ♗×c3+ 6.b×c3 ♘e7 7.a4
♘bc6 8.♘f3 ♕a5 9.♗d2 c4
10.♘g5 h6 11.♘h3 ♘g6 12.♕f3
♗d7 13.♘f4 ♘×f4 14.♕×f4 ♘e7
15.h4 ♗×a4 16.h5 ♕b5 17.♔d1
♖c8 18.♗c1 ♖c6 19.♗e2 ♖a6!
20.♔d2 0-0!? 21.g4 f6!?

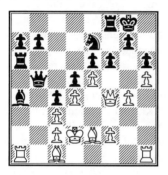

After some interesting complications, the game ended on the 41st move, with a victory for Black.

In *64-Shakhmatnoye Obozreniye* (9/1996), the article, "The French Defense," from Botvinnik's personal archive, in which he held forth on the course of the opening in his own chess praxis. It was a fearsome weapon in the hands of Botvinnik over the course of a number of years. We have before us a position that occurred in his game against Milner-Barry, from Hastings 1934/35. after the moves **1.e4 e6 2.d4 d5 3.♘c3 ♗b4 4.e5 c5 5.a3 ♗×c3+ 6.b×c3 ♘e7 7.♘f3 ♘bc6 8.♗e2 ♗d7 9.0-0 ♕c7 10.♖b1 c4 11.♘e1 0-0-0 12.f4 f6** (D)

Botvinnik wrote: "How many inaccuracies might the modern-day master spot today in White's play! For example, White did not play a4 (with ♗a3 to follow); the move 12.f4 is wrong in principle, as it restricts the sphere of influence of the white pieces,

and weakens the light squares. The diagrammed position, so well-traveled and routine for the contemporary chessplayer, was out of the ordinary then; and so it is no surprise that Milner-Barry was "swimming..."

The blockading pawns split the board in two. White can only switch his pieces from one side of the board to the other via the c1-square, while Black finds it easier to maneuver. In addition, the white queenside pawns are demonstrably weak. There is no realistic compensation for White for these weaknesses. If White did not make the mistakes we have already noted, his position would not be that bad. But play takes on a subtle positional character, where he who has the better prepared plan (before the game begins!) for the middlegame usually wins. In the 1930s and 1940s, when very few persons had studied this position, the variation unrolled without a hitch, and how many games I could win in the decisive moments in those days!"

Later on, when Botvinnik's opponents had discovered the antidote to the French Defense system he used, he decided to play something else. As noted in the above-mentioned article: "Eventually, I began suffering losses with the French in my games against top-class chessplayers, and I had to give up that opening which had so many successful outings over the board connected to it. What can you do: everything must go forward, everything changes. In the years 1941-48, I considerably outpaced my opponents in playing strength, and could allow myself to play, as Black, such complex and dangerous positions. But then, in the years 1951-63, when I was just first among equals, life made me switch to the more solid, but less promising Caro-Kann Defense..."

Does this mean that the French Defense has gone under a cloud, nevermore to be resurrected? Hardly. Time passes, and a new generation comes along, one unfamiliar with its finesses, while simultaneously, there appears a new practitioner, with just as strong a researcher's talent. His fantasy and intuition will show him new ideas in the French Defense, he will try it out in games with leading masters, he will find it to his taste, and once again, the French Defense will become the powerful weapon that it was in the 1930s and 1940s. And what shall we play – the Ruy Lopez, which has been studied even more deeply? The Sicilian, which has been "pulled about" so much that pretty soon, it will shredded to pieces? Or the Caro-Kann, from which it is so difficult to tempt one's opponent into a risky attack?

The first place in Botvinnik's chess repertoire, after the French Defense, became the Caro-Kann Defense. In the colorful words of Garry Kasparov, this tough defense became "both shield and sword in the same hands" – Botvinnik's

major weapon in three of his matches for the world title, where he "most successfully neutralized the energetic activities both of Smyslov and of Tal." As Botvinnik showed, the Caro-Kann Defense, with resourceful play, taking careful note of the psychology of one's opponent and the situation as it developed, could serve, not only as a stubborn defensive tool, but eventually for the creation of counterplay. By way of an example, where Botvinnik successfully extinguished the "aggressive strivings of Smyslov and Tal," Kasparov presents, in the second volume of *My Great Predecessors*, two games, the first game of the return match against Smyslov, and the ninth game of the match against Tal (cf. both games, in *World Championship Matches.*)

We present, again, the opening of the second of these two games, against Tal, from 1960.

1.e4 c6 2.d4 d5 3.♘c3 dxe4 4.♘xe4 ♗f5 5.♘g3 ♗g6 6.♘1e2 ♘f6 7.h4 h6 8.♘f4 ♗h7 9.♗c4 e6 10.0-0 ♗d6 11.♘xe6!? fxe6 12.♗xe6 ♕c7 13.♖e1 ♘bd7 14.♗g8+ ♔f8 15.♗xh7 ♖xh7 16.♘f5 g6!! 17.♗xh6+ ♔g8 18.♘xd6 ♕xd6 19.♗g5 ♖e7 20.♕d3 ♔g7

This position already favors Black, who has, in the interval from moves 16 through 19, broken up his opponent's plans with his sharp play and created the basis for organizing a counterattack. "It looks as though Tal was unprepared for such a turn of events, and from this point (the 20th move) began playing very irresolutely," concluded Kasparov. After a lively struggle, the game concluded in victory for Botvinnik on the 59th move.

Botvinnik not infrequently disappointed opponents who made use of the Caro-Kann Defense against him, in hopes of reaching a draw haven. As White, he gave preference to a system of play called the Panov Attack (1.e4 c6 2. d4 d5 3.e×d5 c×d5 4 c4). But, at the decisive moment, he found an improvement, bringing to theory new, more effective methods of attack. They were highly rated lines in Konstantinopolsky and Weiss' monograph *Zashchita Karo-Kann* (Moscow 1983). Here are some variations:

4...♘f6 5.♘c3 ♘c6 6.♗g5

Botvinnik's move with the bishop, which he first used in his match with

Flohr (1933), and is now popular. Its aim is, by means of an attack against the d5-pawn, to determine his opponent's intentions in the center, and depending on what these are, to set up his own plan of active play. The effectiveness of Botvinnik's opening strategy became particularly evident in the ninth match game (cf. *Flohr-Botvinnik match, 1933*).

Botvinnik's striving for the initiative was interesting also in this variation when Black defended in other ways. For example:

5...e6 6.♘f3 ♗e7 7.c5 0-0 8.♗d3 b6 9.b4 a5 10.♘a4 ♘bd7 11.b5 bc 12.dc e5! 13.c6 e4 14.cd ♘×d7 15.0-0, as in the game Botvinnik-Pomar (13th Olympiad, Munich 1958).

In other circumstances, Botvinnik played 7.cd ♘×d5 8.♗c4, with the idea of inducing Black to trade knights (♘×c3), strengthening his center and making effective use of his bishop on the a2-g8 or b1-h7 diagonal.

Botvinnik also executed original ideas in a number of other openings – the Sicilian Defense, the Ruy Lopez, the Four Knights' Game, the King's Indian Defense, etc. Some of them were the fruit of home preparation; others smacked more of over-the-board improvisation in a tournament or match game. But in either event, it reflected the depth of his research work, the breadth of his opening survey, his farseeing strategy, and his tactical acumen. And, of course, the fact that, in Botvinnik's games, the opening stage was closely bound up, strategically, with the middle- and endgame.

Defense

One of the notable aspects of Botvinnik's creations was his stubbornness in the defense of tough positions, and his mastery of analysis of adjourned games. Max Euwe wrote, on the occasion of the Soviet champion's 70th birthday, in 1981: "As an analyst, Botvinnik at this time is surpassed by none: his analysis of adjourned games is always at the very summit of thoroughness."

And the Dutchman had experienced this himself when, at the Groningen tournament of 1946, Botvinnik drew a rook endgame against him that had seemed completely hopeless to everyone. Among the famous games that Botvinnik surprisingly won or drew thanks to his deep analysis of adjourned positions, we should also mention Reshevsky-Botvinnik, in the USA-USSR match of 1946, Szabo-Botvinnik, Budapest 1952, and Botvinnik-Fischer, Varna 1962.

Here are two of them that became especially widely known. The Botvinnik-Euwe game was a Queen's Gambit Declined in which, after a tense struggle in which the initiative changed hands repeatedly, Black finally managed to obtain a favorable endgame.

(127) Botvinnik – Euwe
Groningen 1946
Queen's Gambit Accepted [D27]

1.d4 d5 2.♘f3 ♘f6 3.c4 d×c4 4.e3 e6 5.♗×c4 c5 6.0-0 a6 7.a4 ♘c6 8.♕e2 ♗e7 9.♖d1 ♕c7 10.♘c3 0-0 11.b3 ♗d7 12.♗b2 ♖ac8 13.d5 e×d5 14.♘×d5 ♘×d5 15.♗×d5 ♗g4 16.♕c4 ♗h5

17.♗×c6!? ♕×c6 18.♘e5 ♕e8 19.♖d5 ♖d8?! 19...b5! 20.a×b5 a×b5 21.♕c2 ♖a8 is almost equal.

20.♘d7? White does not want to exchange the annoying knight, so 20.g4! ♗g6 21.♖ad1 (Botvinnik) 21...♖×d5 22.♕×d5 ♕c8 23.♘d7± as given in MegaBase is called for. **20...♖×d7 21.♖×h5 ♕d8! 22.♖f1 g6 23.♖h3** A sad necessity, as the queen cannot enter the attack: 23.♕c3? ♗f6!–+; 23.♕g4? ♖d2–+ **23...♖d1 24.g4?!** Moving pawns in front of the castled position is always a risky business. The direct 24.♕c3? backfires directly: 24...♖×f1+ 25.♔×f1 ♕d1+ 26.♕e1 ♕d3+ 27.♔g1 ♕×b3 28.♕e2 ♕a2 29.g4 ♗f6–+; 24.♕c2 ♖×f1+ 25.♔×f1 ♕d6 26.e4 is better, but Black's position is still much easier to play of course. **24...♖×f1+?!** White's kingside attack should be met by the direct counter-strike 24...b5! 25.a×b5 a×b5 26.♕f4 f6 27.e4, when, in contrast to the game, Black has 27...♕d2! with a strong initiative. **25.♔×f1 b5! 26.a×b5 a×b5 27.♕f4** 27.♕×b5? plays into Black's hand as he can active all pieces quickly: 27...♕d1+ 28.♔g2 ♕×g4+ 29.♖g3 ♕e4+ 30.♖f3 ♖a8 **27...f6 28.e4 ♕d1+ 29.♔g2 ♗d6** 29...♕c2 is answered by 30.♗c1= **30.♕f3 ♕×f3+ 31.♖×f3 ♗e5 32.♗×e5 f×e5**

33.♖c3 Trading down into a pawn endgame loses: 33.♖×f8+? ♔×f8 34.♔f1 g5 35.♔e2 ♔e7 36.♔d3 ♔e6 37.♔c3 ♔d6 38.♔d2 ♔c6 (38...c4? 39.b4=) 39.♔c3 b4+ 40.♔c2 ♔b6 41.♔d2 and now a triangulation decides: 41...♔a6 42.♔c2 ♔a5 43.♔d2 (43.♔d3 ♔b5 44.♔c2 c4–+) 43...c4 44.b×c4 ♔a4 45.♔c2 b3+ 46.♔b2 ♔b4 47.c5 ♔×c5 48.♔×b3 ♔d4–+ **33...♖c8 34.♔f3 ♔f7 35.♔e3 ♔e6 36.f4 e×f4+ 37.♔×f4 c4 38.b×c4 b×c4 39.h4 h6**

It is really amazing that Botvinnik managed to hold this endgame despite his passive rook: **40.g5! h5** Here the game was adjourned. **41.♔e3 ♔e5 42.♖c2! c3 43.♔d3 ♖d8+** The usual *zugzwang* strategy 43...♖c7 does not help here as the pawn ending is surprisingly drawn after 44.♖×c3 ♖×c3+ 45.♔×c3 ♔×e4 46.♔c4 ♔f4

47.♔d4 ♔g4 48.♔e5 ♔×h4 49.♔f6= **44.♔e3! ♖d4 45.♖×c3 ♖×e4+ 46.♔f3 ♖×h4 47.♖c6 ♖f4+** 47...♔f5 48.♖c5+ ♔e6 49.♖c6± **48.♔e3 ♖e4+ 49.♔f3 ♔f5**

50.♖f6+ ♔×g5 51.♖×g6+! ½-½

"A fighting draw!," wrote Botvinnik, remembering the reaction in the hall. "And the fifteen hundred spectators who followed our game spent some time in open-mouthed amazement, for during the break, everyone knew that Euwe must win."

The first reaction of spectators and commentators to the adjournment of the Botvinnik-Fischer game, played 16 years later at the Olympiad in Varna, Bulgaria, was similar. This dramatic game was the first – and turned out to be the only – game to be played between the then world champion and 19-year-old grandmaster Robert Fischer, the subject of great hopes and already quite popular. The emotional level for this game was so great, and the desire of both sides to achieve victory was expressed so distinctly that the top-level mastery of both players was shown in the course of the struggle, as well as the errors they made...

The energy and resourcefulness of the young American chessplayer is overwhelming – he succeeded in finding, over the board, an effective refutation of his opponent's opening novelty. At the same time, the game once again demonstrated the exceptional mastery of Mikhail Botvinnik in his defense of tough positions. Already, his selection of an opening, and within it, the system of play worked out by grandmasters Smyslov and Ragozin, gave promise of a sharp fight, in which neither side would compromise.

After the event, both Botvinnik and Fischer would return again and again to this game in their analysis. Concerning some of the moves and continuations, their annotations had a contentious character.

(128) Botvinnik – Fischer
Varna 1962
Grünfeld Defense [D98]

1.c4 g6 2.d4 ♘f6 3.♘c3 d5 4.♘f3 ♗g7 5.♕b3 d×c4 6.♕×c4 0-0 7.e4 ♗g4 8.♗e3 ♘fd7 9.♗e2 ♘c6 10.♖d1 ♘b6 11.♕c5 ♕d6 12.h3 12.e5 is the main line **12...♗×f3 13.g×f3 ♖fd8 14.d5 ♘e5 15.♘b5 ♕f6 16.f4 ♘ed7 17.e5 ♕×f4!!** A very unpleasant surprise for Botvinnik, who had already analyzed this position when preparing for his return match with Smyslov in the winter of 1958. **18.♗×f4 ♘×c5 19.♘×c7 ♖ac8 20.d6 e×d6 21.e×d6 ♗×b2 22.0-0 ♘bd7 23.♖d5 b6 24.♗f3?** From here the bishop only hits air. 24.♗c4 ♘e6 25.♗g3 ♘dc5 (Botvinnik) is stronger and should be about equal **24...♘e6! 25.♘×e6** Geller's idea, 25.♗h2 ♘d4 26.♖×d4 ♗×d4 27.♖e1,

is interesting but most probably not sufficient for equality **25...f×e6 26.♖d3 ♘c5 27.♖e3 e5! 28.♗×e5 ♗×e5 29.♖×e5 ♖×d6 30.♖e7 ♖d7 31.♖×d7 ♘×d7 32.♗g4 ♖c7 33.♖e1 ♔f7 34.♔g2 ♘c5 35.♖e3 ♖e7 36.♖f3+ ♔g7 37.♖c3 ♖e4 38.♗d1 ♖d4 39.♗c2 ♔f6 40.♔f3 ♔g5 41.♔g3 ♘e4+?** it was not at all necessary to make such a radical decision before the adjournment. Furthermore, rook endings have a very large drawish tendency. So 41...♖b4 42.a3 ♖d4 43.f3 a5−+ (Botvinnik) was correct. **42.♗×e4 ♖×e4 43.♖a3?!** 43.♖c7 ♖a4 44.♖×h7 is more active, but not sufficient for a draw according to Kasparov. **43...♖e7?!** 43...a5 44.♖b3 ♖b4 (Kasparov) is better, as Black is more active. **44.♖f3 ♖c7?!** In view of what follows, 44...♔h6 is more circumspect. **45.a4** The game was adjourned here, and Fischer sealed. **45...♖c5 46.♖f7 ♖a5 47.♖×h7** The Soviet team had analyzed almost all night long and established that Geller's fantastic idea was sufficient for a draw. This concept to fight against Black's queenside pawns had escaped Fischer's attention. **47...♖×a4 48.h4+ ♔f5 49.♖f7+ ♔e5 50.♖g7 ♖a1 51.♔f3**

51...b5?! 51...♔d4 52.♖×g6 b5 53.h5 b4 54.h6 b3 55.♖g4+ ♔c5 56.♖g5+ ♔c6 57.♖g6+ ♔b7 58.♖g7+ ♔a6

59.♖g6+ ♔a5 60.♖g5+ ♔a4 61.♖g4+ ♔a3 62.♖h4 b2 63.h7 b1♕ 64.h8♕ ♕b3+ 65.♔e2 ♕d1+ 66.♔e3 ♖b1 and Fischer claimed that Black wins in his work *My 60 Memorable Games*. But Botvinnik found that 67.♕f8+ ♔a2 68.♕c5 draws, while the 13-year old Garry Kasparov even found a second drawing method in a session of the Botvinnik school: 67.♖c4!=. **52.h5! ♖a3+ 53.♔g2 g×h5 54.♖g5+ ♔d6 55.♖×b5 h4 56.f4 ♔c6 57.♖b8 h3+ 58.♔h2 a5 59.f5 ♔c7 60.♖b5 ♔d6 61.f6 ♔e6 62.♖b6+ ♔f7 63.♖a6 ♔g6 64.♖c6 a4 65.♖a6 ♔f7 66.♖c6 ♖d3 67.♖a6 a3 68.♔g1** "With a face as white as a sheet, Fischer shook my hand and left the hall with tears in his eyes." (Botvinnik) ½-½

Famous Games

At the very start of Botvinnik's career, the exceptional gifts of this young Leningrad master drew the attention of the chess world. At the start of the 1930s, one of the games he played in the eighth USSR championship against Vsevoldod Rauzer was circulated worldwide. According to grandmaster Flohr, it created a powerful impression: "I heard about this game while I was still in Czechoslovakia. The energy, power, elegant and careful calculation, deep strategy and creativity sent me into ecstasy."

(129) Rauzer – Botvinnik
Leningrad 1933
Sicilian Defense [B74]

1.e4 c5 2.♘f3 ♘c6 3.d4 c×d4 4.♘×d4 ♘f6 5.♘c3 d6 6.♗e2 g6 7.♗e3 ♗g7 8.♘b3 ♗e6 9.f4 0-0 10.0-0 ♘a5 11.♘×a5 ♕×a5 12.♗f3 ♗c4 13.♖e1 ♖fd8 14.♕d2 ♕c7 15.♖ac1 e5 16.b3

16...d5!? A fascinating try to start dynamics. 16...e×f4 17.♗×f4 ♗e6 is the alternative. But 16...♗e6? 17.♘b5 ♕e7 18.c4 is too passive. **17.e×d5** 17.b×c4? d×e4 18.♘d5 ♘×d5 19.c×d5 e×f3 plays into Black's hands. **17...e4 18.b×c4** 18.♘×e4!? ♘×d5 19.♗f2 ♘×f4 20.♕e3 ♗b5 21.♔h1= **18...e×f3 19.c5 ♕a5 20.♖ed1?!** The computer suggests 20.♕d3= **20...♘g4**

21.♗d4? 21.♘e4 ♕×d2 22.♗×d2 ♗d4+ 23.♔h1 f×g2+ 24.♔×g2 ♖×d5 25.h3 limits the damage. **21...f2+! 22.♔f1 ♕a6+ 23.♕e2 ♗×d4 24.♖×d4 ♕f6 25.♖cd1?! ♕h4 26.♕d3 ♖e8 27.♖e4 f5 28.♖e6 ♘×h2+ 29.♔e2 ♕×f4** The game was awarded the first brilliancy prize. (Botvinnik in *Izbrannye Partii 1926-1936*, Moscow-Leningrad 1936) **0-1**

Botvinnik's best-known game, of course, has become the game won by him in brilliant style over Capablanca in AVRO 1938.

(130) Botvinnik – Capablanca
AVRO 1938
Nimzo-Indian [E49]

1.d4 ♞f6 2.c4 e6 3.♞c3 ♝b4 4.e3 d5 5.a3 ♝×c3+ 6.b×c3 c5 7.c×d5 e×d5 8.♝d3 0-0 9.♞e2 b6 10.0-0 ♝a6 11.♝×a6 Nowadays 11.f3 is the main line. **11...♞×a6 12.♝b2?** 12.♕d3 or 12.f3 are more precise. **12...♕d7 13.a4 ♜fe8 14.♕d3**

14...c4? Closing the queenside gives White a free hand on the other wing. 14...♕c8 is more circumspect. **15.♕c2 ♞b8 16.♜ae1 ♞c6 17.♞g3 ♞a5** 17...♞e4 is met by 18.♞h1! f5 19.f3 ♞d6 20.♝a3 g6 21.♞g3 (Kasparov) followed by e4. **18.f3 ♞b3 19.e4 ♕×a4 20.e5 ♞d7 21.♕f2 g6 22.f4 f5 23.e×f6 ♞×f6 24.f5 ♜×e1 25.♜×e1 ♜e8?** In principle, it is good to exchange attacking potential, but Botvinnik has prepared a way to break through. So 25...♜f8 was the last chance to fight, e.g., 26.f×g6 (26.♕f4 ♞e4) 26...h×g6 27.♜e6 ♚g7, and White has a strong attack but no direct knockout blow. **26.♜e6!** After 26.f×g6?, Black can defend with 26...h×g6 27.♜f1

(27.♜×e8+? ♞×e8 plays into Black's hands.) 27...♜e6 28.♕f4 ♕d7 **26...♜×e6** 26...♚g7? runs into 27.♜×f6! +– **27.f×e6 ♚g7 28.♕f4 ♕e8** 28...♕a2? 29.♞f5++– **29.♕e5** 29.♕c7+!? might even be more precise: 29...♚g8 30.♕e5 ♕e7 (30...♚g7 31.♝a3 ♞a5 32.♕c7+ ♚g8 33.♝e7+–) 31.♝a3 ♕×a3 32.♕×f6 ♕f8 33.♕e5 ♕e7 34.♕×d5+– **29...♕e7?** Running into a thunderous shot. 29...♞a5? 30.♝c1 ♕e7 31.♝a3+–. 29...h6 is relatively best, but it is not likely that Black can defend with his b3-knight so far away.

30.♝a3!! "If the first move of the bishop, 12.♝b2?, was just a bad joke, then the second little step from b2 to a3 has created a drama! The kamikaze act forces the black queen to leave her king again, this time not voluntarily, and to unblock the ambitious pawn which is running for the biggest prize." (Kasparov) **30...♕×a3 31.♞h5+!!** The knight opens the gates. **31...g×h5 32.♕g5+ ♚f8 33.♕×f6+ ♚g8 34.e7** 34.♕f7+ ♚h8 35.g3!+– (35.e7? ♕c1+ 36.♚f2 ♕d2+ 37.♚g3 ♕g5+ 38.♚f3 ♞×d4+! 39.c×d4 ♕g4+= Kasparov) **34...♕c1+ 35.♚f2 ♕c2+ 36.♚g3 ♕d3+** 36...♕×c3+ 37.♚h4 ♕e1+ 38.♚h3 ♕e3+ 39.g3+– **37.♚h4 ♕e4+ 38.♚×h5 ♕e2+ 39.♚h4 ♕e4+ 40.g4 ♕e1+ 41.♚h5 1-0**

"Many years after the game," wrote Botvinnik, "I did not understand why the Cuban, giving check to the white king, did not prefer to leave his queen at c2, d3 or e4. Practical genius that he was, he hoped that in time-pressure, White would avoid the exchange of queens and accept a perpetual check."

Among other notable games by Botvinnik, we can cite the ones he played on first board of the 1945 radio-match USSR-USA in 1945 with Denker; in the 1968 Monte Carlo tournament against Portisch (cf. both games in the section on *Attack*); in the Olympiad in Bulgaria 1962 against Fischer; and two against Euwe, in Groningen 1946 (cf. *Defense*); and the match-tournament of 1948.

Combinations
Tactical alertness was one facet of Botvinnik's play. In a number of his games, we see many multiple-move combinations – as, for example, in the game with Capablanca from the AVRO tournament, or in his game with Portisch, from 1968, where his twelve-move sacrificial combination led to complete destruction of his opponent's kingside castled position (cf. *Attack*).

The following game against Tartakower was awarded a special prize as the most beautiful combination in Nottingham 1936. It received high marks from the great master of combinations, Alexander Alekhine.

(131) Botvinnik – Tartakower
Nottingham 1936
Old Indian Defense [A55]

1.♘f3 ♘f6 2.c4 d6 3.d4 ♘bd7 4.g3 e5 5.♗g2 ♗e7 6.0-0 0-0 7.♘c3 c6 8.e4 ♕c7 9.h3 ♖e8

10.♗e3 ♘f8 11.♖c1 h6 12.d5 ♗d7 13.♘d2 13.♘h4!? **13...g5?** Tartakower also opens his kingside up. 13...c5! stops White's attacks on both flanks. **14.f4** The alternative breakthrough, 14.c5 dxc5 15.♘c4±, is also very strong. **14...gxf4 15.gxf4 ♔g7?** 15...♘g6 16.fxe5 dxe5 limits the damage. **16.fxe5 dxe5 17.c5! cxd5** 17...♕c8 18.♕f3 ♘g6 19.♘c4+– **18.♘xd5 ♕c6 19.♘c4 ♘g6 20.♘d6 ♗e6** 20...♗xd6 21.♖xf6+– **21.♘xe7 ♘xe7**

22.♖xf6 A strong king hunt sacrifice, but the normal 22.♕f3 wins as well, e.g., 22...♘fg8 23.♕h5 ♘g6 24.♘f5+ ♗xf5 25.exf5+– **22...♔xf6 23.♕h5 ♘g6 24.♘f5 ♖g8** 24...♗xf5 25.exf5+– **25.♕xh6 ♗xa2 26.♖d1 ♖ad8 27.♕g5+ ♔e6 8.♖xd8 f6 29.♖xg8 ♘f4** 29...fxg5 30.♖xg6+– **30.♕g7 1-0**

Another combination, not so deeply calculated, this time, as those mentioned above, but also most spectacular.

(132) Botvinnik – Alexander
England-USSR Radio Match 1946
Nimzo-Indian [E49]

1.d4 ♘f6 2.c4 e6 3.♘c3 ♗b4 4.e3 d5 5.a3 ♗xc3+ 6.bxc3 c5 7.cxd5 exd5 8.♗d3 0-0 9.♘e2 b6 10.a4

♗a6 **11.♗×a6 ♘×a6 12.♗a3**
12.♕d3 ♕c8 13.♗a3 ♖e8 14.0-0 ♕b7
15.f3 ♖ac8 16.♘g3 ♖e6 17.♖fe1 ♖ce8
is a better black setup, Corral Blanco-
Franco Ocampos, Mondariz 2002.
**12...♖e8 13.♕d3 c4?! 14.♕c2 ♕d7
15.0-0 ♘b8?!** Very slow. **16.♖ae1
♘c6** 16...♘h5 17.♗c1 f5 18.f3 ♘c6
19.h3± **17.♘g3 ♘a5 18.f3 ♘b3
19.e4 ♕×a4 20.♕b2 a5 21.e5 b5?**
21...♘d7 22.♘f5 ♔h8 23.♗d6 ♘f8 is
more tenacious.

22.♗d6?! The direct 22.e×f6! is even
stronger, e.g., 22...b4 23.♕f2 b×a3
24.♘f5 ♕d7 25.♕g3 g6 26.♘e7+ ♖×e7
27.♖×e7 ♘c6 28.♕e5 ♖f8 29.♖f2 ♘c1
30.♕g5 ♘d3 31.♖fe2+− **22...♖e6
23.e×f6 ♖×d6 24.f×g7 b4 25.♖e5
♖e8?** This should lose, but Black's
position is very precarious in any case.
25...♕c6 or 25...♕d7 was better. **26.f4
♕d7?! 27.♕e2! ♖de6 28.f5 ♖×e5
29.d×e5 b×c3 30.f6?** 30.e6 wins, e.g.,
30...♕a7+ (30...f×e6 31.♘h5 ♕a7+
32.♔h1 ♕f7 33.f×e6 ♕e7 34.♕f3+−)
31.♔h1 f6 32.♘h5 ♕d4 33.♖f4 ♕d2
34.♘×f6+ ♔×g7 35.♘×e8+ ♔f8
36.♕×d2 c×d2 37.♖f1+− **30...♕a7+?**
The following line is more or less
forced: 30...♘d4 31.♕e3 ♕g4 32.♔h1
(32.♕×c3? ♕×g3–+) 32...c2 33.h3 and
now one way to draw is 33...♕d1
34.♔h2 ♕d3 35.♕f4 ♕d1 36.♕e3
♕d3= **31.♔h1 ♘d4 32.♕e3 ♖a8
33.♕×c3 a4 34.♕×d4!? ♕×d4**

35.♘f5 h5 35...♕×e5?! 36.♘h6#
36.♘×d4 ♖e8 37.♘f5 d4 38.e6 1-0

Botvinnik wrote more than once about
the role of combinations in the game of
chess, and in the creativity of the
chessplayer, defining the game of chess
as an aspect of skill (cf. (*Esthetics*). In
1939, he appeared in the magazine
Shakhmaty v SSSR, with a small article
"Concerning the Definition of a
Combination." And almost forty years
later, in the fourth volume of *Analytical
and Critical Works* (Moscow 1987), he
continued to insist on the genuineness
of his definition: "Combination – a
forcing variation with a sacrifice."

Many chess authorities did not agree
with this definition. Is a sacrifice a
necessary ingredient? Why must it be
only a forcing variation? Does the
combination consist only of the
sacrifice, or all of the moves which
follow, leading to a change in the
position in the initiator's favor? Etc.,
etc. All of these and other questions
became a subject for discussion in the
pages of the chess press. There is still
no single viewpoint.

Compositions
Botvinnik was always quite interested
in chess studies. And the main criterion
of his evaluation was its proximity to
practical play. Regarding problems:
"Although problems are also in great
measure independent of practical play,
they undoubtedly help to popularize
chess." In a number of publications,
mostly forewords to books by Soviet
composers, Botvinnik continuously
emphasized his inclination toward
studies. The studies of Sergey Kaminer
(1908-1938), Mark Liburkin (1910-

1953), and Gia Nadareishvili (1921-1992) inspired him particularly. For instance, he wrote that "...the basis of Nadareishvili's talent is that he knows how to transform clear and clever ideas into natural, everyday forms, familiar to the chess practitioner. This is, perhaps, the difficulty, but also the joy of his compositions." (1976) And in his foreword to the book of studies by Kaminer and Liburkin (1981), he expressed the hope that "...readers will get genuine esthetic pleasure out of these artistic compositions."

His mind's analytical bent and its striving for the truth in endgames – the most difficult part of a game – led to Botvinnik's finding, in a practical game, purely study-like continuations – that is, the sole route to the win or draw, which is known to be usually achieved in a chess composition.

Some years, Botvinnik would, drawing from experience, compose studies himself, all of which would be published in the chess press. The first of these was constructed in 1925, and was a reworking of the ending of his game with the first-category Leningrad player N. Lyutov. Later on, the ideas for his studies would, as a rule, also be suffused with practical play. In all, from 1925 to 1958, he composed ten studies, the years of publication being 1925, 1939, 1941, 1944, 1945, 1949, and two studies each in 1952 and 1958. Here are three of them.

1939

White to move and win

1.♔f5! ♔b6 2.♔f6! ♔b7 3.♔f7 ♔b8 4.♔e6 ♔c7 5.♔e7! ♔c6 6.♔d8 ♔d6 7.♔c8 ♔c6 8.♔b8 ♔b6 9.♔a8! and White wins, for the black pawn at a6 deprives its king of the square it needs to maintain the opposition. As a result, Black loses both his a-pawns.

1949

White to move and win

1.e7 ♖e4 2.♖c5+ ♔a4 3.♖f5!! e2 Black also loses after 3...♖e6 4.♖f7 ♖e5 5.♖f4+ ♗c4 6.♖xc4+ and 7.♖c8; or 3...♗f7 4.♖xf7 ♔b3 5.♖f4 (5.♗h6 e2 6.♗d2) 5...♖e6 6.♖b4+ and 7.♖b8 **4.♖f4 e1♕ 5.e8♕+** and White wins.

1952

White to move and draw

1.d5+ If 1.♔c3? f5 2.d5+ ♔e5, and back to the main variation. But Black could play the stronger 2...♔f6!! and then, it is Black who wins: 3.exf5 ♔xf5 4.♔b2 ♔e5 5.♔xa1 ♔xd5 6.♔b2 ♔d4! 7.♔c2 ♔e3 **1...♔e5 2.♔c3 f5 3.d6! ♔xd6 4.exf5 gxf5 5.g4! fxg4 6.♔d4 ♔e6 7.♔e4 ♘c2 8.♔f4** Draw

As an advocate of study composition, Botvinnik proceeded from the position that "these compositions influence the development of the esthetic taste, combinative alertness, and calculating ability of the chessplayer."

So it was no accident that in the foreword to the book by Nadareishvili, *The Study Through the Eyes of a Grandmaster* (Moscow 1982), he noted that study composition was one of the important spheres of chess creativity, and that, in this connection, the book "well serves the propagation of the art of chess." And among the over three hundred notable compositions presented therein, we see nine (three studies each by Kaminer, L.Kubbel, and Nadareishvili), annotated in detail by the sixth world champion.

Preparing for Tournaments

This was first worked out by Botvinnik at the start of his competitive career, and he made it clear in 1939, when he published the article, "My Methods of Event Preparation: A Regimen for Tournaments." With this statement, the USSR champion and acknowledged world championship candidate was apparently stating openly that he wanted to achieve something more in chess: "Please, my friends, take this, and make use of it. All of it has already been tested in practice, and apparently it has brought me decent results." These methods can be boiled down to the following:

(1) Above all else, before an event, it is necessary to consider your own health, for only if you are in good condition can you hope for success.

(2) Learn interesting new games; study the games of your intended opponents.

(3) Prepare the openings you intend to use in upcoming events.

(4) Test them in games against an opponent, and keep it confidential.

(5) Cure yourself of the illness of time-pressure.

(6) Study the endgame, giving great attention to studies.

(7) Five days before the tournament, stop studying, so you do not lose your taste for chess play.

In conclusion, Botvinnik wrote: "Each master must approach these rules carefully, and employ them while considering his own individual peculiarities and habits."

The system he offered was carefully thought out, tested by Botvinnik himself in practice in a number of tough matches and tournaments in the second half of the 1930s. "You should not think that I was the first one to prepare for events; sometimes I, too, experienced this weapon," Botvinnik said. "Alekhine was a great master of preparation. I was inspired, upon reading his article in the collection of the games of New York, 1927 – there he wrote of how he prepared for his match with Capablanca. I became convinced of his mastery in 1936."

This all-embracing method of preparation outlined above, was first, not just worked out, but also effectively used by Botvinnik in the period of his primary struggles for the crown of the king of chess. 1942-48 was the time of triumph for his new method of preparation. Even in the war years, After this, Botvinnik was not afraid of the noise in the hall, nor of the cloud of smoke, wafting from that inveterate smoker, Mikhail Tal!

We know Botvinnik was way ahead in working out opening theory. *In those days, when his method of preparation was being set up and used, there were not any computers for storing information. My entire search library consisted of big general notebooks, and small ones, too. In a general notebook, I would enter the text of the opening phase of a game (until the 20th move)* *of those openings I was interested in, if there was something new in it. All of this was systematized by opening, and I would underline similar variations with colored pencil. So getting around in such a library was easy.*

"When I prepared for an event, my material for analysis was already collected, and the results of analysis were related to what had been analyzed out beforehand. And all of my personal theory of the openings went into a small notebook that I kept in reserve, which easily found a place in my pocket, and traveled with me to those events. Perhaps, this method was of greater value than referring to a computer!

His return-matches for the world championship are the clearest testimony to the effectiveness of Botvinnik's preparation, with the combination of all sides of his method. When, many years later, during his lectures for foreign guests of the 1962 Moscow Chess Festival, Botvinnik was asked: "You have been world champion five times. How do you explain this achievement?" This was his response:

"Most likely, I was a decent practical player, and along with that, I was a good researcher. Thus, when I arrived at the start of a new event, I was not going to be the person my opponent was expecting. Some of my qualities in chess would turn out to be unexpected. I would play differently than before. It was for exactly this reason that I succeeded in winning two of those return matches. From my loss in the former match, I extracted a lot of material for the study of both myself and my opponent. In the return match, my opponent remained the same as he had been, while I became someone else. And that's how I won the return match!"

Botvinnik was forced to acknowledge, sadly, that some components of his system of preparation had lost their popularity by the close of the 20th century. "I think that, with the appearance of computers, the method of preparation we are examining has faded somewhat. Nowadays, the art of chess is not going through the best of times. But the day is coming when everything will go back to its accustomed place, and then this method will once again perform as before."

However, it is too soon to consign Botvinnik's method to the dustbin. It lives on, and today it is effectively utilized in battles on the highest level. This was shown by Garry Kasparov, who, as Botvinnik said, "is perhaps, of all the world champions who followed me, the one who best assimilated my method of preparation."

Middlegame
Botvinnik looked at play in the middle of a game as an unbreakable connection with its beginning and its ending. That explains both the depth of a number of his opening discoveries and his skill at moving a game into a favorable ending, which he would then play out to completion. But in the heart of the middlegame, he demonstrated an entire array of new strategic ideas and plans, which totally raised the level of positional play.

Here we have the game Botvinnik-Keres, from the 20th USSR

championship, Moscow 1952, which had great significance for the final prizewinners. In it, Botvinnik, by advancing his f- and e-pawns in the opening, created a powerful center. Then, combining his control of the center with the harmonious cooperation of his pieces, obtained a strategically won game. Next, on the 30th move, he delivered a pretty tactical blow which signaled the onset of a strong attack, which led, in just six moves, to his opponent's resignation.

(133) Botvinnik – Keres
Moscow 1952
Queen's Gambit Declined [D36]

1.d4 ♘f6 2.c4 e6 3.♘c3 d5 4.c×d5 e×d5 5.♗g5 ♗e7 6.e3 0-0 7.♗d3 ♘bd7 8.♕c2 ♖e8 9.♘ge2 ♘f8 10.0-0 c6 11.♖ab1 ♗d6?! 11...a5 is played most often and 11...g6!? might be interesting. **12.♔h1 ♘g6 13.f3 ♗e7 14.♖be1 ♘d7 15.♗×e7 ♖×e7 16.♘g3 ♘f6 17.♕f2 ♗e6?! 18.♘f5** 18.f4!? **18...♗×f5 19.♗×f5 ♕b6?** 19...♘e8, with the idea 20.e4 d×e4 21.f×e4 ♘d6 22.♗g4 f6, is more circumspect. **20.e4 d×e4 21.f×e4 ♖d8 22.e5 ♘d5 23.♘e4 ♘f8 24.♘d6 ♕c7 25.♗e4 ♘e6?!** 25...♘g6 and 25...♖×d6 26.e×d6 ♕×d6 27.♗×d5 c×d5 are more tenacious. **26.♕h4 g6?! 27.♗×d5 c×d5 28.♖c1 ♕d7 29.♖c3**

The second rook joins White's attack with decisive effect. **29...♖f8 30.♘f5 ♖fe8** 30...gxf5 31.♖g3+ ♘g7 32.♕f6+– **31.♘h6+ ♔f8** 31...♔g7 32.♕f6+ ♔xh6 33.♖h3# **32.♕f6 ♘g7 33.♖cf3 ♖c8 34.♘xf7 ♖e6** 34...♔g8 35.♘h6+ ♔h8 36.♕f8+ ♖xf8 37.♖xf8# **35.♕g5 ♘f5 36.♘h6 ♕g7 37.g4 1-0**

As we cannot uncover the entire panoply of Botvinnik's contribution to middlegame theory and practice, we shall restrict ourselves to two more examples, the first of which is characteristic of his skill at the control and effective exploitation of a weak square (in this case, c6).

(134) Botvinnik – Donner
Amsterdam 1963
English Opening [A14]

1.c4 ♘f6 2.♘f3 e6 3.g3 d5 4.♗g2 ♗e7 5.0-0 0-0 6.b3 b6 7.♗b2 ♗b7 8.cxd5 ♘xd5 9.d4 c5 10.dxc5 ♗xc5 11.♘bd2 ♘d7 12.a3 ♘5f6?! 12...a5 gains more space. **13.b4 ♗e7 14.♘d4 ♗xg2 15.♔xg2 ♕c7 16.♕b3 ♖fc8 17.♖fc1 ♕b7+ 18.♕f3 ♘d5?!** The computer prefers 18...♕xf3+ 19.♔xf3, but Black's defense is an uphill struggle here as well. **19.e4 ♘5f6 20.b5**

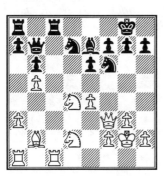

20...a6? 20...♘e5 21.♕e2 ♗d6 was better, to meet 22.f4 ♘g6 23.♘c6? with 23...♗xf4! **21.♘c6 ♗f8 22.a4 axb5?!** The computer prefers 22...h6, but Black's position looks very unpleasant in any, because of the mighty knight on c6. **23.axb5 ♖xa1 24.♖xa1 ♖a8 25.♖d1 ♘e8?!** 25...♖c8 26.♖c1 ♗c5 27.♘c4 ♖xc6 28.bxc6 ♕xc6 is a better practical chance. **26.♘c4** 26.e5!?+– **26...♘c5?!** 26...♘ef6 27.e5 ♘d5 28.♘d6 ♗xd6 29.exd6+– **27.e5 ♖c8?! 28.♖a1 ♖c7 29.♖a7 ♕xa7 30.♘xa7 ♖xa7 31.♘xb6 1-0**

The strategic idea of exploiting isolated, doubled pawns for the control of central squares with one's own pieces is interesting, and not often seen in Botvinnik's games.

Kasparov, in his notes to the well known game Botvinnik-Alekhine, from Amsterdam 1938, had this to say about White's pawn-based strategy (cf. *Endgame*):

Positions with isolated pawns have always been part of Botvinnik's game. Thanks to his efforts, all the possibilities present under such positions have been discovered; players have felt an almost mystical awe when playing with isolated central pawns. This awe was universal, back in the day of Steinitz's impressive victories over Zukertort, and the powerful logical arguments of the first world champion, who later published articles against the creation of unnecessary weaknesses. Botvinnik became the first one to show that piece activity, combined with pressure in the center, quite often more than compensates for the insignificant pawn structure defect.

This is also correct as regards the doubled pawns, which Botvinnik intentionally created, and with the same idea in mind,

(135) Botvinnik – Kan
Leningrad 1939
Nimzo-Indian Defense [E24]

1.d4 ♘f6 2.c4 e6 3.♘c3 ♗b4 4.♘f3 c5 5.a3 ♗×c3+ 6.b×c3 ♛a5 7.♗d2 ♘e4 8.♛c2 ♘×d2 9.♘×d2 d6 10.e3 e5 11.d×e5 d×e5

Regarding this position, Botvinnik wrote: "A typical position. At first glance, White has an inferior pawn position; so Black can face the future with confidence. This would be correct, if you took all the other pieces off the board. But there are still many pieces there, so the weakness of the d5-square in Black's camp is more important than White's defect: doubled, isolated pawns on the c-file. More than that: the presence of such pawns actually favors White! When, in order to secure the d5-square, he wishes to advance his pawn at e3 to e4, the pawn on c3 will secure the d4-square against the incursion of black pieces. I have proven the usefulness of such a pawn setup in a number of games."

12.♗d3 h6 13.0-0 0-0 14.f4 ♘d7 15.f5 ♘f6 16.♘e4 ♛d8 17.♘×f6+ ♛×f6 18.♗e4 ♖b8 19.♖ad1 b6 20.h3 ♗a6 21.♗d5 b5 22.c×b5 ♖×b5 23.c4 ♖b6 24.♖b1 ♖d8 25.♖×b6 a×b6 26.e4 ♗c8 27.♛a4 ♗d7 28.♛a7 ♗e8 29.♖b1 ♖d6 30.a4 ♔h7 31.a5 b×a5 32.♛×a5 ♖a6 33.♛×c5 ♖a2 34.♛e3 ♛a6 35.♖b8 ♛a4 36.♔h2 ♖a3 37.♛c5 ♖a2 38.♖a8 ♛×a8 39.♗×a8 ♖×a8 40.♛×e5 ♗c6 41.♛c7 1-0

The examples presented bear witness to Botvinnik's deep penetration into the secrets of the positional struggle which, in his words, is "the most delicate in chess. Material targets (the pieces) need not be created. Meanwhile, positional ones ("holes," weak squares, open lines, isolated pawns, and so forth) can and must be created."

An interesting episode in this regard, told by Tal concerning Botvinnik's positional sense, which astonished even elite chessplayers: *There is an impression that every position has its little key. I recall how astonished I was by the postmortem we did of the ninth game of our world championship match in 1960. In one of the variations of the Caro-Kann Defense, I executed an interesting piece sacrifice, prepared at home, which led to the following position, after the 19th move:*

"After the game, I showed him what seemed to me very interesting forcing variations. Mikhail Moiseevich listened to all of them, as it seemed to me, purely out of respect, but then he said, "This is all fine. I was also afraid of the piece sacrifice, at first: but then I came to the conclusion that, in this case, I only had to trade rooks, and keep the queens on." I was totally shocked by such a "pronouncement." His evaluation of the position seemed much too abstract for me. But later on, as we continued our examination of the position, with horror I began to see that Botvinnik was absolutely right. If I had been able to exchange queens, White's pawns would have become much stronger than the opposing knight; while with queens still on, it and the knight together could create uncomfortable threats against White's king.

But Botvinnik was the great master of tactical operations as well when they required sharp combinative alertness and the calculation of concrete variations. Therefore, along with deep evaluation of position, Botvinnik often demonstrated the high level of mastery of a "calculator," which was also emphasized by Tal, who characterized his creativity thus: "Botvinnik, in his collection, has a large number of games he has won, thanks to far-seeing and exact calculation." Some idea of this is given in the games presented in the chapter, in the sections on *Attack, Defense, Combinations, Endgame* and in the second chapter on tournaments with Botvinnik's participation.

Losses

As a rule, when unfortunate things happened in Botvinnik's games, it was a result of his poor competitive form: occasionally, excessive self-confidence; or, finally, his opponent's striving, at whatever cost, to rehabilitate himself, in his struggles with the veteran, and take revenge for a previous defeat. But a "great moment of misfortune" would also sometimes happen to the champion, as Matsukevich so accurately called the unforgivable blunders or cases of astounding "blindness," which no great chessplayer has ever been able to avoid.

(136) Botvinnik – Bronstein Moscow 1951 17th Match Game

34.♘g4 d4 35.♘f6+?? ♛×f6! and White resigned in view of 36.e×f6 ♖×e1+.

Endgame

Botvinnik's mastery of the final stages of a chess game was universally acknowledged. Here, even a small advantage was enough for him to bring the encounter to victory with elegant technique. And his skill at saving what at first sight would appear to be hopeless positions turned out to be just as amazing – as, for example, in his well-known games against Euwe (Groningen,1946), or Fischer (Varna

1962) (see *Defense*). These qualities said a lot about Botvinnik: his wide-ranging knowledge in the area of the theory and practice of his predecessors, his high level of analytical mastery, the ability to find paradoxical solutions, and finally, his inclination towards the art of the study, which allowed him to find the elegance in endgames which would not infrequently go missing from the thinking of his opponents.

Very often, Botvinnik would, after an uncomplicated middlegame struggle, move the game into the "quiet" harbor of the endgame, where a "small advantage" was crystallizing – but it would be enough for him to win with. As in his well-known game with Alekhine at AVRO 1938. The first half of the game was relatively quiet, and by the 22nd move, the game had turned into an endgame, with a small number of pieces, but with a positional advantage to White. It is interesting to follow how White's advantage grew.

(137) Botvinnik – Alekhine
AVRO 1938
Queen's Gambit [D41]
Notes based on those by Kasparov from
ChessBase MegaBase

1.♘f3 d5 2.d4 ♘f6 3.c4 e6 4.♘c3 c5 5.c×d5 ♘×d5 6.e3 Botvinnik wisely decided to avoid 6.e4 ♘×c3 7.b×c3 c×d4 8.c×d4 ♗b4+ which was tested in the Alekhine-Euwe rematch, and instead went for a lesser known (at the time) type of position. **6...♘c6 7.♗c4 c×d4 8.e×d4 ♗e7 9.0-0 0-0 10.♖e1** Positions with isolated pawns always were favored by Botvinnik. Thanks to his efforts to discover all the possibilities that such positions held, chessplayers have lost their almost

mystical fear of playing with isolated pawns in the center. This fear had been pervasive since Steinitz' impressive victories over Zukertort and the powerful logical arguments the first world champion put forth against creating unnecessary weaknesses. Botvinnik was the first to prove constantly that active piece play with pressure in the center very often more than compensates for a slight defect in the pawn structure. **10...b6?!** A very dubious decision. This move is playable after an exchange on c3. After 10...♘×c3 11.b×c3 b6 12.♗d3 ♗b7 13.h4! ♗×h4 (otherwise 14.♗g5 is unpleasant) 14.♘×h4 ♕×h4 15.♖e3, with a very strong initiative for the sacrificed pawn, as was proven in later practice. The best alternative is probably 10...a6. **11.♘×d5! e×d5 12.♗b5** Despite the symmetrical pawn structure, Black is now doomed to a passive defense. Weaknesses on the c-file and the slightly uncoordinated black pieces give White an easy game in which he can develop his initiative. **12...♗d7?** Now after the inevitable exchange of the light-square bishops, the black position becomes even more vulnerable. 12...♗b7 13.♕a4 ♖c8 (or 13...♕d6) offered much better chances for a successful defense. 14.♗f4 a6! **13.♕a4 ♘b8** A sad retreat, but after 13...♖c8 14.♗f4, Black has problems with his next move, while ♖a1-c1threatens to finish him off. **14.♗f4 ♗×b5 15.♕×b5 a6 16.♕a4** Keeping the b8-knight in its misery. **16...♗d6** In order to relieve pressure. **17.♗×d6 ♕×d6 18.♖ac1 ♖a7 19.♕c2 ♖e7** Black's position looks reasonable, but unfortunately for him all the weaknesses remain permanent, e.g., 19...♘d7 20.♕c6 ♕×c6 21.♖×c6 and the endgame does not promise any respite. On 19...f6, there follows

20.♕f5, heading again for a queen exchange. **20.♖×e7 ♕×e7 21.♕c7 ♕×c7 22.♖×c7** After these useful exchanges, the white rook penetrates the black position. But Alekhine rightly estimated that this rook alone was not able to cause serious damage.

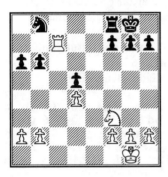

22...f6! 23.♔f1 Because after 23.♖b7? ♖c8! 24.♔f1 b5, Black has taken control of the c-file and is out of any danger. So the white rook is pushed from the seventh rank. **23...♖f7 24.♖c8+ ♖f8 25.♖c3!** Going back into the bushes, to pounce again at the right moment. Do not be fooled by the pawn symmetry. Black is not able to restore the coordination of his pieces. **25...g5** A smart idea. Pushing his pawn on the kingside, Alekhine reduces the importance of the seventh rank, which will sooner or later be dominated by his opponent's rook. On 25...♘d7 or 25...♔f7, the rook reappears in his camp with resounding effect.

26.♘e1 h5 26...h6 27.♘c2 ♔f7 28.♘e3 ♔e6 29.g4 is hardly satisfactory, but after the text move this line is playable, because the white knight does not get a stronghold on f5. Alas the problem comes from a different side. **27.h4!!** Forcing new weaknesses on the kingside. Now

Black's defensive lines are being breached and his passive pieces cannot operate effectively all over the board. **27...♘d7** 27...g×h4 28.♘f3 cannot be considered seriously. 27...♔f7 may have been the better option, though after 28.h×g5 (less clear is 28.♘f3 g4 29.♘e1 ♖e8! 30.f3 [but even here 30.g3 ♖e4 31.♘g2 ♖×d4 32.♖c7+ ♔e6 33.♘f4+ ♔d6 34.♖h7 and the h-pawn gives White excellent chances] 30...g×f3 31.g×f3 ♖e6! and with the knight back in the game, Black is still kicking.) 28...f×g5 29.♘f3 ♔f6 30.♘e5 and the difference in the knights' positions make a draw a miracle result. **28.♖c7** Back in full control. **28...♖f7 29.♘f3! g4 30.♘e1** A pendulum maneuver, preparing the f4-square to collect the bonuses, the pawns on d5 and h5. **30...f5 31.♘d3 f4** The key square is temporarily under control, but the pawn on f4 is added to the long list of objects for White to attack.

32.f3 32.♘b4 wins a pawn, but Botvinnik fixes the new weakness with mathematical precision. He knows that material benefit is just a short-term affair. **32...g×f3 33.g×f3 a5 34.a4 ♔f8 35.♖c6 ♔e7 36.♔f2 ♖f5 37.b3** There is no need to hurry. **37...♔d8 38.♔e2 ♘b8** desperately trying to activate the poor steed. **39.♖g6!** No way! One cannot escape one's destiny. 39.♖×b6 ♔c7 and 40...♘c6 give Black counter-chances. **39...♔c7 40.♘e5** Making sure its counterpart will not participate in the game. **40...♘a6** (D)

41.♖g7+ 41.♖g5 wins a bit quicker, the rook exchange leading to the promotion of the white pawn: 41...♖×g5? 42.h×g5 ♔d6 43.g6 ♔e7

44.g7 But in fact the way to win the position is a matter of taste. **41...♔c8 42.♘c6 ♖f6 43.♘e7+ ♔b8 44.♘xd5** At last! **44...♖d6 45.♖g5 ♘b4 46.♘xb4 axb4** In the end the two knights, with such different histories, both disappear together. But it gives Black no satisfaction, since the rook endgame is absolutely lost. **47.♖xh5 ♖c6** 47...♖xd4 48.♖f5 ♔c7 49.h5 and the weak pawns are still around. **48.♖b5 ♔c7 49.♖xb4 ♖h6 50.♖b5 ♖xh4 51.♔d3 1-0** Black had enough. "Of the 14 games I played in this tournament, only once did I feel that my opponent outplayed me – it was the game with Botvinnik in round seven" said Alekhine later. No further comments are needed!

We conclude with Botvinnik's own comments to the game: "One of those endgames in which there are no pretty moves, nor complicated calculations. All the moves look simple, but not one can be omitted, since they are all firmly tied together. And this is its genuine power."

Botvinnik did not have any "favorite" piece, which he could maneuver most adroitly in an endgame. He was adept at every endgame phase, from pawn to queen endings; and in every one, he found the nuances required to win, or for stubborn defense. Here are a few examples of his great skill in handling endgames. The pawn ending against Taimanov (1967); the knight ending with Keres (1948), the opposite-color bishops ending against Kotov, the rook ending against Najdorf (1956); and the queen ending against Minev (1954).

(138) Taimanov – Botvinnik
USSR 1967
Grünfeld Defense [D70]

1.d4 d5 2.c4 c6 3.♘f3 ♘f6 4.♘bd2 g6 5.e3 ♗g7 6.♗e2 0-0 7.0-0 b6 8.b4 ♗b7 9.♗b2 ♘e4 10.♘xe4 dxe4 11.♘d2 f5 12.c5 ♘d7 13.♕b3+ ♔h8 14.d5 cxd5 15.♗xg7+ ♔xg7 16.♗b5 bxc5 17.bxc5 ♖c8 18.♕c3+ ♖f6 19.♘b3 ♔g8 20.♖ac1 a6 21.♗xd7 ♕xd7 22.♖fd1 ♗c6 23.♘a5 f4 24.exf4 ♖xf4 25.♘xc6 ♖xc6 26.♕e5 ♖f5 27.♕xe4 dxe4 28.♖xd7 ♖fxc5 29.♖e1 ♖c1 30.♔f1 ♔f7 31.♖d4 ♖xe1+ 32.♔xe1 ♖c2 33.♖a4 e3 34.fxe3 ♖xg2 35.h4 h5 36.♔f1 ♖g4 37.♖xg4

At first glance, White seems sure of a draw: 37...♔f6 38.♔g3 ♔f5 39.e4+ ♔xe4 40.♔xg4 e5 41. ♔g5, and the pawns queen together. Botvinnik found a paradoxical way of winning.

37...hxg4 38.♔g2

38...g5 39.h5 ♔g7 40.♔g3 ♔h7
Giving the move to White! **41.♔×g4**
♔h6 42.e4 This move was sealed by
White, but then he resigned, since he
cannot avoid falling into *zugzwang*:
42.a5 ... 52. e8♕ ♕f1+, and White loses
his queen.

(139) Botvinnik – Keres
The Hague/Moscow 1948
Queen's Gambit [D06]

1.d4 d5 2.♘f3 ♗f5 3.c4 e6 4.c×d5
e×d5 5.♕b3 ♘c6 6.♗g5 ♗e7
7.♗×e7 ♘g×e7 8.e3 ♕d6 9.♘bd2
0-0 10.♖c1 a5 11.a3 ♖fc8 12.♗d3
a4 13.♕c2 ♗×d3 14.♕×d3 ♘d8
15.0-0 ♘e6 16.♖c3 b5 17.♕c2
♖cb8 18.♘e1 ♘c8 19.♖c6 ♕e7
20.♘d3 ♘b6 21.♘b4 ♖d8 22.♕f5
♖d6 23.♖fc1 ♖×c6 24.♖×c6 ♖d8
25.♖×b6 c×b6 26.♘c6 ♕c7
27.♘×d8 ♕×d8 28.♕c2 ♕c7
29.♕×c7 ♘×c7 30.♘b1 ♔f8
31.♔f1 ♔e7 32.♔e2 ♔d6 33.♔d3
♔c6 34.♘c3 ♘e8 35.♘a2 f6 36.f3
♘c7 37.♘b4+ ♔d6 38.e4 d×e4+
39.f×e4 ♘e6 40.♔e3 ♘c7 41.♔d3
In this position, the game was
adjourned.

The continuation was: **41...♘e6**
42.♘d5 ♔c6 43.h4 ♘d8 44.♘f4
♔d6 45.♘h5 ♘e6 46.♔e3 ♔e7
47.d5 ♘c5 48.♘×g7 ♔d6 49.♘e6
White wins a tempo in order to seize

control of the e5-square. After the
exchange of knights, the ending is lost
for Black. **49...♘d7 50.♔d4 ♘e5**
51.♘g7 ♘c4 52.♘f5+ ♔c7 53.♔c3
♔d7 54.g4 ♘e5 55.g5 f×g5
56.h×g5 ♘f3 57.♔b4 ♘×g5 58.e5
h5 59.e6+ ♔d8 60.♔×b5 1-0

(140) Kotov – Botvinnik
Moscow 1955
Semi-Slav Defense [D45]

1.d4 d5 2.c4 c6 3.♘c3 ♘f6 4.♘f3
e6 5.e3 ♘bd7 6.♗d3 ♗b4 7.0-0
0-0 8.♗d2 ♗d6 9.b3 ♕e7 10.♕c2
e5 11.c×d5 c×d5 12.d×e5 ♘×e5
13.♘d4 ♘×d3 14.♕×d3 ♕e5 15.f4
♕e7 16.♖ac1 ♖d8 17.♖c2 ♗c5
18.♘a4 ♗×d4 19.♕×d4 ♗f5
20.♗b4 ♕d7 21.♖c3 ♘e4 22.♖cc1
b6 23.♖fd1 f6 24.♘c3 ♘×c3
25.♖×c3 ♗e4 26.♕d2 ♕g4 27.h3
♕g6 28.♕f2 h5 29.♔h2 a5
30.♗a3 b5 31.♗c5 b4 32.♖cc1
♖dc8 33.♗d4 ♗c2 34.♖d2 ♗e4
35.♖dd1 ♕f5 36.♕e2 ♕g6 37.♕f2
a4 38.♖×c8+ ♖×c8 39.b×a4 ♕e8
40.♖d2 ♕×a4 41.♕h4 ♖c2
42.♖×c2 ♕×c2 43.♕g3 ♕×a2
44.♗×f6 ♕×g2+ 45.♕×g2 ♗×g2
46.♗d4 ♗e4 47.♔g3 ♔f7 48.h4
g6 49.♔f2 ♔e6 50.♔e2 ♔f5
51.♔d2 ♔g4 52.♗f6 ♔g3 53.♗e7
♔h3 54.♗f6 ♔g4 55.♗e7 ♗f5
56.♗f6 ♔f3 57.♗e7 b3 58.♔c3
♗e6 59.♗c5

59...g5!! 60.f×g5 60. hg h4 ... 63. Bd6 K:e3 loses.
60...d4+ 61.e×d4 ♔g3 62.♗a3 ♔×h4 63.♔d3 ♔×g5 64.♔e4 h4 65.♔f3 ♗d5+ 0-1 Botvinnik: "Probably the most elegant opposite-color bishop in my whole career."

(141) Botvinnik – Najdorf

Moscow 1956
Nimzo-Indian Defense [E42]
Notes based on those by Chekhov from ChessBase MegaBase

1.c4 ♘f6 2.♘c3 e6 3.d4 ♗b4 4.e3 c5 5.♘ge2 d5 6.a3 c×d4 7.a×b4 d×c3 8.♘×c3 0-0 8...d×c4 9.♕×d8+ ♔×d8 10.♗×c4 ♘bd7 11.0-0 ♔e7 12.e4 b6 13.f3± Uhlmann-Larsen 1957 **9.c×d5 ♘×d5** 9...e×d5 10.♗e2 ♘c6 11.b5 ♘e7 12.0-0 ♗e6 13.b3 a6 14.♗b2 a×b5 15.♘×b5 ♖×a1 16.♕×a1± Hort-Karaklajic, Palma de Mallorca 1967 **10.♘×d5 ♕×d5** 10...e×d5 11.♗e2 ♗e6 12.0-0± Garcia-Sanguinet, Buenos Aires 1962 **11.♕×d5 e×d5 12.♗d2± ♗f5** 12...♘a6!? △ ♗d7, ♘c7, ♗b5 **13.♗c3 ♘a6!** 13...♘d7 14.♗e2± **14.♗×a6** 14.♗e2 ♘c7 15.0-0 ♗d7 △ ♗b5 **14...b×a6 15.♖×a6 ♗d3 16.♖a5 ♗c4 17.♔d2 a6 18.♖c5!± ♖fd8 19.g4** 19.♔c2 ♖d7 20.e4 ♖ad8 21.♖d1 ♗e2 22.♖d2 ♗b5 23.e×d5 f6± **19...h6 20.h4 ♖d7 21.♖b1 ♖e8** 21...♗b3 22.b5± 22.b3 ♗b5 23.♖g1 ♔h7 24.♗d4 ♖e6 25.f3 ♖e8 26.h5 f6 27.♖gc1** 27.f4 ♖f8 28.♖g3 ♖e8 29.♖c1 △ g5, ♖cg1 **27...♔g8 28.♖c7?!** 28.♖g1! **28...♖×c7! 29.♖×c7 ♖d8 30.♗c5 ♖a8?!** 30...♖d7!? 31.♖c8+ ♔h7! (31...♔f7?? 32.f4 △ f5, ♖f8#) 32.♖a8 ♗f1 33.f4 ♗b5 34.f5 ♖b7 35.♗d4 ♖f7 36.♖d8 ♖d7 37.♖f8 ♗f1 38.g5 h×g5 (38...f×g5 39.f6 g6 40.♖h8+!+−) 39.h6 g4 40.h×g7 ♖×g7 41.♗×f6 g3! **31.♔e1 ♗d3?!** 31...♖d8!? **32.♖d7! ♗c2**

33.♖×d5 ♗×b3 34.♖d3 34.♖d7?! ♗c4 35.♖c7 a5! **34...♗c4 35.♖c3 ♗b5 36.♗d4 ♗e8** 36...a5? 37.♖c5 **37.♖c5 ♖b8 38.♗c3 ♖d8 39.♗d4 ♖b8 40.♗c3 ♖d8 41.e4 ♗d3?!** 41...♖d6!? 42.♔f2 (42.e5 ♖c6! 43.e×f6 g×f6) 42...♖c6 43.♔e3 ♖×c5 44.b×c5 ♔f7 45.♔d4 ♗e6 46.f4 ♗c6 47.f5+ ♔f7 48.♔e3 ♗d7 49.♔f4 ♗c6 50.e5 ♗b7! 51.e6+ ♔e7 52.♔e3 ♗c6 53.♗d2 ♗b7 54.♗d4 ♗f3 55.g5 h×g5 56.♗×g5 ♗×h5! (56...f×g5 57.h6 g×h6 58.♔e5+−) 57.c6 ♔d6= **42.♔e2 ♗b5** 42...♖d6 43.e5! f×e5 44.♗×e5 ♖c6 45.♗c3 ♖×c5 46.b×c5± **43.♖×b5 ♖×c3 44.♖b8+ ♔f7** 44...♔h7 45.f4 ♖g3 46.e5 f×e5 47.f×e5 ♖×g4 48.♔d3± **45.♖b7+ ♔f8 46.♖b8+ ♔f7 47.♖b7+ ♔f8 48.♔f2 ♗b3 49.♖b6 ♖a3 50.♖b8+ ♔f7 51.♖b7+ ♔f8** 51...♔g8 52.f4 **52.♔g3 a5 53.b5 a4 54.♔f4 ♗b3 55.b6?!** 55.♔f5 ♖×f3+ 56.♔e6 ♔g8 57.♔d5+− **55...♔g8?!** 55...♖b5! 56.♖a7 ♖×b6 57.♖×a4 ♖b5 58.♖a3 ♔f7 **56.♔f5 ♖b5+** 56...♖×f3+? 57.♔g6+− **57.♔e6 a3 58.f4! a2** 58...♔h7 59.♔d7 a2 60.♖a7 ♖×b6 61.♖×a2± **59.♖a7 ♖×b6+ 60.♔f5 ♖b7** 60...♖b2 61.♔g6 ♔f8 62.♖a8+ ♔e7 63.♔×g7 ♖g2 64.♖a7+ ♔e6 65.f5+ ♔e5 66.♖a5 ♔×e4 67.♔×f6 ♔d3 68.g5!+− **61.♖×a2 ♔f7 62.♖a5 ♖c7 63.♖d5 ♖a7 64.e5 f×e5 65.f×e5 ♔e7** 65...♖b7 66.♖d7+!

66.e6 ♖a4 66...♖a6 67.♖d7+ ♔f8 68.♔g6! ♖×e6+ 69.♔h7+− **67.g5!**

**h×g5 68.罝d7+ 舍f8 69.罝f7+ 舍g8
70.舍g6 g4 71.h6! g×h6** 71...罝a8
72.h×g7 g3 73.e7 g2 74.罝f8++- **72.e7
罝a8 73.罝f6** 73.罝f6 g3 74.罝d6 罝e8
75.罝d8+- **1-0**

Rook endings would arise often in
Botvinnik's games, and in them, his
play was always instructive. One such
endgame was the 20th game in his 1961
return match against Tal, which lasted
122 (!) moves, and ended up a draw.
And on his opponent's 95th move, he
found a beautiful stalemating idea –
which, however, his equally resourceful
opponent also saw – and avoided.
Botvinnik evinced interest in the theory
of this sort of endgame, as witness to
his widely published analysis, entitled
"Rook Endings with f- and h-pawns" in
the magazine *Shakhmaty v SSSR* (7-
8/1949).Many positions appeared
therein: winning as well as drawing. He
concluded that these would be
important for endgame theory, and
useful in practical play.

And, finally, an example of a queen
ending of theoretical significance.

(142) Botvinnik – Minev
Amsterdam 1954
Semi-Slav Defense [D47]

**1.匂f3 匂f6 2.c4 c6 3.d4 d5 4.匂c3
e6 5.e3 匂bd7 6.奧d3 d×c4 7.奧×c4
b5 8.奧d3 b4 9.匂e4 奧b7
10.匂×f6+ g×f6 11.e4 奧d6 12.0-0
罝g8 13.嘗e2 嘗a5 14.匂d2 0-0-0
15.匂c4 嘗c7 16.f4 c5 17.a3 f5
18.a×b4 匂f6 19.匂a5 c4 20.匂×b7
c×d3 21.匂×d6+ 罝×d6 22.嘗×d3
f×e4 23.嘗e2 嘗b7 24.f5 匂d5
25.嘗×e4 匂×b4 26.嘗×b7+ 舍×b7
27.f×e6 f×e6 28.罝f7+ 舍c6 29.奧e3
舍d5 30.罝×h7 匂c6 31.奧f4 罝dd8
32.奧c7 罝h8 33.罝g7 罝hg8 34.罝h7**

**罝h8 35.罝g7 罝hg8 36.罝f7 罝gf8
37.罝af1 罝×f7 38.罝×f7 罝c8
39.奧e5 匂×d4 40.奧×d4 舍×d4
41.舍f2 a5 42.g4 罝c2+ 43.舍g3
罝×b2 44.g5 a4 45.g6 罝b1 46.舍h4
罝g1 47.舍h5 舍c4 48.罝f4+ 舍b5
49.罝f3 舍b4 50.罝f4+ 舍b5 51.罝f3
舍b4 52.罝g3 罝×g3 53.h×g3 a3
54.g7 a2 55.g8嘗 a1嘗 56.嘗g4+
舍a5 57.嘗×e6 罝h8+ 58.舍g6 嘗c3
59.g4 嘗d2 60.g5 嘗d4 61.嘗f5+
舍a4 62.舍h5 嘗h8+ 63.舍g4 嘗h1
64.嘗f4+ 舍a5 65.嘗e5+ 舍a4 66.g6
嘗d1+ 67.舍g5 嘗d8+ 68.舍f5
嘗c8+ 69.舍f4 嘗c1+ 70.嘗e3 嘗c7+
71.嘗e5 嘗c1+ 72.舍f5 嘗c8+
73.舍g5 嘗d8+ 74.嘗f6 嘗d5+
75.嘗f5 嘗d8+**

**76.舍h5 嘗e8 77.嘗f4+ 舍a5
78.嘗d2+ 舍a4 79.嘗d4+ 舍a5
80.舍g5 嘗e7+ 81.舍f5 嘗f8+
82.舍e4 嘗h6 83.嘗e5+ 舍a4 84.g7
嘗h1+ 85.舍d4 嘗d1+ 86.舍c5
嘗c1+ 87.舍d6 嘗d2+ 88.舍e6
嘗a2+ 89.嘗d5 嘗e2+ 90.舍d6
嘗h2+ 91.舍c5 1-0**

Esthetics
The deep strategic plan, the sudden
tactical strike, the original combinative
ideas, the far-seeing calculation – these,
and other criteria were characteristic of
many of Botvinnik's games, and
together, they constitute a milestone of
beauty in chess. The best of his
productions were created in games

against elite chessplayers – Capablanca, Alekhine, Euwe, Smyslov, Tal, Petrosian, Portisch, Reshevsky, Bronstein, Keres, Najdorf, Flohr, Tartakower, and others.

Thinking about contemporary practice in chess, and about past treasures, Botvinnik came to a conclusion about the philosophical content of the essence of the game of chess. His article, which was published in 1960 and formed an afterword to the games collection, *Smyslov-Botvinnik 1958, World Championship Return Match*. Already, its title forewarned the reader that Botvinnik intended to deal with a sharp and arguable question: "Is chess an art?"

"It is universally acknowledged," Botvinnik noted there, "that chess has three sides to it: play, learning, and art. But, of course, there is no one who affirms that chess is learning." But since there can (and must!) be research, then it indubitably possesses one element of learning. And he goes on to affirm that "taking into account the strength of its esthetic influence, and also its worldwide popularity, we can hardly be mistaken if we consider chess an art. Yes, in our day, chess is perhaps at once a game and an art. It apparently became an art when both artists and the general public could appreciate the beauty of chess. However, we must remember that chess is always a game (as distinct from composition), and only rarely a genuine art. It is too seldom a game created which is genuinely valuable in an artistic sense... But if this master has created an interesting game which is an artistic production, this game will live on for decades, to give chessplayers esthetic pleasure."

Botvinnik believed in his "credo" until the end of his days.

Trainers

From time to time, Botvinnik brought experienced trainers, and a number of first-class chessplayers, as sparring-partners in to work with him, in the interests of more effective preparation for events. Among them were Vyacheslav Ragozin, Grigory Goldberg, Ilya Kan... He played a number of training games or mini-matches against grandmasters Yuri Averbakh, David Bronstein and Tigran Petrosian. Later, in the 1960s and 1970s, government support was enabled for other candidates for important events on the highest level, in the interests of retaining the chess crown in the USSR. Gradually, the number of such helpers increased. In 1987, Botvinnik spoke openly on this topic: "Champions, much like kings of old, travel with large "staffs." I think that such staffs are of little benefit. Only one helper is necessary – but he has to be a good one. Such was Ragozin for me. It was with him that I won the world championship."

Nevertheless, it remains a fact that, it was precisely with Botvinnik that the tendency started, showing itself especially during the 1970s and 1980s, to put together impressive teams and "staffs" during the periods of matches for the world championship.

Goldberg, Grigory Abramovich (July 29, 1908, Tsarskoe Selo (today Pushkin City)-December 1, 1976, Moscow), master, international arbiter, teacher, journalist, trainer and second to Botvinnik in three matches for the world championship (1957-60). Talented organizer of USSR chess life.

"Grisha Goldberg was tall, elegant, and had long legs," Botvinnik wrote of his friend, whom he had known since he was 15. "His eyes would flash at you in conversation. He had a manly face, with multi-colored hair." Everything that Goldberg put his mind to came easily to him. When he occupied himself with chess, he became a master in 1939; when he started playing ping-pong, he rapidly achieved the first rank. He thought of organizing, under the auspices of his own club, "Trud," an All-Russian children's chess school, and it would become a fount of talents (1963). It was the career starting point for Karpov, Balashov, Rashkovsky, and Timoshenko.

Within three years, in 1966, on his own initiative, he founded a chess section in the Physicultural Institute, which specialized in the preparation of chessplayers and trainers. Among its earliest graduates were grandmasters Balashov, Chekhov, Akhsharumova, Zaitseva... For many years, the section he had nurtured was to successfully develop the topmost chess education, and a chair (one of 42) at the Russian State University of Physiculture, headed by E. P. Linovitsky. Under this chair today, you can get a B.A, a masters, or a doctorate.

As Botvinnik acknowledged, he first experienced Goldberg's chess strength in 1932, at the Leningrad championship, one of the strongest in the city's history. "Goldberg played the opening and middlegame in an original

way, since he was not too well versed in theory; but he played no weak moves. I sensed that my opponent was breaking the generally-held rules, that he was playing "incorrectly." But I didn't know how to fight against this manner of conducting the battle! We adjourned the game in a position that was objectively lost for me..."

But in the adjournment, Botvinnik nevertheless saved himself. By the way, in this tournament Botvinnik only gave up one point to his opposition, with draws against Goldberg and Ilyin-Zhenevsky, and outplayed all the rest. Goldberg also performed well, taking sixth place among the 12 participants. And here is the above-cited "fighting game," as Romanovsky called it, placing it, with his own notes, in the first volume of his *Chess Creativity of Botvinnik* (Moscow 1965).

(143) Goldberg – Botvinnik
Leningrad 1932
Nimzo-Indian Defense [E35]

1.d4 ♘f6 2.c4 e6 3.♘c3 ♗b4 4.♕c2 d5 5.c×d5 e×d5 6.♗g5 ♗e6 7.e3 ♘bd7 8.f4 h6 9.♗×f6 ♕×f6 10.♗d3 ♘b6 11.♘f3 0-0 12.0-0 ♖ac8 13.♘a4 c5 14.♘×b6 a×b6 15.♕a4 ♕e7 16.♘e5 c4 17.♗b1 ♗d2 18.♖f3 c3 19.♕c2 f5 20.b3 ♕a3 21.♕d1 ♖c7 22.♗c2 b5 23.♖g3 b6 24.h3 ♖f6 25.♔h2 ♕f8 26.♕e2 b4 27.♔b5 ♕d6 28.♘d3 ♗f7 29.♘e5 ♖e7 30.♕a6 ♗e8 31.a3 b×a3 32.♖×a3 ♗h5 33.♖a1 ♖f8 34.♕d3 ♔h8 35.h4 ♕f6 36.♖h3 g6 37.♔g3 ♖h7 38.♔f2 ♔g8 39.♕b5 ♕e6 40.♖a6 ♖b7 41.b4 ♖d8 42.♗b3 c2 43.♗×c2 ♕c8 44.♘c6 ♖d6 45.♗a4 ♗d1 46.♖×b6 ♖×b6 47.♕×b6 ♔h8 48.♗b5 ♗g4 49.♕c5 ♖×c6

50.♕×c6 ♕×c6 51.♗×c6 ♗×h3
52.g×h3 ♗×b4 53.h5 g5 54.♔f3
♔g7 55.♗×d5 g×f4 56.♔×f4 ♔f6
57.♗c6 ♗d6+ 58.♔f3 ♗h2
59.♗d7 ♗b8 60.♔e2 ♗h2
61.♔d3 ♗g1 62.♗c8 ♗f2 ½-½

A quarter-century later, Botvinnik offered Goldberg the post of second for his second match against Vassily Smyslov, in 1957, and did not regret it. "At the time of the match, I knew Goldberg's true strength as a chess master. He knew and analyzed the endgame brilliantly. In the analysis of unfinished games in the ending, he gave me invaluable support." (Botvinnik)

Besides this practical help. Goldberg's *joie de vivre* provided a friendly moral "boost": this was his knowing how to "coin an accurate little phrase" at the right time, his ability to dissipate the tension and dispel accumulated fatigue. To the last day, Goldberg was working at the Physicultural Institute, trying not to think about his cardiac illness...

Starting in 1990, students and teachers of the institute held tournaments daily – memorials to Goldberg, with international master, and sometimes grandmaster norms.

Kan, Ilya Abramovich (May 4, 1909, Samara-December 12, 1978, Moscow), Soviet chessplayer and trainer, second to Botvinnik during the 1954 match against Smyslov.

At 14, he moved to Moscow, when he also learned to play chess. In his youth, his father played Mikhail Chigorin to a draw in an exhibition, and was the undisputed authority on chess in the

Ilya Kan

family. At the first Moscow International Tournament, 16-year old Ilya, who was already a serious student of the self-taught Schiffers, attended the halls of the Hotel Metropole, where the kings of chess were battling. Nor could he have imagined that, in ten more years, he would be battling as an equal against the seemingly unreachable Emanuel Lasker and Capablanca.

At his debut in the 1929 USSR Championship, Kan took third place. Recalling his first appearance among his country's elite, Ragozin wrote: "The twenty-year old chess-player showed himself to be an experienced tournament fighter. And already then there was an incorrect opinion circulating concerning the style of the young master which has persisted to the present day. Kan always strove for clear and positionally healthy setups, and this striving led to the error of his critics, who relegated Kan to the ranks of positional chessplayers, whereas, in many of Kan's games, a most unexpected *denouement* would take place after a complex tactical struggle. It was precisely this top-grade tactical skill, his understanding of how to find the key to complex situations, that moved the young master into the forefront among Soviet chessplayers."

Apparently, the leader among Soviet chessplayers, Mikhail Botvinnik himself, took a long time to accustom himself to Kan's style of play: he lost to him in 19 moves at the 1929 USSR Championship, then in a team match of the professional unions of Moscow and Leningrad, and again after making a fatal error on his 21st move in the Second Moscow International. Kan wrote the following about the second of these victories: "Not an error-free game, but an interesting one, and one of the most difficult and tense games of my chess career."

(144) Kan – Botvinnik
Leningrad 1930
Nimzo-Indian Defense [E22]
Notes based on those by Primel from ChessBase MegaBase

1.c4 ♘f6 2.♘c3 c5 3.♘f3 e6 4.d4 c×d4 5.♘×d4 ♗b4 5...♘c6 6.e4 transposes to a Kan Sicilian! 5...a6. **6.♕b3!?** Bogoljubow's ideas was popular at this time, but in any event, Black has no trouble equalizing. 6.g3, and in particular ♘db5, which became the main line, were not known at that time. 6...0-0 7.♗g2 d5 8.c×d5 ♘×d5 9.♕b3 (9.♗d2=); 6.♘db5!? d5! 7.♗f4 0-0 8.e3 ♘c6 9.a3 ♗×c3+ 10.♘×c3 **6...♗c5** 6...♘a6 ♗d2 Bogoljubow-Przepiorka, Bad Pistyan 1922, 1-0 **7.♘f3 b6** 7...♘c6 8.♗g5 0-0 9.e3 b6 10.♗e2 ♗b7 11.0-0 ♗e7= 12.♖fd1 ♖c8 13.♕a4 Koenig-Bluemich, 1926

½-½ **8.♗g5 ♗b7 9.♕c2N** 9.e3 ♘c6 10.♗e2 h6 11.♗h4 ♕e7 12.a3 g5 13.♗g3 ♘h5 14.0-0-0 ♘×g3 15.h×g3 0-0-0 16.♕a4 ♔b8 17.♘d4 ♗×d4 18.e×d4 ♖c8 Grünfeld-Spielmann, Vienna 1929 **9...h6** 9...♗e7 10.e3 **10.♗h4 0-0 11.e4** A rather risky weakening of the d4-square and the e4-pawn, which may also be subject to pressure after ♘a6-c5. 11.e3!? **11...♗e7!** A multi-functional move, freeing the c5-square for the ♘a6 and releasing the ♗g5 pin. **12.♗e2 ♘a6 13.e5** 13.0-0 ♘c5 **13...♘b4 14.♕d2 ♘e4! 15.♘×e4 ♗×e4 16.♗×e7 ♕×e7 17.0-0 ♖ad8** 17...♖fd8 18.a3 ♘c6 **18.♖ad1** 18.♖fd1 f6 **18...♘×a2** 18...f5 19.♘d4 ♘×a2 20.f3 ♗a8 21.♖a1 ♘b4 22.♖×a7 **19.♘d4** 19.♖a1 ♘b4 20.♖×a7 ♘c6 **19...♘b4 20.♘b5 ♕c5 21.♘×a7 f6** 21...♗c2! 22.♖a1 d5∓ **22.e×f6 ♖×f6 23.♕d4** 23.♘b5 d5! **23...d5 24.c×d5 e×d5 25.♘b5 ♘c6 26.♕×c5 b×c5 27.♖c1 d4!?** 27...c4!? **28.f3** 28.♖×c5 d3 29.♗g4 d2 30.♖d1 ♗g6 **28...d3! 29.♗d1** 29.♖fd1 d×e2 30.♖×d8+ ♘×d8 31.f×e4 ♖b6 **29...d2 30.♖×c5 ♗d3! 31.♖f2 ♗×b5 32.♖×b5 ♖e6 33.♖f1 ♖e1 34.♖c5?! ♘b4 35.♖c4 ♘d5** 35...♘d3 36.♗b3 ♔f8 37.g3 ♖a8!−+ **36.♖e4 ♘e3−+ 37.♖×e3 ♖×e3 38.♔f2 ♖de8 39.♗a4 ♖e1 0-1**

At the Second Moscow International Tournament, Kan shared sixth/seventh places with Grigory Levenfish participants, and earned the plaudits of Emanuel Lasker. And within a year, it was Capablanca's turn to exclaim, "Oh, Kan! Excellent!" when the Muscovite master beat one of his competitors – grandmaster Salo Flohr. In this double-round tournament, Botvinnik at last avenged his losses, defeating his *bête noire* Kan twice.

Thirty years later, the chess paths of the two "friendly enemies" crossed again. On this occasion, the world champion asked Ilya Kan, an experienced analyst, to be his trainer and second for his 1954 match against Vassily Smyslov

Kan was a well-known chess theoretician and writer, an author of a number of books.

Books: *The Chess Creations of N. D. Grigoriev*, Moscow 1954; *Defense*, Mosow 1960; *Chess Encounters*, Moscow 1962; *The Chessplayer Nikolai Ryumin*, Moscow 1968; *Chess Battalions*, Moscow 1970; *The Principles of Chess Battles*, Moscow 1971; *From the Opening to the Middlegame*, Moscow 1978.

Ragozin, Vyacheslav Vasilievich (October 8, 1908, St. Petersburg-March 11, 1962, Moscow) international grandmaster (1950), trainer and second for many years to Botvinnik, when he was fighting for the world championship.

"Slava's course in life," as Botvinnik wrote in his reminiscences about his friend and trainer, "was not an easy one. After his school years, he went into a bread factory; there he was injured – the bone of his right arm was damaged. After that, he only finished the construction institute with difficulty – chess got in the way, because he had given over his life to it..."

It was precisely in chess that Vyacheslav found his calling. He participated in over 60 tournaments (and took first or second place in 17 of them!) and three matches, two of which were for the master and grandmaster

Vyacheslav Ragozin

titles. In the first of these, in 1930, Ragozin defeated the Ilyin-Zhenevsky, +6 -4 =4; and in the second, in 1946, he beat Bondarevsky, score of +7 -3 =2. Only in his match against Botvinnik three years before (cf. *Ragozin-Botvinnik, 1940 Match)*, did he suffer a loss, winning not one of the twelve games, and drawing seven.

Ragozin played in the USSR championships twelve times. His appearances were successful in the second and third Moscow International Tournaments in 1935 and 1936. He took second place in the 1947 Chigorin Memorial, ahead of Keres, Smyslov, Boleslavsky, Kotov, Bondarevsky and Gligoric. In the matches of the USSR Team against the teams of the USA and Great Britain (1945-47, 6½/8!). Finally, Ragozin became the second world correspondence champion, winning the championship of 1955-59.

Talking about the "secrets" of his creative laboratory, Ragozin noted his "affinity for independent analysis. I analyzed hundreds of positions from the opening, middlegame and endgame in the first period of my developing skill. And in practical play, I was always attracted by the process of struggle, the search for original ideas. This brought me much pleasure, but also sometimes a great deal of disappointment. Because of time-pressure and exhaustion, I did not always succeed in carrying out the plans and ideas I had thought of."

His own games were among the splendid productions of the art of chess. He defeated Emanuel Lasker, Spielmann, Ståhlberg, Najdorf, Lilienthal, Reshevsky, and many others. His favorite game was his win over the second world champion. Regarding the ending, Ragozin wrote, "I succeeded in 'lowering Lasker's alertness,' thanks to an original idea, catching the rook with my bishop."

(145) Em.Lasker – Ragozin
Moscow 1936
Sicilian Defense [B73]

1.e4 c5 2.♘f3 ♘c6 3.d4 c×d4 4.♘×d4 ♘f6 5.♘c3 d6 6.♗e2 g6 7.♗e3 ♗g7 8.0-0 0-0 9.h3 ♗d7 10.♕d2 ♖c8 11.♖ad1 a6 12.♖fe1 b5 13.♘×c6 ♗×c6 14.f3 ♕c7 15.♗f1 ♖fd8 16.♕f2 ♖d7 17.a3 ♕b7 18.♗b6 e5 19.♗a5 d5 20.e×d5 ♗×d5 21.♖×e5 ♘g4 22.♖e×d5 ♖×d5 23.f×g4 ♗×c3 24.♖×d5 ♗×a5 25.♖d6 ♗c7 26.♖f6 ♗d8 27.♖d6 ♗e7 28.♖b6 ♕×b6 29.♕×b6 ♗c5+ 30.♕×c5 ♖×c5 31.♗d3 ♔g7 32.♔f2 ♔f6 33.♔e3 ♔e5 34.g5 ♔d6 35.h4 h6 36.g×h6 ♖h5 37.g3 ♖×h6 38.c4 ♖h5 39.c×b5 a×b5 40.b3 ♖e5+ 41.♔f4 ♖d5 42.♗e4 ♖d2 43.g4

♖a2 44.h5 ♖×a3 45.b4 f5 46.♗b1 g×h5 47.g×h5 ♖h3 48.♔g5 ♔e5 49.♔g6 ♖g3+ 50.♔f7 ♖b3 51.♗c2 ♖×b4 52.h6 ♖h4 53.♔g6 b4 54.♗d1 f4 55.h7 55.♗h5 is met by 55...♖×h5 56.♔×h5 ♔f6−+ **55...♖×h7 56.♔×h7 ♔e4 57.♔g6 f3 58.♔g5 ♔e3 0-1**

Ragozin paid great attention to working out methods of rational preparation for the battles of chess. His creative work with Botvinnik in this regard began back in the mid-1930s. Thus, preparing for the Second Moscow International, while living in the village of Zacherenye, not far from Luga, they worked together on competitions, analysis, and played training games. Botvinnik presented one of them in his reminiscences in 1984, clearly demonstrating Ragozin's self-taught gifts.

(146) Botvinnik – Ragozin
Zacherenye 1936
Sicilian Defense [B84]

1.e4 c5 2.♘f3 e6 3.d4 c×d4 4.♘×d4 ♘f6 5.♘c3 d6 6.♗e2 a6 7.♗e3 ♕c7 8.a4 b6 9.f4 ♗b7 10.♗f3 ♘bd7 11.♕e2 ♗e7 12.0-0 0-0 13.g4 d5 White attacks on the wing and so Black counterstrikes in the center. **14.e5 ♘e4 15.♘×e4 d×e4 16.♗g2 ♗d5 17.♖fc1 ♖ac8** 17...g5!? **18.♗f2 ♘c5 19.b4?** (D)

19.g5 limits the damage. **19...♘d3!!** A very deep combination. **20.c×d3 ♕×c1+ 21.♖×c1 ♖×c1+ 22.♗f1 ♖fc8 23.♕b2?** 23.♗e3 e×d3 24.♕d2 was the last chance to fight, but Black is better here as well in view of the strong passed d-pawn. **23...e×d3 24.b5?!** 24.♕d2 ♖8c3 25.♗e3 ♗×b4 26.♕×c1 ♖×c1 27.♗×c1 d2−+ **24...a×b5 25.a×b5?!** ♖d1 **26.♘c6**

♗f8 27.♗×b6 d2 28.♕c2 ♗f3 0-1
29.♔f2 ♖×f1+ 30.♔×f1 d1♕+ -+

Ragozin did a lot for chess, as a theoretician, journalist and organizer. Many of his opening discoveries made their way into tournament practice. Among these were the "Ragozin Defense": 1.d4 d5 2.c4 e6 3.♘c3 ♘f6 4.♘f3 ♗b4. The idea of this defense is

a struggle of the pieces, preparation for the advance e6-e5, and other plans of play in the center and on the queenside.

Starting in 1947, and over the next 15 years, Ragozin carried on the organizational work of FIDE as its vice-president. During the same period, he was the chief editor of the magazine *Shakhmaty v SSSR*.

Author: *Selected Games*, Moscow 1964; *Kandidatenturnir fur Schachweltmeistersschaft*, Bled/Zagreb/Beograd, 1960 (co-author).

Books: Vasiliev, V., *Twice a Grandmaster*; *Chess Silhouettes*, Moscow 1961; Yudovich, M., *V. Ragozin*, Moscow 1984.

Chapter Four

Writer and Journalist

A Literary Man

Botvinnik's activities rested upon "three great pillars," those being chess, teaching and literature. It was not enough for him to attain the highest competitive achievements possible. He felt an inherent need to accompany every step towards Olympus with an open self-expression. That included commentary on his own games, the placement of his analyses and articles in the current press, and his views on national and international chess, ultimately dealing with issues concerning the conduct of the world championship. Such was Botvinnik!

He could not live, or fight, otherwise! And, even when he cut short his appearances in the daily life of tournaments, his thoughts and his pen continued their activity: articles, profiles, essays, and interview were published in both the Russian and the foreign presses. His newest books would be immediately translated and distributed through many countries, testifying to people's interest in whatever came out of the Patriarch of Soviet chess.

It is easy to see that Botvinnik kept current, was witty, and dealt with a wide variety of problems, as well as his involvement with the fourth volume of his *Analytical and Critical Works* (1987). However, the articles and essays he presented in it do not exhaust Botvinnik's activity as journalist and writer. In the general and the specialized press, articles were also published which give an impression of the sixth world champion, including his positions on many issues.

Thus, during the "Cold War" period, he came out with an article, "On International Chess Links" in *Novosti* magazine (October 15, 1951), in which he complained about " the enlivening of international chess life becoming a serious factor in achieving mutual understanding and the cultural *rapprochement* among nations." "Additionally," the world champion asserted, "securely established international links to chess as an art are necessary."

Botvinnik, himself, did a lot to help secure these bonds. In his articles and interviews, he demonstrated a good knowledge of the chess life of many lands and peoples. Whether he wrote a foreword to the book *British Chess* (1983), in which he foretold serious success for 17-year old Nigel Short, or gave an interview for *Magyar Sakkelet* (1981), in which he congratulated Hungarian chessplayers for their brilliant results at recent Olympiads, and talked about his encounters with Szabo, Barcza, Portisch, and Lilienthal. And he visited the Netherlands, East Germany – everywhere he showed affection for his colleagues in those lands, expressed his good wishes to their peoples in their development of chess culture.

Not infrequently, Botvinnik appeared in the Moscow chess journals *Shakhmaty v SSSR* and *64-Shakhmatnoye Obozreniye*, and in the pages of general political editions – in the journals *Ogonyok* and *Nauka i Zhizn*; in the newspapers *Pravda*, *Komsomolskaya Pravda*, *Moscovsky Komsomolets*, *Trud*, *Sovietsky Sport*, as well as in the newspapers of Siberia and the Far East, and a number of the Soviet republics, where he would make appearances with exhibitions and lectures and where his publications aided the increase of chess culture.

As a committee member of FIDE, Botvinnik naturally gave his attention to the most varied problems, noting in some situations critical points in this international organization. In others, underscoring its importance for world chess development, and organizing the world championship. Not accidentally, he gently recommended that FIDE pay special attention to the selection of a new president in 1978. In this regard he announced that under no circumstances would he himself run for the post. And it was not without humor that he explained why: "Of course, the president must be charming, know how to set up contacts, speak in several languages, appeal to the ladies, be above middle age, etc. This is so obvious, as not to require explanation! All three presidents, from 1924 to 1978 – Alexander Rueb and Max Euwe, of Holland and Folke Rogard of Sweden fully met those requirements."

Botvinnik opined that "the new FIDE president should be above any egoistic national interests, so that the Olympiads and other FIDE events would further the progress of chess, and not divide the chess world; I have always considered FIDE's chief purpose to be executing the world championship."

In chess history there had never been a champion who so accurately and clearly defined the worldwide political business of chess, and who so frequently appeared in the press with the expression of his point of view on the various questions of chess life. The collected articles, interviews and essays of Botvinnik could, by his witty observation, "serve as 'advice' about the history of mid-twentieth-century chess." At the same time, they are an excellent depiction of the world champion himself – his individuality and his journalistic and literary talent.

The same might also be said of Botvinnik's several dozen books, which have seen the light of day during his competitive and literary activity.

Matches

As we know, this formula of the meeting of two grandmasters brings out the best, not just of their relative strengths, competitive form, and other personal traits of the two opponents, but also the general level of mastery – that is, the state of the art of chess at a given moment. Therefore, it is no accident that Botvinnik's first book was dedicated to analytical research of the games of his match against grandmaster Flohr, and his next two books to his matches for the world championship against Smyslov.

The Flohr-Botvinnik Match – that was the name of the book published in 1934, immediately after the event itself, ending drawn after a very tense struggle. In the foreword, its author emphasized: "...the particular interest of the whole of Soviet society in every nuance of the event, and to the art of chess, on the whole, gave a most valuable stimulus to my creativity, and to achieving the result that I did." Botvinnik further described how he prepared for the match against Flohr, and how, before anything else, he studied his games. The presentation of all 12 of the games in that book demonstrated one of his greatest accomplishments – his talent for analysis.

Botvinnik released just two game collections of his annotated games about his matches for the world championship – and both of these were the matches against Smyslov. The first was about the 1954 match, while the second was about the return match of 1958. It is notable that the latter was released by the publishing house Iskusstvo (Art), and closed with his article, "Is Chess Art?" (cf. *Esthetics*). This time Botvinnik, along with careful analysis of the games, placed in the beginning of the book an article on the opening statistics of the match. There, he examined five openings that were of interest from the viewpoint of opening theory, including the Caro-Kann, Grünfeld, Sicilian, King's Indian – and the English Opening.

Two works about matches that were played by others stand unique. One of them was the *Alekhine-Euwe 1937, the Return Match for the World Championship* published in 1939. This work would later become the foundation for his preparation for a world championship match against Alekhine.

Botvinnik's final book on matches came out five years after the conclusion of his competitive career. It was witness, on the one hand, to his retaining the acuity of his analytical mastery, and on the other hand, to the continuing interest he had in the highest level of struggle. This work, *Three Matches of Anatoly Karpov*, was released in 1975. Thoroughly analyzing all 43 games of three candidates' matches with Polugaevsky, Spassky, and Korchnoi, Botvinnik showed that "Anatoly Karpov undoubtedly is the strongest chess fighter of our time," and expressed disappointment that there had never been a match with Robert Fischer, "who had earlier aroused such compassion with his fearless play." At the same time, he emphasized that when Fischer refused to play his next match for the world title, Max Euwe, the president of FIDE, was right to proclaim Karpov the 12th world champion, on April 1, 1975.

Tournaments

Botvinnik put out two books about All-Union championships that became classic productions of chess literature. The first of these was dedicated to the 11th USSR championship in 1939, where he took first place without a loss, and outdistanced second-place finisher Kotov by a full point. In the preamble, he wrote that game collections of national championships ought to be prepared by an authors' team, because it would be impossible to give detailed commentary on 150-200 games so quickly. For this book, out of 150 games, Botvinnik analyzed the 23 best games, presenting the rest without commentary. But besides the outstanding analysis, the work took on special value because of some problematical articles about the organization of the championship, the competitive struggle for the champion's title, the players' characteristics, and the tournament results, from the viewpoint of opening theory. What also drew special attention from a wide circle of chessplayers was the article, "About myself in particular, and my methods of preparing for tournaments – My tournament regimen."

This was the first time in chess literature that a maestro had written so honestly about his competitive regime, his system of preparing for a tournament, and of attaining analytical skill. The discussion was not about methods generally, but about the way he himself would prepare for tournaments. Such information great masters, as a rule, hold *inter familias,* or out of print. And this article was reprinted, *in toto* in Botvinnik's book. *Methods of Preparation for Events,* 1996.

Only once did Botvinnik stray from his recommendations, when he did the commentary for all 60 games of an event. This was the match-tournament for the title of Absolute Chess Champion of the USSR, the final prewar tournament, which took place in Leningrad and Moscow in 1941, with the participation of the six strongest chessplayers in the country. In 1947, Botvinnik's work was itself published in book form, and four years later, it underwent a second printing. In his detailed review of it, Alexei Sokolsky noted: "...outstandingly annotated games. Botvinnik's notes are characterized by objectivity, a deep evaluation of position from all sides, simplicity and clarity of exposition. This is why, by studying this book, every chessplayer will extract for himself much that is useful." (*Shakhmaty v SSSR,* 9/1949).

Besides these two game collections which were completely written by Botvinnik, there were also a number of books about tournaments, in which he participated, along with others, as annotator of some games. Among these were the following books: *VII All-Union Chess Tournament, Moscow 1931*; *Tournament of Masters, with the Participation of Euwe and Kmoch,* (four games with his notes); *The Second International Chess Tournament,* Moscow 1935 (seven games); *The Third International Chess Tournament, Moscow 1936* (eight games, including the only one he lost, in the seventh round, against Capablanca); and *The Chigorin Memorial* (9 games). By the way, this game collection came out under the general editorship of Botvinnik, and included his essay about

Chigorin. In it, the first Soviet world champion noted the significance of Chigorin's work for the progress of both his home country and the world's chess culture, as well as his prominent role in the development of a chess movement in Russia.

Four years later, after Botvinnik's death, the Interregional Governmental Fund released the book, *Match-Tournament for the World Championship, The Hague/Moscow 1948* which presented annotations by Keres for all the games, except those played by Botvinnik. Those games contained his own personal annotations. In addition, the book included the first publication of the diary Botvinnik maintained during the course of the event, and chess and psychological portraits of his opponents, as well as his plan of preparation for the greatest tournament of his life. These revealed the inner Botvinnik, both as a person and as a great chessplayer.

Selected Games
In connection with the interest shown by a wide circle of chessplayers in the creations of the USSR champion, and then first Soviet world champion, books of Botvinnik's best games, thoroughly annotated, would periodically appear. The first edition saw the light of day in 1938, and covered the period of his appearances from 1926 through 1937; the second edition appeared in 1949, and comprised his games from 1926 through 1946.

In the following years, the interest in the games of Botvinnik was satisfied thanks to many game collections from international tournaments and those USSR championships in which the sixth world champion was a participant.

In the years 1965-68, a three-volume set was published by V. D. Baturinsky – *The Chess Creations of Botvinnik*, in which Botvinnik's participation in national and international events of 1924 through 1967 was very accurately portrayed, and many of his articles during this period about different chess issues were presented. In 1970, Botvinnik stopped appearing in official tournaments. This fact defines the limit of the period of selected games in his book *A Half-Century of Chess*, which appeared in 1978 as part of the series, "Talented Chessplayers of the World." In it, he gathered and annotated 83 games from 1925 through 1970. Among his opponents were seven world champions: Alekhine (2 games), Capablanca (1), Euwe (2), Smyslov (5), Tal (3), Petrosian and Fischer (1 each). World championship candidates required more than twenty games: Reshevsky (1), Bronstein (2), Lilienthal, Kotov, Larsen (2 each), and one game each from Geller, Boleslavsky, Szabo, Taimanov, Gligoric, Najdorf, and Portisch. A number of games from the early period of the competitive career of Botvinnik against leading Soviet masters at the end of the 1920s and 1930s was also included – Levenfish, Alatortsev, Rabinovich, Ryumin, Rauzer, Chekhover, *et al*. The book also included 10 studies by Botvinnik, 1925-1958, and the articles, "My Methods of Preparing for Events. A Tournament Regime." and "Is Chess An Art?"

Achieving the Aim

Back in his youth, Mikhail Botvinnik dedicated his whole life to the achievement of the highest competitive and creative successes in the art of chess, having as his final goal winning the title of world champion. He focused on this goal unswervingly and consistently, showing implacable will and iron character. In the book, *Achieving the Aim* (1978 Molodaya Gvardia), Botvinnik talked frankly about all the twists and turns of his complicated life and competitive career, along with his teaching activity in the realm of electro-technology and cybernetics. In later years, he wrote books frequently of an autobiographical character, in which he presented many new interesting episodes from his life and teaching activities, including his encounters with world champions Lasker, Capablanca, Alekhine and Euwe.

From Electronics to Cybernetics

Parallel with chess, Botvinnik occupied himself from his earliest years, right up until the end of his life, with solving difficult scientific problems – first, in the field of electro-technology; and then, starting in the 1960s, in cybernetics – more accurately, in the creation of a machine that would play chess at the grandmaster level. In the first of these he succeeded, defending both his master's and his doctoral dissertations, and moving to the practical application of the theoretical problems resolved. Botvinnik's book, *Regulating the Stimulation and Statistical Stability of the Synchronous Machine* (1950 Gosenergoizdat), laid out a method for calculating the coefficients of regulation, which had primary significance for the transfer of energy by alternating current over very long distances. This book was, naturally, aimed at engineers occupied with regulating the initialization of electric generators.

Four of Botvinnik's books, issued in 1968 and 1969, were aimed at a much greater audience: they were dedicated to the programming of computers to play chess. They were aimed at science workers, teachers and students, and also other readers who showed interest in these problems. Botvinnik's book, *An Algorithm for Playing Chess* (1968 Nauka) had a print run of 25,000 and quickly sold out: it attracted interest, not only among mathematicians with whom the former world champion was engaging, but many chessplayers, as well. Contrary to the tendency then holding sway in the world, increasing a program's power by increasing the speed at which it evaluated moves and variations, Botvinnik suggested the idea of creating a program that would play like a real chessplayer, throwing out unnecessary moves first. Two years later, the book was published in the USA.

In 1970, having ended his playing career, Botvinnik dedicated himself totally to the creation of an artificial chessplayer. Continuing to expand his method, and also putting forward the idea of teaching the machine himself to play chess while working out with it an algorithm for chess play, Botvinnik decided to acquaint a wider group of readers with the first results of his work. *The Cybernetic Goal of the Game* (1975 Sovietskoye Radio) was published with a first run of 57,000 (!) copies. In it, the author explains in detail his solving idea and the process of playing an inexact task with limited information, by reducing that information with the "horizon method" (a person sees the world around him only to the limit of the horizon).

Botvinnik, calling his program "Pioneer," continued to work on completing the algorithm of a chess master. In 1979, the same publisher issued his next book, *Solving Inexact Sorting Tasks*. In it, he laid out the general theory of solving such tasks, analogous to chessplaying, and gave a partial description of his program, "Pioneer." His opinion was that it could also be used in practice, in the field of economics, involved with the administrative aspect of government.

Ten years later, in the book *A Chess Method of Solving Sorting Tasks* (Sovietsky Sport), Botvinnik demonstrated practical results obtained by his "Pioneer" program, in the analysis of some chess positions and studies, and also in the solution of strictly economic tasks, i.e., the yearly planning of repairs to the construction of electric stations on the scale of the EES, comparing the weekly graphic of the load of the energy system, etc.

In the foreword to his monograph, Botvinnik said that he started working on a chess program for computer back at the start of the 1950s, and occupied himself systematically with this problem from 1963; and his programming team got to work in 1972. "And why did the work take so long?," asks Botvinnik. And immediately, he replies: "Partly because of the searching nature of this difficult task, and partly because of the insufficient speed and capacity of the operating memory of the computer they were using." Alas, these reasons prevented him, until the end of his days, from ever effectively carrying out the tasks he had thought up in the field of cybernetics.

Analytical and Critical Works

That was the name of Botvinnik's four-volume series about his fundamental work in chess. It came out from 1984-87, and was his contribution to the treasury of chess art. The first three volumes correspond to three periods of his chess career (1923-41, 1942-56, and 1957-70). They included his 380 best tournament and match games, as well as 28 training games. But if the names of some of Botvinnik's sparring-partners were quite well known – Ragozin, Kan, Averbakh, Furman, then it was surprising to find, in 1952, Bronstein playing that role (within a year after their world championship match!) and Petrosian (11 years after the chess crown was lifted from his shoulders!).

On the other hand, there were more than a few surprises waiting for readers in this work, including the profiles which preceded the games in each volume, and the characterization what was different about each stage in the life and creations. Each of the three periods was named: (1) From Chigorin's *Chess Pages* to the Foot of the Chess Olympus; (2) Heavy Art Thou, O Crown of Monomakh!; and (3) From Tournaments and Matches – Understanding the Foundation of the Game.

The fourth volume also turned out to be an interesting collection of new and previously published articles and memoirs. There were also a new section, "Portraits and Descriptions." Here there were profiles of Chigorin; Em. Lasker, Capablanca, Euwe; Keres,

Ragozin, Kotov, Grigoriev, Model, Goldberg; musicians Oistrakh and Gippels; and cyberneticists Lyapunov and Glushkov, etc.

Other sections of that volume included "Creative Problems," "Tournaments and Matches," "Notes Along the Way," "Chess Cybernetics," "Analyses," "Compositions," and finally, "Achieving the Aim."

A perusal of Botvinnik's sections and profiles underscores the breadth of his interests and views, the depth at which he grasped the chess life of the country and the world. He not only actively participated in and outstripped everyone else in the chess world, but also constantly thought about, and strove to do everything possible for its progress.

But the creative legacy of the sixth world champion was not exhausted by these volumes and some dozens of the books that he had published nationally and internationally. This is attested to by the postmortem publication of new books, many of which were prepared by him, but that he had not managed to have published during his lifetime. And there were others that were edited from various archive materials whose publication was unintended, which once again revealed the personality of this great chessplayer.

Chapter Five

Timeless Times

Epilogue

Botvinnik and his times gradually moved into the "endgame" in which the ex-world champion's opposition held an indubitable and, above all, a psychological advantage... But Botvinnik held fast, confidently and peacefully, although much that had previously seemed unshakable collapsed. In the mid-1950s, together with Vladimir Alatortsev, Vyacheslav Ragonzin, and Vassily Smyslov, he managed to obtain an old building on Moscow's Gogolevsky Boulevard for a chess club, and he did much to convert it into a center of the capital's chess life. Since the 1990s, the chess club, open to all, has belonged to the Russian Chess Federation.

Together with Max Euwe, Botvinnik fought to have FIDE run the chess world. Then, at the beginning of the 1990s, Garry Kasparov decided that he would play for the world championship outside the sphere of that international organization. The dissolution of the Soviet Union also did not help the advance of chess, as it deprived the national chess

The encounter between Botvinnik and the times enters its endgame phase.

movement of the former support from the government.

Towards the end of his life, Botvinnik was striving to finish two things: setting up his economic program and his chess program...

"Man's possibilities are limited," said Botvinnik. "Grasping the entire sphere of economics is not possible for him. A compute's assistance is necessary. A computer gives an objective solution of a task. For the program, it is all the same what form the property takes. It gives you maximum return. The task of directing the economy is simpler than chess. I have completed the economic program. But the chess program – that, I have not yet completed. It is more complex..."

His daughter, Olga Fyoshkina, wrote an essay, "My Father – Botvinnik," about his last days: *And for three days, he dictated a thesis of his beliefs about the chess program. The day before he died, he said that he had finished his thesis. He gave the following orders: 'No magnificent funerals [for me]. No chessplayers. Let me go out in peace!' Practically speaking, he only lied down – in the sense that he stopped getting up – two days before his death. His helplessness was a torment to him: "Why should I live on, in such a state?"*

His eyes closed. Quickly, his face became a peaceful, death mask. And that is how they buried him.

Mikhail Moiseevich Botvinnik died on May 5, 1995.

His body was buried in the Novodevichy cemetery in Moscow.

Literature
If we were to gather together all of the articles, sketches, and reminiscences published in the chess press of the USSR, and in many nations of the world, about Botvinnik, they would comprise a number of thick volumes. Many of the most powerful authorities in chess, as well as hundreds of well-known journalists and literati of the

20th century would find themselves depicted therein. All of the world champions have written about Botvinnik – his predecessors Lasker, Capablanca, Alekhine and Euwe, as well as those who followed him: Smyslov, Tal, Petrosian, Spassky, and of course Karpov and Kasparov, who themselves felt the influence of the chess school conducted by the patriarch of Soviet chess...

The first book that was completely dedicated to Botvinnik came out in 1946 in Philadelphia (USA), and came from the pen of the well-known American master and historian, Fred Reinfeld – *Botvinnik the Invincible*. Presenting 62 of his games, among which were victories over Alekhine, Capablanca, Keres, Reshevsky, Fine, and Vidmar, Reinfeld practically foretold his victory in the coming struggle for the world championship: "Literally all the world considers Botvinnik the greatest of contemporary masters. Botvinnik is a deep and penetrating expert in playing chess. He knows how to concentrate his thinking, his will and resistance exceptionally well. The Soviet champion affords desperate resistance in a hopeless position – he does not lose heart when he's down. Nor does success turn his head."

Among books on Botvinnik which appeared when he was still alive, there are also notable works appearing in German: Hans Mueller's *Botvinnik Lehrt Schach* (1967), and by the well-known Soviet grandmaster and chess theoretician, Alexei Suetin, *Botvinnik – Schach-Genie* (Berlin, 1990).

But the greatest work on the sixth world champion was the three-volume work by Baturinsky, published in Moscow in 1965-69 – *Shakhmatnoye Tvorchestvo Botvinnika*. The monograph is notable, first and foremost, for the size of its games collection – 660 tournament and match games, 40 training games. In the three-volume set were also many works on theory, history, methods of preparation, and other problems.

Along with this fundamental work, there also appeared, both in the USSR and abroad, some books which were about Botvinnik's world championship matches. Among these were the monograph, *Botvinnik-Tal Match* (Riga, 1961). with brilliant commentaries on all of the games of the 1960 match, and the book by his trainer, Koblents, *A Chessplayer's Memories* (1986), which related, in many chapters, the story of the match, behind the scenes.

After the death of Botvinnik, more and more materials have appeared in chess periodicals and in chess books, by authors trying to think up something new that the sixth world champion brought to the art of chess, his role in the world history of chess. For example, the seventh world champion's, "Classic," in the magazine *Shakhmaty v Rossii* (1/1995) is of interest. Other articles included Ludek Pachman's "On the Death of the Russian Chess Legend – Dr. M. Botvinnik" in the magazine *Rochade Europa* (June 6, 1995); Genna Sosonko's "His Path to Immortality" in the magazine *64-Shakhmatnoye Obozreniye* (3/1997); and the sketch by Alexei Suetin, titled "Commander," in his book, *Chess Through the Prism of Time* (Moscow 1998). Although some of the conclusions of this article are debatable, its general conclusion is symptomatic: "Botvinnik's contribution, and his methods of positional play, like his means of preparing for events, were genuinely invaluable.

Botvinnik's creative path offers an entire school of the art of chess. His research of a number of standard positions forms a historic epoch in the understanding of chess' secrets. What he accomplished in the 1930s through the 1950s has long outlived his time.

A special edition of the magazine *Shakhmatnyi Peterburg*, published in September of 2001, and dedicated to the 90th anniversary of Botvinnik's birth, and to the 50th birthday of Karpov, was a valuable addition to the examination of the life and creativity of the sixthworld champion.

Garry Kasparov's presentation of Botvinnik in *My Great Predecessors* (vol. 2, Moscow 2003)) was the first attempt to analyze the games of the sixth world champion by means of computer diagnostics. The section, "My Teacher," gets special attention: in it, Kasparov tells in detail his "meetings with the great Master, and of the role he played in what I became."

The World Champions on Botvinnik

Emanuel Lasker Botvinnik' openings are worthy of close analysis, as is his deep positional understanding of the middlegame, and both favorably distinguish his play. The Nottingham tournament was a triumph for Botvinnik. He and his wife made an excellent impression upon the English public. As a chessplayer, he exceeded all their expectations (1936). One does not need to say anything about Botvinnik's achievements: they speak for themselves. In Moscow and Nottingham, the best of the best masters of the chess art were assembled, and none could demonstrate superiority over them... Botvinnik is a candidate for the world championship (1937).

José Raúl Capablanca I am convinced that Botvinnik, for example, would win a match against grandmaster Euwe, who, we know, will play a match with Alekhine for the world championship in 1935. Botvinnik's victory in the Moscow international tournament of 1935 would have brought him great satisfaction. This does not happen often that a young chessplayer achieves such brilliant success in such a very strong tournament (1935). Grandmaster Botvinnik has already become quite strong. I think that, in the forthcoming tournament at Nottingham, the fight for first place will be among Alekhine, Euwe, Botvinnik, Flohr and myself (1936). Botvinnik, in excellent competitive form, played well the entire tournament [Nottingham], without losing a game, winning several games in his best style (1936).

Alexander Alekhine A notable success (at the Nottingham tournament) for the most gifted of our young chessplayers: Botvinnik, champion of the Soviet Union, was not so unexpected, as he had already shown us at the two great Moscow tournaments of 1935 and 1936. His achievement at Nottingham underscores the fact that he is the most likely candidate to earn the title of world champion in the near future. Beside his enormous talent, he has every competitive quality that is of decisive importance for success – fearlessness, endurance, an exact sense for evaluating a position, and finally, youth (1936).

Max Euwe Botvinnik: a great combinative player, a fine positional master, a jeweler of the end-game – a many-sided fighter (1963).

Botvinnik's world record is too well known to stop there. For 13 years, he held the title of world champion; and for over thirty years, he belonged to the small group of elite chessplayer.

How does one characterize Botvinnik's style? More than anything, it was his willingness to fight; his willingness to seize the initiative, even with Black.

Botvinnik was always distinguished by his universality. He might have been compared to Emanuel Lasker, but he was much better equipped with technical mastery of the openings. As an analyst, Botvinnik has not, to this day, been excelled by anyone; his analysis of adjourned positions always proved itself the very acme of thoroughness.

During events, Botvinnik would have been an example of correctness; but he held out stubbornly for his rights, when evaluating the way in which a match or tournament was carried out. Botvinnik was honorable, but never went to extremes. I knew him to be a pleasant conversationalist, a good colleague, and a faultlessly honest person.

Over many years, I was fortunate enough to remain friends with Botvinnik, and many ways, he proved that friendship to me. Although it is possible that, more than anyone, he wanted me to become president of FIDE, more than once I was the object of his stern criticism regarding a few of my decisions. Botvinnik's observations always gave me food for thought, and in some cases made me alter my decisions.

A difference of opinion never adversely affected our friendship (1981).

Vassily Smyslov My rivalry with Botvinnik extended for over a decade, and I was fortunate enough to have played around one hundred games against such a remarkable chessplayer. At the time, we were both in the very flowering of our life force, and I think that the creative results of our encounters played no inconsiderable role in the advance of chess thought.

Mikhail Moiseevich and I belong to chessplayers of a single orientation –classical. But each of us defended his own principles and plans.

I want to add that, in spite of our sharp opposition and the most natural emotion surrounding our encounters, Botvinnik and I remained within the bounds of competitive correctness. Mikhail Moiseevich was a complicated person; some of his requirements seemed excessive, at the time. But everything is relative. And the conflicts of later world championships seem to be child's play, in comparison with them (1961).

Undoubtedly, Botvinnik held to classical views on the art of chess. He was a worthy successor to his great predecessors – Lasker, Capablanca and Alekhine. A clear strategic idea would shine through his game. In his character, he was a researcher; at the basis of his approach to chess creativity lay a search for truth. In a time when computers did not yet exist, Botvinnik, by his deep analyses, foretold the direction of modern chess, which makes extensive use of the accumulation and expansion of information, with the aid of computer science (1995).

Mikhail Tal I have probably met every one of the world's strongest chessplayers; my feelings for them were all different. Playing with Botvinnik, I always felt like a student, under the best of circumstances. We were all students – collegians, perhaps, with himself as the professor.

A former champion, and doctor of the physical sciences, Botvinnik considers that chess is a science. Our school of chess has a scientific approach to chess. And it is precisely in this scientific approach that home preparation, the psychological moment, enormous technique, and exceptional strength of will haves great significance And the synthesis of all this is what Botvinnik brought to the golden treasury that is chess.

Tigran Petrosian Mikhail Botvinnik, who has been leader of Soviet chess for these past 25 years, can serve as a good example for everyone. For chessplayers of the elder generation, he is an example of long-lived competitiveness. Young chessplayers can learn of him self-criticism, the ability to bring oneself to completion, and not to content themselves with what they have already attained. And on the whole, Botvinnik showed that diligence, persistent striving to achieve the aim, and will to win, will lead to the highest achievement (1958).

We all consider ourselves pupils of Mikhail Moiseevich Botvinnik, the acknowledged leader of Soviet chess. And future generations will also learn from his games (1963).

Boris Spassky Mikhail Moiseevich was our Patriarch; a chess academician. Playing against him was very hard – but instructive. And if, during post-mortem analysis, he would say, "Look, old man, you did not choose the right plan here," you did not try to argue with him – he would hit on the true plan, the first time.

The chess world is built like an enormous pyramid; and the king, who stands on top of it, is called upon to strengthen it. This limitless government has its administrative setup – FIDE. And Botvinnik has said, rightly, that the king of chess does not belong to himself alone.

Botvinnik himself was, first and foremost, a political, patriotic figure. Having shown himself as the builder of the Soviet chess school, he was obliged to become world champion – and so he became. Botvinnik was a dedicated Communist citizen. It is true that I was friends with him for a while, and knew that, beneath that dry exterior, he was, in fact, a responsive, warm human being.

Robert Fischer The most powerful impression Botvinnik left on me was his self-discipline. He became a school for how to avoid the superficial. I find myself also under the influence of his self-control and iron logic.

Anatoly Karpov Next (after Steinitz) were the changes noted by Alekhine, but introduced and developed by Botvinnik – the scientific approach to chess.

And Botvinnik started working in this direction. His scientific approach gradually solidified into his primary approach. In my opinion, he did not concern himself, at home, with questions such as, for example, a new move or new idea somewhere around the 15th move, in some variation or other. He would work out an entire system. That was his style. To a great extent, chess was still fertile ground, and he was the "first to plow" it. Today, we have to be satisfied with novelties on the 12th or 15th move. And you do not always get that far! Botvinnik could allow himself lengthy breaks from the game – let's say, he would not play for a long while: take a year off from chess, and do scientific work for a while.

Botvinnik laid the foundation for a serious scientific approach to chess. What does that mean? ... This sharpening of the struggle required chessplayers to prepare themselves, in order to endure previously unheard physical and nervous burdens.

Garry Kasparov My chess worldview was mostly formulated under the influence of the former world champion, Mikhail Botvinnik. I am certain that the five years I spent in the Botvinnik school, from 1973 to 1978, played a decisive role in shaping me as a chessplayer, and defined the path of my later improvement. Of special importance, in my view, was the absorption of Mikhail Moiseevich's chief "axiom": the necessity of constant analytical work: above all, the analysis of one's own games. Following this rule unswervingly, through the years, I was able distinctly to see that it was precisely here that was laid the foundation for the unceasing growth of chess mastery (1985).

Mikhail Moiseevich Botvinnik is indubitably one of the greatest of champions, a genuine chess innovator – a whole epoch unto himself. His style was composed of a deep strategy, based on serious opening and psychological preparation, a high level of technique, and finely adjusted positional and combinative decisions. This scientific approach allowed Botvinnik to devise a system, never before seen, of event preparation, including fundamental examinations of the openings, a systematic study of the opponents' styles, and a scrupulous examination of his own games, with the necessary publication, so that his analysis might then be criticized by others.

Botvinnik coolly removed the cover of secrecy from chess, always comparing it to life situations. He called chess a typical undefined task, like those that people have to resolve in their daily lives, and said, "For the resolution of undefined tasks, it is very important to reduce the size of the problem, in order not to get confused – only then will you have a chance to resolve it successfully. Thus, it would be a mistake to believe that chess does not reflect objective reality. It reflects what a person thinks."

This was a typical Botvinnik approach to chess – as well as to life in general: reducing a problem to directed measurements. I remember that, back in the mid-70s, he warned me against wandering into complexity for complexity's sake, and said to me one day: "You will never become Alekhine, if the variations run your life, instead of the other way around." I was embarrassed by this. But Botvinnik was wise, and of course he was right... In later years, he came out strongly against speedier time-controls, and tried to make a powerful chessplaying program: "Then, grandmasters would have to fight against opponents that would be worthy of them – computers; and then they could return to serious play. This would appear to hold out hope for a return to the best in chess."

He is rightly considered the Patriarch of the Soviet chess school – that so-far unstudied 20th-century phenomenon (2003).

Vladimir Kramnik Botvinnik, of course, represented a new era in chess. I would call him the first real chess professional; the first person to understand that one's result, in chess, did not depend on just the extent of one's ability to play chess. He was the first to think about complex preparation for events: not merely the openings, but sleep also – and one's regime, physical readiness – in this he was, of course, a pioneer.

In pure chess talent Botvinnik was no Capablanca; but he was able to achieve exceptional levels in other components – in his character, his preparation; and to achieve this was in fact no easier. In these areas he was a genius.

On the whole, Botvinnik brought to chess a very great number of conceptual ideas.

I knew Botvinnik in the later years of his life, and he made a very pleasant impression on me.

Of course, Botvinnik could be very categorical. This was, undoubtedly, his strength; it seems to me that, according to his character, he *had* to be categorical (2004).

The "Mikhail Botvinnik Fund"

Created in Moscow by the chess public in 1995, with the goal of maintaining the legacy of the five-time world champion. Anatoly Karpov was elected president. The fund developed energetic activity above all towards the publication of books on the basis of Botvinnik's unpublished material, and also of the reminiscences of contemporaries. The fund set itself the goal of re-establishing the Botvinnik school, and opening a museum, dedicated to the life and works of the sixth world champion. In the fund's first decade, it put out eight books of the archived materials, among which were all eight of Botvinnik's matches for the world championship, and several new editions of some of his books.

The M. M. Botvinnik Memorial

Dedicated to the 90th anniversary of his birth, was held from November 30-December 9, 2001 in Moscow, in the Hall of Columns, Union House. Previously, the 1948 encounters, after which Botvinnik was pronounced the sixth world champion, had been held here. This time, in honor of this notable date, a super-match between two of his students was held. The 13th and the 14th world champions, Garry Kasparov and Vladimir Kramnik played four games with the classic time-control, which concluded with a score of 2-2; then six games of "quick chess" – 3-3; and finally, 10 "blitz" games, which ended 5½-3½ in favor of Kasparov (+4 -1 =5). Grandmaster Igor Zaitsev, reporting on the match, wrote: "In the end, we got a most impressive three-level handicap of 20 games!" Interestingly, he further noted, the result of the lightning contest was about the same as that between Em. Lasker and Capablanca, in the summer of 1914 in Berlin, which wound up with the score 6½-3½ in favor of the Cuban.

Significant Dates in the Life and Works of Mikhail Botvinnik

August 17, 1911 In the little town of Repino, near Petersburg, a second son is born to the family of Serafima and Moishe Botvinnik. They name him Mikhail.

September 1918 Mikhail starts school at the 157th Unified Workers' School, which was previously known as the Vyborgsky 8-class Commercial Academy of Gherman.

1923 An acquaintance of his elder brother teaches Mikhail to play chess. Soon, he enters his first school tournament, where he scores 50%.

1924 Botvinnik studies chess literature – the handbooks of Grekov and. Nenarokov, the games of Emanuel Lasker, a collection of issues of the Chigorin magazine, *Shakhmatny listok* (1876, 1877).

June 1, 1924 Botvinnik is accepted into the ranks of the Petrograd chess collective.

January 1925 "I easily took first place and the first category," wrote Botvinnik, recalling one of the tournaments of his long-ago youth.

November 20, 1925 Botvinnik is included in a number of participants in a simultaneous exhibition given by world champion Capablanca, and scores a memorable victory.

Spring 1926 He plays in the final of the championship of Leningrad, and shares second/third places.

November 1926 The 15-year-old's first excursion over the border, in the Stockholm-Leningrad match, turns out successfully. Botvinnik wins his mini-match 1½-½ against Stoltz, who will later become a Swedish grandmaster.

June 26-August 1, 1927 A double-round tournament with six leading Leningrad chess-players. Botvinnik takes second place, behind Romanovsky, and wins the right to play in the final of the Fifth USSR championship.

September 26-October 25, 1927 Moscow. Botvinnik shares fifth/sixth place in the Fifth USSR championship, and receives the title of Master of Sport in Chess.

August 1928 Botvinnik successfully completes his exams for the Polytechnic Institute, but because of his "social birth" is only allowed to continue his studies in February 1929.

Spring 1930 Botvinnik wins a Leningrad masters' tourney, and receives first prize, a German chess clock.

December 3-March 23, 1930/31 Botvinnik wins the championship of Leningrad, with 14 points out of 17 (+12 -1, =4).

Summer 1931 Botvinnik carries out his student practice in Dnepropetrovsk.

October 1-November 11, 1931 Moscow. In the Seventh USSR championship, Botvinnik confidently demonstrates his superiority, outstripping second-place Nikolai Ryumin by two points, and 3½ points ahead of Vladimir Alatortsev, Fedor Bohatyrchuk, Boris Verlinsky, and Mikhail Yudovich, who share third/sixth places.

September 1932 For the second time, Botvinnik becomes champion of Leningrad.

December 1932 "In December of 1932, I was made a candidate for the electro-mechanical faculty." Botvinnik

November 28-December 19, 1933 Moscow/Leningrad. A match against Czech grandmaster Salo Flohr became, for Botvinnik, a serious test and trial of his preparedness to play against the strongest players of the West. A drawn outcome (6-6) satisfied both players and organizers.

February 1934 Two months after the match, Botvinnik publishes his first book, devoted to the encounter with Flohr. In the preface to it, N.V. Krylenko writes that the match "emphasized that, in the sense of quality of play we have equaled, and as far as the scope of our chess movement goes, we have surpassed bourgeois Europe."

August 17-September 1, 1934 A tournament of the leading Soviet masters, with the participation of world championship candidate Max Euwe and the Austrian master Hans Kmoch takes place in the Great Hall of the Leningrad Philharmonic; the event is won by Botvinnik.

December-January, 1934/35 Hastings. Botvinnik plays in his first foreign event, sharing fifth/sixth places.

February 15-March 15, 1935 The Second Moscow International Tournament takes place in the Moscow Fine Arts Museum, with Capablanca and Emanuel Lasker participating. The battle for first is mainly between Botvinnik, Flohr and

Lasker. At the end, first and second prizes are shared between the younger players. Botvinnik attains the rank of grandmaster. The people's commissar (minister) of heavy industry, G. K. Ordzhonikidze, awards him an automobile and sets Botvinnik up with an elevated candidate's stipend.

April 28, 1935 Leningrad. 21-year old Gaiane Davidovna Ananova, a ballerina with the Kirov (Mariinskovy) Theater of opera and ballet, becomes Botvinnik's wife.

May 14-June 8, 1936 In the Third Moscow International tournament, Botvinnik and Capablanca wage the main battle for first place. At the finish, fate smiles upon the Cuban grandmaster.

August 10-28, 1936 The "Event of the Century" at Nottingham turns out to be one of the strongest in the previous 40 years (since 1899). Four world champions of various eras against four young candidates! And as the "oracles" foretold, Botvinnik and Capablanca win, scoring 10 points, and finishing a half-point ahead of Reshevsky, Fine and Euwe. After the tournament, Alekhine acknowledged that "Botvinnik has every chance to become world champion."

June 28, 1937 Leningrad. Botvinnik defends his doctoral dissertation at the Politechnical Institute. Botvinnik's work is dedicated to the electro-technical problem – the so-called "powerful" regulation of stimulation in the inertial magnetic flow of a synchronous machine...

October 5-November 10, 1937 Moscow/Leningrad. Match for the USSR championship between Botvinnik and Grigori Levenfish, the winner of the 1937 national championship in Tbilisi. After eight games, Botvinnik amasses a sizable advantage, 5-3. But Levenfish succeeds in leveling the score, defending his title.

November 2-27, 1938 The AVRO tournament in Holland is Botvinnik's next test, and he survives it honorably, taking third place and playing a number of brilliant games. His victory over Capablanca becomes one of the highlights of Botvinnik's career;.

January 1939 The Soviet government decides to organize and finance a match for the world championship between Alekhine and Botvinnik. But correspondence on the match is broken off as the Second World War begins.

April 15-May 16, 1939 Leningrad. The 11th USSR championship is Botvinnik's third triumph in the national event.

1939 In Botvinnik's book, about the eleventh national championship, he publishes an article, "My methods of preparation for tournaments, and tournament regime."

May 2-29, 1940 Leningrad. Botvinnik wins a 12-game training match against Ragozin by a score of 7½ -2½ (+5, -0, =7).

September 5-October 3, 1941 A match-tournament for the title of Absolute Champion of the USSR proceeds with the clear superiority of Botvinnik, who wins his matches with all of his opponents and outdistances second-place Paul Keres by 2½ points.

August 19, 1941 Exempted from mobilization by reason of age, Botvinnik and his wife evacuate to the town of Molotov (Perm).

April 1942 The family of Botvinnik experiences a long-awaited addition – daughter Olga.

January 1943 Botvinnik is set to doing foresting, and realizes that that sort of work would spoil his appetite for mental exertion for quite a while. He writes a letter to Molotov, and soon receives a reply through the highest of channels: "Comrade Botvinnik must maintain his fighting form in chess, and secure the time necessary to develop himself further."

April 20-May 16 Sverdlovsk. This first wartime tournament with the participation of Botvinnik ends in a brilliant triumph for him.

December 5-January 11, 1943/44 For the first time, Botvinnik participates in the championship of the capital *hors de concours* and takes first place (+11 -1 =3).

May 21-June 14, 1944 After moving his family to Moscow, Botvinnik again plays in the USSR championship. He wins the deciding game against Vasily Smyslov and takes first place, becoming national champion for the fifth time.

June 1-July 3, 1945 Moscow. In the final of the 14th USSR championship, Botvinnik was first once again, going through the entire tournament without losing a game, with 16 points out of 18, outdistancing second-place Isaak Boleslavsky by three points.

September 1-4, 1945 The famous double-round radio-match USSR-USA takes place, featuring the ten strongest chessplayers on each side. USSR champion Botvinnik plays on first board against the U.S. champion, Arnold Denker, and wins both games. The Soviet team's superiority is overwhelming: 15½-4½. "Great work, boys," was how Stalin characterized the outcome.

February 4, 1946 Botvinnik sends Alekhine a challenge to a match for the world title, offering to have it played in England. Negotiations are underway, suddenly ending when Alexander Alekhine unexpectedly dies (March 24).

August 12-September 7, 1946 In the Dutch town of Groningen, a strong international tournament takes place, the first since the end of the war. The principal rivalry is between Botvinnik and Euwe, At the finish, there was only a half-point between them: Botvinnik is the winner.

September 1946 During the USSR-USA match in Moscow, FIDE makes the historic decision to hold a match-tournament in 1948 for the world championship, inviting six players – Euwe, Botvinnik, Reshevsky, Fine, Smyslov, and Keres.

November 25-December 23 A Chigorin Memorial tournament is held in Moscow. Botvinnik is the winner, while his trainer, Vyacheslav Ragozin, takes second place. "The creative partnering turned out well for both," wrote Botvinnik.

1947 In Moscow, Botvinnik's book*, Match-tournament for the Title of Absolute Champion of the USSR in Chess: Leningrad-Moscow, 1941* is released. According to the author, this was his "best analytical work."

March 2-May 18, 1948 In Holland (The Hague) and USSR (Moscow), the match-tournament for the world championship among the five strongest players in the world (Euwe, Botvinnik, Keres, Smyslov and Reshevsky) takes place. Taking the lead from the outset, Botvinnik holds on to it until the end. As a result of his victory in this tournament, he becomes the sixth chess world champion.

December 1949 Turning from chess to academia, at the end of the year Botvinnik presents his work in electro-technology, in pursuit of his Doctorate in Science, to the instructional soviet of the G.M. Krizanovsky Institute of Energy.

January-June 1950 He occupies himself with the building of a dacha in the Nikolin Hill suburb of Moscow. He designs it himself, and supervises its construction. "A base for the improvement of health and occupations in chess was constructed." (Botvinnik)

March 15-May 11, 1951 Botvinnik's three-year break in chess practice nearly winds up costing him the champion's title. Having passed through the "sieve" of the candidates', Soviet grandmaster David Bronstein takes the lead in the world championship match. And only in the penultimate, 23rd game, did Botvinnik level the score. The match finally ends 12-12, allowing Botvinnik to retain the title.

June 28, 1951 Botvinnik'a second "defense" in six months. This time, it is for his doctoral dissertation. Of the 19 members of the learned Soviet, 14 vote "Yes"! The world champion becomes a Doctor of Science.

November 11-December 14, 1951 In Moscow, the 19th USSR championship takes place. Botvinnik was in the lead most of the way, but at the finish, he could not withstand the pressure – it was a "difficult year" for him – and finishes sharing fifth place, breaking his string of victories in the years 1941-48.

November 29-December 29, 1952 In the 20th USSR championship (Moscow), Botvinnik shares first/second places with Mark Taimanov, and quickly wins a subsequent match with him for the title of national champion.

March 16-May 13, 1954 Moscow. Botvinnik plays a second match for the world championship and draws again (12-12), but this time, against a new candidate, Vassily Smyslov, retaining his champion's title for another three years.

August 1954 At 43 years old, Botvinnik debuts in the worldwide Olympiad, leading the USSR team at the event in Amsterdam. The world champion was in good sporting form and turned in the best performance on first board.

February 11-March 15, 1955 Moscow. The 22nd championship, and the 12th in which Botvinnik participates. This tournament would be his last appearance in national championships. He shares third/sixth places, a half-point behind the winners, Keres and Smyslov.

September 1-25, 1956 Moscow. The 12th World Olympiad. Botvinnik, playing on first board, wins six games, and draws seven. He takes second place on board one, behind Denmark's Bent Larsen, drawing their mutual game.

October 8-November 2, 1956 Moscow. The Alekhine Memorial. Botvinnik goes through this event successfully (+8, -1, =6), sharing first/second places with Smyslov.

March 5-April 27, 1957 Moscow. Botvinnik's third match for the world championship and his second against Smyslov, who has once again won the candidates' tournament. This time, his opponent demonstrates not just the highest level of mastery, but also great will to win, while with his own play, Botvinnik is less than satisfied. By his own admission, he "...showed his lack of preparation. I displayed neither accurate opening systems, nor genuine skill in analysis of unfinished games, nor sporting stubbornness." Losing by a score of 9½-12½, he ends by ceding the title of world champion. He then begins preparations for his rematch.

March 4-May 8, 1958 As Alekhine did two decades before, Botvinnik manages to win the rematch. "Smyslov's loss had a psychological subtext – he underestimated his experienced opponent" (Botvinnik).

October 1-23, 1958 Munich. The 13th World Olympiad. Playing first board once again, he scores well, +7, -1, =4. "We played in an ancient hall: very beautiful, but dark. Because of nearsightedness, I was not playing, I was suffering," recalled Botvinnik. "When I lost to Dückstein, the Austrian, I needed a table lamp." In the final, Botvinnik played excellently.

1959 The FIDE Congress takes away the champion's right to a rematch, starting in 1963.

1960 Botvinnik's book is published by Gosenergoizdat: "Asynkronizirovannaya synkron-naya mashina" (which was translated by Oxford 4 years later), devoted to his scholarly research in the area of electro-technology. In the same year, the publishing house Iskusstvo is out with Botvinnik's work, *The Smyslov-Botvinnik*

Return Match for the World Championship, Moscow 1958. It was a collection of games which he annotated. At the back of the book his essay, "Is Chess An Art?" appears. Botvinnik is selected as president of the "USSR-Netherlands Society."

March 15-May 7, 1960 Moscow. Two Mikhails, 48-year old Botvinnik and 23-year old Tal, fight a battle for the world's top title. The entire chess world "roots" for the young pretender, exulting in his combinative genius. Botvinnik the chessplayer loses the match +2, -6, =13. But Botvinnik the researcher manages to identify the "creative gaps" in the play of the talented player from Riga, and vows to exploit them in the last return match FIDE was going to allow him.

March 15-May 12, 1961 This time, Botvinnik wins the match against Tal convincingly, +10, -5, =6. He is soon awarded the order of the Workers' Red Banner. Presenting this honor, the President of the Presidium of the Upper Soviet of the USSR, Leonid Brezhnev says: "I was rooting for you, while my son was rooting for Tal..."

December 27-January 5, 1961/62 Hastings. After a 27-year hiatus, Botvinnik participates in this traditional holiday tournament, and confidently finished in first place (+7 -0 =2).

September 16-October 31, 1962 Varna. The 15th World Olympiad. Here, Botvinnik plays his first (and last) game with the 19-year-old Robert Fischer, who manages to find an improvement in one of the variations of the Grünfeld Defense, and gets the advantage. However, in overnight analysis, Botvinnik and his cohort on the team, Efim Geller, finds a saving line in a difficult rook endgame.

March 23-May 20, 1963 Botvinnik's seventh world championship match takes place, like the previous ones, in Moscow. This time his opponent is Tigran Petrosian. Known for his defensive prowess, Petrosian is a formidable foe and defeats Botvinnik 12½-8½ (+5 -2 =15) to become the ninth world chess champion.

1963 On the initiative of master Grigori Goldberg with the sports club "Trud," an All-Union children's chess school is organized, overseen by Botvinnik. Among those in attendance is future world champion Anatoly Karpov, future grandmasters Yuri Balashov, Yuri Razuvaev, Naum Rashkovsky, Gennady Timoshchenko, and others.

1964 Botvinnik starts working on the creation of artificial chess intelligence; he will dedicate the next 30 years of his life to it.

November 2-25, 1964 Tel Aviv. The "promised land" was the site of the next, 16th Olympiad. Appearing on second board, Botvinnik scores 9 points out of 12 (+7 -1 =4).

May 1965 Botvinnik makes the acquaintance in Moscow of the gifted American mathematician and author of information theory Claude Shannon, who is well acquainted with a number of the works of the ex-world champion on the theme of "People and Machines. Over the Board." They play some chess, and Botvinnik observes that "Shannon plays at the strength of today's computer."

1965 and 1968 August Appearances with Euwe and Muhring in cities of Siberia and the Far East.

1965-68 A three-volume set, *The Chess Creativity of Botvinnik*, appears in Moscow. It features 700 games, from 1924 to 1967, as well as published articles. The book was put together by Baturinsky, working together with Botvinnik.

July 5-15, 1966 "Once again, I am playing chess," as Botvinnik could have ironically said to himself at the International Tournament at Amsterdam. "This tourney is organized by the company IBM. But we are playing in a modern church!" As before, this trip to Holland ends up being one more success for him.

September 23-October 5, 1966 Moscow. Appearing in the USSR team championship, Botvinnik defeats his old rivals Smyslov and Keres, in excellent style, along with the challenger for the world title, Boris Spassky.

December 28-January 6, 1966/67 His third appearance at Hastings, this time assembling one of the youngest assortments of players in the history of these holiday events – Balashov, Mecking, Keene, Hartston... But it was the "eternally young" Botvinnik who wins! After the close of the tournament he toured "chess Albion" as a guest.

1967-68 Over the course of six months, Botvinnik plays in two powerful international tournaments with Smyslov – in Palma de Mallorca and Monte Carlo. Truly, their "evil genius" is the normally peaceable Dane, Bent Larsen, who has studied Russian well, and twice "barely" outstrips the Russians by a half-point in each tournament.

January 1969 Botvinnik's final victory in an international tournament came his way in the Dutch town of Wijk aan Zee (first/second places with Geller).

March 29-April 5, 1970 The "Match of the Century" at Belgrade, in which a team from the USSR meets a team from the rest of the world in four rounds of play. Botvinnik played eighth board, against the Yugoslav grandmaster Milan Matulovic, and achieves an important victory for his team, 2½-1½.

April 18-May 8, 1970 Leiden (Holland). Botvinnik closes out his sporting career with a four-player match-tournament. His result, +1, -2, =8. "I had a hard time playing. In the school where the tournament was held, it was damp, and unventilated. I did not get any creative satisfaction out of my play..." (Botvinnik).

1970-1980 Distancing himself from tournament practice does not mean leaving chess entirely, As before, Botvinnik continues to supervise his chess school. Among his students were the those who would become some of the strongest grandmasters in the world, Garry Kasparov, Artur Yusupov, Elena Akhmylovskaya, Anna Akhsharumova, and many others.

1975 The next book by Botvinnik appears, from the publishers "Sovietsky Radio": *The Cybernetic Playing Objective.*

December 1976 Botvinnik's chess computer program was entitled "Pioneer!"

1977 Botvinnik attends the second computer world chess championship in Toronto.

1978 The publishing house "Fyskultura and Sport" publishes Botvinnik's monograph, "A Half-century of Chess," as part of its series, "Gifted Chessplayers of the World." It presents 83 of his best games (1925-70), and 10 studies, as well as two works, "Methods of Preparation for Events," and "Is Chess An Art?"

1978-1987 The publishing house "Molodaya Gvardia" releases Mikhail Botvinnik's autobiographical *Achieving the Aim.* It is the first time in chess history that a world champion has delved so deeply and honestly into events of his life. It was soon translated into other languages. Years passed. "Times have changed, and many events can now be spoken of with greater candor," says the author. And a second edition of these reminiscences appears in 1987. Finally, after another seven years, a third volume is put together – which appears after his passing, in 1997.

1979 Botvinnik's next book appears, *From Chessplayer to Machine.*

1979-1989 Under the heading, "Cybernetics," the publishing house "Sovietskoye Radio" releases a new work by Botvinnik, *The Resolution of Inaccurately Addressed Tasks.* Ten years later, in 1989, the publishing house "Sovietsky Sport" publishes his monograph, *A Chess Method of Solving Addressed Tasks.* In it, he attempted to depict "the algorithm of searching for the move by a chess master, which forms the basis of the chess program "Pioneer."

1983 Journey to the fourth world computer chess championship in New York. He also meets with Fine, Reshevsky, and Capablanca's widow, Olga. The publishing house "Sovietskaya Rossiya," under the heading "Shakhmatnoye Isskustvo," releases the book *Episodes of Chess Battles.*

1984-87 The publishing house, "Physkultura and Sport" releases Botvinnik's 4-volume work, *Analytical and Critical Works.* The first three volumes contain 380 of his best games, played in tournaments and matches. The fourth volume has articles and reminiscences, written during the time of Botvinnik's lengthy creative and sporting activities.

1990 The Italian Chess Association awards Botvinnik the Gioacchino Greco prize for "A Life Given to Chess."

August 1991 Botvinnik travels to Brussels, where he observes the quarterfinals of the candidates' matches, and celebrates his 80th birthday.

May 5, 1995 Moscow. Mikhail Botvinnik passes away after a serious illness. His body is interred in the Novodevichy Cemetery alongside his wife and mother.

Tournament Record

			W	L	D	Place
1926	Leningrad	Semi-finals 5th City Ch.	11	0	1	1
1926	Leningrad	5th City Ch.	6	1	2	2/3
1927	Leningrad	Tmt.	6	1	3	2
1927	Moscow	5th USSR Ch.	9	4	7	5/6
1928/29	Leningrad	Teachers' Union Ch.	8	0	5	1
1929	Odessa	Quarter-finals 6th USSR Ch.	6	0	2	1
1929	Odessa	Semi-finals 6th USSR Ch.	2	2	1	3/4
1930	Leningrad	Masters Tmt.	1	1	1	-
1930/31	Leningrad	6th City Ch.	12	1	4	1
1931	Moscow	Semi-finals, 7th USSR Ch.	6	2	1	2
1931	Moscow	7th USSR Ch.	12	2	3	1
1932	Leningrad	9th City Ch.	9	0	2	1
1932/33	Leningrad	Masters Tmt.	6	2	2	1
1933	Leningrad	Masters Tmt.	7	0	6	1/2
1933	Leningrad	8th USSR Ch.	11	2	6	1
1934	Leningrad	Masters Tmt.	5	1	5	1
1934/35	Hastings	International Tmt.	3	2	4	5/6
1935	Moscow	International Tmt.	9	2	8	1/2
1935	Moscow	International Tmt.	7	1	10	2
1936	Nottingham	International Tmt.	6	0	8	1/2
1938	Leningrad	Semi-finals 11th USSR Ch.	12	1	4	1
1938	Holland	AVRO	3	2	9	3
1939	Leningrad	11th USSR Ch.	8	0	9	1
1940	Moscow	12th USSR Ch.	8	4	7	5/6
1941	Leningrad/Moscow	Absolute Ch.	9	2	9	1
1943	Sverdlovsk	Tmt.	7	0	7	1
1943/44	Moscow	23rd City Ch.	11	1	3	1
1944	Moscow	13th USSR Ch.	11	2	3	1
1945	Moscow	14th USSR Ch.	14	0	4	1
1946	Groningen	International Tmt.	13	3	3	1
1947	Moscow	Chigorin Memorial	8	1	6	1
1948	The Hague/Moscow	World Ch. Match/Tmt.	10	2	8	1
1951	Moscow	19th USSR Ch.	6	3	8	5
1952	Budapest	Maroczy Memorial	7	2	8	3/5
1952	Moscow	20th USSR Ch.	9	1	9	1/2
1954	Amsterdam	11th Olympiad	6	0	5	-
1955	Moscow	22nd USSR Ch.	7	3	9	3/4
1956	Moscow	12th Olympiad	6	0	7	-
1956	Moscow	Alekhine Memorial	8	1	6	1/2
1958	Munich	13th Olympiad	7	1	4	-
1958	Vageningen	International Tmt.	3	0	2	1
1959	Tbilisi	2nd USSR Spartakiad	1	0	6	-
1960	Leipzig	14th Olympiad	8	0	5	-
1961	Oberhausen	2nd European Team Ch.	4	1	4	-
1961/62	Hastings	International Tmt.	7	0	2	1
1962	Stockholm	International Tmt.	8	0	1	1
1962	Varna	15th Olympiad	5	1	6	-
1963	Amsterdam	International Tmt.	3	0	2	1
1964	Moscow	USSR Team Ch.	3	0	3	-
1964	Tel-Aviv	16th Olympiad	7	1	4	-

1965	Noordwijk	International Tmt.	5	0	2	1
1965	Hamburg	3rd European Team Ch.	2	3	3	-
1966	Moscow	USSR Team Ch.	5	2	2	-
1966/67	Hastings	International Tmt.	5	1	3	1
1967	Moscow	4th USSR Spartakiad	5	1	2	-
1967	Palma de Mallorca	International Tmt.	9	1	7	2/3
1968	Monte Carlo	International Tmt.	5	0	8	2
1969	Beverwijk	International Tmt.	6	0	9	1/2
1969	Belgrade	International Tmt.	5	3	7	7
1970	Leiden	International Tmt.	1	2	9	3/4

Match Record

1933	Moscow/Leningrad	Flohr	2	2	8
1937	Moscow/Leningrad	Levenfish	5	5	3
1940	Leningrad	Ragozin	5	0	7
1951	Moscow	Bronstein	5	5	14
1953	Moscow	Taimanov	2	1	3
1954	Moscow	Smyslov	7	7	10
1957	Moscow	Smyslov	3	6	13
1958	Moscow	Smyslov	7	5	11
1960	Moscow	Tal	2	6	13
1961	Moscow	Tal	10	5	6
1963	Moscow	Petrosian	2	5	15
1970	Belgrad	Matulovic	1	0	3

Bibliography

Books and brochures by Botvinnik

11th All-Union Chess Championship, Moscow/Leningrad 1939
Achieving the Aim, Moscow 1978
Alekhine-Euwe: Return Match for the World Championship, Moscow/Leningrad
    1939; 2nd ed. Moscow 2002
An Algorithm for Playing Chess, 1968
Analytical and Critical Works, vols. 1-4, Moscow 1984-1987
Botvinnik-Smyslov, Match for the World Championship, 2nd ed., Moscow 1957
Botvinnik's Best Games, 1947-1970, Leningrad 1977
A Chess Method of Resolving Sorting Tasks, Moscow 1989
Concerning the Chess Match for the World Championship, Stenographed Lectures,
    Moscow 1954
Concerning the Cybernetic Goal of the Game, Moscow 1975
Concerning the Solving of Indefinite Selecting Tasks, Moscow 1979
Dr. Michail Botvinnik, Hamburg 1959
Episodes of Chess Battles, Moscow 1983
Flohr-Botvinnik Match, Leningrad 1934
From Chessplayer to Machine, Moscow 1979
Geschichte, Stuttgart 1981
The Grünfeld-Indian Defense, Moscow 1979 (co-authored with Ya. Estrin)
A Half-Century of Chess, Moscow 1978
Match-tournament for the Title of Absolute Chess Champion of the USSR, 2nd ed.,
    Moscow 1951
Match-tournament for the World Championship, The Hague/Moscow 1948,
Kharkov 1999 (co-author, P.Keres)
Meine 100 schonsten Paartien 1925-1970, Heidelberg 1980
One Hundred Selected Games, Dover 1960
Schach in Russland: 1941-1945, Hollfeld 1979
Selected Games, 1926-1946, Moscow/Leningrad 1949
Selected Games: 1967-1970, Oxford, 1981
Smyslov-Botvinnik, World Championship Return Match, Moscow 1960
Soviet School of Chess, Moscow 1951
Three Matches of Anatoly Karpov, Moscow 1975
To the Goal. Memories. Games, Moscow 1997

Books on the Life and Works of Botvinnik

Alatortsev B., Stepanov A., *Botvinnik-Smyslov, Match for the World Championship*, Moscow 1954

Botvinnik-Tal Match, Riga 1961

Botvinnik's Best Games, Vol. 1-3, Olomouc 2000-2002

Baturinsky, V.D., ed., *The Chess Works of Botvinnik, Vols. 1-3*, Moscow 1965-1968

Botvinnik, I.Yu. ed., *Botvinnik-Bronstein Match*, Moscow 2001

Botvinnik, I.Yu. ed., *Botvinnik-Petrosian Match*, Moscow 2005

Botvinnik, I.Yu. ed., *Botvinnik-Tal Return Match*

Botvinnik, I.Yu. ed., *Portraits*, Moscow 2000

Botvinnik, I.Yu. ed., *The Three Botvinnik-Smyslov Matches*, Moscow 2004

Kasparov G. (co-written with D. Plisetsky), *Mikhail the Sixth* (in the series *My Great Predecessors*, vol. 2, Moscow 2003)

Levin K., *Mikhail Botvinnik*, Moscow 1951

Linder B. I., Linder I., M. *Mikhail Botvinnik* (in the book, *Kings of the Chess World*, Moscow 2001)

Müller H., *Botwinnik lehrt Schach!*, Wien-Stuttgart 1949

Pedersen S., *The Botvinnik Semi-Slav*, 2000

Reinfeld F., *Botvinnik the Invincible*, Philadelphia 1946

Soltis, Andy, *Mikhail Botvinnik: The Life and Games of a World Chess Champion*, McFarland 2014

Index of Games

(36) Kholmov-Botvinnik, Moscow 1963
|(37) Botvinnik-Petrosian, Moscow 1964
(38) Botvinnik-Keres, Moscow 1966
(39) Averbakh-Kotov, Zürich 1953
(40) Botvinnik-Kotov, Groningen 1946)
(41) Botvinnik-Levenfish, Moscow 1937 (m2)
(42) Botvinnik-Levenfish, Leningrad 1937 (m12)
(43) Botvinnik-Larsen, Leiden 1970
(44) Botvinnik-Alatortsev, Leningrad 1934
(45) Botvinnik-Kmoch, Leningrad 1934
(46) Alatortsev-Botvinnik, Leningrad 1930/31
(47) Chekhover-Botvinnik, Leningrad 1932
(48) Lilienthal-Capablanca, Hastings 1944/34
(49) Lilienthal-Botvinnik, Moscow 1940
(50) Matulovic-Botvinnik, Belgrade 1970
(51) Matulovic-Korchnoi, Sochi 1966
(52) Bronstein-Botvinnik, Moscow 1951 (m14)
(53) Botvinnik-Bronstein, Moscow 1951 (m23)
(54) Botvinnik-Smyslov, Moscow 1954 (m12)
(55) Botvinnik-Smyslov, Moscow 1954 (m18)
(56) Botvinnik-Smyslov, Moscow 1957 (m13)
(57) Smyslov-Botvinnik, Moscow 1958 (m1)
(58) Botvinnik-Smyslov, Moscow 1958 (m2)
(59) Tal-Botvinnik, Moscow 1960 (m9)
(60) Botvinnik-Tal, Moscow 1961 (m7)
(61) Tal-Botvinnik, Moscow 1961 (m14)
(62) Botvinnik-Petrosian, Moscow 1963 (m14)
(63) Petrosian-Botvinnik, Moscow 1963 (m11)
(64) Botvinnik-Euwe, The Hague 1948
(65) Botvinnik-Keres, The Hague 1948
(66) Botvinnik-Euwe, Moscow 1948
(67) Smyslov-Botvinnik, Moscow 1948
(68) Botvinnik-Reshevsky, Moscow 1948
(69) Keres-Botvinnik, Leningrad 1941
(70) Bondarevsky-Botvinnik, Moscow 1941
(71) Botvinnik-Padevsky, Monte Carlo 1968
(72) Benko-Botvinnik, Monte Carlo 1968
(73) Zhivstov-Botvinnik, Moscow 1943/44
(74) Ryumin-Botvinnik, Moscow 1935

(75)   Botvinnik-Lilienthal, Moscow 1936

(76)   Najdorf-Botvinnik, Groningen 1946

(77)   Najdorf-Fischer, Santa Monica 1966

(78)   Botvinnik-Larsen, Norway 1965

(79)   Botvinnik-Donner, Norway 1965

(80)   Alekhine-Botvinnik, Nottingham 1936

(81)   Botvinnik-Vidmar, Nottingham 1936

(82)   Gligoric-Botvinnik, Palma de Mallorca 1967

(83)   Petrosian-Botvinnik, Moscow 1963 (m5)

(84)   Petrosian-Spassky, Moscow 1966 (m10)

(85)   Botvinnik-Ragozin, Leningrad 1040 (m5)

(86)   Janowski-Reshevsky, New York 1922

(87)   Reshevsky-Capablanca, Margate 1935

(88)   Reshevsky-Botvinnik, Moscow 1955

(89)   Alekhine-Romanovsky, Petersburg 1909

(90)   Romanovsky-Botvinnik, Leningrad 1927

(91)   Ryumin-Capablanca, Moscow 1935

(92)   Ryumin-Botvinnik, Leningrad 1934

(93)   Szabo-Ståhlberg, Leipzig 1960

(94)   Botvinnik-Szabo, Hamburg 1965

(95)   Botvinnik-Konstantinopolsky, Sverdlovsk 1943

(96)   Smyslov-Botvinnik, Moscow 1954 (m9)

(97)   Smyslov-Botvinnik, Moscow 1957 (m6)

(98)   Smyslov-Eingorn, Moscow 1988

(99)   Botvinnik-Ryumin, Moscow 1931

(100) Botvinnik-Yudovich, Leningrad 1933

(101) Kotov-Botvinnik, Leningrad 1939

(102) Dubinin-Botvinnik, Leningrad 1939

(103) Smyslov-Botvinnik, Moscow 1944

(104) Lilienthal-Botvinnik, Moscow 1945

(105) Tolush-Botvinnik, Moscow 1945

(106) Botvinnik-Boleslavsky, Moscow 1945

(107) Botvinnik-Moiseev, Moscow 1951

(108) Bronstein-Botvinnik, Moscow 1952

(109) Taimanov-Botvinnik, Moscow 1953 (m5)

(110) Taimanov-Hort, Tallinn 1975

(111) Taimanov-Botvinnik, Moscow 1953 (m1)

(112) Botvinnik-Taimanov, Moscow 1953 (m4)

(113) Tal-Smyslov, Bled 1959 (1-0, 26)

(114) Botvinnik-Tal, Moscow 1960 (m6)

(115) Tal-Larsen, Yugoslavia 1965 (m10)

(116) Flohr-Botvinnik, Moscow 1933 (m6)

(117) Flohr-Vidmar, Nottingham 1936

(118) Botvinnik-Flohr, Leningrad 1933 (m9)

(119) Pliater-Botvinnik, Moscow 1947

(120) Botvinnik-Kottnauer, Moscow 1947

(121) Botvinnik-Ragozin, Leningrad 1927

(122) Ståhlberg-Nimzovich, Göteborg 1934

(123) Ståhlberg-Em. Lasker, Zürich 1934

(124) Denker-Botvinnik, 1945

(125) Botvinnik-Tal, Moscow 1961 (m21)

(126) Botvinnik-Portisch, Monte Carlo 1968

(127) Botvinnik-Euwe, Groningen 1946

(128) Botvinnik-Fischer, Varna 1962

(129) Rauzer-Botvinnik, Leningrad 1933

(130) Botvinnik-Capablanca, AVRO 1938

(131) Botvinnik-Tartakower, Nottingham 1936

(132) Botvinnik-Alexander, 1946

(133) Botvinnik-Keres, Moscow 1952

(134) Botvinnik-Donner, Amsterdam 1963

(135) Botvinnik-Kan, Leningrad 1939

(136) Botvinnik-Bronstein, Moscow 1951 (m17)

(137) Botvinnik-Alekhine, AVRO 1938

(138) Taimanov-Botvinnik, Moscow 1967

(139) Botvinnik-Keres, Moscow 1948

(140) Kotov-Botvinnik, Moscow 1955

(141) Botvinnik-Najdorf, Moscow 1956

(142) Botvinnik-Minev, Amsterdam 1954

(143) Goldberg-Botvinnik, Leningrad 1932 (m7)

(144) Kan-Botvinnik, Leningrad 1930

(145) Lasker, Em.-Ragozin, Moscow 1936

(146) Botvinnik-Ragozin, Zacherenye 1936

Index of Openings